SMALL BUSINESS PERSPECTIVES

PETER GORB
PHILIP DOWELL
PETER WILSON

Foreword by
JOHN BOLTON

INSTITUTE OF SMALL BUSINESS
LONDON BUSINESS SCHOOL

PUBLISHED BY ARMSTRONG PUBLISHING

London Business School, Sussex Place

London N.W.1. Tel : 01-723 3902

ISBN 0 9506540 7 8

Printed in Great Britain by
Biddles Ltd, Guildford, Surrey

SMALL
BUSINESS
PERSPECTIVES

American Journal of Small Business

SMALL BUSINESS PERSPECTIVES

FOREWORD

By John Bolton, C.B.E., D.S.C., D.L.

This book of readings in small business, the first of its kind in
Britain, has been produced in response to a need which has been
recognised for some time. The three editors of the book all work at the
Institute of Small Business at the London Business School and participate
in its various teaching programmes. They, in common with others, have
always found it difficult to guide students towards appropriate background reading in small business.

The amount of material available has been growing over the past ten
years. But it comes from widely dispersed sources and is not always
available to students in U.K. libraries. In addition the material has
differing purposes and its quality varies significantly.

The provision of an appropriate selection of readings in book form
appeared to be a daunting task until a resource came to hand at London
Business School which made its collation much easier. This resource was
the Small Business Bibliography published in 1980 by the Institute. With
over two thousand titles classified, cross-referenced and stored on a
computer, identifying appropriate content for the book had been made
much easier.

And yet the sum total of the written word about the small business
sector in Britain, the research and teaching being done in this field and
the numbers studying the science (and art!) of managing small businesses, are each miniscule in relation to the importance of the sector to the
British economy. The sector accounts for some 20% of GNP and 30% of
the employed population, as revealed by the Committee of Inquiry on
Small Firms (1969-71). Moreover, the importance of small businesses
can scarcely be over-rated in terms of their leverage relative to resources
available in creating new jobs, fostering innovation, providing a more
balanced industrial and social structure and in contributing to export
growth.

The tax and financial climates have both improved significantly in the
past ten years in Britain - the risk reward ratio has moved (even if not
far enough) so as to encourage entrepreneurial activity; it also

encourages the hope that our small firm sector can at last have the opportunity and the incentive to emulate its U.S. counterpart.

In that country, between 1969 and 1976, two thirds of net new jobs were created by firms employing fewer than 20 people and a further 20% by firms employing 20 to 500 people. Cutting the "cake" in another way, 80% of net new jobs were created by firms which were less than five years old (1). The record of small businesses in innovation is equally staggering. Research by the U.S. National Science Foundation, covering the years 1963-1973, showed that a comparable amount invested in research and development in small firms yielded twenty-four times the "quantum" of innovation compared with large firms and four times a similar investment made in medium sized firms. Innovation, as the history of new developments has shown, truly takes place in small groups, and often even through the determination of one person to show that he's right and the rest of the world is wrong.

We have many recent examples of the disastrous effects on an industry or a town in Britain of the collapse of a dominant company in the industry, or a major employer in the town. These examples illustrate the importance of a dynamic and balanced industrial structure, new firms starting and others continuing to grow to fill the gap inevitably created by the decay and collapse of whole industries or of mature companies.

As for exports, we have evidence in Britain of the valuable contribution of small exporters. As a member of the Queen's Awards to Industry Committee for the past ten years, I have seen some two thirds of all the applications come from the small firm sector, usually exporting innovative products. In 1980, small firms won 50% of the Awards.

So I trust this innovative book of readings in small business will be of considerable value not only to guide students, but also teachers and practitioners in the small business field. With three million unemployed and much of our traditional industrial base in decline, U.K. Ltd. certainly needs all the guidance it can get.

(1) *D. Birch : The Job Creation Process, MIT 1979*

SMALL BUSINESS PERSPECTIVES

SMALL BUSINESS PERSPECTIVES

INTRODUCTION

The debate about the role of small business in the British economy
has generated a wealth of literature over the past decade. Indeed, this
debate now has a dimension arguably surpassing the most optimistic
dreams of Schumacher himself when he argued in his classic work *"Small
is Beautiful"* for a change from the "idolatry of large size" to the
"convenience, humanity and manageability of smallness".

The range and diversity of that literature has created problems for
students eager to undertake further reading in the subject. It is the
purpose of this book to help those students on their way and to do so by
providing a perspective view of the field. However to sharpen the focus
the readings have been organised under a number of broad sections. A
short note describing the content of each section is included in the text.

The articles we have selected are likely to be of interest to all kinds
of students of small business whether graduates, undergraduates or
businessmen themselves. For this reason, although the subject matter
is serious and densely argued, we have tried to avoid articles with
special technical or academic appeal. We have preferred shorter rather
than longer pieces and have welcomed controversy. Most of the articles
are recent and only one is as much as ten years old. What we hope the
book will do is to lead the reader to a deeper and more reflective view of
the small business world than it is possible to get from the media or the
classroom.

Much of the content has been determined by a constraint which arises
from a view we hold about small business teaching. It is obvious that to
the extent to which any business teaching is useful, it is also useful to
both large and small businesses. However it is not our intention in this
book to regurgitate the whole of business studies in micro form. We
have instead concentrated on those aspects of small business which are
specially relevant to the smaller firm; for example, start-up, financing
and the relationships between large and small firms.

This emphasis on the characteristically small is one which we have
adopted in our work at the London Business School in order to avoid
repeating work done in other fields. This has lead us to believe that
there is a fundamental problem arising from reiterating for the small
business world the problems and precepts of the large. It is that

practically all of the current skills and knowledge which have been developed are derived from big business experience. It has been argued elsewhere that there are potential dangers in transferring skills from one field to another : skills which are irrelevant or even harmful(1). The context of that argument was that of management education itself, and it is worth summarising it here, if only to sound a caution about the extent to which formal management education can be helpful in encouraging the growth and development of small business.

In a much simplified and polarised argument, the following diagrams are used to delineate the small and large environments in which typical "small" and "large" managers work.

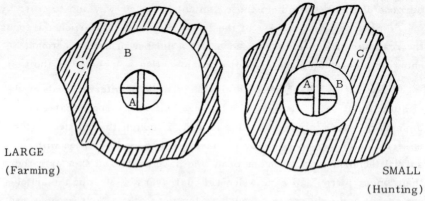

LARGE
(Farming)

SMALL
(Hunting)

The centre circle(A) represents in each case the manager as he sees himself in his operating world. The white area(B) represents the known and predictable world in which he works, and the shaded area (C), the unknown and unpredictable world. The large company world can be compared to farming, a high level and sophisticated activity employing well established techniques to deal with complex but reasonably predict- able situations, and dealing with the unpredictable by making it predictable; by taking into cultivation a small piece of jungle and enlarging the perimeter fence. The management word for this is planning. These valuable and legitimate skills are of little use to the small man, who can be compared to a hunter, who lives in a small clearing in the jungle. This is so easy to look after that he leaves it to the children and the old people to manage whilst he is out there in the unpredictable jungle. Most of the time he is scratching for berries, at subsistence level, and prey to unpredictable predators. Sometimes, however, he goes after the big game, taking high risks for high reward with a high chance of failure. That failure is often bearable because when it comes it is unpredictable, and so not his fault. For these reasons the honest small businessman will admit that his successes are equally unpredictable and so not necessarily due to his efforts.

No such attitude towards success and failure is acceptable in the predictable, planned and cultivated world where the "large" businessman lives and works. There the application of hard won skills and knowledge are expected to show results, and usually do. It is the transfer of these skills to small business where they are usually less relevant, and sometimes counterproductive which forms the basis of much management education for small business. Conversely, when the large company executive transfers to small business, he lacks not only the skills to operate in the jungle but is unprepared for the new measures of success and failure which are being placed upon him.

It is by emphasising the special characteristics of small business operation that one can help to bridge the gap in understanding between small and large, and help to bring to bear the resources of large industry and indeed Government in encouraging the growth of new small businesses. This book hopefully contributes to that purpose.

Acknowledgements

Our thanks are due to all the authors and publishers who have allowed the reproduction of readings in this book. Each author and source is acknowledged at the beginning of each article.

We would also like to thank Mr John Bolton specifically for his preface and more generally as the progenitor of the current interest in small business in the U.K. This year is the tenth anniversary of the publication of the report which bears his name(2). It is hard to over-estimate its influence. Indeed, it is doubtful whether the wide and intense interest in small business would exist without the stimulus provided by the Bolton Report.

Finally, we would like to acknowledge our debt to the Small Business Bibliography produced in the Institute of Small Business with the help of the Library and Computer Services at London Business School. Without that bibliography as a source, this book could not have been produced.

Introduction - References

(1) *Gorb, P. : The Management Development Needs of Small Business:
     Farmers and Hunters (Management Education & Development, Dec.
     1978)*
(2) *Report of the Committee of Inquiry on Small Firms (Chairman : J.
     Bolton, Cmnd. 4811, HMSO, 1971)*

Peter Gorb
Philip Dowell
Peter Wilson
Institute of Small Business, London Business School

November, 1981

PART I

STARTING UP
IN BUSINESS

CHAPTER 1 : VENTURING FORTH

Introduction

Many aspiring small businessmen are unwilling to accept the view that their own time should be included as a cost in all calculations. Once their businesses are established, they soon realise that there is not enough time available to do everything. Forced at least to contemplate employing someone else for the extra tasks, they soon appreciate that, while time may not actually be money, the two are at least interchangeable, and that the choice between them will never go away.

However, before there is a business, there must be a business "idea", and it is to the nature, origin and circumstances surrounding this idea that this chapter is addressed. The use of the term "idea" does not necessarily imply uniqueness, novelty, or even creativity - most new businesses are mere copies of existing ones - but rather reflects the thought processes that inevitably precede the action.

In fact, the interchangeability of time and money is involved at this stage. It is likely that at least some knowledge of the activity will be necessary somewhere in the business, and the would-be entrepreneur has the choice between investing time - either as experience or research - and money. It is quite possible to purchase knowledge such as a patent or licence (or an existing business) or by recruiting skilled staff or partners. Many new ventures involve a mixture of time and money.

In the third article in this chapter, Stanworth and Curran deal with the most sophisticated form of the "all-money" option, franchising, whereby the entrepreneur can acquire a "new" yet tried-and-tested business, complete with reliable expectations and all the necessary training. Franchising is essentially a new phenomenon in the U.K. and deserves mention because of its recent growth (and its economic significance in the U.S.).

The authors point out that new ventures seeking to grow via franchising may stand to make more money through the sale of franchises than from their operations, and should be viewed with some scepticism.

Reliable franchisor companies are then essentially "big business" with a specific orientation towards new ventures. In the second article, Gorb discusses the circumstances in which big business proves to be a source of business ideas by virtue of its orientation <u>away from</u> new or small ventures. The phenomena of Demerger, Hive-Off and Spin-Off are of greatest interest for their social implications (rather than as a recommended route to entrepreneurship) and readers may like to compare the evidence presented here with the prognostications in the last article in this book.

It may seem curious that this introduction should end with a discussion of the first article. It is equally curious that the Harvard Business Review should begin a small business feature with an article stressing the relevance of experience to new venture ideas. Common sense suggests that some prior experience is usually found amongst entrepreneurs, and many people would go so far as to claim it was a prerequisite. (Indeed, the significance of a 'track record' is discussed in Gorb's article.)

Readers, particularly those who, in the author's words, believe that "good managers can manage any type of business", are recommended to adopt a "looking-glass" view with Karl Vesper's article, and take note of the approaches to the development of ideas which do not involve experience - remembering that necessary knowledge can sometimes be purchased.

Most new businesses do involve some prior experience on the part of the entrepreneur, but the nebulous issues are "how much?" and "of what?". What does the knowledge that someone can handle the production of a product imply about his or her ability to sell it, and vice versa? Anyone capable of answering this question consistently would be worth a lot of money to a lot of investors, for an essential ingredient is the nature of the entrepreneur, discussed in Chapter 2.

1. NEW-VENTURE IDEAS : DO NOT OVERLOOK EXPERIENCE FACTOR

Karl H.Vesper

Discovering workable new-venture ideas is no easy feat. Many would-be entrepreneurs have unsuccessfully gambled huge sums testing seemingly profitable concepts.

Even a man as creative as Mark Twain came up a consistent loser when he bet on new business ideas. In his autobiography, he recalled the first in a series of failures he encountered backing the invention of a friend :

"At last, when I had lost $42,000 on that patent I gave it away to a man I had long detested and whose family I desired to ruin. Then I looked around for other adventures. That same friend was ready with another patent. I spent $10,000 on it in eight months. Then I tried to give that patent to the man whose family I was after. He was very grateful but he was also experienced by this time and was getting suspicious of benefactors. He wouldn't take it and I had to let it lapse.

"Meantime, another old friend arrived with a wonderful invention. It was an engine or a furnace or something of the kind....."

The best of Twain's business attempts was an invention of his that he patented and characterized as "the only rational scrapbook the world has ever seen". On that enterprise, he invested $5,000 and managed to recover $2,000.

Unfortunately, sound guidance on where to find profitable venture ideas is nearly as sparse today as it was in Mark Twain's day. And the guidance that exists is of questionable quality because systematic research on the subject is almost non-existent.

Many books on entrepreneurship completely neglect the subject of new-venture ideas. In the most widely used text in entrepreneurship courses, *New Ventures and the Entrepreneur*, Patrick R.Liles devotes eight chapters to various aspects of entrepreneurship but fails to examine the origination of venture ideas(1).

A book by Charles B.Swayne and William R.Tucker, *The Effective Entrepreneur*, offers a "road map by means of which any venture can be formed" but does not indicate how to formulate venture ideas(2). Robert S.Morrison's 558-page *Handbook for Manufacturing Entrepreneurs* presents guidance on whether to start a company, who should start one, and how to "select" a product but fails to offer advice on how to find alternatives from which to do the selecting(3).

More popularized books on entrepreneurship typically recommend various mental exercises. In *How to Think Like a Millionaire and Get Rich*, Howard Hill recommends dreaming up ways to "add color or a new twist to commonplace products and services"(4). Russell Williams, author of *How to Wheel and Deal Your Way to a Fast Fortune*, advises the reader to "pick a product in your home and ask yourself, how is it marketed? How is it manufactured? Could you introduce a competitor?"(5).

In *The Poor Man's Road to Riches*, Duane Newcomb tells the reader, "Ideas are everywhere...... To find them, you generally decide on an area of interest like the restaurant business.... then as you go about your daily business you simply let anything that comes close to your interest area trigger your imagination"(6).

A composite list of recommended venture idea sources from these and other books on entrepreneurship appears in the *Exhibit* below. Of course most items on the list are categories that could be further sub-divided into many other lines of action. Thus it is clear that the number of possible activities for seeking venture ideas is enormous and could consume nearly endless amounts of time.

Is there a better way of formulating new-venture ideas? A study of the histories of approximately 100 highly successful entrepreneurs suggests that there is. The cases were drawn primarily from five books about entrepreneurship as well as from magazine articles and interviews with successful entrepreneurs(7). The objective was not so much to obtain a scientifically representative sampling as to discover the range of sources prospective entrepreneurs can draw on to find promising venture ideas.

Exhibit – Idea sources advocated in entrepreneurship books :

Mental gymnastics :
Brainstorming
Observation
Seeking new twists

Personal contacts with :
Potential customers
Potential suppliers
Business brokers
Business owners
Successful entrepreneurs
Property owners
Professors
Graduate students
Patent attorneys
Product brokers
Former employers
Prospective partners
Bankers
Venture capitalists
Chambers of Commerce
Plastic molders
Corporate licensing
    depts.
Editors
Management consultants
Technology transfer agencies
Regional development agencies

Visits to :
Trade shows
Libraries
Museums
Plants
Invention
    expositions
Universities
Research
    institutes

Reading of :
Trade publications
Trade directories
Bankruptcy announce-
    ments
Business Opportunities
    Classified
Old books & magazines
Commerce Business
    Daily
Other commerce dept.
    publications
NASA's Tech Briefs
Patents & Patent Gazette
New product publications
Doctoral dissertations
Idea books & newsletters
Best seller lists
New technology publications
Licensing information services

Observation of trends :
Materials shortages
Energy shortage
Waste disposal
New technology
Recreation
Nostalgia
Fads
Legal changes
Pollution problems
Health
Self-development
Personal security
Foreign trade
Social movements

One key finding was that instead of searching randomly, as many popularized entrepreneurship books seem to suggest, the entrepreneur should closely examine his or her own education, work experience, and hobbies as idea sources. The large majority of the entrepreneurs studied primarily used their own expertise rather than that of others.

The pattern of close connection between prior work and new-venture ideas was common to a large majority of the successful start-ups - between 60% and 90%, depending on the industry - the correlation being highest in advanced technology areas like computers and medical instruments and lowest in enterprises of a relatively unspecialized nature such as nursing homes, fast food franchises, and other consumer-oriented businesses.

Variations in Background

Not surprisingly, the entrepreneurs differed in how they acquired their expertise. Nearly all entrepreneurs involved in starting successful advanced technology companies had earned one or more college degrees and had had substantial work experience in scientific research or engineering design before formulating their venture concepts. Entrepreneurs who conceived successful machining businesses, however, usually had not attended college but had put in five years or more working for other people on shop floors.

A spectacular, fairly typical example of an advanced technology start-up was that of Intel Corporation : Robert N.Noyce, an M.I.T. physics Ph.D., and Gordon E.Moore, a Cal.Tech. chemistry Ph.D., had worked for Fairchild Semiconductor since its inception in 1956. By 1968, Noyce was general manager, Moore was director of research, and Fairchild's annual sales had grown to $150 million.

At about that time, the two men became aware of a promising related area of semiconductors that had been neglected by big companies. Their observation coincided with their own growing frustration with long commuting times and the difficulties of working within a corporate bureaucracy. They convinced a venture capitalist to invest $300,000 and raised another $2.2 million through private placements.

The entrepreneurs used the money to start a new semiconductor memory company with Noyce as president and Moore as executive vice president. Seven years after the company's inception, sales had grown to $134 million and profits to $19.8 million.

Although it involved exceptionally large seed capital, this venture was not unusual for advanced technology start-ups. A team of technical specialists employed a clear product concept and sought fast growth - a classic pattern carried out, albeit on a smaller scale, by many such companies.

In contrast, consider the following more conventional manufacturing start-up : In 1961, Al Richards was fired as a machinist for a small cutting tool company. The dismissal was a shock, made more painful by the fact that he had only meagre savings. He was not unaccustomed to adversity though, for he had been raised in orphanages, employed in a shipyard at age 16 by falsifying his age, and battle-tested in the Seabees. Because he had worked in several machine shops while he was taking related evening courses, he was confident of his knowledge of the cutting tool business.

Against the advice of his lawyer, he sold his boat, car and guns and took a second mortgage on his house to raise the $18,000 necessary to start his own shop. With rented space and used machinery, he began soliciting orders. He also moonlighted to cover his business and personal expenses. Orders came in slowly, and the company, after losing money the first year, moved into the black the second year. Eight years after start-up, the company's sales had reached an annual level of about $300,000.

Similarities stand out

Though different conditions inspired creation of these two ventures - Noyce and Moore were motivated by dissatisfaction with secure jobs and Richards by unexpected discharge from a job he liked - a basic similarity stands out. Both enterprises represented activities similar to those performed for years in the entrepreneurs' prior jobs.

Working for Fairchild had given Noyce and Moore very special know-how, both in dealing with a particular advanced technology and in identifying and exploiting the technical frontier. The leap to the new-venture idea thus appears not to have been particularly difficult or surprising but rather a natural outgrowth of their work. Richards similarly did not have to search far for his new-venture idea.

Another important source of venture ideas can be hobbies, as the following example illustrates : Bill Nicolai dropped out of college in the late 1960s and hitchhiked to Yosemite to climb mountains. For several years he worked sporadically, supplementing his income with food stamps and spending much of his time climbing mountains in Yosemite and elsewhere.

Then one night a mountain blizzard blew his tent apart, bringing death too close for comfort and setting Nicolai to thinking about alternative tent constructions. He designed a tent made from a tube of fabric held open by circular metal hoops and borrowed a sewing machine to make it a reality. It worked, and he began to imagine an enterprise to fabricate and sell a product he would call "the omnipotent".

He then rented a booth at an annual Seattle street fair and put several tents on display. "I don't think we actually sold any at the fair," he recalled, "but we did sell a few a short while later after people had had a chance to look the flyer over". Sales began to drift in, and Nicolai moved the fledgling business from a friend's basement to a storefront with manufacturing space in the back. After two years, he was employing four of his friends, and annual sales were $60,000. "It wasn't much of a living," he said, "but we were surviving and enjoying the work".

At this point, we might note the source of the business idea and where it led. Nicolai used his substantial hobby experience to conceive his product and enterprise. In a sense, his hobby had been his job because it had been a relatively full-time commitment for several years. It had given him knowledge of the market and available technology. The tent collapse revealed a need, which in turn led to discovery of a product and creation of a business. Again, the moral for successful venture discovery seems to be to work from what one is familiar with - from a hobby if not from one's occupation.

Importance of subsequent events

Nicolai's venture was not particularly successful at this point. The meagre $56,000 gross sales did not allow him to escape food stamps. By the usual standards for wages and profits, the business was, after two years, a loser with no salvation in sight.

Then things changed : A salesman tried to interest Nicolai in using a new tent fabric that boasted the unique property of venting vapor without leaking water, so that breath moisture could escape the tent but rain could not enter. Producers of the new fabric "went to all the big companies first, because we were nobody", Nicolai recalled, "but each big company assumed the material was no good because none of the other big companies used it".

Seeing little to lose, Nicolai introduced a tent made of the new material and threw all his resources into advertising it. Within a month, sales leaped from $5,000 a month to $6,000 a day. Over the next three years, sales rose to $2 million annually, at substantial margins.

This shift from a modest enterprise with little promise to a fast-growing highly profitable business was another important characteristic common to a large proportion of other extremely successful ventures. Except for the advanced technology enterprises, which virtually all started with high expectations, roughly 40% of the ventures studied began as relatively small-time enterprises. Some event occurred later that induced fast growth. Thus another reasonable conclusion to draw from the cases studied is that highly successful venture ideas can easily emerge from apparently small-time businesses as entrepreneurs gain experience, expertise and business exposure.

The successful entrepreneurs' experience thus contrasts sharply with advice offered in the how-to-succeed books. Jobs, the main idea source, are not stressed at all. Though some of the books suggest hobbies, they neglect to emphasize the importance of accompanying experience. What the books mostly suggest - daydreaming, visiting museums, browsing in libraries, and studying world trends - produced few ideas used to start the businesses studied.

This is not to say that following the advice in the popularized books is likely to cause failure. It is just difficult to find examples of success- ful entrepreneurs who have systematically used those approaches. While it seems plausible to expect that hopeful entrepreneurs who deliberately use such advice should achieve some success, this question might benefit from academic research.

Other idea sources

Occasionally, winning ideas are discovered the way the popularized entrepreneurship books say they should be. Ole Evinrude thought up the outboard motor when ice cream melted in a boat he was rowing to a summer picnic. King Gillette conceived the safety razor when his straight razor dulled. Such incidents are extremely rare, however, and nobody has demonstrated that a skill for creating them can be deliberately learned.

But there are some systematic approaches besides background and experience that sometimes work, as the following three examples illustrate:
- E. Joseph Cossman, author of *How I Made a Million Dollars in Mail Order*, tells of finding unexploited products by visiting trade shows, reading classified advertisements, and seeking unused tooling from products previously judged unsuccessful at plastic molding companies(8).
- One entrepreneur adopted a strategy of calling or visiting at least one person daily who might be able to help him find an opportunity, any opportunity. After a year, he had located a partner. After two years, they had a product - a blood-testing device produced under a licensing agreement. And after three years, their company was profitable and nearing $1 million in annual sales.
- A prospective electronics manufacturer discovered a successful product by asking purchasing agents what items they were having trouble obtain- ing. He identified the need for a certain sophisticated electronic component, got it designed and into production, and wound up with a multi-million-dollar publicly held company.

Each of these enterpreneurs unearthed a venture opportunity through someone else. Cossman bought products other people had developed and then applied his merchandising talents to sell them. The medical product manufacturer obtained a license (some entrepreneurs form partnerships with inventors). The electronics maker obtained information about a need and then developed a product.

But they all made use of others who had the specific idea they needed. Thus the idea search process was largely one of making personal contacts until one paid off in a usable concept. For the prospective entrepreneur in search of a venture concept, the message is to seek new contacts for ideas.

A further possibility is to look to others not only for venture concepts but also for complete ongoing ventures - that is, for acquisitions. This approach comprised about one-fifth of the cases examined in this study. What is striking about this approach is that more than half of those who used it had no prior experience in the business areas they suddenly adopted through acquisition. Yet all emerged extremely successful.

Thus the acquisition approach seems well suited to those who either cannot or prefer not to find new-venture ideas based on their own work or hobby experience and who are not content to wait and hope someone else will come to them with a venture proposition.

Where do these findings leave the generalist manager? Does the view widely held among business schools that a good manager can manage any type of business also hold for entrepreneurs? Or can only a specialist start a particular type of business? No general answer has been demonstrated, but it can be observed that technical expertise must be brought into the new enterprise *somehow*, whether by the entrepreneur or by those he recruits.

One way to recruit needed talent is to buy a going concern in which the specialists are already employed. Another is to buy a franchise that comes with the opportunity for special training and guidance. A third is to hire or become partners with someone who has the needed special know-how.

In conclusion, it seems significant that none of the entrepreneurs in the cases examined discovered winning ideas through random mental reflection or even concentrated brainstorming. Those who scouted ideas out applied action, not just thinking, to find them. Hence, some final advice for the person desiring a venture who hasn't yet identified a

suitable concept : don't just sit and think; move around, contact people
and act.

(1) *Homewood, Ill. : Irwin, 1974*

(2) *Morristown, N.J. : General Learning Press, 1973*

(3) *Cleveland, Ohio : Western Reserve Press, 1973*

(4) *West Nyack, N.Y. : Parker Publishing Co., 1968*

(5) *Parker, 1977*

(6) *Parker, 1976*

(7) *The five books used were : Orvis Collins & David G.Moore, The
Organization Makers (New York : Appleton-Century-Crofts, 1970);
Richard Lynn, The Entrepreneur (London : G.Allen & Unwin, 1974);
Harry Miller, The Way of Enterprise (London : Andre Deutsch,1963);
Lawrence A.Armour, The Young Millionaires (Chicago : Playboy Press,
1973); and Gene Bylinsky, The Innovative Millionaires (New York :
Charles Scribner's Sons, 1976).*

(8) *Englewood Cliffs, N.J. : Prentice-Hall, 1963*

2. HIVE-OFF, SPIN-OFF AND NEW SMALL BUSINESS

Peter Gorb

Tenth European Small Business Seminar
Financing The Smaller Company
Amsterdam September 17th-20th 1980

Most of the issues relating to the financing of the smaller business are based on a model which in the U.K. is popularly described as the "seed bed model". Given its official place in public policy in 1971 when the Bolton report was published (1), the seed bed model is based on encouraging the proliferation of new small business and nursing them through their early stages so that some if not all of them will grow and develop into substantial organisations contributing to employment, economic growth and technological advancement.

Policies based on that model have flourished, with some success in the U.K. They are no longer politically controversial, encouraged as they are by both the last Labour and the current Conservative governments. Furthermore an extensive financial network ranging from regional and specialised agencies to the pervasive overdraft and medium term mechanisms of the U.K. banking system has developed to support this model. Indeed, there are current signs that U.K. government is beginning to look with renewed favour on tax concessions designed to encourage "Aunt Agatha"; the ultimate financial mechanism for this model of small business growth. Aunt Agatha is the private investor prepared for risk taking. Because, (like the "seed bed" small business) the private investor is networked over the country he (or she) is in a position to act as a guardian of his interest in a way that no centrally organized lending institution can, however good its information system.

All this is particularly encouraging for the seed bed model, which can be called the "bottom up" approach to promoting small business growth. However, in the last year or so a new model has begun to emerge in the U.K. which can roughly be described as a "top down" approach to small business growth. It is a model which is developing in a number of directions, and which carries a number of important implications for those who make policy designed to support small business, including of course financial support.

Peter Gorb

The model is too new to have developed a clear terminology and I have dubbed it here the "Fragmentation" approach. In essence it is the encouragement of smaller business by breaking up the larger ones. Fragmentation has had a number of manifestations in the U.K., not all of them new. They have been variously named as "Demerger", "Hive Off" and "Spin Off", each of them describing ways to fragment, which though different from each other have a common thread.

That thread is the acceptance of the problems created by dis-economies of scale. Some of the larger companies, who it must be emphasised are themselves the promoters of fragmentation, are explicit about some of the social and economic disadvantages which are implicit in bigness. These disadvantages are various and numerous ranging from their inability to exploit new ideas, to the social disruption caused by small percentage manpower reductions in big organizations based in small communities. They are best described in some detail under the three sub-divisions of fragmentation:Demerger, Hive Off and Spin Off. These names have been variously used for some time, often overlapping in meaning. My definitions, particularly the distinction between Spin Off and Hive Off, are arbitrary ones and are intended only to clarify the arguments in this paper. There is however a strong reason for describing each of these subdivisions separately. It is to give particular emphasis to the changes to the support and encouragement systems, (and particularly financial support) which the third of these ways of fragmenting, Spin Off, is likely to require. Spin Off is the newest and the most interesting of these fragmentation developments, but before we come to it let us first deal with the other two, Demerger and Hive Off.

Demerger usually refers to the splitting up of a major and publicly quoted corporation into a number of smaller ones; smaller in relation that is to their original parent. They are usually still quite big by any other measure. Demerger was given enormous impetus this year by the announcement by G.E.C. (the U.K. giant electrical manufacturers) that it intended to divide into a number of quoted companies based on its existing divisional structure. Whilst the reasons were never made explicit they were fairly obvious. G.E.C. had a market quotation which tended to be dragged down to a level determined by its worst performing divisions thus constraining its ability to grow by acquisition. Its

- 19 -

commercial progress was being inhibited by regulations relating to monopolistic practice. Finally the extent to which so large and widely based a business can continue to be purposefully managed from the centre was under doubt. Management control G.E.C. is largely decentralised anyway.

There are of course well tried financial and support services which are capable of handling Demergers. Their interest to us here lies only in the climate they set, which reinforces that disenchantment with economies of scale.

Hive Off, the second aspect of fragmentation has a well established place in the history of business organisation. I define it as the separation of an existing and operating part of an organization into an independent operating business; usually a small one in relation to its parent, and often small by other measures. In the U.K. Hive Off was actively practiced in the heady days of the sixties as mergers between disparate groups, mainly for financial considerations, created organizations from disparate operating units. The asset strippers were particularly adept in using Hive Off; and as professional managers succeeded financiers at the head of new conglomerates the process developed apace. "Make or Buy" logic began to determine policies for Hive Off for subsidiaries originally acquired as "upstream" suppliers or "service" providers; and market position decisions began to condition the disinclination to own small customers.

This "cleaning up" was reinforced as the U.K. moved into economic decline, when the cost of management diversion from the central purposes of a business began to count heavily in favour of Hive Off. So too did the recognition that Hive Off would be better than the alternative, which was closure, redundancies and social hardship.

In general the financing for Hive Off has been found in traditional places. There have been a number of Hive Offs where an individual buyer has purchased the new independent business to run it himself. But more often the line manager who runs the subsidiary and divisions has sought finance to buy himself out. He and his colleagues may provide some collateral, but finance comes in the main from the recognized lending institutions who generally favour this form of small business creation.

The reasons are obvious. In the first place, unlike a new or relatively new small business starting from scratch the Hive Off and its managers usually have a track record. In the risk spectrum which runs from "collateral to confidence", and which determines a lender's attitudes, a track record is of vital importance. Secondly, no Hive Off is possible without the willing co-operation of the parent. That co-operation is nearly always expressed in contractual arrangements relating to the supply of goods, or services, or to the payment of accounts; all of which reinforces the confidence of lenders. Thirdly quite often the Hive Off used to be an independent operating company and some experience - albeit tenuous - was often still available to assist the management to live in an independent and commercially based world.

We can be confident that Hive Off will continue to grow, relying on the services of existing financial institutions to service and encourage it. Spin Off on the other hand, which often takes place under two of the three conditions described above, poses greater problems of financial and general support. It is probably the most fragile, but potentially the fastest growing of all the three aspects of fragmentation.

I define Spin Off as the process by which an individual leaves a large organization to start a new small business. The concept of Spin Off was given its first public expression by the late C.C.Pocock, the last Chairman of Shell. In a seminar(2) paper he proposed the following way of encouraging small business growth.

"Most of us (in large industry) will know of products which are of commercial interest but not worth developing in a large company........
Why not encourage a retiring employee to take an idea with him, develop it, hiring people for the purpose, and sell us back the product.......?"

This proposal has implicit in it a number of clear opportunities of benefit to both sides of the Spin Off deal :
1. The opportunity to develop new business ideas which, because of the need for management not to be diverted from central issues, would otherwise have low priority within the parent.
2. The opportunity to create employment when the parent company can perhaps only expect employment rundown in its efforts to improve productivity and performance.

3. The opportunity to find new and refreshing employment for managers, perhaps demoralized by the length of the queue for promotion. Indeed to create a pro-active way of dealing with management redundancy.

4. The opportunity to re-examine and exploit Make or Buy decisions over a wide range of existing functions, as well as the new business proposals outlined above.

The idea of Spin Off has gained general approval amongst policy makers in the U.K., and has been reinforced by tax legislation designed to encourage the senior managers in their late forties and early fifties to use Spin Off as a route to a new career. It is gaining increasing support from industry and at a recent one day conference(3) at the London Business School, an impressive number of Britain's larger companies were present to learn more about and to help to develop the ideas behind both Spin Off and Hive Off.

However, for the lenders who need to translate general support into practical financial help there are some new problems to consider. The first concerns the pro-active nature of support being given to the Spin Off by the large company, and the extent to which that company is a good judge of the business proposition behind the Spin Off. If the proposition is closely linked to the company's own business, either by a licence or franchise, then the lender operates in a known and tried situation. But if the proposition is either a downstream or upstream trading arrangement, or a production, marketing or technological by-product, then the lender's view of the large company's judgement of the proposition may rely more on that company's general reputation than on the validity of the proposition itself. And very large companies are notoriously bad judges of new small business ideas.

The second problem concerns the ability of the senior executive with twenty years experience of large company operations to perform effectively in the new environment of the small business world. Many of the skills he possesses are either irrelevant or counter productive in a small business. Often too his attitudes and style of operation successfully developed in the one environment are inimical to success in the other. To the lender, none of this is necessarily apparent.

Finally there is the problem of employment. Unemployment in the developed world is nearly always a regional problem. A large company may for this reason encourage the new business to start in an area in which its employment commitments are high and where it perhaps foresees some inevitable increases in unemployment. As long as the large company remains a major customer for the new small one this may not matter. But where this is not the case, problems arise. Most new small businesses have either local or special customers and need them to be prosperous ones. Small businesses starting in areas of high unemployment may need more support than is readily available from traditional financing if they are to survive.

All these examples demand a repositioning of the lender's stance along that spectrum which runs from collateral to confidence when determining the terms of a loan. A new business proposition actively supported by a major corporation may suggest less collateral requirement and more confidence than might otherwise be the case. In fact the opposite may well be true.

A new set of tasks for the funding of small business is arising out of Spin Off and a whole new set of skills is going to be required to deal with them. They are skills to see beyond the distorting mirror of large company support. They are also the skills to determine the new characteristics of the Spun Off business in its relationship to its parent, once independence is achieved. For example, well struck contracts may matter rather more than sound management information systems; and pricing policy, more than productivity.

The acquisition of these skills is likely to be of some priority, as is the necessary investigation and research into the small/large relationships arising from all three aspects of fragmentation. The differences between the three aspects are of course not as sharp as has been suggested in this paper, which has been concerned to differentiate in order to identify. The frontiers between them are blurred, particularly between Hive Off and Spin Off; and are likely to become even more blurred and complex as the pace grows at which large organisations purposefully discard pieces of themselves.

It is certain to grow for the various reasons indicated above and also for some others. Those reasons can be summarised as follows :

1. An increasing disenchantment with the concepts of economies of scale – both social and economic.

2. The expense in a high cost energy economy of moving people and goods to centre in order to work.

3. The options offered by new information technology which, by the decentralization of information and feed back, provides the freedom to speed the fragmentation process.

Because the movement is purposeful (and whether it takes the form of Hive Off or Spin Off or some other mechanisms) it will make formal demands on the financial institutions to develop resources. For those who deal in funding early preparation is needed if they are to provide those resources effectively, and with profit to themselves. This will mean that studies in the relationships between small and large are likely to take priority in the work of academics and others who deal with small business problems over the next decade.

(1) *The Bolton Report – Report of Committee of Inquiry on Small Firms – November 1971 – HMSO*

(2) *C.C.Pocock : More Jobs – A Small Cure for a Big Problem – The Ashridge Lecture 1977*

(3) *Joint meeting at the London Business School with the London Enterprise Agency – April 1980*

3. FRANCHISING, A SPECIAL KIND OF SMALL BUSINESS

John Stanworth and James Curran

The Bankers' Magazine. Volume 222 Number 1606. January 1978

Franchising is becoming an increasingly important form of small business activity in Britain. One estimate of the current turnover of the frachised outlets of the eight founder members of the recently formed British Franchise Association, is £180m. The members include Wimpy International, the best-known franchise operation in Britain, with over 600 outlets, while other members operate in areas as diverse as domestic and industrial cleaning, car hire and car servicing, printing and hotels. Franchising has also emerged in ice-cream distribution, contract employment, central heating and elsewhere.

Franchising is frequently seen as a very recent phenomenon imported from America but the real innovators of modern franchising were almost certainly the 18th-century brewers who created a system of 'tied' agreements with publicans which remains widespread in Britain today. It is true, on the other hand, that franchising is economically more important in the United States than in Britain. Franchise activities in America now account for just over 30% of all retail sales and 10% of the gross national product. It is estimated that, in 1977, there were over 460,000 franchised outlets in the States with a combined turnover of around $240bn. Although some companies operating in Britain today, such as Wimpy International and Dyno-Rod originated and developed in this country, others such as Kentucky Fried Chicken, ServiceMaster, Ziebart and McDonalds had their origins in America.

How it works

Defining franchising is not easy since there are a variety of forms it can take. Essentially, however, an organisation (the franchisor) with a market-tested product or service, established contractual relationships with individuals (franchisees) who set up their own business to operate under the franchisor's trade name in a specified manner to market the product or service. The franchisee finances his own business operation which usually involves buying or renting premises, purchasing equipment and supplies from the franchisor and the payment of any staff employed. A fixed sum is paid to the franchisor for the use of the trade name and initial training. Thereafter, the franchisee pays a continuing royalty which may be a percentage of annual turnover or may be included in the price of supplies of materials required for the business. The relationship is, therefore, an ongoing one and in exchange for the royalty the franchisee pays, the franchisor provides any required further training, advice, administrative back-up, and the benefits of local and national advertising.

Franchise 'packages', though they share certain core elements, vary from company to company and similarly, initial capital requirements also vary considerably. Wimpy, for instance, require new franchisees to invest between £15,000 and £25,000. A standard fee of £750 is paid for the right to use the trade name but the precise capital requirement depends on the size, type, locality and estimated customer-potential of the particular Wimpy Bar. Dyno-Rod, drain cleaning and hygiene specialists, offer contracts based on an investment of between £6,000 and £30,000. The licence fee is around £1,000 for a new area but is higher for an already established area. Otherwise the formula is much the same as for Wimpy.

ServiceMaster, specialists in indoor cleaning services, ask for an initial licence fee of £1,750 and a further investment of £1,750 for specialist chemicals and equipment. Thereafter, a franchisee requires only a van and a modest amount of working capital since special premises are not strictly necessary. Prontaprint, a relatively new franchise offering rapid printing services, charge a licence fee of £2,500 and around £5,000 for equipment. Working capital requirements are about a further £7,000. This is estimated to be sufficient to establish the business and generate a satisfactory income for the franchisee.

The amount of royalty paid to the franchisor as well as the way it is paid can vary. For instance, Wimpy derive their income from a mark-up on supplies of hamburgers to their franchisees. Dyno-Rod, on the other hand, take a 25% royalty on franchisees' turnover and this, like the Wimpy mark-up, covers the cost of advertising and promotion. On a similar basis, ServiceMaster and Prontaprint each take a 10% royalty.

The main marketing services provided by franchisors are usually advertising and promotion but sometimes include initial customer contact and subsequent referral to the appropriate franchisees, and dealing with customer queries and complaints.

Advantages of the system

The foremost advantage of franchising to the franchisor is that it enables him to quickly achieve national coverage for his product or service. Most of the necessary capital is put up by franchisees and the latter, being self-employed, are usually motivated to work much harder in building up their business - thus, no doubt, ensuring success for the franchisor.

The franchisee, on the other hand, gets the chance to run his own business, training, use of an established trade name, usually a guarantee of exclusive rights to a particular geographical territory, head-office advice and administrative back-up, plus the benefits of market research and product/service development. Of course, there can be disadvantages. In addition to the possible need to work long hours, the franchisee may feel that the terms of his contract, which emphasise consistency and standardisation, limit his freedom to impose his own individual personality on his business. In addition, whilst his contract ensures that his franchisor will not promote direct competition for him by selling the same geographical area twice over, there is nothing to stop a rival franchise organisation from creating on-the-doorstep competition.

The cost of setting up as a franchisee is similar to or can exceed the cost of setting up a totally independent small business. However, the franchisee buys himself a commercial advantage through the franchisor's expertise in a specific field thus avoiding many of the pitfalls which often trap the independent small man. So it is not surprising that available evidence suggests that the failure rate is much lower than among conventional small businesses.

Banks backward in coming forward ?

A recent survey among franchisees from three leading franchise organisations in this country, supported by the Social Science Research

Council showed that 45% had raised loans from banks in order to buy their franchises. The sums involved ranged from £500 to over £10,000. Some franchisees claimed that raising bank loans to buy into an established franchise was easier than raising loans for a totally independent business. Often the franchisor assisted the potential franchisee in his dealings with his bank by providing professionally prepared projections of likely turnover and profits. However, on occasions, franchisors and franchisees alike were critical of the banks for their conservatism. Some respondents felt that local banks did not really understand how franchising worked and seemed to regard it as an unproven business method. One factor which may have contributed towards the conservatism of bank managers here is the bad publicity attracted by a number of illegal or unethical schemes in the past. These schemes have frequently been labelled 'franchises' and in some respects have resembled the genuine franchise operation. Prominent among these dubious practices were 'pyramid' selling schemes where the investor paid for a 'distributorship' of a product or service but could only make a profit by subsequently recruiting sub-distributors. Typically the product or service was worthless or one for which there was little or no demand and the investor usually lost his money. In some cases the investment was financed by a second mortgage and investors lost their homes as well as their savings.

The laws have now been tightened up to discourage this kind of fraud but it is difficult to legislate comprehensively. The 'get-rich-quick' claims of promoters of these pseudo franchises would make most people cautious but many apparently intelligent people were among the victims. More commonly, the victims were ambitious but inexperienced ordinary people who failed to seek proper advice.

If, as expected, genuine franchising continues to grow in Britain to become an important legitimate alternative opportunity for self-employment, bank managers and others involved in advising and assisting would-be investors, will need to be armed with a check-list of questions designed to distinguish the genuine franchise operation from the spurious variety :

1. Is the franchisor a member of the British Franchise Association? The Association has eight founder members : Budget Rent-a-Car, Dyno-Rod, Holiday Inns, Kentucky Fried Chicken, Prontaprint, Service-Master, Wimpy International, Ziebart. All are well established,

legitimate operations and the Association states that additional
applicants will be carefully vetted before being admitted into membership.

2. How long has the franchisor been in operation and how many outlets
   does he currently have?

3. Has the franchisor's product or service been properly market-tested
   before being franchised and is it being properly promoted by means
   of local and national advertising?

4. Has the potential franchisee been allowed to visit one or more existing
   outlets - preferably freely selected from a complete list of operations
   - and to talk to franchisees? An introduction to somebody who claims
   to have *previously* operated a successful franchise is no adequate
   substitute.

5. Has the would-be investor seen an independent solicitor or accountant
   about the contract and background financial data supplied by the
   franchisor? 'Franchise consultants' do exist but may be more
   interested in selling franchises than giving fully independent advice.

6. Is the franchisor's own long-term success dependent upon the
   franchisee's success? If this is not the case, then there are grounds
   for suspicion. If the initial 'buy-in' fee appears high for what the
   franchisor is offering and/or if there is a *fixed* annual royalty
   unrelated to the franchisee's future turnover or profits, then the
   offer may well be a spurious one.

7. Does the potential franchisee appear to have the qualities required to
   both work on his own as an operator of his own business *and* maintain
   a proper, amicable working relationship within a larger organisation?
   Put another way, is the franchisor selective in offering contracts?
   Unscrupulous operators, interested in short-term gains, are likely to
   accept anybody willing to part with his money. Previous experience
   in the industry in which the franchise operates is *not* a prerequisite.
   Reputable franchisors provide a full training and continuing support.
   Previous experience may even be a disadvantage because the franchisee
   may feel he 'knows better' than the franchisor how to operate the
   business.

8. What does the franchisee get if he decides to end his contract? How
   easy is it to end the contract and what, if any, are the penalties
   imposed by the franchisor? In a genuine franchising operation, an

outlet that has been developed into a flourishing small business can be sold as a going concern just like an independent small business. However, franchisors will usually insist on approving any buyer before the sale is completed.

Separating sheep from goats

The number of franchisees seeking assistance from the clearing banks is likely to increase, and it is to be hoped that the publicity attracted by unethical, pseudo-franchise operations will not blind bank managers to the real merits of legitimate franchise operations. Bank managers are busy people and may not have the time to check out in detail all of the points raised above but if at least most of the right questions are asked, the chances of a wrong decision should be greatly reduced. At the same time, banks and others who help franchise operations will be further assisting the small businessman - now belatedly being recognised by Government, politicians of all parties and other serious commentators, as crucially important to Britain's future.

CHAPTER 2 : THE ENTREPRENEUR

Introduction

However brilliant a new venture idea, its conversion into a successful business depends on one or more people having the necessary abilities and aptitudes to nurture the venture through its gestation period and infancy. Not everyone is prepared to work long hours, to weather hardship, to ride ill fortune, and perhaps, to be ready to capitalise on good fortune, yet these attributes and more are usually required in the course of new business development. What then, is known of such people?

The term entrepreneur means different things to different people. To some it conjures up the almost romantic figure who builds empires overnight; others think of the second world war spiv who could always obtain anything through the black market provided the price was right. However, the small business literature defines an entrepreneur as anyone who starts a new business.

This leaves considerable scope for subsequent classification. For example, there are discernible differences between Sir Freddie Laker and say, a fish and chip shop owner, and much of the literature concentrates on the former type. In the second article in this chapter, Brown provides an interesting perspective on Clive Sinclair and his approach to what is, by the standards of the 1980s, perhaps the most romantic of all British companies.

But does entrepreneurship involve essentially mystical qualities? After all, there would be nothing particularly romantic about selling individually-wrapped tablets of soap - were it not how Unilever started. Perhaps then, entrepreneurs are not men apart, but rather become men apart, as contended by Liles. In the first and principal article in this chapter, Liles summarises the 'state of the art', in terms of current knowledge of entrepreneurship, and while he may not explain what makes entrepreneurs, he provides many insights into what prevents their emergence from amongst the 'professional classes'.

European readers who detect a cultural difference in the attitudes expressed in Liles' article, will be encouraged by the final article in which Karger demonstrates that the phenomenon does occur in the U.K., and presents interesting reasons why business graduates have the potential to become entrepreneurs. It appears that planning and technique can replace instinct, although luck is still important.

Of course, Karger offers evidence based on a sample of one - but this is typical of the subject. It is far easier to produce anecdotal counter-examples than it is to offer even general theories of entrepreneurship. Fortunately for the alchemists, the subject was not around in their time, and they were able to concentrate on their search for the philosopher's stone.

1. WHO ARE THE ENTREPRENEURS ?

Patrick R.Liles

MSU Business Topics. Volume 22 Number 1. Winter 1974

Most American businessmen have at some time in their careers thought about starting their own company. Some have envisioned their own enterprise as an avenue to personal wealth through large capital gains. To them, there is a beautiful formula for financial success : a) start a small company, preferably in a glamour industry; b) generate rapid growth in sales and profits; c) then sell out either to the public or to some large acquisitive conglomerate.

Others have seen their own company as an opportunity to do what they really wanted to do : to get close to a sport by developing a ski area, or to reduce a new technology to practical use. Still others have sought an escape from stultifying large-company constraints, politics, or career impasses. In their dreams, their own venture would be a means to gain the top position in a business.

Despite dreams, wishful thinking, and even plans, few people actually take the step of trying to start a company. Why is this? Is there a special breed of man which is particularly inclined to become an entrepreneur? Are there special characteristics or conditions which stimulate entrepreneurial activities?

The basic questions we are asking here are classic ones : Are entrepreneurs born or are they made? If they can be made, what are the ingredients? I have reached the conclusions that, given a degree of ambition and ability not uncommon to many individuals, certain kinds of experiences and situational conditions - rather than personality or ego - are the major determinants of whether or not an individual becomes an entrepreneur.

If we examine some of the attitudes in the sub-culture of American businessmen we find that there are significant connotations to starting a company as a career alternative. Almost everyone gets a glow - a tingle - at the idea of being an entrepreneur. To men in their thirties and forties the idea of starting a company means "free enterprise" and "opportunity", as reflected in Horatio Alger stories. In value terms of the younger generation, starting a company is a way to "do your own thing". For such businessmen and for many business school students, starting a successful company is a very attractive idea, yet only rarely do they seem to consider it a serious alternative. When a possible opportunity presents itself, there is somehow too little time to investigate it properly and too little time to determine whether or not the idea really makes sense. Thus, it appears that *most* would-be entrepreneurs stop before they get started. Unfortunately, there is very little information on people who have had ideas about starting companies but never seriously pursued them.

We might think that we already know a lot about the entrepreneurs themselves - those who actually go ahead and start companies. Yet, do we really? We find that there are people who think of entrepreneurs being formed by school systems and child raising(1), by rejecting fathers (2), or by the business environment(3). However, efforts to measure and predict entrepreneurial potential are, at best, still in the development stages(4).

Perhaps one of the best broad-based studies on entrepreneurs was carried out by Orvis F.Collins and David G.Moore at Michigan State University in 1964. Using a series of personal interviews and psychological tests, they reached a number of rather unsettling conclusions regarding people who start their own company :

"Throughout the preceding analysis, obviously we have been having difficulty deciding whether the entrepreneur is essentially a 'reject' of our organizational society who, instead of becoming a hobo, criminal, or professor, makes his adjustment by starting his own business; or whether he is a man who is positively attracted to succeed in it. We have, perhaps without intention, regarded him as a reject.

"Entrepreneurs are men who have failed in the traditional and highly structured roles available to them in the society. In this.......entrepreneurs are not unique. What is unique about them is that they found an outlet for their creativity by making out of an undifferentiated mass of circumstances a creation uniquely their own : a business firm.

"The men who travel the entrepreneurial way are, taken on balance, not remarkably likeable people. This, too, is understandable. As any

one of them might say in the vernacular of the world of the entrepreneur
'Nice guys don't win' "(5).

Several small-sample studies at Harvard and MIT have yielded results
different from the Collins and Moore study(6). Entrepreneurs were
found not to be failures. Instead "most of the founders had experienced
a generally higher than average level of success in their previous
employment. Several had established outstanding records of achievement"
(7). These entrepreneurs seemed more typical of the successful, hard-
charging, young business executive or engineer than a reject figure(8).

One possible explanation, of course, is that people in Michigan are
very different from those in New England. It might be more helpful,
however, if we categorized in some detail : a) the kinds of business which
are used in studies of small business fatality rates and in the Collins and
Moore study, and b) the kinds of business which might be started as
alternatives to professional management or engineering careers. The
survey-type studies are comprehensive in that they essentially look at
all companies which are started within a particular period of time. This
includes a wide range of business ventures : dry cleaners, retail shops,
electronics manufacturers, computer software firms, gas stations, and
so forth. Each of these is used in the computation of a wide range of
statistics about the rise and demise of new companies. There should be
no reason to doubt the aggregate figures or the results of in-depth
studies made of these situations. The Collins and Moore study looked at
110 manufacturing firms started between 1945 and 1958 in Michigan but
made no further distinctions as to the nature of the business, size, or
potential.

If we consider kinds of ventures which might be of interest to a
professional manager or an engineer, the vast majority of the enterprises
started each year (and, therefore, the bulk of those considered in large,
broad-based studies) would not be included. A dry cleaning establishment or a small metal fabricating shop is not the basis for the dreams of
these people. From their perspective (and therefore the perspective of
this article), we should label this subcategory of small business as
marginal firms.

Who Are the Entrepreneurs?

That leaves us with the task of considering the kinds of venture situations which are potentially attractive career alternatives. The first, which I have labeled the *high-potential venture*, is the company which is "started with the intention that the venture grow rapidly in sales and profits and become a large corporation"(9). In its planning stage the high-potential venture is the extreme of personal economic opportunity, the entrepreneur's big dream : such as Polaroid, Digital Equipment, Scientific Data System, Cartridge Television, Viatron, and so on.

Another type of enterprise, less obvious than the high-potential venture, also holds a strong interest for many would-be entrepreneurs. This type of venture we might call the *attractive small company*. In contrast to the high-potential venture, the attractive small company is not intended to become a large corporation, probably will never have a public market for its stock, and will not be attractive to most venture capital investors. However, in contrast to the marginal firms, attractive small companies can provide salaries of $40,000 to $80,000 per year, perquisites (company car, country club membership, travel, and so forth) to its owner/managers, and often flexibility in life-style such as working hours, kinds of projects and tasks pursued, or geographical location. In this subcategory we find such businesses as consulting and other service firms and some specialized manufacturers.

Both the high-potential venture and the attractive small company are interesting beyond the scope of the benefits they may provide to their founder/owners. In the high-potential venture we find the genesis of the major corporations of the future and, therefore, the source of a growing number of jobs and other contributions to the economy. The attractive small companies provide less spectacular but stable inputs of a similar nature. Both of these kinds of companies must gain and maintain their position by providing competitive discomfort to the existing corporate giants through innovation, flexibility, and efficiency.

The marginal firms, on the other hand, provide support for their owners/employers but frequently at a lower level than might be obtained by employment if they could or would work elsewhere. However, these people are not likely to seek employment elsewhere because of their difficulties in functioning in larger and more structured organizations(10).

Without question, some of the businessmen and engineers who start high-potential ventures or attractive small companies *are* compulsive entrepreneurs. They cannot function effectively in a large organization. They must be their own boss and they may have known this all their lives. It may seem as if they could have behaved in no other way. But what about the others who started companies? What about the entrepreneurs who are basically well-adjusted people and who had given little previous thought, if any, to the idea of their own company? How did these people happen to become entrepreneurs although most were already successful in the pursuit of a more conventional career? What factors play a leading role in determining who becomes an entrepreneur? Which factors might be largely fortuitous and which might be controlled by the individual?

A Basic Prerequisite : Achievement Motivation

Not all people are inclined to take on significantly more than they have to. A high-potential venture or an attractive small company is usually recognized as requiring a tremendous amount of determined effort and commitment. These kinds of activities are not attempted unless an individual is willing to expend more effort and energy than would be required in a more conventional career.

People high in achievement motivation are the people who strive to make things happen - in the laboratory, on the production floor, in the sales office, in the classroom(11). Obviously this factor alone is insufficient to determine who starts companies and who does not. But it is a beginning. People without this kind of orientation are unresponsive to the other influences which might encourage starting a venture. However, people with achievement motivation together with other influencing factors may become entrepreneurs.

Achievement motivation can be developed(12). It would appear unlikely, however, that someone would try to develop achievement motivation in himself in order to start a high-potential venture or an attractive small company. One would expect that it would take a highly achievement-motivated person to want to start either of these kinds of enterprises in the first place.

A Disqualifying Influence : Social Self-Image

The majority of people trying to do exceptionally well in their careers never seriously consider starting a company. Even among the professional managers or career businessmen the number is small. This is not to say that many of these people would not gladly be successful entrepreneurs in their own companies. They are unwilling, however, to take what they see as a backward or downward step necessary to achieve that success.

An acquaintance of the author's, a Yale graduate, has described the effect of his college experience on his own thinking about his career :

"It all came clear one night when I was arguing and describing how Charlie had not been able to go to college, but instead after working in a restuarant had bought a second-hand dump truck. That's when it dawned on me that *because* I went to college I could *never* buy a second-hand dump truck, not even a brand new one with someone else to drive it. When I ran across an old friend, I could not afford to explain that I was the owner of a dump truck. No, I was "with" the ABC Corporation. Not necessary to explain that they are the largest producers of this and that in the world. I was "with" them, and my friend was "with" someone just like them."

Because of recent increasing sentiments favoring personal independence and relevance, we might expect to find in the future a greater general public acceptance of entrepreneurial activities and, therefore, to discover less and less of a conflict between this kind of a career and a person's social self-image. In this sense, it may be becoming easier for someone to decide to strike out on his own than it has been in the past. Perhaps we shall come to the point where becoming an entrepreneur is recognized as a socially legitimate, and even attractive, career alternative.

Influence on Entrepreneurial Careers

For the person who has achievement motivation and whose social self-image is not in conflict with starting a company, there are two kinds of conditions which become critical : a) how *ready* he sees himself for undertaking such a venture, and b) how many *distractions* or *obligations* he sees holding him back.

The reader will note that what an individual does depends upon how he perceives a situation rather than upon what the situation actually is. This is particularly critical in considering a person's readiness or his restraints because there is no way for anyone to make direct, objective measurements of these characteristics. Instead, a personal assessment of readiness or restraints is going to be a combination of knowledge, insight, judgment and personal values.

Readiness

In terms of his decision to initiate a company and to try to run it successfully, a person's own assessment of how ready he is probably is a good approximation of how ready he really is. One would not likely find a runner expecting to run a four-minute mile without having some objectively valid reasons behind those expectations. Similarly, an individual who believes that he is ready to start a company is probably reaching that decision from some background of experience, exposure, special skills, and industry knowledge. This is not to say that some people do not try to initiate businesses when they are totally unprepared. It would imply, however, that in most of such instances the individual himself knows very well that the odds are against his being able to make a go of it.

It might be useful to think of an individual's readiness in terms of levels of specific and general self-confidence. Specific self-confidence in this context represents an individual's feeling of mastery over the kinds of tasks and problems he would expect to encounter in starting a company and making it successful. General self-confidence would be his feeling of well-being and his universal assurance that he can accomplish things.

What people learn through a variety of business and related experience accumulates over time. Most people learn relatively more and learn relatively more rapidly early in their careers when much of what they do and see is new to them. And although the relative rate of learning may diminish over time, the cumulative effect is an increasingly competent individual. The evolution of a person's readiness as reflected in his specific self-confidence to master various elements of a venture is depicted

- 39 -

graphically in Figure 1, below.

FIGURE 1 - <u>READINESS TO START A VENTURE</u>

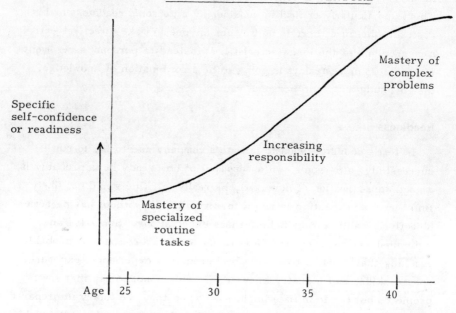

General self-confidence, which is necessary for someone to want to try something new, is an elusive idea. Most people can identify in their own lives those periods when they were confident and up for doing big, new things. They can also recall other times when they were anxious, and uncertain - unwilling to get away from the sure and the known. Given the high degree of uncertainty for most people in starting a company, a high level of general self-confidence is necessary for them to be willing to try.

Restraints

Perhaps the most effective restraint on someone who otherwise might start a company is his continuing success and satisfaction in pursuing his present job. Why should anyone want to change if things are going well? Especially with the passage of time, increasing seniority for such people means a larger salary, greater responsibilities, and greater benefits. In addition, an individual develops a personal power base within an organization : key knowledge and skills, confidence and loyalty of associates, and so forth, which enables him to assert himself and to be effective. At some point, even in the face of a grave disappointment or disenchantment with the company, it becomes almost prohibitively "expensive" to resign and pursue another career direction.

A would-be entrepreneur's freedom to break away and start a company also becomes hindered by financial and other obligations typical of the U.S. male life-cycle development between the ages of twenty-five and forty years. A man gets married, buys a house, and starts to raise a family. He may immediately incur a sizable mortgage and heavy real estate taxes. With children he acquires the cost burdens for their future education. In addition, he assumes responsibility for his family in the event of his death or disability. These immediate and future costs tie him to a schedule of direct expense payments, a plan for savings, and the costs of insurance.

In addition, the usual pattern is for expenditures on living expenses to rise as a person receives promotions and increases in salary. He now has two cars instead of one, a larger house, and takes more expensive vacations. These costs, closely following if not sometimes overtaking income, as a practical matter are only adjustable upward. And until the children have finished school, it is unusual to find sufficient funds for anything approaching financial flexibility.

Other commitments created by marriage and families may do as much to restrict the freedom and flexibility of would-be entrepreneurs as do his financial obligations. Few women marry with the intention of becoming nurses and housecleaners for absentee husbands. Moreover, personal relationships among people take time, including even the minimum of spoken communication, the ritual of certain courtesies, and the recreational activities people pursue together. And some part of evenings, weekends, and holidays are expected by the family to be devoted to these activities. The family life cycle experience usually creates an increasing time requirement upon the husband until the children go away to school. As small children begin to lose physical dependence upon their mothers, the role of the father increases in both depth and scope. In the wisdom of everyday life, "This is the time when the children need a father".

Two other interesting phenomena frequently appear as part of the male life cycle. The first is an evolution of values as the family, especially children, enters into his thinking. Their security is related to his career security and, therefore, his career security becomes more important to him. The time spent with wife and children is more than the minimal to satisfy physical or emotional obligations, but it is a part of a change in the importance he places on what he does - a transition from preoccupation with a career to a realization of new interests in his life. The other aspect, closely related to a change of values, is a change of pace. The drive and physical and emotional energy expended by so many young executives in pursuit of a career do not lend themselves to the pursuit of many other interests. Perceived at the office, Joe at the age of forty is slowing down. Perceived by his wife, Joe is beginning to live. Perceived by himself, Joe is just doing other things - not necessarily enjoying himself more than when he was hotly pursuing his career interests, but enjoying himself in other ways.

For starting a company, an individual's self-perceived *effective capacity* can be derived from a combination of readiness and freedom from restraints and distractions. The results, depicted graphically in Figure 2, show that effective capacity for starting a company typically increases with age between twenty-five and thirty as the individual learns rapidly from his early experiences. As a person grows older, however, this trend is modified and then reversed as the marginal learning experience becomes less, and the influences of successful employment plus family-related interests and obligations are incurred. If we identify a certain level of capacity as being necessary for a person to be able to act, we can define a certain period - a *free choice period* - when the individual sees himself as able to act. During this period the capability, the self-confidence, and the career commitment on balance can be more of an influence than are his economic or emotional commitments and interests in other areas.

FIGURE 2 - THE FREE CHOICE PERIOD FOR THE WOULD-BE ENTREPRENEUR

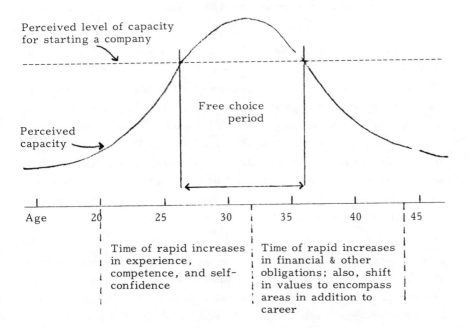

Precipitating Events

For some people, the combination of circumstances is such that they never attain sufficient capacity to start a company. They never reach a free choice period. Their other commitments become too large before they reach a point where they could strike out on their own. On the other hand, there probably are thousands and thousands of people who pass through a period when they could choose to start a company (when they have sufficient capabilities and few restraints) but they don't do it. It would appear that most people need something more : something to help break established ties, to create resolve, and something specific to pursue.

Three additional kinds of conditions appear to be major influences on decisions to start ventures. The first, *deterioration of job satisfaction*, disposes the individual to consider seriously other career alternatives. The second, *identifying a new venture opportunity*, helps to focus upon what might otherwise be a largely undefined possibility. The third, *encouragement to start a company*, helps an individual make what becomes a very subjective decision.

Dissatisfaction : This element - a negative outlook on his present and future job situation - appears to have a strong influence on the would-be entrepreneur. Relative to his expectations, something disturbs him. A budget for product development is cut back, the right promotion or salary increase does not occur, an addition to his staff is denied. Although entrepreneurs will cite such specific events or unfulfilled expectations as the triggering event which brought them to leave, the reasons usually are more complex. The last straw is but one of a number of disquieting and disappointing incidents which occurred over time and which produced a general feeling of dissatisfaction and, perhaps, resentment.

Job dissatisfaction - for whatever reasons - is not an unusual condition. Changing jobs in most instances is the easiest and more common occurrence. Frequently, it is the opportunity of another job that triggers a critical assessment of one's current employment situation. The transition from one job to another is relatively quick, and its results - at least in the short term - are predictable. In addition, it usually achieves direct use of special skills and knowledge accumulated in prior positions. The unusual thing is when an individual, instead of expressing his objections in the conventional way by changing jobs, elects to start a company.

Identifying a new venture opportunity : Opportunities for new ventures, like most other opportunities, usually emerge over time instead of suddenly appearing. In a technical area, an individual may find or learn of a solution to a particular kind of problem and see the potential for using this approach in areas where it has not been applied before. Or in dealing with his employer's suppliers, he may identify key features of purchased products or services which he believes he can handle better, or at less cost, than others in the business. Or he may discover that there are needs for particular products or services that no one else supplies.

An individual in any part of a business enterprise may see potential opportunities for new ventures related to areas in which he is active. The alternative of starting a company becomes possible only when an individual perceives the basis for a viable enterprise and can see himself playing a major role in it. Whether or not a person interprets a situation as an opportunity is determined to a large degree by his perception of his own ability to take advantage of it.

Encouragement and support : Today when most middle managers or engineers begin to think of leaving their jobs they never *seriously* consider the possibility of starting a company. Unlike the established training programs and junior positions created by major corporations, there are no recognized patterns or channels for getting into one's own business. A few individuals have the special insights from their fathers' having been entrepreneurs, but the majority do not. For many, any substantial encouragement or help in the direction of becoming an entrepreneur is happenstance or luck.

Inputs which expand an individual's thinking about starting a company may range from an encouraging word to assistance with a detailed plan and analysis. It may be offered in a casual way or directed toward achieving some specific objective of the helper. In any case, it frequently plays a significant initial role.

One source of support comes from other individuals who share in the feelings of job dissatisfaction and would like to join in pursuing a venture or to become part of a team that undertakes such an effort. These people may represent a logical combination of diverse talents and personalities needed to overcome the problems and inertia of getting the venture started and continuing it as a profitable operation. Moreover, they may be known to each other and therefore represent a degree of certainty about how specific tasks will get done. But at the outset, a key role for these people and for others outside the immediate founder group can be to provide psychological support and encouragement. At the initial stage, momentum for the venture originates from talking it up, proposing different ways to solve the problems of starting, and giving helpful criticism to each other.

Who Are the Entrepreneurs?

A wife's reaction to the idea of starting a company usually is a major influence upon how long and how seriously an individual considers starting a company. Eventually, she will be directly affected. Her husband's happiness, her life-style and the family's financial future are at stake. I have seen wives who have responded with extreme anxiety at the prospect of their husband's starting a company, and I have seen those who have become a key part of the new venture. At either extreme the wife's role is critical.

Another source of support emerges from people to whom the would-be entrepreneur goes for help : potential suppliers, lawyers, bankers, other entrepreneurs, government officials, and so forth. These people can help an individual clarify his own thinking. They can assist in clarifying some of the specific uncertainties associated with starting the venture and can indicate their potential role in providing future information, assistance, or service should the venture be actively pursued. The existence of this kind of readily available help is part of the process of transforming an individual idea into a realistic alternative. If these sources of help are not apparent, then real and imagined problems of getting a venture going may appear insurmountable.

What About Risk?

Up to this point we have not dealt with risk as a factor *per se*. Entrepreneurs, in fact, have been described as people who *like* to take risks. (I believe the entrepreneurs I know would describe such people as fools.) There is more than a little difference between the person who likes risk and the person who finds risk to be a challenge. Risk covers a multitude of areas, all of which impinge in most instances upon entrepreneurial decisions.

Only when an individual considers starting a company as a serious alternative does his perception of risk become a key factor. Risk in this context has three elements : a) the perceived "odds" of various good and bad events occurring, b) the perceived consequences of these events, and c) the perceived seriousness of these consequences. It should be noted that all three aspects of risk are subjective. The individual's assessment of the risk is what influences his decision.

When an individual is in a free choice stage of his career, and when he is considering starting a company as a specific alternative, the perceived risks in a situation will influence whether or not he goes ahead with it. Below are briefly described four critical risk areas.

FINANCIAL RISK

The problem most people would think of first is whether or not they can afford to work with little or no salary for a period of several months to several years while the venture is getting started. This is particularly significant for the successful young executive or engineer who has improved his standard of living as he received promotions and salary increases. What would happen to the family budget without the monthly paycheck? How many families are willing to take a severe cut-back in their living expenditures?

But this is more a question of financial *sacrifice* than financial *risk*. In most new venture operations the individual will put a significant portion of his savings or other financial resources at stake. This money *is* risked and will in all likelihood be lost if the venture fails. The entre-preneur *may* also be required to sign personally on company obligations which far exceed his personal net worth. When such obligations significantly exceed the tangible net worth of the company, the individual exposes himself to the extreme condition of financial risk : personal bankruptcy.

CAREER RISK

A question raised by most would-be entrepreneurs is whether or not they will be able to find a job should they experience a failure in their own company. Obviously many people who are unsuccessful in their own firms *do* get jobs afterward with major corporations. The question, of course, is how difficult is it to get such a job and how will an employer look upon this kind of prospective employee?

FAMILY RISKS

As already mentioned, the requirements of starting a new venture frequently consume the energies, emotions, and time of the entrepreneur. As a result, he has little to give elsewhere, and his other commitments suffer. Entrepreneurs who are married, and especially those with child-ren, expose their families, at best, to the risks of an incomplete family experience and, at worst, to permanent emotional scars from inattention, quarrelling, and bitterness.

THE PSYCHIC RISK

An entrepreneurial effort by an individual has special features which subject a person to high psychic risk. First, everyone, including the entrepreneur himself, identifies the venture with one or two men. The company *is* these people. In addition, the magnitude of effort required to start a venture has given those activities priority over everything else in their lives - family, friends, and other interests. The greater the commitment, the more the identification with the venture is internalized.

If an individual fails, the experience can be shattering. In addressing the causes of a venture's failure, the entrepreneur himself is always one of the reasons. He planned poorly, he executed poorly, he followed through poorly, or in some way he did not allow sufficient margin for the unexpected. If an individual concludes that his failure in a particular effort was because of an inherent incapacity or inadequacy, he has lost his self-confidence. *The* risk to an individual is the risk of losing his self-confidence. The individual without self-confidence loses not only his abilities to function effectively in his career or profession but also loses his ability to deal effectively in his personal life. Moreover, once begun, such a process gains momentum and tends to whirl into a relentless downward spiral.

Summary and Conclusions

We have examined the entrepreneur who is involved in substantial ventures and have considered what we found in light of traditional thinking that he is a special type of individual - somehow an unusual and uncommon man - a man apart. It probably is true that very successful entrepreneurs *become* men apart. But, at the beginning, when they make the decision to start an entrepreneurial career, they are in most respects very much like many other ambitious, striving individuals. It appears, moreover, that the entrepreneurial interests for those who elect that path are more a function of *external* differences than internal ones - more the result of practical readiness and cost/income constraints than of individual psychology or personality. This is not to suggest that starting a successful company is a game that anyone can play. It is, however a statement that far more people could become entrepreneurs than ever do, and that the inclination of people to move in this direction could be increased by an increased awareness and recognition of this as a career alternative.

(1) *William F.Whyte & Robert R.Braun, "Heroes, Homework, and Industrial Growth", Columbia Journal of World Business, Spring 1966*

(2) *Manfred F.R.Kets de Vried, "The Entrepreneur as Catalyst of Economic & Cultural Change" (Ph.D.diss., Harvard Graduate School of Business Administration, 1970)*

(3) *Arnold C.Cooper, "Entrepreneurial Environment", Industrial Research, September 1970*

(4) *Michael Palmer, "The Application of Psychological Testing to Entrepreneurial Potential", California Management Review, Spring 1971*

(5) *Orvis F.Collins & David G.Moore with Darab B.Unwalla,"The Enterprising Man"(East Lansing, Mich. : Division of Research, Graduate School of Business Administration, Michigan State University, 1964), pp.241,243,244*

(6) *Herbert A.Wainer, "The Spin-Off of Technology from Government Sponsored Research Laboratories : Lincoln Laboratory" (M.A. thesis, Massachusetts Inst.of Technology, 1965); Paul V.Teplitz, "Spin-Off Enterprises from a Large Government Sponsored Laboratory" (M.A.thesis, Massachusetts Inst.of Technology, 1965); and Patrick R.Liles, "The Use of Outside Help in Starting High-Potential Ventures" (DBA diss., Harvard Graduate School of Business Administration, 1970)*

(7) *Liles, "The Use of Outside Help"*

(8) *Walter Guzzardi,Jr.,"The Young Executives"(New York : The New American Library, 1964)*

(9) *Liles, "The Use of Outside Help"*

Who Are the Entrepreneurs?

(10) *Collins, Moore & Unwalla, "The Enterprising Man"*

(11) *David C.McClelland, "Business Drive & National Achievement"*
Harvard Business Review, July-August 1962

(12) *David C.McClelland, "Achievement Motivation Can be Developed",*
Harvard Business Review, November-December 1965

2. THE SINCLAIR SYNDROME

Rosemary Brown

Management Today. June 1977

Entrepreneur extraordinary or spectacular flop? A decade hence,
what will be the verdict on Clive Sinclair, founder and managing director
of Sinclair Radionics? The question has important implications, and not
just because the National Enterprise Board has invested £650,000 of
taxpayers' money in what is, by any criterion, a high risk venture. The
success or failure of Sinclair could be - and is certainly so regarded by
many people - as a barometer of Britain's ability to compete at the fast-
moving consumer end of high-technology industry in world markets.

However you judge him and his company's potential, a man who
started from nothing, challenged the Japanese on their own ground and
- in spite of colossal setbacks - is still competing with world giants; who
made and lost hundreds of thousands of pounds in the space of a few
years and now, at the age of 36, is pioneering a pocket television that
he, at least is convinced will be a world-beater, is well worthy of
attention. Four years ago, with his company's profits at £306,000 before
tax, Sinclair was the golden boy of consumer micro-electronics. He
seemingly never put a foot wrong. But that was back in the heyday when
mini-calculators were selling at around the £80 mark, when the stylish
Executive was roaring up the export charts and Sinclair was being hail-
ed as the latest 'wizard' and 'genius' of British business.

It was common knowledge then that management was low on Sinclair's
scale of interests. But this only added to the mystique of the new young
tyro who invented and designed amazing products, then strode out into
the wide world where he found insatiable markets. In the rave press
notices he received in those days, there was no mention of the frequent
fiery scenes ('when Clive shouts, the mill trembles' remarks an ex-
employee); few reservations about the fact that the company sub-
contracted its entire production. The story of Clive Sinclair was far too
compulsive to mar with snide comments. Even in the trade, his tearaway
image was gradually replaced by grudging respect when, following the

launch of the pocket Cambridge in August 1973, Sinclair seized number one position in the U.K. calculator market.

By any standard, it was a remarkable feat for a boy who finished his education at 18, started life as a technical journalist, and whose entrepreneurial début began - as a spare time occupation - assembling radio components in his bedsitter. The beginning was so crude, so hilariously cheeky, that it smacked more of a schoolboy lark than the strategy of a tycoon in the making. What it boiled down to was that with £25 of his own money, and £25 borrowed from a friend, Sinclair purchased a load of reject transistors from Plessey. He tested and graded them; then, with his own specifications and name on them, resold them via mail order advertisements in the technical journals. It was the complete brash, one-man operation. As well as the 'production' end, Sinclair handled all his own promotion, and this included - as he unabashedly recalls - writing up the merchandise in glowing terms in the publication for which he worked.

Brazen or not, business prospered sufficiently to allow the introduction of phase two : radio kits. Again the method was essentially mail order - the only practical means of getting cash in advance. Compared with the make-or-break situation Sinclair faces today, the risks involved then seem paltry. But, at the time, this modest expansion was a highly precarious undertaking. The greater capital outlay needed for spare parts meant that life became a balancing act between getting money in and keeping suppliers sweet. If it says something for Sinclair's charm that he persuaded the trade to allow him to exist largely on credit, it says something for his drive and technical flair that he was able to launch the company proper at the age of 22. A year later, he could report a profit of £1,400 before the managing director's salary.

People who knew Sinclair then say he has changed since those buccaneering days 15 years ago. But his essential philosophy and outlook seem to have remained strikingly consistent. In spite of the knocks, his confidence in his ability is as buoyant as ever. The same attitude that decided him not to go to university 'because it had nothing to offer me from the point of view of electronics' is piercingly evident when, in the face of doubting sceptics, he insists with utter conviction that, whatever the cynics maintain, his Microvision Pocket T.V. will rank as a big-time winner. Right or wrong, Sinclair has the unswerving faith of which both fools and heroes are made.

Another echo from his youth is the compulsion to be constantly innovating. Though development work on the T.V. is calculated to take another five or six years, Sinclair is already leaping mentally ahead to his next major creation : a new form of electric motor. This restlessness combined with the shoe-string conditions of his early days, undoubtedly shaped his approach to business. It is no accident that, until recently, all his production was sub-contracted. It was a deliberate policy designed both to maximize return on limited capital and to minimize the management structure : its weaknesses only appeared with the electronic watch venture.

Until this Black Watch disaster, the strategy paid off handsomely. Without manufacturing overheads, there was more money to plough into research and development. Equally, relieved of some of the burden of normal management duties, Sinclair had more time to devote to the activities he was best at and which interested him most : technology, design and marketing. With the wisdom of hindsight, his critics can accuse him of rashly over-delegating quality control. However, it is arguable that, had he stuck to a safer and more conventional course, he would never have had the funds, or the impetus, to grab himself a place among the leaders in the world of pocket calculators.

Sinclair blames his catastrophic losses - £335,600 in 1976 - on the suppliers of the chip for his digital Black Watch. The dispute is now subject to litigation. The problems were certainly, to say the least, far-reaching. Not only did the chip itself run into trouble, the mercury-oxide batteries also caused reliability difficulties and there was a static electricity problem associated with the plastic 'anti precious' case. But whatever the principal reasons, the watch proved a stunning disaster. Reports of its failure rate vary from 30% to 70%. Although, to be fair, other companies trying to cash in on the new digital craze also suffered technical setbacks, the fact is that - but for the NEB rescue - Sinclair Radionics would have been in desperate straits.

The Sinclair Syndrome

Fast-moving, Cut-throat Industry

The saga vividly illustrated the hazards facing a minnow who dares to take on the world's giants in a fast-moving, cut-throat industry. The daunting moral is that if you are small and under-capitalized, one major mistake can easily prove fatal. But there is another angle to the story which casts an even more glaring light on the high-risk stakes for which Sinclair has been playing. At the height of his success in 1973, he described his formula for reaching the top in the following terms : "You look for a market which seems bound to develop, you find a product with a definite plus and then you out-advertise the competition". Diverse as it is, the Sinclair range - transistor radios, hi-fi, calculators, digital watches and now the pocket T.V. - has a common thread, apart from its obvious electronics link. Each product line is (or was) a potential trend-setter in a market highly susceptible to the vagaries of fashion.

While this description might apply equally to the cosmetics industry, the crucial difference between lipsticks and calculators is, of course, the technology factor. Both are ferociously competitive fields. But give or take a few refinements, a lipstick is a lipstick; whereas when the pocket calculator boom suddenly exploded, the technology was changing so fast that the unique selling qualities of one month could be obsolete the next. At the same time, the arena was crowded with vast, rich rivals who could afford to lose money for several years in the hope of emerging with a sizable slice of the market. In the struggle for supremacy, price-cutting quickly became the order of the day. As consumer demand for the new gadget grew beyond wildest expectations (it is estimated that one American household in four now has a calculator), the price crashed from a nice profitable £80, down to £20, then £10. Today, the basic Sinclair model retails at around £5.

The digital watch market proved almost equally erratic. If Sinclair and others suffered a bloody nose, they at least had the consolation of catching a rising trend, unlike most of the Swiss watch manufacturers, who are paying the penalty of their conservatism. Unemployment in the Swiss watch industry is currently reckoned to be 30%; and the forecast is that, within five years, digitals could be grabbing over 75% of total watch sales. Meanwhile, Sinclair is attempting the most difficult marketing feat of all : the relaunch of a dud product. The technical faults have now been corrected and, for better or worse, the revamped Black Watch is back on sale.

Not everyone shares his optimism that the gamble will succeed. Sinclair still has his admirers, but capitalism awards no prizes to an entrepreneur for having tried and failed. In City circles, where the comment is positively waspish, about the kindest remark anyone has ventured was : "You can't be a whiz-kid and go to the NEB, begging bowl in hand". But to write Sinclair off as a dilettante showman who got too big for his boots is not only to misjudge him but to belittle his very considerable achievements.

No one will deny him credit for having isolated three mass markets - for hi-fi, pocket calculators and digital watches - ahead of the trend; and for producing the goods to meet them - even though one has so far been a failure. It also needed courage to go in fighting against big corporations that could afford to finance loss leaders without serious risk to their shareholders or established reputations. Nor can Sinclair be denied his remarkable design flair, which has been recognized on both sides of the Atlantic.

His export achievements have been equally formidable. Sinclair is currently exporting products to more than 40 countries. The 'Executive' alone notched up over £2½ million of export revenue. His marketing acumen is not in doubt either : in 1974, he won the Institute of Marketing Award. Six months later Sinclair Radionics scored another triumph, as one of only two companies to win the 1975 Queen's Award to Industry for both export achievement and technological innovation - in scientific electronic calculators.

Whether or not you would pay £2,750 for a solid gold 'Sovereign' calculator, you have to credit the imagination that could promote the idea of lifting calculators out of the utility class, into the sphere of personal jewellery. Who cares what a calculator looks like, as long as it is functional!? The answer, it seems, is thousands of people. Several retail organizations are currently reporting 'tremendous sales' of the Sovereign gold finish (£60) and the brushed chrome (£30) models. Sinclair's latest slogan, 'A pocket calculator is as much a part of the business man's survival kit as his watch or cuff-links' could point to yet another trend. The test will be whether, before long, his competitors will be flaunting prestige lines.

Although, in the event, bankruptcy was staring him in the face, Sinclair's conceptual approach was textbook for the head of a small innovative company trying to break into the big time. The 'get in first, establish the market and then cut the price when volume sales allow and competition compels' is in the classic market tradition. Sinclair's biggest achievement of all, however, is his continued survival. In spite of the dramatic swoops in fortune, his loss of financial credibility, the sneers of the City and the gallons of cold water that have been poured on the prospects of the pocket T.V., Sinclair is still there, pioneering away and elaborating confidently on the new mass markets he says he is about to capture.

The pace of life has altered remarkably little at Sinclair Radionics since the débâcle. There have obviously been changes. The NEB cash and its 43% shareholding have added a new dimension. (For that matter, there is also the £700,000 from the National Research Development Corporation which is specifically ear-marked for further work on the pocket T.V.) It is also true that the company no longer consists merely of the mini go-go team, plus engineers, with its corps of secretaries and clerical staff dancing attendance. The clerical side has been streamlined. More to the point, most of the production has been moved in-house, swelling the workforce to 320, and 'quality control' has become the new motto on everyone's lips. Certainly, too, there has been a considerable tightening up on the management/supervisory side, and people who knew the organization in the old swashbuckling days say they detect a definite new air of formality. Possibly so. But the company's head office, in an old converted mill out at St.Ives, Huntingdon, nevertheless still radiates youthful casualness, with none of the trappings that might be expected in an organization that has moved from turbulent adolescence to sobering maturity. Sinclair's own office is a large, airy room at the top of the building. With its stark white brick walls and contemporary furniture, the style is downbeat Habitat : practical rather than comfortable, designed for work, devoid of signs of affluence.

"I'm not a brilliant manager"

But then Sinclair has no particular yearning for money as his driving force. The question 'What does motivate Clive Sinclair?' is one that is bound to arise often. Power? Yes, in the sense that he wants to be listened to, feels strongly about the tax structure, the climate for enterprise and the need to encourage new technology to replace the old, dying industries. "I want to change things. If I succeed, people will talk to me", he explains with real emphasis. But power in the sense of being the big boss, of making million-pound deals, controlling other people's lives? Not really. "I'm not a brilliant manager", he confesses. "I loathe firing people, almost to the point of funking it. And though it's absurd, I still find it horribly difficult to give a lecture".

If not power, then the freedom and independence of running his own company? "It's what I always wanted. On the other hand I enjoyed working for other people. My ambition was to design and produce products, so to the extent that I'm free to do that, Sinclair Radionics gives me enormous satisfaction. I'm excited by the technical side, solving problems, getting it right". No problem he has ever faced is more fascinating, nor needs to be got right more urgently, than the newest baby - the pocket television.

After 12 years of research and over £500,000 invested in its development, the Microvision Pocket T.V., launched last January, has a 2" screen, is 4" wide, 6" from front to back, $1\frac{1}{2}$" deep and weighs $26\frac{1}{2}$ozs. It works by internal rechargeable batteries or off the mains, is capable of receiving transmissions in most parts of the world, operates in a car and train as well as in the home, and costs £200 plus VAT. The question is : Who will buy it?

In the immediate future, Sinclair sees it essentially as an executive purchase. But once the price comes down and the product is adapted along less sophisticated lines, he estimates the potential to be virtually limitless : as big, say, as the current transistor radio market. The strategy he envisages is the standard Sinclair blueprint : be first in the field, get cracking on the developments; and when the competition moves in, be ready to slash the price and cash in on volume sales. The formula has time as one critical factor. Sinclair reckons on having an 18 months to two-year lead over the rest of the world but he is acutely conscious that the Japanese are not all that far behind. (National Panasonic produced a dwarf, if not a pocket size set a couple of years ago.) He is equally aware that once the demand is established, they will attempt to come in and swamp him : just as a firm like Casio now offers a range of calculators and digital watches which is far more comprehensive than Sinclair can hope to market.

But will the T.V. demand be established? Why should a travelling businessman want a pocket television, when virtually every hotel room contains a full-size set? And can the price ever be brought sufficiently low to appeal to any other than the rich who can indulge a whim by buying the latest toy? Sinclair has gallant answers to such questions. The current model was designed to be the ultimate in perfection : over-engineered, if you like. Without the international transmssion features, for example, the cost could be substantially reduced. An exclusive market for Arab sheiks? In America, where the set has also been launched, orders are apparently flooding in. Obviously, if the product proves to be only a status symbol with transient appeal, disaster will loom. But Sinclair talks of extraordinary developments under investigation and is sure that the potential spin-offs are immense.

Behind the fierce pride, there is a suspicion of defensiveness. For all the brave enthusiasm, Sinclair is still on the raw from his rejection by the City. It is no secret that, when he was in trouble last year, he approached several City houses, plus GEC. 'Trying to raise finance in the City wasn't so much difficult as downright impossible' is his summing up of a situation that angers him, and that he wants to forget.

Polite cynicism, downright doubt

While undoubtedly treated with the utmost courtesy, he could hardly fail to have missed the polite cynicism - not to say downright doubt - with which his chances were assessed. Choosing his words carefully, a Charterhouse spokesman observes : 'Though we thought he was a very impressive chap, Charterhouse was always an unlikely source of finance given our policy of investing in consistently successful businesses'. Other comments from other sources are strictly non-attributable : 'The chances of making any money at all are less than 1%'; 'If I had several hundred thousand to spare and tossed in a couple of hundred, I should regard it strictly as a charitable donation'; 'If he had come to us to ask for cash, we should have told him in so many words that we don't believe in selling miniature televisions to fishermen who should be watching the fish and not some little screen'.

Leaving aside the gibes and the gratuitous rudeness, some very legitimate doubts are being expressed. For a start, there is the uncomfortable feeling that the calculator boom has run its course. There have already been casualties and over the next couple of years the market could be littered with corpses. And if Sinclair's major money spinner were to collapse, which is conceivable, what then? There is real concern about the prospects of the Black Watch. Although the product is now technically sound, there are many more attractive models available, some of which are only marginally more expensive. It is difficult to forecast fashion appeal, of course, but after Sinclair missed the boat at the initial launch, can he really expect to succeed at a second attempt? If he does, some marketing textbooks may have to be rewritten.

As for the television, most people agree that it is a fantastic toy. Equally, most will concede that if it were selling for £10 or £20, it could be sure of a huge market. But at £200 a time, will sales ever become sufficiently buoyant to permit the price-slashing and streamlining that would obviously make sense?

Although Sinclair argues that the same doubts were attached to pocket transistor radios, there are undeniable differences between the two. You can listen to the radio while getting dressed, typing a letter or doing the cooking; a television set is more demanding and time-consuming in that it has to be watched. But assume that Sinclair is right, and the pocket T.V. booms, one of two very nasty possibilities could still loom on the horizon very quickly indeed. The company could be under-capitalized once again, and need a further massive injection of cash. Alternatively, as Sinclair himself admits is conceivable, the Japanese could enter the fray and indulge in a vicious price-cutting battle, if necessary sustaining substantial losses for a few years until they had swept the Microvision out of the market.

The Sinclair Syndrome

'Risky and innovative projects'

All these risks must have been known to the NEB and NRDC. So why, between them, did they invest over one and a quarter million pounds of taxpayers' money? The NRDC's answer is forthright. Our business is to invest in risky and innovative projects. In the sort of league we deal in £700,000 comes about middle-rank. Quite simply, we are backing two things : Clive's entrepreneurial flair and what he is proposing in relation to the next generation of T.V.tubes. The NEB is more overtly optimistic. "The attraction for us was that Sinclair Radionics is the only genuinely British effort in the consumer micro-electronics field, so we couldn't afford not to consider it seriously. Look at the thing in perspective : a relatively small company with a number of sound innovations under its belt that took on the Japs and, despite some battle scars, has survived. We are under no illusions about the risks but our judgment is that we expect to make some money - and quite a lot of money at that."

Clearly, the Microvision is a considerable commercial risk. It could be an intelligent speculation, and it could be lucky. It might even make a small contribution towards getting Britain back on its feet. Old industries are dying and are not being replaced. Jobs are disappearing. Yet inventiveness and daring can still be found, and the best hope of national recovery must be to encourage individuals with these qualities to attempt new breakthroughs. It did look at one point as if Clive Sinclair had found a way round the obvious financial difficulties by the inspired method of sub-contracting his manufacturing.But marketing a product without control of its production is no substitute for the integrated operation whose future Sinclair's critics are now questioning.

Like Sinclair's backers at the NEB, the business world (including the bankers who disregard his chances) will have to wait and see. The odds are that in so fast-moving a market, they will not have to wait long. What is already clear is that the insouciant attitude to management of the past is one luxury Clive Sinclair can no longer afford : a luxury that would prove far more extravagant than a solid gold calculator or even a £200 midget T.V.

3. BIG FISH IN LITTLE PONDS - THE BUSINESS GRADUATE AS ENTREPRENEUR

M.H.Karger

Business Graduate. Volume 4 Number 4. October 1974

Summary

In this article I describe my experience in starting my own business, manufacturing decorative candles, after graduating from the MSc class at the London Business School. The gestation and growth of the company is described from the genesis of the idea in 1970 to the present time.

In the following sections some of the reasons for the low number of MBAs from U.K. business schools who start out on their own are discussed and the reasons why, in the opinion of the author, more should, are put forward.

In a final section we consider the main advantages which a business graduate brings to the role of entrepreneur compared with his non-MBA counterpart.

The number of business graduates from U.K. Business Schools who start up in business on their own after graduation is remarkably low. In the 1972 class at L.B.S., for example, they numbered two from a total of over ninety. Of these one went into an established family firm, leaving the other, the author of this article, as the sole entrant into the ranks of the classical entrepreneur.

It is the purpose of this article, in describing the starting up of a company with negligible experience and resources, to show that it is still possible in the age of the multi-national corporation to start a manufacturing company from scratch, and, in a surprisingly short space of time, to bring it to the point where it is able to support a business graduate in the style to which he hopes to become accustomed.

My own company, Kandell Designs Ltd., was started on a part-time basis in 1970, becoming a full-time occupation in mid-1972. Today, just two years later, turnover is approaching £100,000 with projected earnings before tax (but after extracting a salary roughly twice that I might have expected as a business graduate) of between £15,000 and £20,000. The starting capital was a little over £200 and even today the total capital input by the owners (my brother being an equal partner in the venture) is under £2,000.

Our interest in candles was sparked, quite by chance, when a particular type of candle seen in a film proved unobtainable. A friend and I decided to attempt to make our own in lieu, and I began to look into methods of manufacture. At the time I was working as a research chemist prior to beginning a two-year course at L.B.S. I was able to carry out some limited research into the means of production and design of decorative candles and even to investigate via the scientific library at my disposal the early history and technology of the subject. By August 1970 we had designed a number of different styles of decorative candles which were felt to be already superior to those available on the market, which were of very limited appeal as well as being very expensive. We felt that, to use the jargon, we had perceived a gap in the market for a low technology consumer product.

At this stage we decided to set about marketing the product in a small way. A three-way partnership between myself, my brother, and the friend who had originally suggested the idea, was set up, using £200 scraped together from personal savings.

This starting capital was used to purchase raw materials and equipment, a garage providing 120 square feet of work space was fitted with gas and electricity and we were in business.

Sales were initially made on an ad-hoc basis to friends and following their enthusiastic reception of our efforts we did a small test market, approaching six or seven gift shops. Over £250 of sales were made and this ready acceptance by the retail trade gave a tremendous boost to morale, confirming the product's competitiveness.

Further marketing information, particularly with regard to such parameters as colour, shape and design preferences, as well as price elasticity was obtained via street market sales to the public.

In December 1970 the power workers' strike led to a massive demand for candles. Although we were at capacity prior to the Christmas trading peak and were thus unable to capitalise on the situation, we found that the enormous amount of free product publicity had a pronounced long-term effect (reinforced by subsequent power and coal crises). The British public began to become candle-conscious, and the growth of the overall market became prodigious.

During the following year our product range became increasingly sophisticated. Many different and unique styles and shapes were produced and the packaging, in glossy red cartons with gold foil labelling, approached cosmetic industry standards. We now felt ready for a wider market and approached several major London department stores, with some success. The John Lewis group in particular proved most encouraging, giving us national distribution throughout their 25 stores and placing orders of over £600. Since this store buyer had available competitive products from all over the world we felt we were now fully the equal of any of our competitors both here and abroad.

By the end of 1971 sales of over £5,000 had been achieved (1970 : £500) and our garage was looking increasingly inadequate as production rose to over 500 candles per week.

With a very high gross margin and virtually no overheads the expansion in turnover was comfortably self-financed, and by early 1972 it had become obvious that sufficient potential existed to justify a decision to go into the venture on a full-time basis.

After much thought both my brother and I decided to take this step and bought out the third partner, who felt unable to give up his job and join us.

As part of the MSc programme at London Business School, a five-year plan with fully detailed finance, marketing and budgetary forecasts had been made. Armed with this document, which called for a level of turn-over of £100,000 by 1976, our friendly local bank manager was approached. Much impressed by the mass of figurework and heavily jargonised text he allowed us sufficient overdraft facilities (amounting to over ten times our own equity stake in the company) to enable us to begin a major expansion of our activities. A 2,000 square feet factory was leased in November and the first staff taken on and trained in the means of making the candles. (Up to this point the entire output had been manufactured by the three principals.) By the end of 1972 sales had risen to £13,000, a level just sufficient to provide living expenses, but no more.

At this stage we were a company with a highly competitive product with woefully inadequate marketing, depending on sales to one or two large customers and perhaps seventy or eighty retail outlets obtained in a fairly sporadic and haphazard way.

The first step in systemising the marketing of the product was to set up, over a period of a year or so, a network of agents each selling to one particular area of the country. By the end of 1973 some 80% of the country was covered in this way and the number of retail accounts was approaching six hundred.

In addition, the company was increasingly participating in retail trade fairs which, allied with a certain amount of trade advertising, was making the company extensively known throughout the giftware trade as a supplier of high quality candles.

Thus by the end of 1973 sales had reached over £50,000 and it was becoming possible to draw a salary more in line with that of a business graduate than that of his secretary.

Up to the time of writing, expansion has continued unchecked aided by diversification of the existing products into new markets, particularly exports. (In May 1974, for example, exports, particularly to the U.S.A. and W.Europe, accounted for over 50% of total sales during the month.) In addition our existing U.K. distribution network enables us to feed in other high quality giftware products which are bought in rather than manufactured. Currently such products account for some 20% of U.K. turnover and this is expected to rise, thereby reducing our dependence upon a single product, however excellent.

The situation of the company today is a healthy one. Turnover is expected to appraoch £100,000 in 1974, two years in advance of the original target date. With a current staff level of twelve the company is fully able to meet this demand and the present premises can probably support at least double that, before larger ones need be sought. With a very low overhead structure and high gross margins, the level of profit is substantial, currently yielding a healthy return on owners' equity.

Thus the decision to take the risk of starting one's own business from scratch has been fully justified.

As the story of the gestation and growth of a small business, the above description is typical of hundreds of others. Indeed, many major companies today can trace their origins back to a similar garage/kitchen sink type of operation. What is perhaps unusual, in a U.K. context, is that the founders of this particular business should both be such highly qualified people. (As well as my own MSc in Business Studies both my brother and myself have PhDs in scientific subjects.)

I should like to now go on to consider the inverse question of why so few highly qualified people (particularly those with business degrees) start up their own businesses in this country (in the U.S.A. and Germany two of the most highly developed free-world economies such a situation is far from unusual), but why in my opinion they should. Finally, I shall discuss some of the advantages which the MBA brings to running his own enterprise which would serve to give him a head and shoulders start over his less privileged fellow entrepreneur.

WHY NOT?

1. Status. A side effect of the cult of big business is the enhanced social status of those associated with large companies ("He's Assistant Marketing Manager with Prentice and Thompson, you know") and, conversely, the diminished social status of the owners of small businesses. Most owners of smaller businesses seem remarkably unconcerned about this. In fact they commonly take a rather derogatory attitude towards the executive in the large corporation, regarding it as almost unbeliev- able that for managing perhaps £10m worth of assets an executive will take home less than the owner-manager of a business perhaps one- hundredth or even one-thousandth of its size.

2. Risk. Undeniably the small business has a far higher risk of failure than the large, with its sophisticated forecasting staff and high reserves of capital and technological resources. But the risk element in the small business is far more controllable by the relatively sophisticated graduate owner than appears at first sight. Once the business is off the ground (and if it does not get off the ground very little is lost anyhow), an extensive panoply of choices for expansion or for product or market diversification is available to the business graduate, trained as he is to take the longer view.

In the larger company while the risk of the company failing may be very low, not so the risk of personal failure for the executive, particularly in middle age, when he realises that he has progressed as far as he can in the organisation. Executive unemployment in these days of frequent takeover and merger is no longer a rarity, but the owner of a successful small business is immune from loss of livelihood.

On a slightly different level, many graduates who would otherwise be eager to start on their own feel unable to do so, feeling that the step from full-time employment to complete self-reliance is too drastic to take, particularly if family responsibilities weigh heavily. By no means, how-ever, does the decision have to be an all or nothing leap in the dark. In my own case two years of careful preparation were invested before deciding upon the venture as a full-time occupation. During these two years, I was fully occupied during the day at London Business School but used the available spare time to bring the business to the stage where it could support me immediately, albeit at a level not much higher than my student grant of £1,300 per annum.

In a similar way, a fully employed graduate could initially progress on a part-time basis, gradually building up to the point where he could leave his company and not suffer too drastic a cut in his standard of living.

3. Capital. Lack of capital is often considered the main stumbling block to the prospective entrepreneur. Again, I have shown in our case how as little as a couple of hundred pounds sufficed to get the business under way, whilst, when more substantial sums were required, a reasonably well-documented case was sufficient to enable borrowing requirements to be met. The business graduate with his ability to present a well researched and logical investment proposal has a tremendous advantage over his less educated counterpart. In general if the business proposal is sound someone can be found to put up the required capital.

4. Reward. Undeniably, the steadily rising salary levels offered to management by large companies provide a secure and attractive basis for a high and rising standard of living, particularly in comparison to the often years of self-denial that may be necessary before the entrepreneur can claim an equivalent "take", compared to his big business counterpart. But from that point on the management executive is unlikely to match the owner of a small business in the rewards for his labour. As well as suffering unfavourably on a straight salary comparison, the executive is unlikely to be able to take advantage of the numerous perks available to the self-employed. In particular the tax authorities are far more lenient on the self-employed than on the salaried, and many major items of expenditure, particularly cars, foreign travel and entertainment expenses, may legitimately be made through the company in a manner denied to lower and middle level executives in the larger enterprise.

5. Ideas. Another major reason often put to me to justify an action is that ideas such as mine filling a market need are very hard to produce. But such an attitude could be viewed in a slightly different perspective. If your managing director called you in and told you to examine the future direction for your company you would work to produce an answer. You would soon be beavering away with market research, etc., and would, no doubt, soon emerge with a sparkling set of ideas for new markets to attack, complete with a fully detailed corporate plan of action. After all, that was what Business School was all about. Strengths and weaknesses, markets and competition, etc. Surely then, if you can do it for your company there is no reason why you cannot do it for yourself.

6. Temperament. Many graduates simply feel temperamentally unsuited to operate in the small business world, feeling perhaps that their talents are more attuned to the organisational requirements of large companies. Certainly the world of the small business can rarely approach the degree of complexity and extent of functional fragmentation that holds, as a rule, in large corporations. For those more at home in the world of the committee, the departmental memo and the organisation chart there would appear to be little reason for going into the more personal world inhabited by most smaller enterprises.

7. Power. Although many would be loth to admit it, much of the appeal of working in a large organisation stems from the opportunity it affords for supervising the working lives of large and growing numbers of people. Empire building a personal power structure enables control of numbers of talented and educated subordinates. In short, power over others.

There is no doubt that the smaller business cannot provide such satisfaction to the same degree. The difference lies at the other end. For all but a handful, the large corporation will always have a pyramid above, the mirror image of the one below. The difference being, of course, that you are at the bottom accountable to your immediate boss, for the management of your own pyramid. In your own business the pile beneath may be a lot smaller and less talented but above is only the clear blue sky.

8. Job satisfaction. Finally, perhaps the most valid reason of all for continuing to work in a large organisation concerns the question of job satisfaction. Without doubt the larger company can provide work which is far more demanding intellectually, and may be far more stimulating than the work involved in building up a small business. (Whether it does or not is another question.) This can be trivial, often boring and, horror of horrors, will often involve a degree of manual work which may be felt to add little to the dignity and self-esteem of the business graduate, unaccustomed as he is to having his hands dirtied by anything other than ink, or to carrying around anything heavier than computer print-out.

For those who relish complexity in their work and wish to have their mental capacity strained to its limits there is, perhaps, every reason to avoid the path of the entrepreneur. Having said this, many of today's most successful small businesses have come about as a result of technically advanced products being born in research departments, only to be neglected by the company, to the dismay of the originators, who have then left the company to develop and market the product themselves. Certainly on the technological side larger companies by no means have a monopoly of either products or innovative talents.

Balanced against the relative lack of this sort of job satisfaction must be set the immense feeling of achievement in creating a company and an organisation, often from nothing, and, in a very real and tangible sense, having added to the wealth of the community.

One of the notable features of any analysis of the positions which business graduates occupy is the large proportion involved in manipulating wealth rather than creating it. In the 1974 BGA Address Book, for example, out of some 1,400 entries no less than 620 were in the banking/finance/consultancy/educative sectors, and of those who did enter manufacturing industry, very few indeed entered the production field. While it is, of course, true that the more advanced an economy the greater the importance of its finance and service sectors, it is equally true that one of the main reasons for Britain's poor economic performance is the weakness of the manufacturing sector relative to our international competitors. Such a situation is not helped by the draining of our most talented managerial recruits overwhelmingly into the non-manufacturing sectors. Starting one's own manufacturing company represents, in however small a way, a reversal of this trend for the benefit both of the entrepreneur himself and of the community.

Britain's wealth in the past has been largely created by processing imported raw materials into finished products and exporting the higher valued end-product. It is the increasing erosion of this strength and the progressively greater importation of manufactured goods which has contributed greatly to the ever-worsening balance of trade. Germany on the other hand, weathers oil crises in her stride, actually producing record trade surpluses while we suffer the reverse. It is perhaps only when we address ourselves to this larger problem, North Sea oil notwithstanding, that we may, as a nation, begin to make a more efficient use of our talents.

These then cover the majority of reasons put forward for not starting your own business. Turning to the other side of the coin - what are the positive advantages to the business graduate (or anyone else) in going it alone? There are four major reasons which I feel most entrepreneurs would readily agree with -

1. Freedom. Relative to his cousin in the large corporation the little entrepreneur enjoys a personal freedom which is almost intoxicating in its totality. Virtually the only limitations are those imposed by the scale and success of his enterprise. He is in total control of all facets of his business. He can devote himself to day-to-day production or to long-term planning; to marketing or to finance; to home or overseas; or to all of these at once. He can decide to enter a dozen new markets or none at all; to take one week's holiday, or ten; to go to Sidcup or Sydney. He can even devote himself to writing overlong articles for "The Business Graduate"! There is no-one to veto any course of action, no superior to placate, no subordinates to worry over in case they covet your own job.

Conversely there may be no-one in a position to disagree with wrong decisions, or with whom to discuss genuine doubts, and the business may suffer if the head absents himself for too long. Even these disadvantages, however, can be minimal, since many small businesses (my own included) have two or more partners who can shoulder the burdens of absence and share the often lonely responsibility of ownership. In short, you are your own boss.

2. Salary. I have already pointed out how the small businessman can draw a salary out of all proportion to the size of his enterprise. Certainly, compared with U.K. manufacturing industry the rewards appear substantial.

The abysmally low standards of remuneration prevailing in the manufacturing sectors relative to the financial and service sectors and to manufacturers overseas, were recently brought home to me most forcibly. I was informed that the managing director of a major subsidiary of one of our largest mining/chemical groups, responsible for a company making £2m profit, was paid £7,000 per annum, a salary comparable with my own even at this early stage in the growth of our company, a company moreover with profits less than 1% of the larger company.

3. Capital. The entrepreneur enjoys one priceless advantage over his big business counterpart. As his company grows so does its capital value representing an enormous if unrealised potential capital gain, which is comparatively lightly taxed at the present time. With current marginal tax rates on earned income at 83% but capital gains tax at 30% it has become virtually impossible to accumulate wealth from salaried income alone, leaving capital gains as virtually the sole legal method of wealth accumulation still available. The growth of a solely owned small enterprise need only proceed to a relatively limited extent, before the owner is a wealthy man (or woman). Whilst large companies have attempted to give capital gains to their executives by such means as share options, this avenue has now been closed by legislation. Not so the capital gains of the entrepreneur.

4. Finally, if for no other reason, running your own business is such bloody good fun! Each day brings the unexpected, every other week a major triumph or failure. No long interminable meetings with faceless bureaucrats. No tedious report-writing to justify one action, or to seek to promote a new course of action. It is rather like piloting a high-speed launch. You will never carry as many passengers as the QE II, and you will certainly never cross the Atlantic, but you can sure enjoy throwing her around a bit even if you do get drenched in the process.

Advantages of being a business graduate in your own business

In the two preceeding sections, I have tried to present in an open but biased way, the pros and cons of starting out alone to develop one's own business. While no-one can guarantee success, and in fact the majority of small businesses fail, there are powerful reasons why the chances of failure for an MBA setting up on his own are likely to be very much lower than the average.

Firstly, the Business Graduate has the ability to talk to the financial world in its own terms, very often in language it cannot understand but is impressed by. Verbally and on paper the business graduate is able to put over his ideas and proposals in a thoroughly professional way. These ideas may, in fact, be inferior to many others competing for funds, but a superior presentation will often win the backing that the better proposal fails to get.

Secondly, once the business is under way, the MBA, by virtue of his grounding in accountancy and budgetary procedure, can ensure that the day-to-day running of the business is of a high order of efficiency. Short-term cash flow analysis, regular audits of profitability and good short-term planning techniques ensure that problems are anticipated well in advance and appropriate remedial action taken in time. Too often the small business run by less well trained entrepreneurs flounders on

its own success, over-trading in the period before a sudden credit
squeeze being a common cause of business failure. The business graduate
can readily avoid such pitfalls since, in general, his overall control of
his business will be of a much higher level than his competitors.

Thirdly, the business graduate has been trained to take a much
longer-term view than is usual. He will above all be aware of the dangers
of dependence upon one or two customers or markets. He will have a
clear idea of where his business is now, and where it is heading in two,
five and ten years' time. His ear will be more finely tuned to the needs
of the market, because he knows what becomes of companies who remain
unchanged for long periods of time. He will have had drummed into him
ad nauseam, the need for analysis of company strengths and weaknesses
and for diversification. In our own case for example we very early
recognised the need to diversify both our markets and our product range,
with the result that we were selling in overseas markets even before we
had fully covered the U.K. market, and are rapidly diversifying our
product range to reduce our dependence on candles alone.

Finally, the MBA will have had at least a theoretical grounding in all
aspects of business. Whilst many of the more advanced analytical
techniques are unlikely to be of use as long as the business remains small,
it is surprising just what facets of a business school education do prove
useful. In our own case, for example, we were able to take the concept
of the autonomous work group, examined in the course on organisational
behaviour, and develop it to its logical end.

Our production system is now such that it almost entirely runs itself.
The teams of girls work virtually unsupervised, switching and changing
tasks as they feel like it within entirely flexible working hours. As a
result the loudest noise on the factory floor at Kandell is the sound of
girls' laughter, and there is a waiting list for jobs with the company.
Productivity is exceptionally high, even higher than that calculated as
an ideal to aim for. Since the despatch department and the U.K. sales
effort also virtually run autonomously the owners of the business are in
the happy position of having virtually worked themselves out of a job.
This does enable a lot of long-term thinking and planning to go on, far
more than in the usual small company, where management is usually beset

by day-to-day problems and rarely has a chance to sit back and examine the business and its markets from afar.

In a similar vein we have used much of the finance and accounting teachings from L.B.S. to install a simple management accounting system which throws up week-by-week analysis of such things as overall profitability and labour productivity.

The sales force is also managed in a manner calculated to yield the maximum of both sales force effort and informational feedback, after one of the innumerable case studies examined at L.B.S.

In these and many other ways the business graduate is enabled to exhibit considerable advantages over his less well trained counterpart in the small business world.

In this article I have tried to indicate some of the positive results which a business graduate may hope to achieve in business on his own, illustrating where possible from my own experience. I have also tried to indicate why some of the reasons often advanced for preferring large companies to starting on one's own, have only limited validity. I hope that some of the classes graduating in the future from British business schools may thereby be encouraged to try their hand on their own. Certainly life may be a bit more risky than being a corporate planner or a financial analyst but there is a good chance that it will be a lot more exciting and leave you at the end of the day considerably better off, both materially and mentally.

Small Business Perspectives

PART II

FINANCING SMALL BUSINESSES

CHAPTER 3 : SOURCES OF FINANCE

Introduction

It should be apparent by now that writings about small firms are not characterised by definitive conclusions drawn from statistical analyses of large samples. Because they tend to operate in small, specialist or embryonic markets, small firms are a disparate, heterogeneous group.

It follows that there is no 'usual' pattern to the financing of new firms. In the U.S. it is not uncommon for entrepreneurs to borrow several million dollars against their own personal assets of a few tens of thousands. In contrast, the £80 million JCB Excavators was started with fifty shillings and a second-hand welding kit. Indeed it is rumoured that JCB borrowed only once during the early years - on a Friday afternoon. This is supposed to have caused the proprietor such anxiety over the weekend that he repaid the loan on Monday morning and managed without it.

The financial structure with which a firm starts is influenced by many factors. From the backer's viewpoint, the risk of the enterprise is judged not just against the market uncertainties, but also against the nature and value of the assets to be acquired, and, of course, the collateral available from the entrepreneur(s). On the other hand, the entrepreneur may be unwilling to share the equity with outside investors, or pledge personal assets. In such cases the project is sometimes scaled down, for example, by subcontracting production. Ultimately, lending decisions depend upon the lender's assessment of the borrower's ability to execute the plan, and are therefore largely subjective. The entrepreneur needs to be prepared to 'do the rounds'.

The sources of finance for new firms in the U.K. are more numerous than is generally thought, but since these sources are frequently described in newspapers and periodicals, this chapter concentrates more on the processes involved. In the second article, Stevens, himself a practitioner, presents his view of the issues involved in appraising and investing in venture capital projects. It is worth noting that although venture capitalists have had a further decade of practice since this article first appeared, their investment records have probably not improved substantially.

In reality, most small firms do not use venture capital, and in the principal article, Tamari makes a valiant attempt to examine some of the widely-held beliefs about the financial structure of small firms. If the nomenclature makes the article a little difficult to follow, and the conclusions appear rather 'soggy', the content is nevertheless valuable, particularly for some of the explanations the author puts forward for the phenomena he observes. Just as the owner-manager's business and private lives are intimately connected, so too are his assets. Managers of public companies do not usually move their personal financial resources around to meet the needs of the business.

Finally, Sibley provides an institutional viewpoint in his description and analysis of the newly-created Unlisted Securities Market on the London Stock Exchange. It seems likely that, for the immediate future, this will represent a means whereby proprietors can get money out of, rather than into, their firms, but nevertheless the development reflects the increasing awareness of the economic importance of small firms. And, if the USM encourages more firms to grow, so much the better.

1. THE FINANCIAL STRUCTURE OF THE SMALL FIRM - AN INTERNATIONAL COMPARISON OF CORPORATE ACCOUNTS IN THE U.S.A., FRANCE, U.K., ISRAEL, AND JAPAN

Dr.Meir Tamari, Bank of Israel

American Journal of Small Business. Volume IV   Number 4.
Spring (April-June) 1980

I. INTRODUCTION

An investigation of the financing of the small firm, its profitability, and its pattern of investments is essential to any serious analysis of the small firm and its future development. The financial performance of small firms reveals both the strengths and the weaknesses of this sector of the economy. It is therefore not surprising that in many countries the analysis of financial structure has become an integral part of the research conducted into the behaviour of the small firm, in addition to the various social, political, and psychological aspects of the subject.

The first surveys specifically devoted to the small firm were conducted in the U.S.A. Merwin's (1) pioneering research in 1940 which referred to approximately 900 firms, was followed in 1960 by a far more extensive project carried out by the Federal Reserve System(2). A more recent study of the small firm which also included financial analysis is that edited by Pfeffer(3). Similar studies of the financial behaviour of the small firm have been carried out, *inter alia*, in the U.K., France, Israel and Japan.

The analyses of small firm financial data are usually centered on two main theses :

(a) If one assumes the existence of economies of scale, then the small firm in any economy is likely to be less profitable than its larger counterpart; it therefore constitutes an inefficient use of resources.

(b) Small firms have limited access to the capital and money markets and therefore suffer from chronic undercapitalization. As a result, they are likely to have excessive recourse to expensive funds which act as a brake on their economic development. This hypothesis is usually expressed in two forms : First, that small firms have less equity than large firms, and secondly, that small firms tend to enjoy less liquidity than do large firms.

These hypotheses regarding the financial structure of the small firm may be tested by examining data from the various studies conducted in the five countries mentioned. In each of the countries concerned, one can discern a pattern of financial behaviour which distinguishes the small firm from the large firm in that economy.

II. PURPOSE AND SCOPE OF THIS STUDY

A distinct pattern of financial behaviour in a particular economy, however, is not by itself sufficient evidence that such a difference reflects uniquely the effect of size. It may well be that the institutional framework for economic activity and legal or fiscal restrictions in a particular economy are the real causes of this particular pattern of behaviour.

Numerous examples can be brought to illustrate this; two may suffice.

Meltzer(4) found that small firms in the U.S. tend to rely more on trade credit than do large firms, as a result of their inability to obtain funds from other sources. If this could be confirmed by data in other countries, then it might be concluded that it indeed characterizes small firms, and is not dependent on the structure of the money and capital market of a particular country.

Alternatively, corporate research in Israel shows that small firms tend to distribute part of their profits in the form of excessive managerial salaries paid to the owners, household and personal expenses charged to the firms and the like, rather than as nominal dividends(5). It might be, however, that such practices reflect the country's fiscal policy or the prevalent forms of firm ownership. If it can be shown that the same policy of profit distribution is common to firms of all sizes having the same form of ownership, or paying the same reduced tax income rates, then it may be assumed that these factors rather than the size, determine the pattern of profit distribution.

The purpose of this study, therefore, is to examine the financial structure of the small firm in various countries - U.S., U.K., France, Japan and Israel. If the international comparisons reveal that a common

pattern of behaviour prevails for the small firm in these economies despite
the social, political, and economic differences between them, then it is
suggested that such a pattern does indeed reflect the effects of firm size.
On the other hand, should a particular financial pattern exist only in
one economy, then one may doubt if firm size is the primary cause.

For U.K. the information for this study was drawn from the financial
and nonfinancial data collated by the U.K. Commission of Small Firms,
established in 1970. These data are based on replies to a postal questionnaire of a sample of over 2,000 small firms covering the period 1964-
68. Aggregate data for the same period, as published by the *Business
Monitor*, for quoted firms - assumed to be large - were used as a basis
for comparison.

Income statistics published by the Internal Revenue Service and the
quarterly series published by the Federal Trade Commission, are the
data source for the U.S.A. The former represent all the firms submitt-
ing returns and the latter a statistically representative sample of all
manufacturing corporations operating in a particular year.

The Bank of France publishes annual data on the accounts of
corporations broken down according to industrial sector and size. The
data represent all those firms who have submitted financial statements in
order to qualify for rediscount of their bills by the banking system.

Ever since 1956 the Bank of Israel (Israel's Central Bank), has
conducted a corporate finance project based on the income tax returns
filed by a representative sample of manufacturing corporations in Israel.
Since this project covers firms of all sizes it was possible to draw on it
for data concerning small firms in Israel.

In Japan, data on large firms were collected from the corporate reports
published by the Bank of Japan, and the Ministry of Finance. These
represent all the firms considered leaders in their industrial subsector.
The small firms data were taken from a special study devoted to small
firms in Japan.

In all countries included in this study, the data are so arranged that
they show the financial structure for an average firm in each of the
different size groups. Firms employing fewer than 200 employees were

defined as small in the U.K., France, Israel, and Japan. Medium firms were defined as those employing between 200 and 500 employees in Israel and France. No data were available for medium firms in the U.K. and Japan. For the U.S.A., the firms were classified according to their assets, the smallest asset size, less than 5 million dollars assets, was used to represent the small firms. Medium firms were defined as those having between 5 million and 100 million dollars assets.

In order to eliminate the effect of the industrial sector in which the company operates on its financial behaviour, the study is limited to manufacturing firms only.

The data for the countries concerned do not cover the same period. The data for the U.K., U.S., and Israel are an average of the years 1964-68, while Japan - 1970, and France - 1973. It is suggested, however that this inconsistency does not substantially affect the findings of the data since there is no basis for assuming that the choice of a particular year would provide the same economic conditions in all the economies concerned.

Analysed in this study are those aspects of corporate finance which relate to the two hypotheses described in the introduction - that small firms have greater difficulty in obtaining funds and that they are less profitable. The study follows the following plan : Section III discusses leverage in small firms as compared with that of large firms. The effect of size on the structure of equity is described in Section IV, and in Section V the relative profitability of small firms is examined, including the methods and extent of profit distribution. Section VI comprises a concluding summary.

III. LEVERAGE

It has been argued that small firms in any economy are discriminated against by the banking and financial institutions so that they are unable to raise equity or loan capital necessary for profitability and expansion. In theory this argument would seem to be well founded, since it is clear that small firms do represent a greater degree of risk :

a) Large firms are better known and usually have a more sophisticated and up-to-date system of financial reporting so that both investor and lender can obtain more information than in dealing with a small firm.

b) In all the countries concerned it is commonly accepted that the bankruptcy rate of the small firm is greater than that of the large firm. Although admittedly the failure of a large firm involves investors and creditors in a greater monetary loss, nevertheless it seems reasonable to assume that, as the likelihood of small firms going bankrupt is greater, investors and lenders will be more careful with regard to this type of firm.

c) The often closely-knit ownership of the small firm - either that of a family or of a small group of shareholders who are also active in the firm's management - makes it difficult for the non-active investor or lender to separate the activities of the firm from the activities of the individual major shareholders. This mingling of accounts is one of the major causes of bankruptcy. In commercial banks, for example, this type of ownership has enabled the management to syphon funds from the depositors' accounts in order to shore up their own, often high-risk investments outside the bank(6).

d) Although many small firms do earn profits higher than those of large firms, the dispersion of small firms around the average rate and the fluctuations in the profit rate over time are much greater.

In order to determine whether such discrimination against small firms on the part of the lenders does indeed exist, the leverage ratios of manufacturing firms in the five countries are presented in Table 1.

Two indicators of leverage are provided in the table; equity as a percentage of the total liabilities (or funds invested in the firm), and equity as a percentage of long-term financing.

The table shows that in the first case the small firms almost always operate with ratios equal to or higher than the large ones. When leverage is calculated, however, as the ratio of equity to long-term debt, then Table 1 shows that large companies do tend to have a higher degree of leverage. *i.e. lower gearing.*

The use of this latter ratio assumes that short-term debt financing is not of a permanent nature or is limited to investment in current assets.

TABLE 1

EQUITY AS A PERCENTAGE OF TOTAL FUNDS AND OF LONG-TERM FINANCE ACCORDING TO SIZE GROUPS

Country	Equity as a percentage of total funds				Equity as a percentage of long-term finance			
	Small	Medium	Large	Average	Small	Medium	Large	Average
U.S.(1)	57	58	57	57	85	80	74	74
U.K.	56(2)	–	52(3)	52	92	–	76	76
Japan	22(4)	–	22(5)	22	52	–	45	45
France(6)	34	37	38	36	56	60	56	56
Israel(7)	45	36	36	38	75	68	56	56

Sources :

(1) *Quarterly Reports – Federal Trade Commission*
(2) *M.Tamari, A Postal Questionnaire Survey of Small Firms.An Analysis of Financial Data.London 1972*
(3) *Business Monitor, London : H.M.S.O.*
(4) *T.Yamanaka, "Small Business in Japan's Economic Progress", Ashai Evening News, Tokyo 1971*
(5) *Statistics Department, Bank of Japan*
(6) *Bank of France, Financial Reports of Manufacturing Companies*
(7) *Bank of Israel Corporate Finance Projects*

This assumption is questionable, however. Current liabilities often turn out to be of even longer duration than long-term borrowing. The firm's overdrafting or access to other credit is not terminated at the end of the year. Unless a sudden deterioration has occurred in the company's performance or some radical change has taken place in the whole economy, this credit will usually be renewed automatically or even increased. In the same way, trade credit, a major constituent of short-term liabilities, is not terminated at the end of the year, but is continued for as long as the firm continues to buy from its suppliers. Furthermore, where companies have a current ratio of less than one, these short-term liabilities are used to finance long-term assets. In France, Israel, and Japan, for example, many companies are in such a situation. Even in the U.S. and U.K. numerous corporations use their current liabilities to finance investments in long-term assets, if not in fixed assets, at least in the long-term element of such assets as inventory and trade credit, which the company is required to maintain as long as it continues its operations.

Despite these reservations as to the meaningfulness of the distinction between short term and long term, Table 1 includes this definition of leverage as the ratio of equity to long-term debt as well, because it does highlight an important difference between the various size groups. The table shows that small firms do indeed have substantially higher equity/long-term debt ratios than do large firms, especially in the U.S.A. and the U.K. Since the overall equity/total debt ratios are not radically different, it would seem that the small firm does tend to substitute current borrowing for long-term borrowing. One can argue that since short-term credit costs more than long-term credit, it is precisely here that the disadvantage of the small and medium-size firms in the capital markets becomes apparent.

It can be shown (see Table 2), that in all the countries concerned, smaller firms tend to borrow a greater share of their funds from trade and other non-bank creditors. Such credit is generally more expensive than long-term or short-term bank credit since the lender of non-bank funds agrees to accept a greater risk since he receives none of the securities that banks usually require, such as mortgages or lien on some or all of the borrowers' assets. This reliance on non-bank credit is even widespread in those countries such as Israel and Japan where subsidized bank credit is made available to most manufacturing firms in accord with government policy.

The reliance on such funds does not, however, only reflect the preferences of the suppliers of long-term finance or short-term bank funds. Research done in the U.S. and the U.K. shows that small firms themselves prefer non-bank credit. For example, in the study of the Federal Reserve System on the financing of small firms, over 75% of the companies interviewed had never applied for bank credit(2). A more recent study of U.K. firms shows that only a third of the companies interviewed had attempted to avail themselves of short-term funds; of those who had applied, only a small minority (33%) had been turned down (7). The Israeli research shows also that most small and medium-size firms were able to satisfy their demand for bank funds(8).

TABLE 2

BANK CREDIT AS A PERCENTAGE OF CURRENT LIABILITIES ACCORD-ING TO SIZE GROUPS

| Country | SIZE | | |
	Small	Medium	Large
U.K.	16	–	24
Japan	21	–	33
Israel	23	24	35
France	2.5	3.8	20.8

Data for the U.S. companies, bank credit as distinct from other short-term borrowings, are not available and therefore were not included in the table.

From the experience in these three countries it would be reasonable to assume that, at least in part, the use of short-term non-bank credit, despite its higher nominal cost, flows from the preferences of the users themselves. In this case, the preference for non-bank credit would seem to be due to the following factors :

a) The demand of underwriters of bond bank issues for access to detailed financial information and their active intervention in the every-day affairs of the company are not likely to be welcomed by small firm owners. The demand of large creditors for a seat on the board of directors and the necessity of using a firm's assets as security present similar drawbacks.

b) Non-bank credit can be obtained with relative ease. Suppliers' credit, for example, is usually available simply with the ordering of goods.

c) The ability to stretch suppliers' credit at no charge beyond the date fixed for repayment also appeals to small firm owners. For instance, if the terms of trade agreed upon, entitle the customer to a 30-day credit, it is often possible to stretch this for a longer period. It may well be,however, that many small firms are ignorant of the real costs of this credit as often there is no direct formal interest charge. In such cases a discount for payment in cash is available, which constitutes an interest payment for non-utilization which is far in excess of bank interest(9).

Despite these considerations, it still seems that the major factor behind the use of short-term credit lies in the discrimination by the suppliers of such funds against the small firm. This may be seen from the results of the structure of the capital markets. The introduction in any economy of special types of quasi-public sector lenders usually leads to a change in the financial structure of the small firm. These lenders are established with additional motivation other than minimizing risk and maximizing profit and they result, *inter alia*, in an increase in the relative borrowing of long-term funds and short-term bank credit by the small firm. For example, small firms in the U.K. eligible to borrow from the I.C.F.C. (an institution for assisting small firms in that economy) had an average equity/total funds ratio 45% lower than both that of the average small firm and that of the quoted company (56%) (10).

Similarly, 60% of the many S.B.I.C's studies did not have any requirements regarding the degree of leverage whereas most ordinary banking institutions limit borrowing to 70-80% of the amount of owners' equity(10). These examples serve to reinforce the argument that a change in the investment policy and lending practices of the usual suppliers of funds would result in a similar change in leverage, even measured as an equity/long-term debt ratio in all small firms.

IV. THE STRUCTURE OF EQUITY

In addition to the differences with respect to sources of debt, important differences also exist between the size groups regarding the structure of equity. Ignoring these differences may lead to faulty conclusions concerning the degree of leverage in the different size groups.

For purposes of this paper, loans from shareholders and major office holders have been included in equity. Although legally such loans are not part of the firm's equity, yet since the availability and conditions of repayment of such funds differ so radically from those of ordinary loans raised from external lenders (external in the sense that they are not shareholders), such loans seem to have more of the character of equity than of borrowed funds. These loans often do not even bear interest charges and, even when such interest charges are included in the formal conditions of the loan, they may be waived by the owners according to the financial situation of the firm.

Table 3 shows the relative importance of the various components of equity according to size groups. The table shows that in all the countries the primary difference between the different size groups is the greater reliance on owners' loans as a source of equity in the small firm.

In the U.S. and the U.K. owners' loans to the small firm constituted respectively 16 and 18% of equity, compared with less than one percent in the large firms. In Japan, small firms financed 25% of their equity from this source while only 18% of the equity in the large firms was raised from such loans. In Israel the small companies raised over half their equity from owners' loans, whereas in the medium and large ones these loans accounted for approximately a third of the owners' equity.

The advantages of owners' capital raised in the form of loans over that of share capital or retained earnings lie both in the greater flexibility and lower relative cost of this form of equity.

TABLE 3

THE STRUCTURE OF EQUITY ACCORDING TO SIZE GROUP
(Percentages)

Country	Size	Share capital	Retained earnings	Loans from owners	Total
U.S.	Small	69	11	20	100
	Medium	55	45	–	100
	Large	56	44	–	100
U.K.	Small	33	61	6	100
	Medium	–	–	–	–
	Large	42	58	–	100
Japan	Small	33	42	25	100
	Medium	–	–	–	–
	Large	45	37	18	100
Israel	Small	22	28	50	100
	Medium	32	29	39	100
	Large	60	14	26	100
France	Small	21	26	53	100
	Medium	21	48	31	100
	Large	54	30	16	100

Raising equity through issues of share capital involves considerable expense such as the commission paid to underwriters, the cost of publishing financial statements, etc. An attempt to diminish share capital in order to enjoy the advantage of leverage will involve the firm in intricate and costly legal procedures. Reducing equity by distributing retained earnings requires that the owners pay income taxes on the dividends. These disadvantages exist over and above the drawback to the present shareholders of their having to share profits and control with others when new shares are issued to outsiders.

Owners' loans, on the other hand, suffer none of these disadvantages. In most cases they may be granted or withdrawn almost at will and neither their infusion into the firm's equity or their withdrawal involve the company's paying taxes or incurring other costs.

Furthermore, the repayment of such loans and the interest paid to the owners on such loans is a method of withdrawing profits without paying corporate tax. The recipient of the interest payment, like the shareholders in the case of dividends, is liable to personal income tax; yet for the firm the interest paid is tax deductible whereas dividends paid on the share capital are not. This difference constitutes a saving to the shareholders who in this case are identical to the firm.

Further analysis can show that the small firms use owners' loans to adjust their leverage in accordance with changes in profitability and overall economic conditions in the economy. In the case of large firms, a return to the previous level of leverage is possible, *inter alia*, by distributing the increased profits in the form of dividends; the recipient paying income tax whereas the repaid loan carries no such liability. For example, an analysis of Israeli data shows that the small firms achieved the same results by adjusting the loans made to the company by the owners(11). Table 4 shows the trend in manufacturing profits in Israel between 1956 and 1970 together with the changes in owners' loans during the same period. The average annual percentage growth in total profits of all the manufacturing sector was calculated for each period and this was related in the table to the proportion of funds raised through owners' loans relative to total funds raised by the sector. When profits in the economy and in the manufacturing sector rose, owners' loans as a proportion of total funds declined. The firm repaid these loans which, in view of the general prosperity in the country at that time, could then be reinvested in attractive alternative assets outside the firm. The prevailing economic conditions also encouraged increased leverage as the expectations of rising profits allowed both the borrowers and lenders to accept increased risks.

As the rate of profits levelled off after 1962, the share of owners' loans ceased to decline. When aggregate profits fell in the 1966-67 recession years, owners' loans rose drastically for the first time since 1956-57. This rise resulted from the owners' desire to buffer the firm against the danger of bankruptcy if the recession continued and also from the reduced profitability of alternative financial investments. Subsequent to the recession in the period 1968-72, the marked increase

TABLE 4

AVERAGE ANNUAL CHANGE IN PROFITS AND PROPRIETARY LOANS -
ISRAEL 1956-1970
(Percentages)

	1956-60	1960-64	1965	1966-67	1968-70
Incremental owners' loans as a percentage of the growth of total funds	-8	2	4	13	-11
Average annual percentage growth in profits	100	27	decrease	decrease	120

NOTE : The data are for all the companies operating during the period.

in profits and the restoration of boom conditions in the economy caused
the ratio of owners' loans to equity to decline once again. A detailed
discussion of the relationship in other countries between profitability
and the non-dividend forms of profit distribution is to be found in the
following section.

It is often assumed that the use of owners' loans as a source of finance
flows solely from the effect of size. Further analysis, however, shows
that this may not be the sole factor. The degree of diffusion of ownership seems to play an important role in determining the use of this form
of equity. In France, Israel, and Japan many large companies are also
financed by owners' loans as may be seen from Table 3. In these three
countries only a relatively small number even of the large firms are listed
on the stock exchange; in the majority of cases their shares are owned
by a relatively small number of shareholders, who are active in the day-
to-day operations of the firm. These shareholders are usually members
of a family or constitute a tightly knit group with related interests. The
information for the U.K. and the U.S. shows that there too are large
companies, albeit a minority, in which owners' loans form a substantial

part of the equity. For instance a subsample of 70 U.K. firms listed on the London Stock Exchange, which would imply that they are not small, shows that in over a quarter of the sample, owners' loans constituted more than 15% of equity. The existence of owners' loans in these large firms therefore supports the hypothesis that the use of this type of finance at least partially reflects the type of ownership which exists even in some large corporations in all countries, either that of family comprising the major shareholders of a firm, or a small number of major shareholders who are also active in the firm's management.

Another difference exists in these countries between the structure of equity in the large and small firm, the latter operating with negative equity whilst this phenomena does not seem to exist for large firms. For example, negative equity was found to exist in the U.K. in 7% of a sample of small firms(7). In the U.S. the data do not allow for the analysis of individual small firms and therefore reference has to be made to aggregate data. Such data show that in the smallest size group of manufacturing companies (those with assets of less than $25,000) the total equity was negative in 1968.

If such negative equity were only the result of sustained losses, one could assume that such firms would be wound up or would be liquidated as a result of bankruptcy proceedings. In all the countries, however, such companies continue to operate for relatively long periods of time. In some cases negative equity is the result of the withdrawal of profits from very profitable firms primarily through repaying owners' loans or granting loans from the firm to the major shareholders; such withdrawals in excess of the retained profits are in actual fact a syphoning off of funds supplied by creditors to the firm.

Another explanation for the continued existence of negative equity lies in the fear of major creditors that bankruptcy proceedings would lead to greater loss than the extension of credit to such companies even when the negative equity is caused by sustained losses.

IV. PROFITABILITY

Before analyzing the profitability of the small firm it is necessary to correct the available data for two reasons :

The Financial Structure of the Small Firm

a) Small firms tend to distribute their profits to the major shareholders in the form of personal and household expenses paid for by the firm, interest-free loans, excessive managerial salaries, etc. These expenses of the major shareholders and members of their families appear in the accounts of the company as tax deductable expenses so that the net profit figure presented in the financial statements is in effect not a profit but rather a retained profit figure. Large firms and listed companies, however, distribute their profits in the form of dividends and their reported profits are usually shown before distribution. To compare the retained profit figure of the small firms with the profit figure before distribution of the large firms would be incorrect.

For instance Stekler(12) in his study of American small firms showed that rectifying or adjusting the profit figure to account for excess managerial salaries defined by him as the difference between the average wage paid to the managers of loss-declaring companies and that of the profit-earning companies, on the assumption that the loss-reporting companies were unable to pay salaries in excess of the market rate, increased the declared profits by 50%.

Tamari's study of Israeli corporations(13) adjusted the declared profits by adding back not only excessive salaries but also the household expenses, the cost of foreign travel, automobile allowances, entertainment charges, etc. which the tax officers ascribed to the personal accounts of the major shareholders. The study shows that profits would have to be increased by 50% for these non-dividend withdrawals.

b) In most countries the ability of the small firm not to declare all its profits is far greater than that of the large firms. This understatement of the profits affects not only the tax liability of the firm but also the decisions of creditors and analysts of macro-economic data. In the absence of any statistical measurements, it is difficult to know by how much the profitability rate would be altered. Nevertheless, some studies demonstrate conclusively the existence of undeclared profits. The declared income of Israeli firms in 1970, for example, differed from their final tax assessment by an average of 30% in the case of large companies while small firms understated their income by 100% (13). Despite the inability to systematically measure the true extent of the downward bias in the profitability of small firms, it is nonetheless clear that the declared profit figures can not be accepted at their face value.

Table 5 shows the profitability rates of the small firms in the countries concerned. Profitability is defined as profit before interest as a percentage of the total investment, returned (return on capital invested), and profit after interest as a percentage of equity (return on the shareholder's capital). It may be seen from the table that, in each of the countries concerned, the profits of small firms are often higher than those for large firms, this even without adjusting the profits of the small firms as described above.

TABLE 5

PROFITABILITY OF MANUFACTURING CORPORATIONS
ACCORDING TO SIZE GROUPS

Country	Profit before interest as a percentage of total funds employed			Profit after interest as a percentage of owners equity		
	Small	Medium	Large	Small	Medium	Large
U.S.	12	11	10	16	20	12
U.K.*	11	-	9	19	-	17
Japan	11	-	10	24	-	22
Israel	12	14	11	25	24	21

*Pretax profit after interest but before deducting directors' fees, etc. are 32% of equity in the small firms in the U.K. in 1968.

It should be noted, however, that the statistical dispersion of the rate of profits does differ significantly according to the size of the company. The rate of profitability in small firms varies much more than that for large companies. In any particular year the profitability rate of most large firms is close to the average for the economy whereas the profit spread among small firms is greater. This may be seen from the results of the study on small firms in the U.K. reproduced in Table 6.

The variability of profits within a particular size group is very wide amongst the smallest firms. Table 6 shows how the range of profitability (measured by profits in relation to both sales and assets) narrows as the firm grows in size; the data are based on the survey for 1968. Similarly results were obtained for 1964 and for other indicators of profitability.

TABLE 6

VARIABILITY OF PROFITS BY SIZE OF FIRM
IN THE U.K. - 1968

Number of employees	1-5	6-24	25-99	100-199
Profits as a percent of sales				
Lower quartile	1.9	1.1	0.9	1.5
Median	6.2	3.6	3.5	4.3
Upper quartile	16.1	8.7	8.5	8.5
Variability(a)	14.2	7.6	7.6	7.0
Profits as a percent of net assets				
Lower quartile	3.2	2.4	1.8	3.5
Median	20.0	12.0	9.1	12.3
Upper quartile	58.8	32.3	25.5	22.6
Variability(a)	55.6	29.9	23.7	19.1

NOTE : a) Upper quartile less lower quartile
SOURCE : *Tamari,M., A Postal Questionnaire Survey of Small Firms :
An Analysis of Financial Data, London : H.M.S.O., 1972*

There is also a suggestion in the survey data that small firms are concentrated in those branches with high mark-ups in relation to turn-over. For example, while 32% of the smallest manufacturing firms(under 5 employees) earned a profit of over 10% of their turnover, only 14% of the firms employing over 100 employees showed a similar profit rate.

These figures are consistent with what is known from other studies of the higher mortality of smaller firms(10). The greater rate of failure amongst some of them is compensated by the higher profitability of others.

V. SUMMARY

1. In all countries, small firms operate with ratios of equity to total sources similar to, or higher than, large firms. If, however, leverage is defined relative to long-term loan capital then small firms in the countries considered function with lower leverage. This is due to the

reliance of small firms on short-term funds, primarily non-banking credit. It is not clear whether such reliance is from choice or results from the demands of the suppliers of long-term funds.

2. There exists an important difference between the size groups regarding the structure of equity. In small firms, loans made to the firm by the major shareholders comprise a greater percentage of equity. It seems, however, that this is not solely an effect of size, as this form of equity is found in many large firms in which ownership is closely held.

3. The average small firm is not less profitable than the large ones. The dispersal of small firms about the median is however, greater, as is their mortality rate.

(1) Merwin, C.L., Financing Small Corporations in Five Manufacturing Industries, 1926-36. New York : N.B.E.R., 1942
(2) Financing Small Business, Washington D.C. : Board of Governors of the Federal Reserve System, 1960
(3) Pfeffer,I.,ed. The Financing of Small Business. New York : MacMillan, 1967
(4) Meltzer,A.M. Mercantile Credit Monetary Policy & Size of Firms, Review of Economics & Statistics, Vol.XLII,No.41,Nov.1960,pp429-436
(5) Tamari, M. The Pattern of Industrial Corporate Profit Distribution in Israel, 1956-64. Bank of Israel Bulletin, No.29,1967, pp.23-49
(6) Smith,J.E. Comptroller of the Currency, Washington,D.C. - Some Lessons from Recent Bank Failures, The Journal of Commercial Bank Lending, January 1975
(7) A Postal Questionnaire Survey of Small Firms : An Analysis of Financial Data. London : H.M.S.O., 1972
(8) Bank of Israel Corporate Project (unpublished data)
(9) Tamari,M. The Cost & Use of Trade Credit, International Management Review, Vol.13, No.1, 1973, pp.93-102

(10) *Tamari, M. Some International Comparisons of Industrial Financing Stonehouse, Glos. : Technicopy Ltd., 1977*

(11) *Tamari, M. Financing Long-Term Investments in Industrial Companies in Israel, 1950-70. Quarterly Banking Review(Tel Aviv) No. 52, Dec. 1973, Vol.XIII, pp. 58-71 (Hebrew)*

(12) *Stekler,H.O. Profitability & Size of Firms. Institute of Economic Research, Berkeley : University of California, 1963*

(13) *Tamari, M. Industrial Corporate Profits in Israel, 1956-70, Economic Review (Jerusalem), No. 40, Sept. 1973*

2. CRITERIA FOR SELECTION OF VENTURE CAPITAL PROJECTS : REASONS BEHIND SUCCESSES AND FAILURES IN THE PAST

H.A.R.Stevens

R & D Management. Volume 3 Number 1. 1972

Abstract : This paper looks at the area of venture management from the viewpoint of a company which is interested in providing financial support for new areas of activity. It discusses the problems associated with entering new markets and argues that many investments have not been the success that was hoped for because insufficient profit margin was obtainable or built in at the outset. However, by far the most crucial criterion for a venture capitalist is the calibre of the people who are to manage the risk funds, and the motivation of the entrepreneur or team wishing to establish the new enterprise.

Though hardly an innovative approach it is perhaps nonetheless sensible to start by defining terms and the scope of this paper. Venture capital is here seen as finance for new and relatively new high-risk, high-profit-oriented projects. In the United States where the term was created it is often associated with advanced technology but low technology products, processes or services are not excluded. A high-risk project is one in which there is a large number of unknowns about its outcome. These unknowns are functions not only of the project itself but also of the knowledge of the potential investor. Venture capitalists are usually thought of as private individuals or financial institutions with little experience of the project field. However the financier can also be an industrial or commercial company.

The marketing of a 'new' chocolate product such as Rowntree's After Eight by an established confectionery manufacturer or a 'new' detergent by a company already in the business is not seen as a venture capital operation. This is because there is a large amount of relevant production skill, cost data and market intelligence available to the financial decision maker. Such information reduces the level of risk from what is here regarded as high to a level more appropriately referred to as 'normal commercial'. If, however, a confectionery manufacturer were to launch a detergent or to enter the business of, say, commodity vending or ticket issuing machines, as Mars is believed to be doing, then this would be a venture capital operation.

In the literature - mostly American - venture capital is written of in three categories depending upon the timing of the investment. Phase One or 'Seed Capital' is that which is invested at the early stage of development of an idea into a prototype and is expected to take a new project or company to the point where it has some potential or one or two actual customers and an embryonic organization ready to organize production and exploit the product, process or service in the market place. Phase Two investment is intended to prove the product in the market, build up a modest volume of sales and produce the first profits. This phase could last from 1 to, say, 5 years. Third phase, or so-called Development Capital, is investment in a more mature company which has a track record of survival, but a low return on assets and which needs gearing up financially, and possibly managerially to exploit fully the potential which is by now fairly apparent. While any investment in a private company is perhaps of a higher order of risk than 'normal commercial' it is proposed that Phase Three finance be excluded from discussion in this paper. Exclusion of the last category means that venture capital is clearly long-term investment that is of 5 or more years. Moreover the money at risk is not readily convertible to cash or marketable securities and, although part may be provided in the form of loans, it is effectively equity investment.

INVESTMENT CRITERIA

Criteria for investment vary to some extent between types of invest- or. Private individuals tend in the main to act less 'professionally' than institutions. They comprise relatives and friends of entrepreneurs to whom they may provide seed capital for emotional reasons or wealthy strangers who are ready at any stage to take quick gambles rather than analyse investment opportunities in the depth that institutional venture capitalists usually do. A third class of individual, the previously successful entrepreneur, can be expected to act more rationally.

The venture capital companies of which there are many in America, very few in Europe, and signs of some emerging in Japan have, now that the 'industry' has gained some experience, a fairly standard approach to investment appraisal. The five main ingredients of a project to be financed are the product, process or service itself, the market demand for it, the relationship between cost and selling price, the managerial resources and the size of the initial investment required.

It is relatively easy to appraise the technical merits of a new project particularly because the applicants for funds often include technical people and their past record is a good guide to the likelihood of their being able to design and build something which will work and at an acceptable cost. Also they usually manage to reach at least the proto-type stage on their own financial resources. Nonetheless the sophisticated venture capitalist will have on his staff or employ as a consultant an engineer who can probe this aspect of the project in considerable depth. One of the criteria to be considered is the technological strength of the applicants to develop eventually a full range or family of products as opposed to the model which they intend to exploit commercially at the outset.

An important consideration is the extent to which patents or the applicants' know-how will give the project protection from attempts by potential competitors to copy the new product. Also applicants' estimates of prime costs can be checked but even if agreed to as being reasonable should always, experience suggests, be increased by a contingency factor.

Assessment of the market potential for an innovation is not easy. For a new project to become very profitable it is necessary for the product or process to sell in large quantities, since a new enterprise cannot for long make big profits on the basis of relatively low sales volume at high margins per unit. Unfortunately it is exactly these market opportunities which established companies are constantly search-ing for. Thus the chances of an entrepreneur coming across one are remote. However it occasionally happens and it is such situations that make history. Xerox and Polaroid are well-known cases in which the products were actually offered to and turned down by large corporations, presumably because their managements thought the market not big enough for them. It is probable also that the promoters of many successful ventures which started from small beginnings did not them- selves realize they were entering so big a market area as subsequently proved to be the case. Even IBM, who of all people should have known, have twice, in 1950 and 1960, substantially underestimated the eventual demand for their own computers. Thus when a financier is assessing a new venture it behoves him to beware of falling into the same trap as the market research departments of big companies and reject propositions in which there is not an obviously large market.

There must on the other hand be a market of some sort, and to discover whether this is the case it is useful to investigate the history of the creative process. Two extreme situations can be simply stated. On the one hand there is the inventor who has devised a product, perhaps because he is fascinated with the technology, which he thinks everybody would like or should have. Against this there is a potential customer for a product who has told a commercially oriented development engineer what he would buy were it available. The existence of a genuine need in the market, however weakly it is expressed, is a vital clue. In the case of the Polaroid camera it is related that it was Dr Land's two year-old daughter wanting to see her photograph immediately after it had been taken that caused him to switch to cameras from Polaroid windshields in which the automobile industry was showing no interest. Similarly Dexion slotted angle was developed when Comino felt a desperate need for more flexible storage and racking for his printing business than was available from existing suppliers. More remotely, Sir Frank Whittle recognized that the customer's need for aeroplanes to go faster presupposed their flying in thinner air and their having to be driven by turbines because propellers could not work at high altitudes.

Under the heading of market assessment comes also the question of selling price. Many venture capital investments have not been the success that was hoped for because insufficient profit margin was obtainable or built in at the outset. A new growth-oriented enterprise needs high margins to help finance product and organizational development and the rapid rate of sales which it must achieve and also to produce the profits which are needed to attract the further external funds which it will eventually require.

By far the most crucial criterion for a venture capitalist is the calibre of the people who are to manage the risk funds. It is tempting at this point to set out the long list of qualities which they would ideally have. However since this is a short paper rather than an academic thesis, it is probably more useful to concentrate discussion on the essentials. These can be summarized as : entrepreneurial motivation, youth and intelligence, technical ability, market orientation and commercial 'nous'.

The reason or motivation for the entrepreneur or team wishing to establish the new enterprise is important. The investor is seeking to go into partnership with people who have a genuine desire, amounting ideally to a need, to make a commercial impact by building up a fast-growing business. Most applicants for venture capital come from employment in established companies and the reasons for their leaving must be probed. Clearly it is not enough that they should have been made, or expect to be made, redundant. Nor is frustration with the employer merely because he axed their development project. One must also beware of the man who cannot live with other people and is seeking finance to start a hermit-like, one-man business. Then there is the perpetual technical development engineer who wants to build and modify prototypes but is not truly interested in their being the basis of a product line which is sold for profit.

The entrepreneur must as the psychologists say be strongly achievement-oriented but have only a moderate need for power. He must want to be the cause of success but one which is obtained through others, whom therefore he must be able to inspire and lead. He must paradoxically be both daring and realistic, imaginative and analytical. He must be able to tolerate and even enjoy risk, but only moderate risk.

The entrepreneur and his team should ideally be young enough to have the enormous energy and the confidence required for success, and both the youth and intelligence which is necessary to learn about business and learn from the inevitable errors which will be made.

Criteria for Selection of Venture Capital Projects

Applicants for venture capital usually have adequate technical ability but not often enough, at least in Britain, market orientation. Arnold Weinstock has said succinctly that all successful companies are run by men who understand the market and Professor Ed.Roberts of M.I.T. has found from his researches of Boston's Route 128 companies that the successful ones had a well-developed marketing function early in their development.

The last ingredient, commercial 'nous', is intended to cover that instinctive feeling for and satisfaction from buying and selling which all successful entrepreneurs have. Half of Professor Roberts's sample of successful men had fathers who had been in business on their own account. From them the sons had obtained a perhaps inborn appreciation that success results from buying at the lowest price, rigidly controlling costs and selling at the highest price the market will bear.

The discussion thus far has been of the qualities sought by a venture investor in his potential partner. They are not however sufficient in themselves to provide a good chance of success. There are other essential ingredients of which some must be provided by the financier and the others can only come from the partnership itself. The fact that there is a partnership is vital; the history of venture capital operations, particularly those financed by established industrial or commercial companies, is littered with failures resulting from a full appreciation of this.

The financier must, like his partner, be totally committed at the highest level to the investment. He must understand the nature of the risk being taken and be prepared for the long haul. He must not be too greedy in negotiating terms and must take responsibility for establishing the ground rules of what is effectively an experiment in commercial enterprise. This involves helping to work out, not just accepting, the cash flow projection which is to be funded. An important input here is realistically estimating the size of the down-side risk, that is the maximum amount of finance which can be expected to be required to achieve a break-even trading position. If things go wrong he must be tolerant towards those which are outside the control of the entrepreneurial team and then be prepared to commit greater funds than were originally budgeted. On the other hand he must be capable of stopping projects. All this presupposes close monitoring of progress by the financial partner and his availability to counsel the members of the entrepreneurial team who can properly expect the investor to have more experience than they do of the problems of nurturing a new enterprise. But the financier must be aware of imposing the dead hand of bureaucracy on his entrepreneurial partners. An amusing comment on the monitoring function is reported to have been made by Peter Danforth of one of Gunwyn Ventures' children. She described her father's business as 'giving money to people and then flying all over trying to keep them from spending it'.

No specific reference has yet been made to what is certainly one of the most vital ingredients of a successful venture, namely its management capability. This has been deliberate because an investor of Phase One or Phase Two venture capital cannot by definition expect his entrepreneurial partner to have experience or a so-called 'track record' of successful management. At the assessment stage a venture capitalist can only expect to find potential. There may well be some applicants who have had previous, relevant experience but this must be regarded as a fortuitous bonus rather than an essential prerequisite However once the investment has been made it is one of the important roles of the financial partner to help develop his partner's managerial potential and to take an active part in augmenting it if necessary. Although some additional people will obviously have to be recruited as the enterprise grows a basic element of venture capital investment is that the original applicants will learn the business game and that functional specialists will be brought in as assistants rather than as replacements.

Finally, another not negligible ingredient of success is good luck. This cannot of course be provided by either partner but, as in sport, it is likely to attend the teams which perform well and are able to take advantage of unexpected opportunities.

REASONS FOR SUCCESSES & FAILURES IN THE PAST

There are two approaches to a discussion of reasons for the past successes and failures of venture capital operations : academic analysis and subjective judgement from personal experience. Thus far, little research has been done in Europe and one has to turn to American publications.

The most impressive work is that done under the direction of Prof. Roberts who has already been referred to. His and his students' principal conclusions relate to the qualities of entrepreneurs who had started new businesses after leaving M.I.T., Government research laboratories or big corporations. Last year two students widened the scope of the work by studying in-house ventures financed by establish-ed companies. Of the entrepreneurs we are told that the successful ones had an average age of 32, an M.Sc. rather than Ph.D., had been engaged in development as opposed to fundamental research, were interested in people, had fathers who had businesses of their own and an appreciation of the importance of the marketing function.

Unfortunately the in-house ventures studied were almost all of such recent origin that it was not possible to make a rigorous analysis of success and failure. However the researchers were able to underline, not surprisingly, the overriding necessity that there be complete commitment from, and participation by, the chief executive and a corporate climate which fosters entrepreneurial activity. And of course they noted that the companies had to have in their employ, or be approached by, the entrepreneurs themselves. Also, more usefully, they found that the venture groups must be able to operate as independently as possible from the corporation's main-stream activities. It is perhaps appropriate at this point to quote the President of 3M, a company which has been outstandingly successful in financing new ventures. When asked what business 3M considers itself to be in he replied, 'We are in the business of gambling on individuals'.

Another approach to trying to evaluate the success or otherwise of venture capital is to study the financial accounts of venture capital companies. This Professor Rotch of Virginia University did in 1968, and Novotny and Searles added to last year in their comprehensive

analysis of venture capital in the United States. Both were limited by
a shortage of information but nonetheless some interesting conclusions
were reached.

The U.S. scene is dominated by the now well-known success of
American Research and Development Corporation whose initial equity
capital had by 1966 after twenty years increased at an effective rate
of 14% per annum compound. This can be compared with the increase
in the Dow Jones index of 11.5%. Without wishing to detract from this
performance, which has probably not been matched by any other
equivalent organization of comparable size, it is worth noting that
the return is at the rate of only 8% compounded if one excludes ARD's
investment in Digital Equipment Corporation, in which the equity of
70,000 dollars became worth some 53m. dollars when Rotch's analysis
was done in 1967. But this is unsound reasoning because the nature
of venture capitalism is that the successes must pay for the failures
and the real profit can only come from the one in a hundred phenomena.
It should also be added that ARD's assets multiplied almost exponen-
tially after the Rotch percentages were calculated and not only because
of further growth in the worth of its stake in DEC.

Thus one finds that the spectacular result of the most successful
venture capital company depended largely on one investment out of
about a hundred and very few other venture capitalists have even
approached these heights. Perhaps the next most successful operation
was Davis and Rock's who hit the jackpot with their investment in
Scientific Data Systems. It is concluded that venture capital is not so
bright a star in the financial firmament as the public was led to
believe during the stock market boom in the late sixties. Rockefeller,
who has a considerable venture capital operation, has agreed that it
has been no more rewarding than the stock exchange, but adds that
it is much more fun.

In Europe specialist venture capital companies are too young to be
able to show big gains yet. However Technical Development Capital
Ltd. has already had some failures, particularly amongst the many very
small investments which it has been the policy to gamble on. (TDC
also has an encouraging number of successful ventures, but primarily

amongst its larger investments.) Most of these failures arose, it is considered in retrospect, because neither the product nor the entrepreneur was sufficiently outstanding to carry the other. In too many cases the product did not have either a sufficiently large sales potential or a big enough profit margin to provide the foundation for an independent business but should have been marketed by an established company. TDC and many of the entrepreneurs it backs are fortunate in being closely linked with the Industrial and Commercial Finance Corporation, for it is often possible to introduce the baby business which proves to be too small for survival to one of ICFC's 2,000 customers to whom both the product and its promoter, if willing, can be valuable additions.

Other reasons for failures have been the inadequacy of financial controls, taking on too early more factory space, plant etc. than was necessary and too early diversification. To survive, the small developing company must become a leader in one, specialist, field. There have also been cases where the technologists, whose skills are the principal assets of the business, have dissipated these by devoting too much of their own time to general management or even such mundane tasks as keeping the books. They and their backers would have been wiser to invest a relatively small amount more and hire experienced personnel to undertake these tasks. At later stages, as embryonic companies grow up there are the dangers that the original management may not themselves grow at the necessary pace or that they develop far too early the ageing characteristics of large companies opting for stability rather than continuity of the risk-taking way of life.

One point which might usefully be made about successes and failures is that as relatively few investments are profitable in their first few years, many eventual successes would have been classified as failures had a halt been called too soon. For example the Polaroid Corporation which was founded by Schroeder, Rockefeller and Kuhn, Loeb in 1937 was still making substantial losses of 96,000 dollars three years later.

FUTURE DEVELOPMENTS

As there has always been - one recalls Queen Isabella's financing of Columbus - there will continue to be investment which can be classified as venture capital. However following the mushrooming of the 'industry' in the United States and the bursting of the bubble in over the counter share trading at the end of the 1960s and after the Autonomics episode in London in 1971, it is probable that there will be less wildcat speculation, particularly on new-technology based start-ups, by non-specialists on both sides of the Atlantic. There will be growth in the stature of well-founded, professionally managed venture capital companies but there are not likely to be so many in Europe as in the United States for a good number of years.

In the United States the publicity given to venture capital and the departure from many established companies of a large number of entre-preneurially inclined employees have created considerable interest in, and some experiment with, in-house venture management. It is too early to say whether this movement is yet successful, but it is already clear that one of the problems encountered is arranging adequate reward for the entrepreneurs and, if they are to have equity in a new company, deciding whether they should have control or only a minority share.

It can be expected that venture management will eventually take hold in Europe. There is little of it as yet though it is claimed that the success of ICI's Dufix adhesive owed something to the technique. And British Oxygen has recently reorganized responsibility for its central R & D activities along venture division lines. With this move-ment there could perhaps also develop tripartite ventures between established companies, entrepreneurs from within or without and venture capital companies. The arrangement whereby the financier reduces the industrialist's risk while at the same time holding the neutral 'middle third' of the equity would seem to have attractions for all parties.

BIBLIOGRAPHY

Morgan, R.F.(1968) 'Making an Idea into a Business', London :
   Technical Development Capital Ltd.

Rotch, Prof.William (1968) 'The pattern of success in venture capital
   financing', Financial Analysis Journal, Sept.-Oct.

Roberts, Prof.Edward B. (1970) 'How to succeed in a new technology
   enterprise', Technology Review, Vol. 72 No. 2. Dec.

Novotny, Carl H. & Searles,David S.,Jnr.(1970) 'Venture capital in
   the United States - an analysis', Cambridge,Mass. : New Enterprise
   Systems

Diederich,Jack L. & Packard,P.K. (1971) 'Venture management in the
   industrial sector', Cambridge, Mass. : M.I.T. Slean School of
   Management

'On the shelf - a Survey of industrial R & D projects abandoned for
   non-technical reasons', London : Centre for the Study of Industrial
   Innovation (1971)

Cooper, A.C. (1971) 'The founding of technologically-based firms',
   Milwaukee : Centre for Venture Management

Cooper, A.C. & Komives,J.(Eds.) 'Technical entrepreneurship : a
   symposium', Milwaukee : Centre for Venture Management

3. SMALLER BUSINESSES : THE STOCK EXCHANGE LOWERS THE HURDLES

Angus Sibley

This article was first published in the February 1981 issue of The Accountant's Magazine, the journal of The Institute of Chartered Accountants of Scotland. It is reprinted here with the permission of the Editor of that journal – and of the author.

For some 30 years the rules of The Stock Exchange have allowed members to arrange deals in the shares of U.K. companies other than those officially listed on the Exchange. Recently, wishing to be seen to be helpfully disposed towards the smaller business, the Exchange has given some positive encouragement to these unofficial trading activities. However, it is clearly anomalous in principle that members of The Stock Exchange should deal in shares of companies that have no obligation to conform with its rules; such trading could, if it developed too far, undermine the Exchange's self-regulatory authority. There have, therefore, been many demands for a modified regime to suit the needs of smaller or newer companies which would have difficulty in meeting the standards required of fully listed companies. These demands have now been answered by the setting up of the Unlisted Securities Market (USM) with its own regulations. Dealings in this market began on 10 November 1980.

The substantive difference between the USM and the main market in officially listed securities is that the conditions of entry to the USM are considerably less onerous than those for listing. However, once a company has been admitted to the USM it has to comply continuously with conditions – regarding disclosure of information, directors' share dealings, issue of further shares and other matters – which differ very little from the conditions imposed upon listed companies. Another difference is noticeable but superficial : no daily closing prices are published for USM companies. However, The Stock Exchange Daily Official List publishes the names of all securities traded in the USM, showing the prices of the most recent bargains in each security.

It will be seen that the term "unlisted" is, in fact, somewhat misleading; its use reflects the deeply ingrained feeling among many

Smaller Businesses : The Stock Exchange Lowers the Hurdles

Stock Exchange members that all "listed" companies should be treated equally, that there should not be a "two-tier market" in listed securities. The necessity of admitting to The Stock Exchange certain companies which cannot be expected to conform with the normal listing requirements has led to the somewhat odd compromise of describing such companies as unlisted, and discriminating between the two classes of company in ways which are, in practice, of little importance. For instance, every contract note relating to a deal in a USM company explicitly states that the company is not listed.

Entry requirements

The real differences between the USM and the main market fall almost entirely under this heading. The chief points are :

(a) *The prospectus*

The Companies Act 1948 made it obligatory for a company to publish a full prospectus, including a five-year accountant's report, when offering new shares to the general public to raise additional funds. Stock Exchange rules oblige any company seeking official listing to publish such a prospectus, even when no new money is being raised (i.e. even when existing shares only are being placed on the market). This rule will be relaxed on the USM; here a full prospectus will be required only (as it is by law) where the company coming to the market is raising new money. In other cases a simpler prospectus will suffice. Instead of the accountant's report, the company will provide a table of financial statistics drawn from audited accounts for the past five years, or such lesser period as the company has been trading.

Another saving for USM companies will be the expense of large-scale advertising in the press. A company making an offer for sale or placing on a listed basis has to publish its entire prospectus in at least one leading newspaper. For USM companies a small "box" advertisement will be sufficient; the text of the prospectus will be available from the sponsoring broker and in the Extel statistical service.

(b) *The length of the trading record*

Normally the minimum acceptable period will be three years, for which audited accounts must be available; but the three-year period is not a rigid requirement. The Stock Exchange "would also be prepared to accept companies seeking finance to put fully researched projects into production". It thus appears that a limited "venture capital" role is envisaged for the USM.

(c) *Proportion of share capital placed*

For a Stock Exchange listing, at least 25% of the company's shares must be made available to the investing public; until 1977 the normal minimum was 35%. In the USM the threshold is much lower. The regulations specify a "guideline" of 10%, but add that "the Council (of The Stock Exchange) intend to treat this question with considerable flexibility in practice". This suggests that markets in some USM company shares may prove to be very narrow.

(d) *Minimum size of issue*

To qualify for listing, a company must have a market value of at least £500,000. In the USM there is no minimum.

These are the main differences in entry conditions between the USM and the fully listed market. They mean that a company can now place its securities in a recognised and regulated public market place at an earlier stage of its development, with a smaller outside participation, and with fewer formalities and costs, than has hitherto been possible within the orbit of The Stock Exchange.

Continuing requirements

Listed companies have to comply with the 20 provisions of the standard Stock Exchange Listing Agreement, most of which are designed to enforce a minimum standard of regular disclosure of information on the company's affairs. The provisions also require the company to seek the consent of its members before issuing new shares to other parties, to regulate directors' share dealings in accordance with the Stock Exchange Model Code and to carry out correctly the routine procedures relating to registration and transfer of shareholdings.

Companies seeking admission to the USM have to enter into a General Undertaking which also contains 20 provisions, the majority of which agree, word for word, with those of the Listing Agreement. One provision is that USM companies must pay a flat-rate annual fee to The Stock Exchange (currently £1,000 per company); there is no initial charge. The differences between the Undertaking and the Agreement are, for the most part, no more than matters of detail.

The only distinction of real substance between the Undertaking and the Agreement relates to the issue of circulars to shareholders disclosing acquisitions or disposals of assets. Listed companies are required to write to all shareholders announcing any acquisition or disposal equivalent to 15% or more of the assets of the company before the transaction. On the view that this requirement is unduly onerous for small companies, the threshold for an obligatory circular has been set at 25% for companies admitted to the USM.

The market mechanism

One interesting difference between the listed market and the USM is that the latter may prove to be, to some extent, independent of the jobbing system. For listed securities, The Stock Exchange adheres to the concept of single capacity. That is to say, jobbers alone trade as principals in listed securities; brokers (and they alone) trade solely as agents; every deal is, in theory at least, a contract between broker's client and jobber with the broker acting as intermediary. The jobber's name does not, however, appear on the client's contract note because the client's contract is deemed to be with "the market", which consists of the whole ensemble of Stock Exchange jobbing firms.

Single capacity presupposes that there are at least two jobbing firms prepared to make a market in every listed security; at least two to ensure a competitive market. In practice it is not unknown for a minor listed stock in which few dealings take place to be traded by one jobber only. The number of jobbing firms has declined sharply in recent years (there were over 100 in 1960, but now there are only 17) and some major provincial centres, including Manchester, no longer have any jobbers at all. Consequently, it has become more difficult to obtain sufficient jobber participation to ensure adequate markets in the shares of smaller companies, particularly those which have a mainly local following in parts of the country where no jobbers are trading.

It has been recognised that the effectiveness of the USM could be seriously limited if this new market were obliged to fit the normal Stock Exchange pattern, with compulsory jobber involvement in every deal. The jobbing system has probably contracted too far to be able fully to meet the needs of the USM. Therefore the principle of dual capacity (brokers acting as both principals and agents) has been admitted for the USM. The Council has concluded that, unless at least two jobbers are willing to register as dealers in a new USM stock, the broker sponsoring the issue will be entitled to apply to the Council for registration. This will mean that the broker is permitted to deal in the stock as principal; where his buying and selling orders from clients do not match, he may himself buy or sell stock to balance the orders.

The future of Rule 163 (2)

Hitherto, dealings in companies not suitable for listing have taken place under this Rule, which provides that the Quotations Department must separately approve every transaction. Approval has, in fact, seldom been withheld and dealings have become more frequent in recent years. One of the purposes of the USM is to remove, as far as possible, the anomaly of Stock Exchange members habitually trading in shares of companies which do not comply with the Exchange's regulations. The recent trend towards liberal use of Rule 163(2) must clearly be reversed, otherwise unquoted companies might well feel that there was no need for them to go to the trouble of complying with the USM requirements.

Accordingly, for future dealings under the Rule, the Council has formulated a new code of practice. It states, *inter alia*, that permission to deal "will normally be withheld where, in the opinion of the Quotations Committee, an active market is developing or appears likely to develop"; it also severely limits the freedom of jobbers to trade under the Rule. The Council intends that, after a transitional period of a year, this code will be interpreted strictly.

The legal position of unlisted securities

The position of USM stocks, in relation to those company and tax laws that distinguish between listed or quoted securities and others, is ambiguous. The interests of investors pull in both directions. Shareholders facing capital transfer tax assessments would clearly prefer to have their shares in USM companies regarded as unquoted; so also would subscribers for newly issued USM shares who subsequently realise losses on selling them. On the other hand, insurance companies would prefer their USM holdings to be regarded as quoted companies so that they can be counted in the computation of solvency ratios; unit trust managers will take the same view, since they are limited by statute to keeping no more than 5% of their portfolios in unquoted securities. The Inland Revenue has indicated that it will regard USM securities as unquoted for tax purposes but will usually accept the recorded dealing prices of such securities as an indication of value where portfolio holdings have to be valued for tax purposes.

The pros and cons

In an earlier article in The Accountant's Magazine (May 1978) I put forward three objections to the introduction of a "second tier" stock market :

a) Listed companies which "traded down" to lower standards of disclosure would become less attractive to investors, especially to the institutions, whose support for the smaller business is particularly sought today.

b) Lower standards of disclosure for smaller companies could encourage abuses by dishonest or incompetent management; The Government might then step in with fresh regulations which would doubtless be more incommoding than any imposed by The Stock Exchange.

c) The private investor, who is often the main buyer of shares in smaller companies, is more in need of high standards of published disclosure than is the institutional fund manager, who generally maintains informal but quite close contact with companies in which he invests.

How well do the USM arrangements stand up against these objections?

First, by permitting only the entry standards to be easier for the USM companies, while imposing almost identical continuing requirements upon both the listed and the unlisted, The Stock Exchange has circumvented my first objection and, largely, my third. Companies will see little point in moving from full quotation to the USM. Nevertheless, "relegation" will be permitted subject to the approval of the shareholders in general meeting.

Second, it has to be accepted that the less rigorous requirements for entry to the USM will make it somewhat easier for companies run by the spivs and the cowboys, who still fray the edges of City life, to rip-off the investing public. That public, and the Quotations Department, will have to be more wary, more conscious of the need sometimes to say "no". This is the unavoidable price of making it easier for the reputable businessman, upon whom the prosperity of our society depends, to finance and develop his business. We live in a fast-changing economy where the industries and the businesses of the past are dissolving before our eyes; we can survive only if we do all we can to encourage those of the future to fill the expanding void.

It would be naïve to expect that there will be no scandals in the USM. We must resist the temptation to react to these in ways that could hamper the development of the entire small business sector. Today's trends in the climate of opinion and the attitudes of the present Government permit a little more optimism on this score than was possible a few years ago.

Third, in terms of disclosure to shareholders, the differences between the main market and the USM will be material for newly-quoted companies but will shrink to insignificance within a few years of entry to the market. *Ceteris paribus*, a company new to the USM will be a riskier investment than a newly listed company. But for companies that have been trading for some years there will be little or no risk differential between the two markets.

Conclusion

Like the Enterprise Zones, the USM is a welcome sign that society today is prepared to shed a little of its cocoon of protective regulations to encourage badly-needed fresh growth. The new market deserves to succeed; the people of Britain can ill afford to see it fail.

CHAPTER 4 : THE BANKS AND SMALL BUSINESS

Introduction

Both the supply of finance to, and the role of the banks in assisting, the small business are two aspects of small business management which are frequently misrepresented. The demand for external finance by the small business and its allocation within the firm are, for instance, two further determinants of the nature of the small business capital market and will tend to limit the role of institutional suppliers of finance. Nevertheless the conventional wisdom states that there is a shortage of finance either for new ventures or for long-term investment : at least convention does recognise that the market is not homogeneous.

The market-place is dominated by the high street banks and whatever their limitations in meeting the financial needs of the small business, their major advantage is that, with some 14,000 branches throughout Britain, they represent a highly visible and accessible network of assistance. But before the aspiring entrepreneur can penetrate this network, he or she needs to be prepared. The first article by Timmons addresses the business plan, the central object of the formal process of preparation.

Timmons discusses the need for a comprehensive business plan and provides a useful outline and some guidance in the course of his article. But his main argument is that a business plan is far more than simply a financing device. The first purpose of the plan is to allow the entrepreneur to crystallise his ideas, to give them direction and to allow him to view the new venture as an integrated whole. A perspective is vitally important since in some cases, as Timmons suggests, entrepreneurial myopia may result in missed opportunities. The second and main purpose is to interest prospective investors in the venture. Timmons confirms the irrelevance of venture capital sources to most new ventures and it is to the "Aunt Agathas" and the local banks that the entrepreneur must turn his attention. In an earlier article, Karger provides personal evidence that a well-argued formal proposal stands a good chance of attracting bank finance.

The overall conclusion of the second article is that the traditional sources of finance for small businesses - trade credit, the banks and

- 117 -

personal funds - are likely to retain their primacy in spite of a proliferation of new institutional sources. Dimson discusses the range of finance
available to the small business, noting the importance of bank borrowing,
particularly short-term borrowing in the form of the overdraft. The
Industrial and Commercial Finance Corporation (ICFC) appears to
dominate the sources of long-term external financing, although even
their relatively small portfolio vindicates the inescapable conclusion that
such external institutional finance has no impact on small business as a
whole.

The final article by Heard identifies the bank manager as an important,
if somewhat undervalued, source of advice and assistance to the small
business. Heard reviews the role of the bank manager in this regard and
concludes that there is considerable scope for improving the relationship
between the bank and the small business, although he notes that an
increasingly complex business environment requires far greater expertise
by the advisers than ever before.

1. A BUSINESS PLAN IS MORE THAN A FINANCING DEVICE

Jeffry A. Timmons

You are enthusiastic about an idea for a new business. You think the business has excellent market prospects and fits well with your skills, experience, personal values and aspirations.

But what are the most significant risks and problems involved in launching the enterprise? What are its long-term profit prospects? What are its future financing and cash flow requirements? What will be the demands of operating lead times, seasonality, and facility location? What is your marketing and pricing strategy?

Once you have convinced yourself and your partners that the answers to such questions are favorable, can you also convince prospective investors? If you seek out investment capital or loans, you will face much skepticism from venture capital firms, banks, insurance companies, and other financing sources. For example, only 3% to 7% of proposals to venture capital sources for start-up on ongoing financing are actually funded.

An effective business plan will convince the investor that you have identified a high-growth opportunity, that you have the entrepreneurial and management talent to effectively exploit that opportunity, and that you have a rational, coherent, and believable program for doing so.

The development of such a business plan is neither quick nor easy. Properly preparing a business plan can easily take 200 to 300 hours. Squeezing that amount of time into evenings and weekends can make the process stretch out to between 6 and 12 months. One might ask if such a time-consuming effort is really worth the trouble.

Wouldn't a more effective approach be to have an outside professional quickly prepare the business plan and then have the founders use their time to obtain financing and start the business?

A Business Plan is More than a Financing Device

Rewards of preparation

Keep in mind that the careful preparation of a business plan represents a unique opportunity to think through all facets of a new venture. You can examine the consequences of different strategies and tactics and determine the human and financial requirements for launching and building the venture, all at no risk or cost.

One entrepreneur with whom I worked discovered while preparing a business plan that the major market for his biomedical product was in nursing homes rather than in hospital emergency rooms as he and his physician partner had previously assumed. This realization changed the focus of his marketing effort.

The business plan is thus another way to evaluate the start-up venture in addition to the two ways I described in an earlier article(1). That article explained how the processes of self-assessment and team assessment can aid entrepreneurs in exerting control over the new venture and improve their prospects for eventual success.

For the investor, the business plan is the single most important screening device. Once the plan has passed initial screening, the investor may request the entrepreneur to make an oral presentation describing key features of the venture. If the investor is still interested, the plan will be given a more detailed evaluation and will become a prime measure of the founders' ability to define and analyze opportunities and problems and to identify and plan actions to deal with them.

A plan's long-term value

Most founders find the business plan to be even more helpful after start-up. As the founder-president of one venture that grew to sales of $14 million in seven years put it :

"Once you are in the business, you realize that everyone, including the founders, is learning his or her job. If you have a thoughtful and complete business plan, you have a lot more confidence in your decisions. You have a reference already there to say, 'Well, I have already run the numbers on inventory, or cost of goods, and this is what will happen' ".

If an outsider prepares the plan, you probably won't have the same sense of confidence and commitment.

The business plan can be especially valuable in the important area of product pricing. In one instance, the initial strategy of the founders of a rotary-drill venture was to price its products below the competition, even though the venture had a superior product innovation in a growing market. When the founders consulted outside experts, they were persuaded to price 10% over the competition.

By its second year, the new company enjoyed pretax profits of $850,000 based on about $9 million in sales. The revised pricing strategy made a significant difference. Without the detailed analysis of the industry and competition that is central to the marketing section of the business plan, it is unlikely that outsiders would have seen the basis for a different pricing strategy.

Feedback on your business plan by trusted and knowledgeable outsiders can help in refining strategy and making difficult decisions. A Nova Scotia entrepreneur who builds commercial fishing boats recently decided to raise his prices more than 40% based on an outside analysis and critique of his business plan. He knew he would lose two orders, but he also knew he would make more profit on the remaining three than all five at the old price. His delivery time would be cut in half as well. He's convinced that the shortened delivery time will lead to additional sales at the higher margins. And with upfront progress payments, he won't have to raise outside equity capital.

The process can also clarify the venture's financial requirements. Another entrepreneur with a three-year-old $1 million business erecting coal-loading sites believed he needed about $350,000 in expansion capital. After reflecting on a detailed critique of his business plan presentation, he concluded :

"The worst thing I could do right now is put more money into the business. The first thing I should do is get my own backyard more in order. But I will be back in two or three years".

True to his prediction, he returned two-and-a-half years later. His company was now approaching $3 million in sales and had a business plan for expansion that resulted in a $400,000 debt capital invesment, without relinquishing any ownership.

Common misconceptions

Entrepreneurs tend to downgrade the business plan because of certain false notions they hold about it. Technical and scientific entrepreneurs share one misconception I call the "better mousetrap fallacy". They frequently place unwarranted faith in a product or invention, especially if it is patented. Indeed, technological ideas must be sound, but marketability and marketing know-how generally outweigh technical elegance in the success equation. The rotary-drill venture discussed earlier reached $40 million in sales last year, yet has no patents on its products.

To further illustrate, less than one-half of one percent of the best ideas contained in the *Patent Gazette* five years ago have returned a dime to the inventors. In essence, the patent is usually a useful marketing tool, but not much else, and may be worth 15% or considerably less of the founding equity.

A second misconception new entrepreneurs often have is that the business plan is essentially a negotiating and selling tool for raising money. It isn't considered relevant or useful beyond that. Indeed, I have heard more than one entrepreneur comment that the plan is "destined for the circular file" once the funds are in the bank.

Such a view is dangerous for several reasons. To prospective partners, investors, or suppliers, it communicates a shallow understanding of the requirements for creating a successful business. It can also signal a promoting quality - a search for fast money and a hope for an early sellout - that creates mistrust of the entrepreneur. If the plan isn't a serious promise of what the team can deliver, should investors believe anything the founders assert?

A third misconception some entrepreneurs have is a belief that the primary and most important task in the start-up process is to determine if they can raise money as an indication that their idea is sound. This "cart before the horse" approach usually results in a hastily prepared business plan and exuberant shopping around among prospective investors.

Because most venture capital firms are quite small - often no more than two or three partners - they generally cannot take the time needed to get to know each entrepreneur and to explain the details for rejection. They use the business plan for initial screening as well as for making investment decisions. I have met many entrepreneurs who, as long as two years later, still do not understand that they were unable to raise capital because their business plans were deficient.

A fourth misconception is a belief among some entrepreneurs that their particular plan has no fatal flaws. These entrepreneurs ignore the need to test the plan's soundness with knowledgeable outside sources. Entrepreneurs must search for flaws in the market analysis that would make further consideration of the venture unnecessary.

One potential flaw is excessive dependence on outside suppliers for important state-of-the-art components that materially affect product development and prices. Suppliers of Viatron, a computer leasing company that obtained substantial public and private financing in the late 1960s, helped drive the company into bankruptcy in large part because they were unable to produce several semiconductors at low enough prices to enable Viatron to meet its own heavily promoted inexpensive prices.

A final misconception among some start-up and early-stage entrepreneurs seeking venture capital is the belief that retaining a minimum 51% control of the company is essential. This view seems to assume that control depends on legal percentage ownership rather than on management's behavior. In short, 51% of nothing is nothing. Compare this with the 20% ownership retained by the four founders of Digital Equipment Corporation.

Sound investment partners do not want to run your company - they invest in you and your team. More than anything else in the early going, the founders' actions are the ultimate controlling influence on the venture.

Putting together a business plan

What format should the business plan take? The outline in the *Exhibit* suggests one commonly used organizational approach. Entrepreneurs should also keep in mind some important general guidelines for preparing such plans :

A Business Plan is More than a Financing Device

Exhibit - Outline for preparing a business plan

Introduction

Summary of business plan & strategy

The company & its industry :

The company
Discussion of industry
Strategy

Products or services :

Description
Proprietary position
Potential
Technologies & skills

Market research & evaluation :

Customers
Market size, trends & segments
Competition - strengths &
weaknesses
Estimated market share & sales
Ongoing market evaluation
Economics - margins, costs

Marketing plan :

Overall marketing strategy
Pricing
Sales tactics & distribution
Service & warranty policies
Advertising & promotion
Profitability & break-even
analysis

Design & development plans :

Development status & tasks
Difficulties & risks
Product improvement &new
products
Costs

Manufacturing & operations plan :

Geographical location
Facilities & improvements
Strategy & plans
Labor force

Management team :

Organization - roles & respon-
sibilities
Key management personnel
Management compensation &
ownership
Board of directors
Management assistant or training
needs
Supporting outside professional
services

Overall schedule (monthly)

Important risks, assumptions, and
problems

Community impact :

Economic
Human development
Community development
Environmental

Financial plan (monthly for first year;
quarterly for next two to three years):

Profit & loss forecast
Proforma cash flow analysis
Proforma balance sheet
Break-even charts

Proposed company offering :

Desired financing
Securities offering
Capitalization
Use of funds

SOURCE : *Jeffry A.Timmons, Leonard E.Smollen & Alexander L.M.Dingee, New Venture Creation : A Guide to Small Business Development (Homewood, Ill. Richard D.Irwin Inc. 1977), p.426*

1. Keep the business plan as short as possible without compromising the description of your venture and its potential. Cover the key issues that will interest an investor and leave secondary details for a meeting with the investor. Remember that venture capital investors are not patient readers.

2. Don't overdiversify your venture. Focus your attention on one or two services or product lines and markets. A new or young business does not have the management depth to pursue too many opportunities.

3. Don't have unnamed, mysterious people on your management team, such as the Mr.G. who will join you later as a financial vice president. The investor will want to know early on exactly who Mr.G. is and what his commitment to your venture is.

4. Don't describe technical products or manufacturing processes in terms that only an expert can understand. Most venture capitalists do not like to invest in what they don't understand or think you don't understand.

5. Don't estimate your sales on the basis of plant capacity. Estimate your potential sales carefully on the basis of your marketing study, and from these estimates determine the production facility you need.

6. Don't make ambiguous, vague, or unsubstantiated statements. They make you look like a shallow and fuzzy thinker. For example, don't merely say that your markets are growing rapidly. Analyze past, present and projected future growth rates and market size, and be able to substantiate your data.

7. Disclose and discuss any current or potential problems in your venture. If you fail to do this and the venture capitalist discovers them, your credibility will be badly damaged.

8. Involve all of your management team, as well as any special legal, accounting, or financial help, in the preparation of the business plan.

9. Don't overstate or inflate revenue and accomplishments; be rigorously realistic and objective in making estimates and discussing risks.

A Business Plan is More than a Financing Device

The search for seed and expansion capital is usually time consuming and exhausting. Failure under such circumstances can leave the founders illiquid and demoralized. A carefully prepared business plan can aid substantially in planning a new venture, screening would-be partners, evolving winning strategies, and joining with a sound investment source, before actually launching the venture. In other words, it can mean the difference between success and failure.

(1) *"Careful Self-Analysis & Team Assessment Can Aid Entrepreneurs"*
(Growing Concerns), HBR November-December 1979, p. 198

2. FINANCING THE SMALLER COMPANY

Elroy Dimson

Long Range Planning. Volume II. December 1978

The deliberations of the Wilson Committee (The Committee to Review the Functioning of Financial Institutions) have been accompanied by increasing general interest in the financing of smaller companies. The Committee has commissioned surveys of the financing needs of medium and small companies, and the small business lobby has been vocal in soliciting support for these firms. In addition, the 1978 budget introduced new measures favouring this sector of the economy.

Despite the interest and support currently being shown for small business, however, there is a paucity of information on the importance of different sources of finance for the smaller firm. Companies which are large enough to have a stock exchange listing have available to them a wide range of financing opportunities. Unfortunately, these are frequently denied to private companies. In this article we examine the relative importance of different sources of finance for companies which are unable to obtain access to stock market funds principally because of their small size.

The Main Sources of Finance

Table 1 shows that the dominant source of finance for the corporate sector as a whole is the earnings which are retained in the business in the form of undistributed profits, depreciation and provisions for future taxation. The owners' interest in the private company consists of these retained earnings plus any finance provided by the directors of the firm. While finance provided by the directors of a small business may be in the form of shares or loans, the latter are to be regarded as equity capital since they have a low priority in the event of bankruptcy.

In addition to the owners' interest, there are three main sources of finance. Firstly, there may be external long-term or permanent finance, raised by means of issues of debentures and convertibles, mortgage and lease contracts, preferred and ordinary shares, etc. Secondly there is

Table 1 - Sources and uses of funds for all U.K. industrial & commercial companies

Sources	Average 1964-1974 %
Retained earnings	69
Bank borrowing	18
Loans, etc.	10
Ordinary shares	3
Total sources	100
Uses	
Capital investment	54
Acquisitions	9
Working capital (net)	27
Other uses	10
Total uses	100

SOURCE : *Walker (1975)*

bank borrowing, in the form of either overdraft finance or term loans. Finally, firms are financed by their current liabilities other than bank borrowing. The most important current liability is trade credit, but other creditors, factors and hirers for example, can also be significant.

Figure 1 summarizes some of the main sources of finance which are available to the smaller company and breaks these down under various headings. However before examining any of these in detail, we will look at the relative importance of each of the four classes of finance discussed earlier : the owners' interest, external finance, bank finance and current liabilities.

Figure 1 - Sources of finance for smaller companies

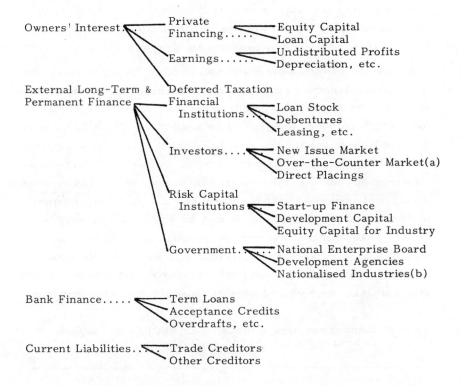

(a) *M.J.H.Nightingale & Co.'s OTC Market & Dealings Under the Stock Exchange's Rule 163(2)*
(b) *British Steel (£750m Available For Companies Using Vacated Sites) and the Coal Industry's Pension Funds*

The Relative Importance of Different Sources of Funds

The importance of each source of funds can be evaluated either from balance sheet data or from statements of the sources and uses of funds. While a balance sheet provides a guide to the capital structure of a firm, it is difficult to compare the balance sheets of small companies to those of a control group of companies for two reasons. Firstly, the balance sheet provides a historical rather than a contemporary summary of financing methods. And secondly, the effect of using book values for non-current liabilities differs between small and large companies. For example, many small firms continue to show very low book values for their equity capital, while companies that have made public offerings of shares have large book values for their share capital.

On the other hand, sources and uses of fund statements also suffer from certain problems. Firstly, there can be different degrees of 'netting out' - in extreme cases this results in the disappearance of sources of funds which can be quite important for small firms. Table 1, for instance, does not indicate any funding from trade credit because this has been deducted from increases in working capital. Secondly, the differences between companies' accounting years make comparisons difficult. Thirdly, a number of surveys of small companies have not published statements of sources and uses of funds, though they have produced summary balance sheets. Even when a source and use statement is available, it may suffer from ex-post bias (such as the exclusion of unsuccessful companies). However, with these caveats in mind, the sources and uses of funds of small companies are compared below to those of large listed companies.

Table 2 - Sources and uses of funds for exempt private companies (averages for 1961/62 and 1962/63)

	Private companies		
	£4-20,000 Profit	£20-50,000 Profit	Listed companies
Sources	%	%	%
Retained earnings	54	70	51
Trade credit	16	12	8
Bank borrowing	18	5	6
Loans, etc.	3	4	11
Ordinary shares	3	3	19
Other sources	6	6	4
Uses			
Capital investment	53	60	58
Acquisitions	8	7	22
Working capital	38	29	20
Other uses	0	4	0

SOURCE : *Board of Trade (1967)*

The most representative study of small firms was undertaken by the Inland Revenue, who examined a large stratified sample of nearly 2,000 exempt private companies' tax returns in the fiscal years 1958/1959 to 1962/1963. The results for the last 2 years of this study are shown in Table 2. There are two striking differences in the sources of funds between the small companies and the listed companies. Bank and trade credit represent twice as large a proportion of total sources for private as for listed companies, and issues of capital have a quarter of the relative importance for private as for listed companies.

The patterns in financing revealed by the Inland Revenue study appear to be stable over the years. For example, a study by Tamari (1972) for the Bolton Report examined the financing of 2115 firms employing under 200 people, and found a remarkably similar breakdown for the sources of funds for manufacturing companies over the period 1964 to 1968 :

	%
Retained earnings	57
Trade credit	16
Bank borrowing	8
Loans, etc.	3
Ordinary shares	6
Other sources	8

A more recent study by Mason (1975) confirms the important role of bank and trade credit. However, this study examined relatively large private companies : those with profits or net assets of at least £50 or £500 thousand respectively and with an Extel card in existence. This may explain her finding that private firms did not rely more on short-term and less on long-term funds than listed companies.

The Capital Structure of Small Firms

For further information on the financing of small companies, we turn to an examination of their balance sheets. A number of studies are summarized in Table 3, and the pattern of financing conforms to what we would expect from studies of the sources and uses of funds. Small firms have a significantly higher proportion of current assets within total assets than larger, listed companies, and much of this is accounted for by trade debtors. This explains the relatively high reliance on current liabilities (mainly trade credit) which characterizes the small businesses' financial structure.

Table 3 - The financing of small companies 1962-1975

| | Various samples of small firms | | | | | Listed companies |
	1962-63	1964-68	1968-70	1970-71	1971-75	1962-75
Total assets	%	%	%	%	%	%
Fixed assets	33	36	37	34	27	45
Current assets	67	64	63	66	73	55
Financed by :						
Owners' interest	58	59	43	53	36	55
Current liabilities	29	30	33	31]	57	26
Bank borrowing	11	7	16	12]		7
Long term loans	2	4	7	3	7	10
Minority interests	0	0	1	1	0	2

SOURCES :

1962-1963 - *348 firms with profits of £4-20,000 (Board of Trade, 1967)*

1964-1968 - *Average for manufacturing firms out of 2115 firms with under 200 employees (Tamari, 1972)*

1968-1970 - *611 firms subsequently financed by ICFC with median & mean net assets of £50,000 and £160,000 (Osborne, 1972)*

1971-1975 - *Average for forty technologically innovative businesses (Beesley and Hamilton, 1977)*

1962-1975 - *Average for 2095 and 746 listed companies respectively (Business Monitor, 1970 and 1977)*

Small firms have traditionally relied on bank borrowing to supplement their equity financing, and since 1962 bank loans have had twice the relative importance that they have in listed companies. A more detailed analysis of the data than that which is presented here also indicates that the relative importance of accumulated reserves is greater for small companies. New issues of equity for cash, including those subscribed by both the proprietors of the business and minority shareholders, are less important for private firms than for public companies.

External finance, whether through long-term loans or sales of equity, is thus of relatively little importance. Even those firms which are not averse to external financing (the 1968-1970 and 1971-1975 samples) have relied much more on current liabilities and less on long-term loans than have the listed companies.

Surveys have also been undertaken on the financial structure of firms which are financed by the Industrial & Commercial Finance Corporation. Though these companies have taken on substantial long-term liabilities, Table 4 shows that the importance of current liabilities and bank borrowing is not diminished.

Table 4 - Aggregate balance sheets of ICFC financed companies

Balance sheet	1967-68		1969-70		1973-74	
	304 ICFC firms	Quoted companies	427 ICFC firms	Quoted companies	557 ICFC firms	Quoted companies
	%	%	%	%	%	%
Fixed assets	67	66	69	67	68	68
-Current assets	97	76	120	89	118	99
-Current liabilities	46	33	66	44	63	52
-Bank borrowing	17	9	22	12	24	15
=Net assets*	100	100	100	100	100	100
Representing :						
Long term loans	26	18	19	20	17	20
Minority interests	0	3	1	4	1	4
Deferred taxation	4	4	4	0	9	6
Preference shares	5	4	7	3	3	2
Ordinary shares	24	30	22	29	16	22
Reserves	41	41	47	44	53	46

SOURCES : *Allen (1970); Biggs (1972, 1978)*
* Items may not sum to 100 because of rounding

Institutions Providing External Finance

It is clear from the evidence that external finance is not a particularly important source of funds for private businesses as a whole. However, the Radcliffe and Bolton Reports, the ICFC surveys (Allen, 1970; Biggs (1972,1978), and the reports of the Wilson Committee have pointed out that the fast-growing company has unusual financing needs. Of these, the most difficult to meet is the requirement for long-term and permanent external finance, notably external equity.

Some indication of the relative importance of institutions providing long-term loan and equity financing is provided in Table 5. Taking into account the fact that much of this financing is for the smaller public company, it is clear that the venture capital companies dominate this market. While they have provided about half the funds used by companies with under £1m of net assets, their role is undoubtedly even more important for the smaller business.

Table 5 - Institutional financing of small & medium-sized companies

Type of institution	Value of holdings in companies with under £1m of net assets £m	New money provided in 1971 £m
Venture capital companies	145	34
Insurance companies	90	47
Banks & merchant banks	40	9
Investment trusts	21	9
Pension funds	2	5
Unit trusts	–	–
All institutions*	296	104

SOURCE : *Mason (1975)*

*Items may not sum because of rounding

Table 6 - Venture and development capital institutions catering for the smaller company(a)

Name of institution	Parent company	Approx.no. of staff	Approx.no. of clients	Minimum investment £'000
Industrial & Commercial Finance Corporation (I.C.F.C.)	Clearing Banks(85%) & Bank of England	200	2500	under 10
National Research & Development Corporation	Dept.of Industry	200	500	under 10
Technical Development Capital	I.C.F.C.	under 10	100	50-100
Charterhouse Development	Charterhouse Group	25-50(b)	50-75	50-100
County Bank	Natl.Westminster Bank	25-50(b)	50-75	25-50
Gresham Trust	Gresham Investment Trust	under 10	50-75	25-50
Abingworth	-	under 10	10-25	50-100
Arbuthnot Industrial Investments	Arbuthnot Latham Holdings	under 10	10-25	Over 100
Barclays Development Capital	Barclays Merchant Bank	under 10	10-25	50-100
Capital for Industry	Grindlay Brandts	under 10	10-25	Over 100
Midland Montagu Industrial Finance	Midland Bank	under 10	10-25	50-100
Natl.& Commercial Dev'ment Capital	Natl.& Comm.Banking Group	under 10	10-25	50-100
Noble Grossart Investments	-	under 10	10-25	Over 100
Safeguard Industrial Investments	-	under 10	10-25	50-100
Small Business Capital Fund	Co-op.Insurance Society	under 10	10-25	50-100
C.P.Capital Partners International		under 10	under 10	under 10

(a) Excluding merchant banks & institutions such as Development Capital Investments & Moracrest Investment. The latter have a minimum investment of around £quarter million. See Bank of England(1978) for details.

(b) Part time

SOURCES : *Springman (1973); Beesley & Hamilton (1977); and Phillips (1977)*

Of the institutions providing external finance two organizations are dominant. The Industrial & Commercial Finance Corporation (and its subsidiary, Technical Development Capital Ltd.) conduct more business than all their competitors put together. In addition, the National Research & Development Corporation, which provides finance on a project-based system rather than to the company as a whole, is an active provider of funds. However, the other institutions providing risk capital continue to conduct a small amount of business, and most of them remain prepared to expand the scale of their activities.

The main risk capital institutions are summarized in Table 6, together with some broad indications of their size in terms of staff and number of clients, and the minimum investment in a company which they are prepared to consider. Many of the smaller institutions have been dormant until recently, and this confirms the dominance of the ICFC. A conclusion which can be drawn from this is that, apart from ICFC clients, the smaller company is likely to continue to seek funds from its traditional sources of finance, trade credit and bank borrowing. While the growth of leasing, factoring and term loans has increased the range of institutions offering fixed interest finance, the private business is likely to continue to rely on its proprietors, and its past earnings for its supply of risk capital for future investment.

References

C. Allen, Small firm survey, I.C.F.C. (1970)

Bank of England & the City Communications Centre, Money for Business, Bank of England (1978)

M.E. Beesley & R.T. Hamilton, An investigation of the institutional venture capital market in the U.K., Unpublished manuscript, London Business School (1977)

C. Biggs, Small firm survey, I.C.F.C. (1972, 1978)

Board of Trade, Patterns of company finance, 'Economic Trends', November (1967)

J.E.Bolton (Chairman), Report of the Committee of Inquiry on Small
   Firms, Cmnd.4811, HMSO (1972)

Business Monitor, M3 : Company finance, HMSO, various annual issues

Inland Revenue, Private exempt companies in manufacturing, distribution,
   etc. Unpublished manuscript obtained from Department of Industry

S.Mason, Small business financing and the capital market. Unpublished
   manuscript, London Business School (1975)

R.C.Osborn, I.C.F.C., financing small & medium-sized businesses,
   I.C.F.C. (1972)

W.Phillips, Businessman's guide to capital-raising outside the market
   system, 'Investors Chronicle', 16 June (1977)

Radcliffe (Chairman), Report of the Committee on the Working of the
   Monetary System, Cmnd.827, HMSO (1959)

M.Springman, Equity & Loan Financing for the Private Company, Gower
   Press (1973)

M.Tamari, A postal questionnaire survey of small firms : an analysis of
   financial data, Committee of Enquiry on Small Firms Research Report
   No.16, HMSO (1972)

J.L.Walker, Structure of company financing, 'Economic Trends', November
   (1975)

H.Wilson (Chairman), Progress report on the financing of industry & trade.
   Committee to Review the Functioning of Financial Institutions, HMSO
   (1977)

H.Wilson (Chairman), Survey of investment attitudes and financing of
   medium-sized companies, Committee to Review the Functioning of
   Financial Institutions Research Report No.1, HMSO (1978)

3. THE CHANGING ROLE OF THE BRANCH MANAGER IN ASSISTING THE SMALL BUSINESS

I.R.Heard

Journal of the Institute of Bankers. Volume 101 Part 2. April 1980

Since the revival of interest in the affairs of the small business, created largely by the Bolton Report (Report of the Committee of Inquiry on Small Firms)(1) in 1971, there has been a wealth of opinion and commentary on the role the banks should play in financing and advising the small business. Unfortunately, some of this opinion has tended to obscure the long-standing relationship which the banks have enjoyed with the small business community and some misconceptions have arisen.

Firstly, from a banking standpoint, the word 'small' is misleading for it tends to suggest that small businesses form a somewhat insignificant part of a bank's business customer base. This notion has even lead to the view that banks discriminate against the small business in favour of their larger corporate customers. The simple fact is, however, that the majority of business customers maintaining accounts with the clearing banks would be considered 'small' within the Bolton Report definition. For the sake of clarity, the word 'independent' is preferable and includes virtually all those businesses which are not owned by the State or by shareholders through the Stock Exchange. These independent businesses, ranging from the sole trader, small partnership to the privately owned industrial company, form the backbone of a bank's commercial business.

Secondly, the High Street branch manager can perhaps be forgiven for being somewhat puzzled by the continuing debate on the small business, for it seems to him that an entity has been created which, until a few years ago, apparently did not exist. He would argue, with justification, that he has been financing businesses to start up and expand their operations over many years, and he would describe with enthusiasm the close rapport he has established with many of his small business customers.

Thirdly, publicity has rightly been given to alternative sources of finance and advice available to the small business from government and other financial institutions. Valuable though these contributions are, the fact remains that in terms of the total market requirement the network of 14,000 branches of the major clearing banks provides the main source of finance and advice to the independent business sector.

A bank's relationship with its business customers of every complexion and size has developed over a long period and, in most cases, is based on a mutual understanding and respect for each other's aims and objectives. It is acknowledged, however, that the pace of change in the business environment has accelerated and the banks have become increasingly conscious of the special problems facing the small business and its growing importance to the economy, particularly in terms of providing employment. Moreover, the fierce competition which exists between the clearing banks behoves each one to review constantly their approach and support to the small business community. Most banks have established specialist units responsible for implementing policy and acting as a focal point for co-ordinating an approach to the affairs of the small business both internally and externally. The effect of these developments on the function of a branch manager is wide ranging, and this paper aims to identify the main areas which are influencing a branch manager's role in financing and advising the entrepreneur.

Types of finance available

It does not seem long ago since a branch manager would satisfy most requests for finance by the provision of an overdraft for trading purposes or a short-term loan for the purchase of fixed assets. It is now a matter of history that the banks have evolved to a stage where they are large financial groups, offering a diverse range of lending and finance-related services which can accomodate almost every need of the corporate customer. In addition to the conventional overdraft, short- and medium-term finance have become increasingly important for the small firm, particularly where assets are to be acquired or a new project is to be financed. More recently, one bank has introduced a long-term loan scheme to support new capital investment with repayments spread over a 20-year term if required. Other services include equity finance (of growing importance to the survival and prosperity of privately owned companies), instalment finance, leasing, block discounting, factoring, export finance and insurance.

The problem for the branch manager is self-evident; it is one thing to be aware of the types of finance available, quite another to identify and evaluate the most appropriate forms of finance for his customer. Nevertheless, with the benefit of training and the support of specialist personnel, a branch manager can mould a financial package which will satisfy his customer's needs and meet the corporate objectives laid down by his head office.

Knowledge of his customer's business

Perhaps the most fundamental change which is taking place in the banker/customer relationship is the increasing knowledge and understanding which a branch manager is seeking to acquire of his customer's business and the problems he encounters. Two major benefits accrue from this development. Firstly, a branch manager is able to evaluate a business proposition across a broader spectrum with the result that he can assess the viability of the business more objectively. Secondly, he will be more qualified to provide advice to the less sophisticated customer, who, though technically able, may be lacking in business acumen. This advisory function is discussed in a later paragraph.

When discussing a business proposition with his customer, a branch manager will develop his appraisal around the amount and purpose of the advance and the proposals for repayment. These three points are simple enough but form the basis for a detailed appreciation of the proposal before him. His perception of its viability will depend on his customer's response to a number of issues which are considered below.

MANAGEMENT CAPABILITY

The honesty and integrity of the borrower, whether a sole trader or small private company, is paramount, but a branch manager will also wish to assess the business expertise of his customer. This is particularly important in the case of the sole trader, for, understandably, there are few who can combine their technical skills with a knowledge of marketing, finance, legislation, etc. In the case of a limited company, a branch manager will wish to evaluate the track record and blend of experience of the directors, and he will be conscious of the problems of management succession, not least where the directors are part of the same family.

By this process a branch manager will identify the strengths and weaknesses of his customer's managing ability, and where there are deficiencies, most commonly in the area of internal financial control, he can offer guidance to his customer, which after all will be of benefit to them both.

THE MARKET/BUSINESS PLAN

It is not suggested that every small business should prepare an elaborate marketing plan and, indeed, this would be quite absurd in many instances. Nevertheless, all small businessmen should be encouraged to plan ahead for all too often they are immersed in the day-to-day operation of their business and are overtaken by events, sometimes with disastrous consequences. It may be encouraging for a branch manager to learn that his customer is expanding his sales next year through entry into a new market or product, but does he have sufficient resources employed in the business to support his plans?

A branch manager must be cognizant of the size and characteristics of his customer's market, his market share and the strength of the competition. He must be alive to any changes in demand for his customer's product or service, for the small businessman is not always alert to changing fashion, the impact of new technology and so on.

PREMISES

In the past there has been criticism that branch managers rarely visit their customer's place of business. This situation is now changing and branch managers are actively encouraged to visit their customer's premises. In addition to creating goodwill in the eyes of the customer, the branch manager is given an excellent opportunity to assess his customer in his own environment and to learn much about his business.

In the case of new premises, the requisite planning permission is sometimes overlooked and its geographical location, ready access to markets
and labour, effective utilisation of space and scope for expansion will be
examined.

Whilst on site, the branch manager will show interest in plant and
equipment in terms of its age and performance, the percentage of capacity
used and any replacement proposals.

PERSONNEL

Even in a small concern the quality of personnel can have a significant
effect on the fortunes of the company, and a branch manager should be
aware of the types of skill employed, recruitment and training programmes,
and any industrial relations problems which could seriously affect its
performance.

FINANCIAL PLANNING & CONTROL

It is no secret that most businesses fail because of bad financial control,
and it is in this area that there is tremendous scope for developing the
skills of financial management. There is already a growing trend in small
businesses towards the introduction of internal management accounting,
but where there is a reluctance to produce management information a
branch manager should provide encouragement. Indeed, where a business
has little track record (and therefore cannot produce audited accounts),
or is experiencing cash flow problems, the submission of regular management information will be essential if the bank is to continue or increase
its support.

In any event the branch manager is now being trained to apply a
'going-concern' approach to a lending proposal so that, in addition to
analysing the last three years' balance sheets in terms of gearing,
liquidity, profitability, etc., he will wish to see budget and cash flow
projections for the ensuing 12 months. This information will be
particularly relevant where, for example, a medium-term loan is required
to finance the purchase of premises or plant. Thereafter a monthly
monitoring procedure may be introduced so that branch manager and
customer can assess actual performance against budget and identify the

reasons for any variances.

In some instances a branch manager will discuss the costing and pricing structure of his customer's business and examine his debtor/creditor/stock control procedures. He will, of course, pay particular attention to these points in cases where he is witnessing frequent pressure on the agreed overdraft limit.

In the last few paragraphs I have tried to identify, albeit briefly, the main points for consideration between branch manager and customer when discussing the provision of finance. It is recognised that where, for example, the bank's support is small in relation to the customer's stake in the business, a comprehensive survey may not be warranted and, indeed, a branch manager runs the risk of losing his customer on the grounds that he is over-cautious or seeking too much information.

Conversely, where the bank's assistance is substantial in relation to the customer's resources, close co-operation is essential on a continuing basis. This involves the regular submission of information, financial or otherwise, to the branch manager so that he can assess the company's progress and offer advice where appropriate.

The advisory role of the branch manager

Despite an increasing number of organisations offering advice to the small firm on aspects such as premises, labour, legislation and marketing, there is clearly a role for a branch manager to play. Branch managers have offered general advice to small businesses for many years but there is growing evidence to support the view that they should provide specific advice on the techniques of internal financial control, particularly to firms in their first few years of existence. The chances of survival can be greatly enhanced if a branch manager is close at hand to ensure that financial disciplines are rigorously applied.

The experience gained by two banks' advisory services during recent years has revealed the dearth of management skills in a number of small firms. The Small Firms Counselling Service receive many requests for assistance on financial matters which, more often than not, relate to a cash flow problem. Simple advice on more efficient debtor or stock control and better utilisation of plant and equipment is invariably the key to the solution.

Thus, as a corollary to acquiring a greater knowledge of his customer's business, there is the opportunity for a branch manager to advise his customer on many aspects of common interest.

COSTING

There is little doubt that a complicated costing system is beyond the understanding of most small businessmen, but the introduction of a basic system is both feasible and desirable. A branch manager can offer encouragement in this direction when he reviews the figures in the latest balance sheet with his customer. He can identify the direct and indirect costs of the business and suggest simple procedures for analysing the cost of materials, labour and other expenses. When asked to provide finance for a specific contract he may request sight of the costing as a means of establishing any omissions in his customer's calculations. He will ascertain whether direct labour costs have been undercharged due to omitting the costs of absenteeism, fringe benefits and impending wage increases. Similarly, he will examine materials costs to see whether his customer has allowed for impending price rises, and the effects of pilfering and wastage. He will ensure that overheads have taken account of the anticipated increase in business and the effects of inflation. Finally, he will look at the rate of mark up and ask himself if this will generate sufficient profit.

PRICING

There is an understandable reluctance in small business to increase prices (for fear of backlash from larger competitors), yet so often this is the simplest way of improving profits. A branch manager should remind his customer of the importance of a regular price review, especially in an inflationary climate. Where necessary, he should endeavour to moderate his customer's obsession for increasing volume and instead extol the virtues of profitability and liquidity. He should stress the importance of the market in determining price, to account not only for costs plus a margin, but also an assessment of what the market will stand. Some businesses deny themselves additional profit by paying scant regard to this point.

BUDGETING

Branch managers are increasingly asking for budgets and cash flow forecasts to support a firm's future plans, particularly when the ability to fund repayments, for, say, five years, out of cash flow is being evaluated.

There will be occasions when a branch manager is required to assist his customer in the preparation of a budget and cash flow forecast, and he will pay regard to the estimated sales figure in relation to the company's past performance, market demand for its product or service and orders to date. He will assess the raw materials figure in relation to projected sales and examine whether labour costs reflect the expected level of activity. An appraisal of other direct costs and overheads should not present any problem.

Initially, some proprietors find this to be a laborious and unnecessary process, but it is apparent that subsequently they become more committed to the discipline of budgetary control and benefit accordingly.

DEBTOR/CREDITOR/STOCK CONTROL

There is little need to refer in detail to the importance of efficient debtor/creditor/stock control, yet so often a proprietor inflicts serious cash flow problems on himself by neglecting one or more of these vital areas. There is, however, little excuse for not maintaining up-to-date ledgers and records, and there will inevitably be occasions when a branch manager insists upon the production of monthly figures as a means of both improving financial control and monitoring progress.

Relationship with the small business community

Most branch managers take pride in the business contacts they have developed in their catchment area, with the obvious benefits which materialise for both bank and customer. Nevertheless, the creation of new sources of finance, advice and training for the entrepreneur means that a branch manager must have a growing awareness of external assistance available to his customer, if only to point him in the right direction.

The experience already gained by the Community of St.Helens Trust, for example, indicates a blissful ignorance by businessmen, bank managers and accountants, of grants available both at government and local authority level. Although a grant is not a means to an end in itself, it could make the difference between a viable and an unacceptable banking proposition, particularly in a 'start-up' situation. Thus, whilst branch managers cannot be expected to be familiar with the plethora of grants available, they can establish a point of reference at the local town hall.

The activities of Cosira and more recently the Small Firms Counselling Service can often play a complementary role to the branch manager in advising and, in the case of Cosira, also financing the small business. The close relationship which these two organisations enjoy with many of their clients indicates that a tripartite discussion can be helpful, especially when the customer is going through a difficult period.

There are a growing number of local initiatives to help the entrepreneur, often supported by large companies and banks. The St.Helens Trust and London Enterprise Agency are two cases in point, and a branch manager will obviously recognise the advantages of such organisations for his customer, and direct him where appropriate.

As far as educating the entrepreneur is concerned, courses funded by the Manpower Services Commission are available at business schools and other academic institutions for new enterprises. These courses aim to instil a practical appreciation of management skills in the mind of the budding entrepreneur and, from the writer's experience, provide excellent training in this respect. From a banker's point of view, the emphasis on the principles of good financial control and preparing a presentation for the bank manager are to be welcomed, and the only regret is that such training is not available for more people.

Conclusions

The changing role of the branch manager is clearly an evolving one and it would be wrong to suggest that all branch managers, or indeed most, have developed the wide ranging expertise which is now required in a business environment of increasing complexity. Moreover, the training of all branch managers in business management skills would be superfluous even if it were practicable, bearing in mind that many branches, particularly in suburban areas, serve the personal sector and have little involvement in the business community.

Much more likely is the continuing development of educating specialist personnel, highly trained in business management skills, with ready access to the small business community. For example, one bank is centralising its management expertise in key business areas, so that the needs of its corporate customers in the locality may be serviced quickly and efficiently. On the other hand, the experience gained by business advisers in two of the clearing banks will prove invaluable when they return to a branch banking environment.

Inevitably, increasing specialism will have to be countered by a release from less onerous tasks if a branch manager is going to devote the time and effort required in this challenging role of being a business-man as well as a banker. The introduction of credit-scoring techniques for personal lending, whereby all requests for personal loans, etc., can be delegated to a senior branch official, is one example of how this can be achieved.

The potential benefits for the small businessman are far-reaching, both in terms of obtaining finance and receiving advice on how to run his business. The realization of these benefits can only be accomplished, however, if there is an equal commitment by members of the small business fraternity to professionalise their approach. Anyone who has a genuine desire to see the small business flourish has a responsibility to offer guidance and encouragement in this direction.

(1)   *Chairman : J.E.Bolton, Cmnd. 4811 (HMSO, 1971)*

Small Business Perspectives

PART III

MANAGING
THE
SMALL
BUSINESS

CHAPTER 5 : SURVIVAL AND GROWTH

Introduction

The questions posed by survival and growth for management strategies in the small business must in most cases be resolved by the owner-manager alone. As Stanworth and Curran point out in the first article, decisions in the small business are frequently the responsibility of one or a few persons who are generally ill-equipped to deal with the complex, strategic considerations posed by growth, even if growth were feasible in the first place. Within the constraints of such decision-making, growth is almost exceptional; indeed in some cases growth may be unplanned, a result of the unpredictable nature of the small business environment. Unplanned growth and stagnation are equally unwelcome.

For most firms, management decisions are made in the context of survival and Stanworth and Curran are critical of the "stage" models of growth which fail to appreciate this. Growth is the manifestation of social, rather than natural, phenomena and the entrepreneur's aspirations, dynamism and limitations will determine the nature and extent of growth. In this view, growth is by no means the natural or inevitable strategy for the small business. The human dimension ensures that strategies for survival predominate.

If large firms are a consequence of the growth of small firms, but growth is a discontinuous social phenomenon, not readily explained by existing organisational theories, then management principles developed for application in large organisations are unlikely to be useful in small ones. Tibbits recognises that both the scarcity of resources within the firm and the limitations of the entrepreneur or owner-manager necessitate a different approach to management and therefore a different set of management principles. The complexity of the management task in the small business is itself no reason for a different approach; the necessity for generalist rather than specialist skills defines the nature of the approach to management. Paradoxically the entrepreneur or owner-manager is likely to be a specialist, having graduated to the small firm from the confines of some specialised functional task in a large company. In this case, the rate at which the specialist can absorb generalist skills will determine the success or failure of the firm in the long-run.

In its attitudes to growth and survival, management in small firms differs from that in large. Strategies oriented to non-growth are perfectly admissible in the small business and in many cases have been quite successful. Frequently non-commercial objectives take precedence over commercial ones; the perpetuation of a family dynasty may itself subordinate all other objectives, whether unintentionally or not. Thus strategic planning in the small firm will tend to be introspective, intuitive and informal, with little recognition of the general business environment. Family managers, unlike their professional counterparts, will accordingly need to react intuitively.

The third article concerns one aspect of the difference in management techniques between small and large firms. In its approach to the market, the small business cannot adopt the extravagent, resource consuming strategies of the large firm, although Mason observes that the need to diversify in order to survive and grow is common to firms of all sizes. Alternative strategies for diversification in the small business proposed by Mason reflect the familiar constraints of resource scarcity, lack of market power and lack of marketing and general management skills.

1. GROWTH & THE SMALL FIRM - AN ALTERNATIVE VIEW

M.J.K.Stanworth and J.Curran

Journal of Management Studies · Volume 13 Number 2. May 1976

Introduction

For most of the 1960s, the small firm, if discussed at all in academic and business circles, tended to be regarded as a remnant of our industrial past inevitably doomed to disappear in an economy dominated by large-scale public and private enterprise. Since then, however, the Bolton Committee report(1), various research studies(2), and a growing disenchantment with the supposed virtues of large-sized economic units(3), have all helped to refocus attention on the small firm.

One aspect of the small firm which has received some attention is its growth and development. The present paper seeks to offer a new perspective on the social processes involved here, and is backed by results from an in-depth longitudinal research programme carried out in a sample of small manufacturing firms from the Surrey area over a six year period(4). Other research data, especially from American studies, is used to provide additional empirical support(5).

The Small Firm : A Definition and Statistical Description

Defining the small firm is in itself no easy task. However, the Bolton Committee saw the small firm as a socio-economic unit with the following characteristics :
1. Economically, a small firm is one that has a relatively small share of its market
2. Managerially, the small firm is administered by its owners or part-owners in a personalized way, rather than through the medium of a formalized management structure
3. Finally, it is independent in the sense that it does not form part of a larger enterprise and owner-managers are free from outside control in taking their principal decisions(6)

This definition may be criticized on several grounds. For instance, some small firms have quite large shares of their often specialized markets.

A methodological drawback here is the lack of available data on ownership, management structures and market shares of firms which precludes
any comprehensive operationalization of this definition. Instead, for
manufacturing industry, the Committee was forced to adopt the less
satisfactory statistical definition of '200 employees or less'. To maximize
comparability between our own work and previous work on small firms,
we have adopted the Bolton Committee's solution to this definitional
problem, though not without reservations for, as our own research
indicates, many of the significant social characteristics of the small firm
become severely attenuated well before the number of participants reaches
200.

The 1968 Census of Production(7) states that there are 58,198 small
manufacturing enterprises, employing nearly 1.4 million personnel and
producing around £2,300m. of goods. Small firms constitute approximately
94% of all firms in manufacturing industry, though the average size of
firm is very much smaller than 200 employees. In fact 44,635, or over
75%, employ less than 25 personnel.

These figures suggest that small firms are an important element of
the manufacturing sector, and a similar pattern emerges from an examination of other areas of the economy. In fact, the figures themselves
understate the importance of the small firm. As the C.B.I. argues, if
our small firms closed down tomorrow 'most of the large firms would grind
quickly and painfully to a halt'(8).

The small firm has declined in importance in our economy during this
century but, in absolute terms, it remains highly significant and, what
is more, the rate of decline appears to have been slowing down(9).
United States experience in recent years underlines this point. The
Bolton Committee Report pointed out that the share of economic activity
held by small firms in the U.S. is larger than in the U.K. Over 98% of
firms in the U.S. employ less than 100 people and between them they
account for about 40% of total employment(10). Further, the decline of
the small firm, in what may be considered the most advanced of industrial
societies, appears to have halted and may even have been reversed(11).

Growth and the Small Firm

Previous Views of Growth in the Small Firm

A survey of the literature on growth and the small firm reveals several contributions to theory construction with certain close similarities between them(12). Without discussing each in detail, and at the risk of some over-simplification, it can be argued that they reveal a dominant and a minor explanatory theme and a shared consistent overall theoretical perspective.

The dominant theme is that of a 'stage' model of growth. The number of stages offered varies, but typically there are three or four, though sometimes as many as ten(13). The small firm here is seen as passing through a sequence of growth stages though there is little discussion on whether this is a necessary progression or whether, under certain conditions, one or more stages may be missed out or variations in the sequence occur. The absence of such qualifications almost certainly stems from a lack of empirical underpinning(14). It is rare for samples of firms to exceed double figures; there is often a tendency to rely heavily on retrospective data or observations at a single point in time instead of longitudinal research strategies, and there is usually insuff-icient linking with data from other studies.

Stage models, regardless of the number of stages offered, also display certain further similarities. The initial stage, as we might expect stresses the individual entrepreneur(s) with an idea for a product or service setting up in business. The next stage (or sometimes the next but one),is usually concerned with the division of managerial tasks(15). The entrepreneur(s) can no longer exercise total managerial control and non-owner managers are recruited, often because they have skills lack-ing in the founder(s). The remaining stages tend to concentrate on organizational maturity and stability. The firm becomes more bureau-cratic and rationalized and takes on the general character of the larger company. It evolves a board of directors who are essentially managers rather than entrepreneurs; it exploits a wide range of management, production and marketing techniques; and there is an acceptance that it must develop systematic working relations with other organizations in society such as trade unions and government departments.

These various approaches do contain a considerable element of truth but this derives at least partly from the definitional procedures used in theory construction. For instance, to define the first stage in terms of an individual or small group deciding to exploit a market for a product or service, is to go little beyond defining the coming into existence of a new independent economic entity.

Another curious aspect of these stage theories of growth is an implied disregard for the size distribution of firms discussed above. The Census of Production data show this to be highly skewed with over 94% of manufacturing firms employing less than 200 people and the typical firm, in a statistical sense, employing less than 30. In other words, most firms do not grow to any considerable size in terms of workforce size (which we may assume is broadly correlated with other dimensions of growth) and that substantial growth is seemingly a rather *exceptional* process. This is reinforced by the data which suggest that the failure rate among small firms, especially in the years immediately following formation, is very high(16).

Finally, an inspection of the implied characteristics of the firm's organizational and managerial structure contained within the later stages in most of the models strongly indicates that the authors concerned are discussing a firm which has long since entered the 6% of large firms in our economy.

The minor theme present in theorizing on growth in the small firm is the so-called 's-curve hypothesis'(17) which can be seen as a special case of the stage theory. This suggests that the small firm will have a short formative period followed by a period of rapid growth perhaps reaching an exponential rate. The thinking behind this is that after the entrepreneur(s) have developed an idea for a product or service, there is an initial establishing period for the firm which ends with the clear demonstration of a market advantage. This leads to a high rate of investment, to further exploit the advantage, sometimes supplemented by outside capital attracted by the firm's performance in the establishing period. This investment fuels the high rate of growth in the next period of the firm's history.

This exceptional rate of growth, however, tails off as competition is offered by other firms who become aware of the market opportunities. A reduction in the rate of expansion further results from a lowering of investment to more conventional levels due to profit-taking by the owner-managers and a decline in the firm's attraction as an investment for outsiders due to the increased competition.

The consistent overall theoretical perspective which unites both the dominant and minor themes in current theorizing concerning growth in the small firm is a highly *positivist* one. The underlying paradigm for theoretical development is an idealized version of that used in the natural sciences. The small firm is seen here as a behaving entity whose elements are related in quantifiable, systematic and highly predictable ways and the object of theory construction is the generation of law-like propositions concerning the growth process.

However, theories of small firm growth, constructed upon this positivist view, fail to meet their self-imposed standards. They seldom, if ever, attain the level of precision required for the development of law-like propositions(18). Nor are they adequately tested against acceptable samples of small firm histories necessary to define limits and boundaries to the relevance of such propositions. Finally, they appear to be inadequately articulated with our present knowledge of the structure of our economy, particularly with reference to the size distribution of firms. Since, in relative terms, so few small firms grow to become large sized, it might be expected that these theories should try to explain the rareness of the process they purport to explain. Their failure to do so suggests a blinkered approach.

The inadequacies of this general theoretical perspective have come in for harsh comment in recent years(19). The main point made is that the assumption that natural and social phenomena belong to the same category of entities for purposes of theorizing and explanation is fundamentally mistaken. The crucial difference stems from the fact that social phenomena *understand* their own behaviour and can act *purposefully* while natural phenomena have neither of these properties.

The Entrepreneurial Spirit in Action Perspective

Our alternative, a *social action* view of the small firm, concentrates heavily on understanding the internal social logic of the small firm as a social grouping. We argue that the key to growth lies in the meanings attached to participation in the firm by the actors involved. The small firm, in this view, is an ongoing social entity constructed out of the meanings and actions of those who participate in the firm or who are 'outsiders' in relation to the firm as social grouping but nevertheless interact with the participants.

It should be stressed that this is *not* a psychological theory of the small firm. It takes the standpoint that definitions and meanings attached to situations are *socially generated, socially sustained* and, of special interest in the present context, *socially changed*. In other words a social action perspective here links the meanings and actions of the small firm's participants with their wider social environment. Moreover, in order to achieve the necessary level of generality for a *social* view of the small firm, the view cannot be limited to specific individuals but is extended to cover tendencies for certain combinations of meanings and actions to recur after the fashion revealed in various studies of small firms in this country and the United States.

This creates a new dimension for analysis because the researcher cannot now simply adopt a theory which assumes that objects in the situation will behave in a relatively positivist and deterministic manner. Purposeful phenomena cannot be treated in this simplistic way. In seeking to interpret the situation, the researcher must now also endeavour to understand what participation means to those involved and the likely changes in these meanings. Only in this way is an adequate account possible.

The resulting interpretation also differs from positivist explanations in that it does not take the form of law-like 'predictions'. Instead, an interpretation of the social situation is provided based upon a knowledge of both internal and external forces (20) influencing the situation. This allows suggestions as to the probabilities of actors attempting certain lines of action, given their interpretation of the situation, and the social forces affecting the situation which originate from the wider social environment.

Given the very strong influence of the owner-manager on the small firm's organizational style, it is important to examine this key role in some detail. Of particular importance are the new owner-manager's reasons for going it alone. Understanding this aids an understanding of attitudes towards growth later on in the firm's life.

Individuals do not generate meanings in a vacuum for most of their social interactions, but rely on an available stock of meanings, 'culture' to make sense of specific social experiences and provide a framework for anticipated experiences aimed at achieving the actor's ends or avoiding certain outcomes. In our society there is a strong cultural bias favouring individualism, and this finds expression in many ways. Economic individualism, it may be argued, in the form of founding and operating a business of one's own, is one of the most legitimate of all culturally prescribed forms of individualism. Indeed, as Weber argued(21), economic individualism, in this form, has been given divine sanction in our culture and in fact was closely associated with the genesis of modern industrial society itself. An American writer on the small firm claimed that starting one's own business has

> .....always been considered an integral element of the American way of life. Our traditional concept of opportunity has carried and still carries, a heavy emphasis on 'freedom', on 'being on one's own', 'being one's own boss' and 'working for oneself'.(22)

While this cultural bias is not quite so highly emphasized in Britain's culture, survey data(23) show that the ideal of self-employment, in order to increase autonomy and personal self-esteem, is none the less widespread.

However, going into business for oneself is a difficult role transition if only because our educational system and vocational guidance processes operate to minimize the practical consideration of this alternative(24). Nevertheless, some people, albeit a very small minority, do take on the owner-manager role. It is important to know something about the social backgrounds and orientations of these people, especially first generation entrepreneurs, if we are to achieve an understanding of the small firm. It is also quite clear from the available data on entrepreneurship in this country and the United States that new entrepreneurs are far from randomly drawn from the population.

As a social category, entrepreneurs tend to share certain character-istics. For instance, they are not, on the whole, well educated. The

Bolton Committee Report stated that nearly three-quarters of a sample
of small manufacturing firms' chief executives had received no higher
education and that only 1% had a management qualification(25). Other
data support this claim for both Britain (26) and the United States(27)
though there have been exceptions reported for the latter(28). The
more general conclusion, derived from the study of the backgrounds of
new entrepreneurs, is that they tend to be people who consider themselves misplaced by the conventional role allocation processes of their
society.

Our main point here of the special social character of those who
embrace the entrepreneurial role is well supported in this quotation from
the largest American survey on entrepreneurship :

.....Entrepreneurs are men who have failed in the traditional and
highly structured roles available to them in the society. In this, as
we have seen, entrepreneurs are not unique. What is unique about
them is that they found an outlet for their creativity by making out
of an undifferentiated mass of circumstance a creation uniquely their
own : a business firm.(29)

We can use the term *social marginality* to refer to this situation in
which there is a perceived incongruity between the individual's personal
attributes - physical characteristics, intellectual make-up, social
behaviour patterns - and the role(s) he holds in society(30). Social
marginality is a common phenomenon due to the very nature of role
allocation processes in society - these are far from perfect in allocating
individuals to social roles - and also because individuals strive to maintain a sense of personal autonomy in social roles in opposition to social
pressures pushing towards conformity. These common forms of social
marginality are, however, unlikely to lead to dramatic social responses.

But, for some individuals and in some areas of society, circumstances
combine to produce high levels of social marginality. The historical
example, *par excellence*, of a group displaying high social marginality
has been the Jews. Being a Jew has, regretfully, been something which
has made a person an 'outsider' in non-Jewish society regardless of his
personal and intellectual characteristics. To some extent Jewish
communities developed patterns of social integration to counter these

deprivations imposed from the wider society but feelings of social marginality were likely to be present to an extent rare in most other parts of
society. For a Jew with only a weak commitment to his religion and
community, feelings of marginality were likely to be much more pronounced.

Other common examples of social marginality are the intellectually
gifted manual worker and the fully acculturated second-generation coloured
Briton. Solutions to intense feelings of social marginality are varied. In
some cases it leads to adherence to 'extreme' political or religious
ideologies which promise to reconstruct social reality and thus 'solve' the
individual's experiences of social marginality. The gifted manual worker
may choose to become a full-time trade union official. For some, a solution
is setting up their own firm.

Examples of the latter solution from our own research include some not
uncommon stories. We discovered social marginality resulting from a
promising academic career being shattered by domestic tragedy, or
through the war, sharply diminishing career prospects in conventional
industrial/commercial life. Or again, we came across social marginality
occurring in middle age when a successful career in the armed services
could not be matched by the attainment of a similarly responsible position
in civilian life. Other cases included instances of demonstrated talents
being overlooked by large employers due to the individuals' unorthodox
attitudes and personal idiosyncrasies.

An Action View of Growth in the Small Firm

Our previously published research, as well as that of others, indicates
that there is no one single, stereotyped entrepreneurial role and thus,
by implication, no single pattern of growth. The classicial economists
offered a picture of the entrepreneur as a rational profit maximizer and
this remains the popular stereotype despite little support from research.
An American study for example, reported that, of a sample of 81 newly
founded businesses, only six approximated to the classical economists'
model of the entrepreneur(31).

Rather, there are several possible constellations of meanings which
may form the core of the entrepreneur's self-definition of the entrepreneurial role. We find it helpful, following Gouldner(32), to distinguish

these constellations of more personal role components from those which may be taken as basic cultural prescriptions by using the concept, *latent social identity*. Research on the small firm - both the research we have previously reported and studies by others - suggest that three such latent identities occur with some frequency in relation to the role of small firm entrepreneur :

1. *The 'artisan' identity*. Here the entrepreneurial role centres around intrinsic satisfactions of which the most important are personal autonomy at work, being able to pick the persons you work with, status within the workplace and satisfaction at producing a quality product backed with personal service.

These are not the only meanings and goals attached to the role, but they are the ones which predominate. Thus, whilst income is important, as it must be for anybody who works and has no other source of income, it is secondary to intrinsic satisfactions.

2. *The 'classical entrepreneur' identity*. This latent social identity most closely resembles the classicial economists' view of entrepreneurship. Earnings and profit become a core component in the entrepreneur's definition of his role and hence in the way he acts out his role. Again maximization of financial returns (consistent with the survival and possible expansion of the firm), is by no means the sole goal of the entrepreneur, but it is given great importance compared to the intrinsic satisfaction associated with the 'artisan' identity.

3. *The 'manager' identity*. Here the entrepreneurial latent social identity centres on meanings and goals concerned with the recognition, by significant others, of managerial excellence. The entrepreneur structures his role performance to achieve this recognition from fellow members of the firm but, and more especially, from outsiders such as other businessmen. Other goals and values stressed here are security and a concern to ensure that the entrepreneur's children will eventually receive the benefits of his enterprise.

These identities are connected to other aspects of the firm's operations and to processes of growth although it should be stressed again that these links should not be seen in a positivist sense. The links occur through the internal social logic generated out of the ways in which the situation is perceived by those involved and the actions which follow on from these perceptions(33).

The *'artisan'* identity is not very concerned with growth and is most frequently found among people who have only relatively recently adopted the entrepreneurial role. It reflects the feelings of social marginality common among entrepreneurs, and is greatly concerned with intrinsic satisfactions likely to minimize the psychological deprivations associated with recent social marginality. However, successful adoption of this identity must be tenuous. Given the data on the instability of new small firms, survival is always problematic. Equally, for the same reasons, it is unlikely that the goals and values associated with the other two identities will be given prominence at this stage.

On the other hand, a small firm which survives the formative period and enters a period of sustained profitability constitutes a social context conducive to the generation of a *'classical entrepreneur'* identity. The goals associated with the artisan identity will have been at least partially realized and the new social and economic situation of the firm is favourable to the possible emergence of a new self-definition for the entrepreneur.

But whether any dramatic take-off into sustained growth is likely, even when the external logic - the economic and market situation of the firm and social relations with outsiders - is highly favourable, is a matter for debate and even scepticism. The internal logic of the firm from the point of view of its chief actor contains certain contradictions. A sustained high rate of growth may change the firm from a solution to social marginality to a situation reinforcing it.

As a firm grows forces emerge, internally and externally, which push it towards a more rational and bureaucratic structure. Management functions have to be delegated as they become too complex and time consuming for a single person to handle. The need for certain skills, almost certainly not possessed by the entrepreneur, becomes crucial and specialists must be recruited. The social relations among participants can no longer be conducted on a highly personal basis but must be more systematically and bureaucratically ordered. From the entrepreneur's point of view, therefore, the firm comes increasingly to resemble previous social situations which produced the social marginality feelings the firm was established to minimize. Entrepreneurs in our own study, who took on the classical entrepreneur identity often claimed, despited financial success, that they were 'beginning to feel like employees in their own firm'.

The emergence of these 'growth effects' depends on a variety of factors, and may not occur until the firm has grown to be of some size. But what is more important is whether the entrepreneur comes to perceive the likely outcomes of these changes and the decisions he makes concerning their desirability as well as his ability to cope with them in terms of the kind of person he has now become. So, again, we return to the internal social logic of the small firm, seen from the point of view of its main actor, and the possible outcomes which can develop.

Some small firm entrepreneurs will have little hesitation in deciding that growth is desirable or even necessary for survival. Having establish-ed that they can maintain a high profit growth company, they may come to redefine their entrepreneurial role in terms of the *'manager'* identity. In addition to the elements listed above, other behaviour patterns indicative of the presence of this identity are an increased interest in management training and development, employers' organizations, using management consultants, and attempts at taking over other firms and merging with larger companies or attempting to go public. Finally, it should be noted that the adoption of this new self-definition of the entrepreneurial role does not, of itself, give immunity against possible contradictions which may emerge as a result. The re-emergence of socially marginal feelings may occur but the entrepreneur, having embarked on a course of action, may find that it is extremely difficult to halt let alone reverse the outcomes(34).

But this particular outcome, the rapid growth and expansion of the small firm, despite its important place in the social mythology of our society, is likely to be less frequent than many expect. The small entre-preneur may well make an assessment of the results of certain courses of action, and decide that, on balance the 'costs' (in social and psychological terms) of some of these are too high.

Growth and the Small Firm

Adopting a conscious no-growth stance in our society is not easy. We live in a society with a strong growth ideology. Growth is 'progress' and businessmen are often judged by this criterion. It is not therefore surprising that small firm entrepreneurs are rather circumspect, even to the extent of self-deception, in not striving too hard for growth. One study of small firms in Britain summed up the attitudes among their sample as being :

> ....roughly divided on this question (the amount of growth thought desirable). Rather more agreed that expansion was desirable than backed the maintenance of the *status quo*. But it was noticeable that they often tended to express their views in a somewhat generalized way, as if they were paying lip service to an absolute abstract ideal of growth.(35)

The reasons given for not growing were often difficult to accept at face value. Relatively minor administrative chores such as collecting insurance contributions and P.A.Y.E. were offered as 'barriers' to growth. Our view is that reluctance to grow has, in fact, much more to do with the consequences, in social terms, of growth than these vocalized reasons.

If this alternative view of the small firm growth patterns is accepted, a number of issues, not adequately covered by previous theories, are resolved. For instance, a social action view of the small firm and growth offers reasons as to why growth is, on the whole, much less common than the prevalent growth ideology would indicate. It explains why, given the data on the low level of rewards(36) (in material terms) of small business-men the popularity of self-employment remains. It explains why the attractions of working for a large firm, with all that this implies in terms of security and material rewards, are rejected by certain people in our society. Also, it explains part of the highly skewed size distribution of firms in advanced industrial societies; it is not simply economic but social and psychological factors which also influence this distribution. Finally, this analysis also tells us something about the growth processes of those small firms who do join the 6% of large firms in our economy.

Earlier theories of small firm growth, such as those discussed above, had, as one of their objectives, that of helping the owner-manager to better understand the growth process of his firm. Few theories in the social sciences would claim not to have practical implications, and ours is no exception. Our alternative approach to understanding the small firm has policy implications for small firm decision-makers, for government attempts to aid the small firm, and for consultants and others who seek to provide expert guidance. By taking a new starting point for analysis and a new theoretical stance, we see that much of the available effort here is likely to be ineffectual. In particular, our analysis and findings points up the fatuity of policies or advice uncritically taken from the experience or techniques of large firms.

Given a knowledge of the way the entrepreneur defines his role in relation to his self-identity, and accepting his decisive position in the firm, we can say quite a lot about how the firm is likely to operate in a wide variety of situations. Thus, the owner-manager with an 'artisan' identity places a high value on independence. This leads to an organizational climate founded on an autocratic leadership style, combined with a strong element of paternalism, which minimizes dependence on others whether they be inside or outside the firm(37). He is likely to perceive the firm as a 'contented team', under-utilize the skills of subordinates and be blind to certain kinds of industrial relations problems. Awareness on the part of the entrepreneur of these possible results of a particular managerial style can help reduce unwanted side effects. Outsiders, wishing to aid the small firm, will be able to evaluate the likelihood of success of proposed strategies against their knowledge of social relation: patterns within the firm dictated largely by the entrepreneurial self-identity.

Probably the most problematic situation identified by our research is that where the owner-manager attempts to make the transition from an 'artisan' to a 'classical entrepreneur' identity. Growth is a strategy normally associated with this transition and the anticipated consequences of this, we argue, are often instrumental in the transition not being made. Even where it is made, the full consequences are often not fully realized, and this results in problems and conflicts - both identity conflicts for the entrepreneur and structural conflicts within the firm.

The administrative necessity to use a more consultative leadership style, to delegate and 'negotiate' with professionally trained managers brought in from outside, is not easily reconciled with the owner-manager's desire for independence. To this extent, he is a captive of the new situation he has himself brought about to meet his changing goals. Problems of a similar nature are likely to arise out of the increasing likelihood of unionization. Entrepreneurs in our study were mostly aware of the positive correlation between organizational size and degree of unionization. However, it was not often that unionization was seen as an extension of the new order of things in a larger firm presenting management with benefits as well as problems. More commonly, a 'communications breakdown' or the actions of 'militants' among new workers were held responsible.

We are not arguing that all those who take on the owner-manager role are socially marginal. In some cases there are exceptional environmental circumstances which make entry into business comparatively easy. For example, an 'open' social and economic environment for entrepreneurship has apparently occurred in many of the developing countries(38). Similarly, within advanced industrial societies some areas of economic activity may also become highly favourable to entrepreneurship as seems to have happened in the U.S. defence and space industries in the 1960s (39). In these circumstances, many people without feelings of high marginality will found firms, and may quite deliberately aim for high growth.

Finally, it must be remembered that much small firm growth results from the management of second and third generation owner-managers. Whether first generation owner-managed firms have lower rates of growth than their second and subsequent generation counterparts is unclear, as they start from different base lines making strict comparisons difficult. The Bolton Committee Report suggested that first generation owner-managed firms grew rather faster than those managed by subsequent generations, but this was based on a very small sample(40). This was countered to some extent also by the further finding that fast growing firms relied to a great extent on borrowed funds. Our own research, and that of Collins *et al*, noted earlier, found that highly socially marginal owner-managers, who are, as we have argued, more likely to be first generation, were strongly opposed to external borrowing because of the threat posed to their personal autonomy.

We feel that second or third generation owner-managers, because they are more likely to have a conventional middle-class background and education are more likely to have a conventional 'managerial' view of economic activity. Their personal life situation is less likely to be one of strong discrepancy between personal attributes and social role, and their socialization will be toward the acceptance of the dominant business ideology of our society with its stress on growth and efficiency achieved through economies of scale. They will, therefore, be more receptive to ideas of expansion, merger and the professionally managed business.

The substantial differences between the view of the small firm growth process presented in this paper and previous views are, we hope, now readily apparent. We have argued against the previous positivist models of growth and our alternative view sees the small firm as a constructed social reality, derived from the meanings which have a central place in the cultures of many modern societies and the activities of individuals suffering role stress in such societies.

Our main focus of attention has been on the entrepreneur and his influence on the social character of the firm. For, although he only shares in the social construction of the firm and cannot achieve this without the cooperation of others, his influence is normally decisive. Small firms do grow though this may often be only to an extent that the firm retains many of the social aspects associated with small size. Where growth proceeds beyond this point certain contradictions between the entrepreneur's self-identity and his participation in the firm are likely to result - at least in the case of a first-generation owner-manager.

Our interpretation is incomplete to some extent since it does not extend detailed attention to the social orientations of other participants in the firm and 'key' outsiders whose orientations and actions have important consequences for social relations within the firm. We have, however, previously discussed(41) some of the relations between owner-managers and wider society and are currently researching small firm worker orientations. This will enable us to greatly enhance our understanding of the firm as a whole and, of course, its growth processes.

(1)   See Bolton Committee, Small Firms-Report of the Committee of Inquiry
      on Small Firms, Cmnd.4811, London : H.M.S.O., November 1971

(2)   See, for example, Wild,Ray & Swan,Kenneth, 'The Small Company,
      Profitability, Management Resources & Management Techniques',
      Journal of Business Policy, Vol.3,No.1, Autumn 1972, pp.10-21;
      Deeks,John, 'The Small Firm-Asset or Liability?', Journal of Manage-
      ment Studies, Vol.10,No.1,February 1973, pp.25-47; Stanworth,
      M.J.K.& Curran,J. Management Motivation in the Smaller Business,
      London : Gower Press, 1973

(3)   Instanced in discussions in Mishan,E.J., The Costs of Economic
      Growth, Harmondsworth : Penguin Books, 1969; Schumacher,E.F.
      Small is Beautiful, A Study of Economics as if People Mattered,
      London : Blond & Briggs, 1973; and in Wild,Ray & Swan,Kenneth,
      ibid.

(4)   See Stanworth,M.J.K.&Curran,J.,op.cit.,where we have presented
      data on nine firms. However, our intention in the current article is
      not to present case material from the book, but rather to mount an
      argument concerning the whole issue of the way in which growth in
      the small firm is viewed. In doing this, we are building not only on
      data presented in our book, but also on additional data collected
      subsequently from the same research programme and data from a
      further ten firm study, the fieldwork of which has recently been
      completed.

(5)   Readers will, of course, be aware of the caution required in apply-
      ing U.S. data to the U.K. - see below our references to Mayer,
      Goldthorpe et al, Roberts & Warner, and Cooper.

(6)   The Bolton Committee Report, op.cit.,pp.1-2

(7)   Report on the Census of Production 1968, Report 158, Summary
      Tables : Enterprise Analysis, London : H.M.S.O., 1974, Table 42
      pp.158/10-11

(8)   Confederation of British Industry, Britain's Small Firms : Their
      Vital Role in the Economy, London : C.B.I., November 1970, p.3

(9)   Wood, Geoff, 'Where Have All the Small Firms Gone?' The Financial
      Times, 14th August 1974. Wood traces Census of Production data
      for manufacturing industry from 1935 to 1968 and concludes '.....
      it appears that the rate of decline is slowing down'. Between 1963

*and 1968 there was a further decline in the number of small firms
(-5%), but the decline in the number of large firms during this
period was even greater(-13%). Hence, the representation of small
firms increased in percentage terms. It may well be the case that
the current economic recession will take a high toll on small firms
as against large, but it would be dangerous to extrapolate any
long-term trend from this.*

(10) *Deeks,J., op.cit.,p.28*

(11) *See the Bolton Committee Report,op.cit,Chp.6 & Deeks,J.,op.cit.
pp.26-8*

(12) *Among the best known are Schumpeter,J.A. The Theory of Economic
Development, Cambridge, Mass.:Harvard Univ.Press,1934; Urwick,
L., 'Problems of Growth in Industrial Undertakings', Winter Proceed-
ings of the British of Management,No.2,1948-49; Penrose,E., The
Theory of the Growth of the Firm, Oxford:Basil Blackwell,1957;
Collins,O.F., Moore,D.G.,with Unwalla,D.B.,The Enterprising Man
East Lansing:Michigan State Univ.Press, 1964; Thomason,G.F. &
Mills,A.J.'Management Decision-Taking in Small Firms', European
Business, No.14,October 1967,pp.29-41; Lupton,Tom, 'Small New
Firms & Their Significance', New Society, 21st Dec.1967,pp.890-92;
Matthews,T.& Mayers,C., Developing A Small Firm, London:BBC
Publications,1968; Steinmetz,L.L.,'Critical Stages of Small Business
Growth', Business Horizons, Vol.XII,No.1,February 1969,pp.29-34.*

(13) *As in, for example, Urwick,L.,op.cit*

(14) *Often the discussion appears to be entirely speculative but even
where it has empirical backing the samples are frequently very small.
For example, the theory offered by Thomason &Mills is apparently
based on a sample of four firms.*

(15) *Urwick,L.,op.cit.,& Thomason,G.F.& Mills,A.J.,op.cit., provide
examples of the division of managerial roles occurring in stage two
while Lupton,T.,op.cit., & Matthews,T. & Mayers,C.,op.cit.,
appear to offer an example of this occurring in stage three.*

(16) *Exact data on the death rates of small firms is very difficult to come
by but see the discussions in Deeks,J.,op.cit., & the Bolton
Committee Report,op.cit.*

(17) *A review of the literature on this view of growth in the small firm is provided in Mueller,D.C.,'A Life Cycle Theory of the Firm', Journal of Industrial Economics,Vol.XX,No.2,July 1972,pp.199–219. See also Steinmetz,L.L.,op.cit.,for one version.*

(18) *A fairly typical example is provided in Urwick,L.,op.cit.,p.9,when he suggests that the limits within which a one-man business can work effectively are approached when the owner-manager has eight people directly reporting to him. The apparent precision here is not qualified by any reference to the kind of small firm the author has in mind; anyone with even the slightest research knowledge of small firms will know that even within a single branch of an industry small firms can display a considerable variation in management structure while remaining economically effective. Between industries such variations can be even greater.*

(19) *For a discussion particularly relevant to economic organizations see Silverman,David, The Theory of Organizations, London:Heinemann, 1970, and more generally, Cohen,Percy S., Modern Social Theory, London:Heinemann Educational Books, 1968, and Berger,Peter L.& Luckmann,Thomas, The Social Construction of Reality, London: Allen Lane,1967.*

(20) *By 'external forces' we mean those factors which influence the structure of social relations in the firm but which originate from outside the firm. Actors in the firm may or may not be aware of these forces and their effects may be actual or potential.*

(21) *Weber,Max, The Protestant Ethic & The Spirit of Capitalism, London: Unwin Univ.Books, 1965.*

(22) *Mayer,Kurt B., Business Enterprise:Traditional Symbol of Opportunity, British Journal of Sociology, Vol.IV,No.2, 1953, pp.160–80.*

(23) *See, for example, Goldthorpe,John H.,Lockwood,David, Bechhofer, Frank & Platt,Jennifer, The Affluent Worker:Industrial Attitudes & Behaviour, Cambridge:Cambridge Univ.Press, 1968, pp.131–6.*

(24) *For instance, a recent survey of material on this topic, Williams, W.M.(Ed.),Occupational Choice-A Selection of Papers from the Sociological Review, London:George Allen & Unwin,1974, contains no discussion of this occupational alternative.*

(25) *Bolton Committee Report, op.cit.,pp.8-9*

(26) *Deeks,J.,'Educational & Occupational Histories of Owner-Managers' Journal of Management Studies, Vol.9,No.2,May 1972,pp.127-49*

(27) *Collins,O.F., Moore,D.G. with Unwalla,D.B., op.cit.,Chp.V*

(28) *Roberts,E.B. & Warner,H.A., 'New Enterprises on Route 128', Science Journal, Dec.1968,pp.78-83; Cooper,A.C.'Entrepreneurial Environment', Industrial Research, Sept.1970,pp.74-6; Miles, Patrick R.,'Who are the Entrepreneurs?', MSU Business Topics, Winter 1974,pp.5-14. These sources seem, however, to refer to a special variety of entrepreneurship which emerged under conditions of a kind not frequently encountered in private enterprise societies. See the discussion below.*

(29) *Collins,O.F., Moore,D.G., with Unwalla,D.B.,op.cit.,pp.243-4.*

(30) *For a comprehensive history of the concept of 'social marginality' see Dickie-Clark,H.P., The Marginal Situation, London:Routledge & Kegan Paul, 1966.*

(31) *Mayer,Kurt B., & Goldstein,Sidney, The First Two Years:Problems of Small Firm Growth & Survival, Small Business Research Series,No. 2, Washington,D.C.:Small Business Association, 1961, reported in Deeks,J.,1973,op.cit.*

(32) *Gouldner,Alvin W., 'Cosmopolitans & Locals:An Analysis of Latent Social Roles', Administrative Science Quarterly,Vol.2,No.3,Dec. 1957,pp.282-92, and Vol.2,No.4,March 1958,pp.444-80.*

(33) *Some readers will note the similarity between this analysis and that of Smith,N.R. in The Entrepreneur & his Firm:The Relationship Between Type of Man & Type of Company, M.S.U.,1967. However, there are fundamental differences between our approach and that of Smith. He assumes a fixed and unchanging entrepreneurial personality type predating entry to the entrepreneurial role. This denies the interplay between role and social experience and the constant reinterpretation of social reality and self which occurs in any role performance. For a further discussion see Stanworth,M.J. K. & Curran,J.,op.cit.,pp.171-6.*

(34) *For an example of this occurring see Stanworth,M.J.K.& Curran,J. ibid.,Chp.7*

(35) *Golby,C.W. & Johns,G., Attitude & Motivation, Committee of Inquiry on Small Firms, Research Report No. 7, London:H.M.S.O.,1971,p 17.*

(36) *See Merrett Cyriax Associates, Dynamics of Small Firms, Committee of Inquiry on Small Firms, Research Report No. 12, London:H.M.S.O. 1971,p. 35, for data for the U.K. Collins,O.F., Moore,D.G. with Unwalla,D.B.,op.cit., suggest that a similar relatively low level of material rewards are received by small firm executives in the U.S.*

(37) *See the Bolton Committee Report,Chp. 2,p. 24,para. 2..17, on the attitude of many owner-managers towards sources of outside help and assistance.*

(38) *This inference may be drawn from the data presented in Warren, Bill, Imperialism & Capitalist Industrialization, New Left Review, Vol. 81, Sept.Oct. 1973, pp. 3-44.*

(39) *Roberts,E.B. & Warner,H.A.,op.cit.; Cooper,A.C.,op.cit.; and Liles,P.R.,op.cit., all provide data on this type of entrepreneurship.*

(40) *The Bolton Report Committee, op.cit.,p. 17.*

(41) *Stanworth,M.J.K. & Curran,J.,op.cit., especially Chp. 6.*

2. SMALL BUSINESS MANAGEMENT : A NORMATIVE APPROACH

G.E. Tibbits

MSU Business Topics. Volume 27 Number 4. Autumn 1979

A number of concepts could assist small business persons in the management of their firms. Rather than seeking out new data on the activities of small business, it is possible to use existing knowledge to arrive at guidelines of value to small business. A major assumption underlying this analysis will be that such principles must take into account the characteristics of small business persons and the environment in which they operate.

Many texts on small business management present the traditional, or classical, concepts of management involving planning, organizing, controlling and staffing as appropriate guides for managers in small firms. This approach can be questioned on two grounds, realism and relevance.

Realism? The research of Henry Mintzberg has indicated that in large firms the work of the manager can be characterized as follows :

'Because of the open-ended nature of his job and because of his responsibility for information processing and strategy-making, the manager is induced to take on a heavy work load, and to do much of it superficially. Hence, his work pace is unrelenting and his work activities are characterized by brevity, variety, and fragmentation. The job of managing does not develop reflective planners : rather it breeds adaptive information manipulators who prefer a stimulus-response milieu."(1)

He goes on to suggest :

"Thus, we can find little of use in the writings of the classical school. They have served to label our areas of ignorance, and may have fulfilled the need of telling managers what they should be doing (even if it did not tell them what they did). But the classical school has for too long served to block our search for a deeper understanding of the work of the manager."(2)

The discrepancies between the classical approaches and reality are so large as to suggest that the traditional ideals are unattainable. Certainly the discrepancies cannot be attributed to a lack of knowledge, since these approaches have been widely publicized for years and have been supported by executive development courses.

Given that the environments of small firm managers are normally as dynamic as or more dynamic than those of large firm managers, there are serious doubts as to the applicability of classical management theory to small business.

Relevance? The adoption of classical management theory in small business texts implies that the same principles of management are applicable to both small and large firms. Unfortunately, no attempt is made to justify this assumption. It seems appropriate to examine the universality of management principles.

Joseph McGuire seems to support the universal application of management principles :

"In the most popular organizational form utilized by large corporations in the contemporary American economy, considerable autonomy and decision-making responsibility is delegated to those operating executives whose performances can be measured objectively by the contributions of their units to corporate profits. Such 'profit centers' whether delineated by product line, geographical location or other attributes, are established on a rational basis in the most efficiently organized large companies. Furthermore, in many large modern corporations, these 'profit centers' possess such a great degree of independence in the scope of their operations that they resemble a small firm. Therefore, it is not inappro-priate to conceive of the modern giant corporation as an assemblage of small companies, each of which is monitored (probably a more apt descriptor than 'controlled') by general policies that inhibit its actions only at the extremes - a company that is supervised largely by ex-post reviews."(3)

This quotation correctly highlights the similarities between the small subsidiary or plant of a large business and the small business. However, there are also important differences not mentioned in the comparison which are likely to require different emphasis in the management of the independent small firm.

The independent small firm has limited access to resources, both financial and managerial. It must build its organization around its key resource(s), often the owner-manager with all his or her limitations and eccentricities. The large organization is able to select the manager for the job. Also, through job rotation, large firms can introduce new managerial talent as the subsidiary outgrows the abilities and personality of the existing manager.

Although the large firm gives its subsidiaries substantial freedom, it can and will interfere when it considers such action desirable. For example, it will generally ensure management succession, and it will introduce specialists when performance is unsatisfactory. It also will provide additional capital when the subsidiary experiences financial difficulties. Furthermore, the survival of the small subsidiary is not vital to the large firm.

It seems probable, then, that the restricted resources of the small firm, together with the impact of the personality of its owner-manager, will necessitate some differences in the approach to management.

The balance of this article will examine alternative approaches to management with a view to isolating guidelines which could assist small business managers.

Decision making as the basis of management

W.J.Byrt and P.R.Masters say that "the simplest of the many descriptions of the task of the manager is 'getting things done through people'. This consists of deciding what to do and getting other people to do it"(4).

A planned, orderly approach to the decision process consistent with the idealized classical approach to management would be to (a) identify the problem, (b) clearly establish one's goals, (c) consider the alternative courses of action which could be taken, (d) evaluate the alternatives in light of one's goals, and (e) select the most desirable course and implement it.

This approach, it is suggested, is appropriate for simple problems but is inadequate in complex situations. Roger A.Golde introduces the concept of muddling through to explain how to deal with complexity : "Much of managerial thinking is presumed to involve analysis and logic - that is, the reasoning mode. Other kinds of thinking are usually thrown into the category of intuition - sometimes called instinct, feeling or hunch. Yet my observations indicate that managers spend a good deal of time operating in still a third mode - a mode that cannot truly be classified as either intuiting or reasoning. This third mode is what....I have called 'muddling'."(5) He defines *muddling* as "conscious but nonlogical thinking" involving "purposive coping focused on a specific problem."(6) He identifies lateral thinking and incrementalism as having similarities to muddling.

Essentially, he is saying that when a problem is too complex for us to analyze in a logical mode, we use a number of techniques to come to grips with the situation without being overwhelmed. These techniques include force-fitting and muddling :

Force-fitting. We grab an existing handle and stuff the boggle into a suitcase already attached to the handle. We do not choose just any suitcase- we try to pick one that worked for seemingly similar kinds of problems in the past......Of course, the problem with force-fitting is that the boggle does not fit into the suitcase very well. We may have to push the problem all out of shape or else resort to major surgery by lopping off a few limbs of the situation. Force-fitting can be a very productive form of muddling if we sincerely try to mould *both the suitcase and the problem over time* so that the force fit gradually improves. We must realise that the initial fit is not a good one and represents merely a way to get moving.(7)

Muddling. Good muddlers utilize a great number of techniques for shifting their perspective, but almost all the techniques can be classified into these three strategies :

1. Changing the medium of expression
2. Changing the way a given medium of expression is used
3. Imagining a change in the situation itself. (8)

The above quotations cannot adequately portray the depth and usefulness of Golde's approach. However, it is important to realize that this is an attempt to legitimize an established approach for tackling complex business problems and to identify the techniques which may assist in such situations.

Managing complex situations is an area in which small business persons particularly need guidance. This is not because the problems with which small businesses are concerned are inherently more difficult than those faced by large firms. Rather, situations are made more complex for the small business person because he or she may lack the appropriate specialized knowledge to deal with the problem, or because this one person must cope with all its dimensions. Furthermore, limited resources and a limited scale of operations rule out the use of some of the more sophisticated techniques which large firms apply to similar problems. The small business person may overcome this lack of appropriate knowledge by hiring consultants. However, this approach may be precluded if (a) the small business person views the use of consultants as an admission of failure, (b) the differences in education and background between the two parties preclude the development of a good working relationship, (c) the small business person does not know how to select an appropriate consultant, or (d) the potential benefits do not justify the cost.

These comments point out that incrementalism is often required to cope with complexity. It is sometimes necessitated by the limited resources of the small firm. This can be illustrated by reference to the analysis of investment decisions. In the large firm, the investment proposal is evaluated in terms of its profitability quite independently of the project's financing. Financing is assumed to be available, and it will be raised in accordance with some longer term plan to maintain an appropriate debt-equity relationship.

The small firm is required to approach such decisions using an incremental analysis involving both investing and financing. In the words of J.A.Langdon and M.J.Francis :
"The small company is further characterized by infrequent dealings in the money market, limited access to external funds, and a precarious liquidity position resulting from the lack of predictable, continuous financial resources and backup finance. Therefore, it is inevitable, even desirable that each capital investment decision be analyzed on a marginal, self-financing basis, contrary to the conventional wisdom. Short run solvency

demands this priority.

So great is the liquidity concern for the small company that investment decisions may be undertaken which favourably conform to the company's liquidity priority, rather than the traditional goal of profit maximization. There is the need for investments to finance themselves, and the specific type of financing available to the firm is often the major constraint on investment decisions, rather than project profitability.

To avoid the.....dangers (of marginal analysis) the small firm must adopt a forward looking attitude. It must be conscious of where it is heading and evaluate each marginal decision as a step along a planned path. It must be appreciated that objective financial planning should be an integral part of overall company strategy.

It cannot be assumed that a series of ad hoc, expedient marginal decisions will miraculously compound into an efficient capital structure."(9)

The limited resources of the small firm, and its inability to have any significant impact on its environment, ensure that immediate environmental factors dominate the decision-making process.

The way in which capital investment decisions are made illustrates another characteristic of decision making in small firms. Decisions tend to be made on a subjective, intuitive basis rather than in a carefully documented and planned manner. Subjective and intuitive decisions may take on overtones of inferiority or badness. Documentation and planning imply goodness and superiority. Are these judgments valid?

It is suggested that small business persons should plan when they can - for example, when the time pressures are low prior to establishment of the firm, prospective business persons should plan their ventures carefully. However, once a firm is operational, time pressures and the lack of resources to commit to detailed analysis of all decisions place the manager in the position of *having to* make many decisions on an intuitive basis.

In the large organization, the need for managers to justify their actions to superiors (for example, other managers or boards of directors)

ensures that detailed analysis is more likely to be justifiable for a large
project than for a small one.

However, when the small business person only has to answer to himself or herself, and the opportunity cost of time for an analysis is high
relative to the magnitude of the decision, intuitive decision making or
back-of-an-envelope analysis may be most appropriate.

Nothing stated above should be construed as denying the considerable
risks associated with intuitive decision making. In fact, the limited asset
base of the firm and the inexperience of the manager may contribute to a
very high risk level. It follows that small business managers need to
develop skills to determine (a) which decisions expose the firm to the
greatest risks, (b) whether incorrect decisions are likely to be readily
correctable, and (c) which decisions can profitably be deferred. Thus,
the small business manager must be selective in deciding which decisions
to subject to detailed analysis.

Another implication flows from the necessity for many small business
decisions to be intuitive. Intuitive decision making requires that managers
know how to structure their experience to assist in a wide variety of
decisions. They also need to know when they can rely on intuition and
when it could be misleading.

Max Gunther points out that "a hunch is a conclusion based on facts
that your mind has accurately observed, stored and processed. But they
are facts you don't consciously know because they are stored on some
unconscious level of awareness.....How do you know whether to trust a
hunch? Says one successful huncher, a retired stockbroker : 'I ask
myself : is it conceivable that I have gathered data on this situation without realizing it? Have I found out all I can about it, done all the work I
can? If the answers are yes, and if the hunch feels strong, I tend to go
with it.' "(10) But never confuse a hunch with a hope.

Another important type of decision in any business is deciding on the
nature and scope of the firm. Peter F. Drucker says :
"In the first place, (the small business) needs *strategy*. The small
business cannot afford to become marginal. Yet this is its perennial
danger. It must therefore think through a strategy which gives it dis-

tinction. It must, to speak in biological terms, find its specific ecological niche in which it has an advantage and can therefore withstand competition. This specific niche may be leadership in a distinct market, whether it is defined by geography, consumer needs, or consumer values. The strategy may lie in a specific excellence, such as a capacity to give service. Or it may lie in a specific technology......For the typical small business has no strategy. The typical small business in not "Opportunistic", it is "problematical" - it lives from problem to problem." (11)

Drucker is arguing that the small firm must identify how it can gain a competitive advantage, and how it can protect that advantage. This does not invalidate earlier comments about tackling complex problems by incrementalism; rather, it suggests that despite all the internal problems managers face, they must make time to keep in touch with the market and the environment. Knowledge of the factors which have contributed to the firm's past successes can be a valuable aid in making decisions under time constraints.(12)

Our conclusions on decision making in small firms are as follows :

1. Small firms need to identify the determinants of the past successes to guide future decision making.

2. The manager must make time to keep in touch with the market and the environment.

3. The limited resources of the firm will mean that many complex problems face the manager. Recent analysis of muddling through provides practical guidelines for coming to grips with these complexities. Furthermore, these techniques are consistent with the incremental approaches to decision making in the firm and should, thus, be readily accepted by practical business people.

4. Decisions are often taken after less detailed analysis than would occur in large firms. The implication is that managers must be able to quickly identify which decisions are most pressing, and which involve substantial risks.

Organization and management

The typical small business is minimally organized; what organization exists is often informal, in the sense that it is not precisely defined. It is suggested here that this often may be an advantage. Hence, the manager should be cautious about imposing a highly structured organization on the firm.

1. The firm cannot afford to have underutilized resources and should, therefore, encourage staff to change activities as the immediate needs of the firm change.

2. Research has shown that the less well defined the organizational structure, the greater the likelihood of prosperity when operating in a dynamic environment.(13) Since small firms often operate in a volatile environment, an informal structure may contribute to their survival.

3. Unless care is taken in determining the tasks to be delegated, the manager may well relinquish the wrong tasks.

In this regard, Drucker has the following comments :
"In many small, and especially in small and growing businesses, the top man is criticized by his associates for spending his time on the wrong things. If by that they mean that the key activities of the business are not being taken care of, their criticism is well taken. But often they mean that he is using his strengths and tackling the activities he is particularly good at, whereas other and equally important key activities are not being done by him. Then the answer is not to talk a man who, for instance, is not very good at handling people but excellent at finance into letting the controller do the finance work, while he himself takes on the management of people. The answer is to recognize that a top man gifted in the financial area is a major asset. But then, somebody else better take over the people responsibility which is a key activity and has to be discharged."(14)

This suggests that the manager should use the concept of comparative advantage in deciding which tasks to perform and which to delegate. The justification, of course, is analogous to the economic theory that countries should export goods in which they are relatively or comparatively more efficient. Naturally, the total amount of delegation will be restricted by the resources available to the firm.

Classical management theory suggests that managers should delegate tasks to allow significant periods of uninterrupted time for consideration of strategic matters. This can be criticized on several grounds. First, an important function of the manager's job in the small firm is to keep in touch with what is happening in the firm and in the marketplace. This cannot be achieved in the abstract. Rather, the best way to accomplish this is by involvement. Second, it is doubtful whether long bursts are the best way of handling a creative activity such as strategic planning. Work on lateral thinking and brainstorming often refers to periods in the vicinity of ten minutes as appropriate time spans. Third, in the words of Mintzberg :

"He develops a sensitive appreciation for the *opportunity cost* of his own time - the benefits foregone by doing one thing instead of another. Thus, he takes on much work because he realizes his own worth to the organization. In addition, he is aware of the ever-present assortment of obligations associated with his job - the mail that cannot be delayed, the callers that must be attended to, the meeting that requires his par- ticipation. In other words, no matter what he *is* doing, the manager is plagued by what he *might* do and what he *must* do.

In effect, the manager is encouraged by the realities of his work to develop a particular personality - to overload himself with work, to do things abruptly, to avoid wasting time, to participate only when the value of participation is tangible, to avoid too great an involvement with any one issue. To be superficial is, no doubt, an occupational hazard of managerial work. In order to succeed, the manager must, presumably, become proficient at his superficiality." (15)

To summarize this section, the organizational guidelines which are most relevant to small business managers are the following :

1. Maintain a flexible organizational structure.

2. Ensure that the manager is involved in those activities which will provide insights into changes taking place in the environment and provide feedback on the major developments in the firm.

3. Only when the manager cannot cope using a superficial approach should delegation be extracted from him or her and then only in those activities in which he or she does not have a comparative advantage, and in which he or she does not need to be involved in order to facilitate strategic decision making.

The Growth Cycle Approach to Small Business Management

A number of researchers have traced the firm through its life cycle. These studies have highlighted the fact that the managerial role and critical skills change as the firm grows. Corresponding with this are changes in the nature of problems facing the firm.

One such growth model identifies the following sequence of managerial roles :

Originator - inventor (initiation)
Planner - organizer (development)
Developer - implementer (growth)
Administrator - operator (maturity)
Successor - reorganizer (decline) (16)

This illustrates that an important managerial skill which a small business manager needs is the ability to develop or modify his or her response/behavior patterns to suit the stage of development of the firm. There is a need to help managers develop the skills to know when behavior should be changed and how to change it.

Managers may want to hold the firm at a certain stage of development. This is most clearly portrayed by the M.J.K.Stanworth and James Curran growth model.(17) They view the firm as passing through three phases. First, there is the artisan stage in which the primary goals and values of the manager are "gaining personal autonomy and independence in the work sphere; being able to pick the people you work with; status in the workplace and the satisfaction of turning out a 'good' product backed up by personal service to the customer".(18) Then, as the firm gets bigger, the manager must act as the classical entrepreneur, and financial goals dominate behavior. As the firm grows even more, the manager adopts a managerial role, that is "the entrepreneur structures his role performance in ways which he hopes will lead others, particularly people outside the firm such as fellow businessmen, to regard him as a first-rate manager capable of building up an enterprise which will survive into the next generation".(19)

Thus, as the firm grows, the values which the firm will satisfy also change. Many small business persons just do not want to make the transition from one stage to the next because of the drop in satisfaction. It is, therefore, necessary that managers who want to stabilize the size of their organization be equipped with means to eliminate or slow growth *without* affecting the vitality of the firm. One possible strategy would be a policy of planned obsolescence for products. By this is not meant changes of styling just for the sake of differentiating one year's product from the next. Rather, what is envisaged is the replacement of products with technically superior ones. The challenge of continual improvement should replace the challenge of growth as a means of stimulating staff. This approach may have to be supported by the selection of a limited product or geographical market. Obviously, this suggestion would be applicable to only a minority of companies.

The point is that, to date, small business managers have not been provided with assistance in this area, and yet many view the nongrowth strategy as appropriate. It would be helpful to identify and explain a range of successful strategies to small business persons so they may be guided and stimulated in the development of policies suitable to their situation.

The desire to remain within a certain size category is supported by economic studies, among them the following :
"In the battery industry, the small-scale operator might actually enjoy lower unit production costs than his much larger rivals if he can employ strongly motivated non-unionized help and imputes to himself modest opportunity cost. Even when small-scale plants have higher production costs, they may enjoy a production-plus-distribution cost advantage over large plants in serving densely populated local markets. As a result, both small and large paint and battery plants coexisted profitably in nearly all the nations covered by our study, while medium-sized plants realized lower profits and exhibited a long-run tendency to disappear." (20)

Smaller firms often can operate with low overheads, whereas medium-sized firms begin to manifest the overhead relationships of large firms without the advantages of high volume production to offset such costs. Thus, growth restraint may be economically advisable.

Transition from one size category to the next involves considerable risk. Expansion often necessitates changes in the approach to management. It is difficult to ascertain both the appropriate timing of the change and the types of changes required : "Using data from fifty firms engaged in commercial printing, they were able to demonstrate empirically that companies during growth apparently go through alternating phases during which they perform well economically and then through critical phases when they perform poorly and have a high probability of failing". (21)

The manager who seeks stability may be aware of the problems associated with expansion and may be merely following a risk-avoidance strategy. "There is something about the fear-wracked period of seeing whether a venture will survive that turns the mind against a repetition of the experience. That is why most small firms should become conservative about risk after they become successfully established."(22)

Another way of depicting the growth cycle of the firm is to identify the series of major crises which many firms encounter. These are the starting, cash, delegation, leadership, prosperity, and management succession crises.(23) Many small business managers find this orientation to management training most acceptable becuase they can more easily relate to the practical situations portrayed than to abstract management principles or guidelines.

The above commentary on growth cycles highlights the changing roles managers must perform as the firm grows. There is a need to synchronize the response patterns of the manager and the needs of the business. The manager must change his or her behavior to match the situation of the firm, or the growth of the firm should be curtailed to match the behavior patterns which the manager is able or willing to display, or both. Management principles should guide the manager in the choice of strategy and its implementation.

Interpersonal Relationships and Management

A most interesting statement on interpersonal relationships and management is provided by J.W.Hunt :

"The autocrat has traditionally begun organisations. Here is a new situation in which the relations with the initial group are nonexistent, where the leader is the authority figure and where the situation is unstructured. In this situation the output oriented style of leader role performance has been particularly effective in the past. Yet this style of leading is in sharp contrast to the research evidence which suggests the modern manager should adopt a supportive, couselling, guiding role rather than a directing, controlling role.

The entrepreneur who successfully creates organisations is often characterised by a tendency to be autocratic and over-confident, even arrogant. No research has shown that a people-oriented or dependent leader would be more effective in this situation. When organisations begin, the prime objective is to increase output to make a return so that the organisation can survive. High concern for human relationships in this output-oriented situation may not be as relevant as in a bureaucracy which may be compensating for an abundance of formal and technical structure by people-oriented managers. However, when the growth stage is reached where profit appears certain, the autocratic, field-independent, production-oriented entrepreneur may begin to kill his own creation because of his failure either to consider the human relationships in the organisation and/or to structure the relationships so that most member behavior is predictable. " (24)

This is consistent with the earlier comments on growth cycles but does emphasize two points :

1. Management theory is situation specific, and the provision of small business managers with a brief overview of concepts developed in a large environment may be more harmful than useful.

2. Small business managers need more specific guides as to when their style of management needs to be modified.

While not specifically mentioned in the article, behavior change is difficult, and exhortation is not sufficient to achieve it. Managers need guidance.

Closing Comments

This article has attempted to identify areas of management (as opposed to functional activities) in which small business persons need assistance. Need in this respect refers to an absence of generally recognized management principles to guide choices and actions. The key areas identified were handling complexity, deciding on the amount and nature of the work which the manager should handle personally, and synchronizing the role requirements and managerial responses.

The underlying philosophy of this article was that small business management principles could be further developed. It was suggested that existing guidelines are not adequate because they give insufficient attention to situational constraints, particularly limited resources, time and expertise. It is hoped that the analysis has justified this viewpoint and provided positive suggestions for improvement.

(1) *Henry Mintzberg, The Nature of Managerial Work (New York: Harper & Row, 1973), p. 5*

(2) *Ibid., p. 11*

(3) *J.W.McGuire, The Small Enterprise in Economics & Organization Theory , Journal of Contemporary Business 5 (Spring 1976) : 117*

(4) *W.J.Byrt & P.R.Masters, The Australian Manager (Melbourne: Sun Books, 1974), p. 70*

(5) *R.A.Golde, Muddling Through : The Art of Properly Unbusiness-like Management (New York : Amacom, 1976) p. 152*

(6) *Ibid., pp. 154-55*

(7) *Ibid., pp. 9-10*

(8) *Ibid., p. 20*

(9) *J.A.Langdon & M.J.Francis, Business Finance, Investment Decisions & Small Companies & Firms , Chartered Secretary 27(1975) : 14*

(10) *Max Gunther, Five Ways to Improve Your Luck , Readers Digest (October 1977) : 94*

(11) *Peter F.Drucker, Management (London : Heinemann, 1973) p. 649*

(12) *See Theodore Cohn & R.A.Lindberg, Survival & Growth : Management Strategies for the Small Firm (New York: Amacom, 1974) and*

C.R.Christensen, Management Succession in Small & Growing Enterprises (Boston : Harvard Univ.,1953), p.197

(13) Tom Burns & G.M.Stalker, The Management of Innovation (London :
Tavistock Publ., 1961)

(14) Drucker, Management, p.652

(15) Mintzberg, Nature of Managerial Work, p.35

(16) C.V.Kroeger, Managerial Development in the Small Firm , California
Management Review 17 (Fall 1974) : 41-47

(17) M.J.K.Stanworth & James Curran, Management Motivation in the
Smaller Business (Epping : Gower Press, 1973)

(18) Ibid., p.98

(19) Ibid., p.99

(20) F.M.Scherer et al., The Economics of Multi-Plant Operation : An
International Comparisons Study (Cambridge,Mass.:Harvard Univ.
Press,1975), quoted in Rein Peterson, Small Business - Building a
Balanced Economy (Erin,Ontario : Porcepic, 1977), p.106

(21) B.Bernholtz & J.P.Rives, The Stage Model of Growth & Small Firms
-An Alternative Hypothesis , Working Paper No.77-002, Dept.of
Industrial Engineering, Univ.of Toronto, February 1977, quoted in
Rein Peterson, Small Business - Building a Balanced Economy, p.107

(22) Cohn & Lindberg, Survival & Growth, p.3

(23) R.B.Buchele, Business Policy in Growing Firms (Scranton,Penn. :
Chandler Co., 1967)

(24) J.W.Hunt, The Restless Organization (Sydney : John Wiley, 1972)
pp.176-77

3. PRODUCT DIVERSIFICATION AND THE SMALL FIRM

R.S.Mason

Journal of Business Policy. Volume 3 Number 3. Spring 1973

In recent years, considerable resources have been channelled into the
development of sophisticated programmes and techniques suitable for
organizations seeking to diversify and extend their product range.
Financial, technological and organizational constraints are acknowledged,
but often taken as being minimal. While such analyses are valuable to
the larger firm, they are often irrelevant to the needs and constraints of
the smaller organization; and although many problems associated with
product planning are clearly common to all companies regardless of size,
this paper looks at the process of new product development and product
diversification with particular reference to the small firm.

The smaller company is severely limited in the extent to which it can
devote money and resources to new product search and evaluation. In
addition, no research and development unit may exist within the
organization to serve as a chrysalis for new ideas, and the level of
managerial expertise and breadth of skills is often likely to be inadequate.
Capital available for new plant or new production processes is insignificant
in comparison to that of the giant companies which have come into being
over the last 20 years. Product ideas which demand too great a level of
technical expertise must rapidly be rejected at the screening stage and
the small firm is constantly seeking new products which can be introduced
'painlessly' into the company range, without making significant demands
on existing production processes, on marketing and distribution
organizations and, above all, on the limited financial resources of the
company.

Clearly, the large organization has considerable advantages over its
smaller counterpart, with regard to product innovation and diversification.
At the same time, these advantages are, to some degree, offset by the
fact that the large and small firm do not effectively compete against each
other, but rather against those companies of a similar size to their own.
Consequently, the performance criteria for new products are far higher,
technically and financially in the larger company. What both types of

firm do have in common, however, is a continuing need to diversify, in order to survive and prosper in their respective markets.

The need to diversify may, in fact, be generated by a variety of changing circumstances, either within the firm or in the market place. At the broadest level, diversification can be seen either as a defensive or as an aggressive promotional factor in company strategy(1). In its defensive role, it is required to ensure financial and organizational stability and may be designed :

a) to reduce or eliminate seasonal variations in sales

b) to reduce or eliminate cyclical variations in sales

c) to counteract any trend towards a decline in demand for the company's existing product lines

d) to utilize excess productive capacity arising from a sudden decline in demand.

Diversification in its more 'positive' role is concerned firstly with the efficient utilization of company resources, and secondly with ensuring that market potential is fully exploited. Andrews(2) puts forward the following motives for diversification under these two headings :

1) *Efficient utilization of company resources :*

    (a) to make use of accidental or planned laboratory discoveries

    (b) to capitalize on unforeseen demands for a product developed for a company's own use

    (c) to capitalize on a unique production process

    (d) to make new use of basic raw materials

    (e) to utilize profitably the by-products of the production process

    (f) to make full use of developing management and staff.

2) *Efficient marketing :*

    (a) to increase sales of basic products

    (b) to meet retail or wholesale pressure to extend lines

    (c) to meet specific requests of individual customers

    (d) to exploit the value of an established trademark

    (e) to reduce the ratio of sales costs to total sales.

The pressure to diversify need not come from one single source : indeed, it is more likely to be the result of the recognition of several weaknesses within the firm or unexploited opportunities within the market.

Similarly, pressure in certain areas may be continuous, as, for instance, with the development of management/staff skills and creativity. In more progressive companies, the need to diversify is recognized as a permanent feature of short, medium and long-term planning.

While sharing many of the motives for diversification, the contrasting requirements and necessary performance of new products introduced by the large and small firm have already been noted. In view of these substantial differences in company requirements with regard to new products and product diversification, the product search and evaluation procedures of the two types of firm cannot be compared realistically, other than at the most superficial level. The constraints and objectives of each type of organization are clearly not related. Brion(3) further develops this distinction by defining the different 'product scope of interest' of large and small organizations :

"Contrary to general belief, the product scope of interest of a firm is roughly inversely proportional to its size and resources; the largest have the most limited areas of interest for development and expansion. This is because a product can ordinarily be manufactured most efficiently by the smallest business that can manage to produce it due to lower and more flexible overhead costs. If a large firm involves itself in a low investment undertaking, smaller producers might enter the market with lower overheads and threaten the whole price structure. On the other hand, small firms make a serious mistake venturing into products with high enough volume demand to permit the low unit costs of mass production. The optimum company-size range of the industry the firm is in should be determined and placed in its industry portfolio and determined for the industry of any prospective diversification".

Brion is arguing that, ideally, the small firm should look for diversification within its existing industry through products whose demands on new financial, technical and managerial resources are low. Secondly, if the resources problem is not severe, an untenable assumption for the vast majority of small firms, it should seek diversification into other industries dominated by firms of a similar (small) size.

Kline(4) draws the distinction between the interest differences of large and small companies by illustrating (Table 1) the new product

TABLE 1 : New product performance criteria for large and small firms

Product requirements	Company A (large)	Company B (small)
Capital investment	High	Low
Sales volume	(1) Large volume (2) Mass markets (3) Many applications (4) National distribution	(1) Small volume (2) Specialized markets (3) Many too few applications (4) Local or specialized distribution
Similarity to present distribution	High to moderate	High
Effect on existing products	Good to fair	Good
Competition	(1) Relatively few companies (2) Sound pricing (3) Good possibility of securing a large %age of the market	(1) Few too many companies (2) Sound pricing (3) Desirable market position variable
Cyclical stability	High	High
Technical opportunity	Great	Moderate to small
Patent protection	Great	Great to none
Raw materials	(1) Basic materials (2) Many suppliers	(1) Intermediate or basic materials (2) Many too few suppliers
Manufacturing load	(1) Standard products (2) Mass production (3) Few grades & sizes	(1) Standard or custom products (2) Specialized production (3) Few too many grades & sizes
Value added	High	High to moderate

requirements of two hypothetical chemical companies whose only major differences are those of size.

Clearly, financial and technological capabilities, together with the production and distribution constraints of any organization, determine to a great extent the pattern and objectives of product search. Larger organizations, as a general rule, seek a technologically sophisticated product which lends itself to mass production and which, potentially, can achieve a significant market share for the company in any particular segment. In contrast, the smaller firm prefers and searches for a relatively "easy to make" product calling for only limited technological and financial inputs. Custom products are acceptable and the performance target certainly is not that of achieving long-term market leadership, but rather of maintaining a "satisficing" market share over time.

New Product Innovation and Adoption in the Small Firm

Having already acknowledged market, financial and technological limitations, the small firm is, in broadest terms, faced with two major constraints on new product development. Firstly, there are the "internal" constraints associated with the organization and operation of the company itself; secondly, the "external" limitations imposed by factors outside the company's area of influence and by the market structure in general. Often these internal and external forces interact, each serving to offset or reinforce the effect of the other.

Before examining these constraints, it is necessary to differentiate small firms on the basis of managerial philosophy. Small firms fall essentially into two categories. On the one hand, a significant number of small companies are family owned, long-established and have built up a traditional "conservative" philosophy in business matters. In contrast, many more modern companies tend to adopt a "progressive" and comparatively radical approach to business development. This distinction does not necessarily imply, however, that product innovation and development will more easily take place in the latter category of companies. Indeed, many newly established small firm successes have been achieved through the development and exploitation of one particular product and come to an abrupt end when falling demand or other factors show a need for new product diversification which is not forthcoming.

Having issued the "caveat", it is a fair generalization to say that the traditional family-based business is, by its very nature, less likely to generate new product ideas and to develop them than is the more progressive organization. The strength of the long-established family business lies in its product reputation, its consistent service over many years and its generally close relationships with its customers. These strengths are clearly seen as predominantly historical, i.e. they are based on past performance measured over a considerable time period. It is the record of past service upon which the company asks its customers to assess present and future efficiency, and, in consequence, the firm's outlook tends inevitably to be retrospective rather than forward-looking; the future is taken as a function of the past. This militates against new product development and product diversification and limits any significant product changes only to those brought about through external market forces, making existing product lines inefficient or obsolete.

In contrast, the "new" small firm has little or no past performance as a recommendation on which to attract present sales. There is no historical perspective in which to place either product efficiency or company service. To compete, therefore, such firms must be progressive and control that sector of the market which the traditional firms lose by default, i.e. they must develop and exploit, as far as possible, any technological opportunities leading to significant product improvement which make traditional lines comparatively inefficient. It is for this reason that product innovation is more likely to be considered an important aspect of sales expansion by the *new* firm, the "late arrival" in a particular industrial or commercial sector, rather than by the long-established and arguably more reactionary family firm.

Having drawn a necessary distinction between progressive and conservative company philosophies and their effects either as a stimulant or as a deterrent to product diversification, the analysis now concerns itself with those internal and external conditions conducive or obstructive to new product development within small firms taken as a whole. The conditions can apply equally to all types of small organization, irrespective of their maturity or philosophy. Again, while many advantages and disadvantages apply also to the large organization, the nature of small firms makes them more likely to benefit or suffer from the conditions examined.

The key to product innovation lies ultimately in the quality of top management, i.e. in the ability of managers to be not only a creative force themselves, but also to ensure that conditions within the organization as a whole positively encourage creative work at all levels. Larger organizations are fortunate in that, by the separation of staff and line responsibilities, and by the existence of R & D and market research units, creativity is built into the structure. For the small firm, a separate staff function is a luxury that cannot be afforded. By far the greater percentage of employees are line managers or "productive" workers. In such circumstances, the responsibility falls on top management, to a far greater extent than in the larger organization, to ensure (a) that their own contribution to product innovation and new product search is significant, and (b) that the formal and informal organization of the firm is such that ideas do come up through line managers and that the need for product development is recognized at all levels within the company.

With regard to (a) above, the degree of innovation will depend again primarily on the quality of the people at the top. Certain "qualities" are particularly conducive to high creativity levels : firstly, a general ability to think constructively about present and anticipated future problems, i.e. creative intellect; secondly, a willingness to look for problems rather than react to them only in a crisis. A major problem facing the small firm is its frequent inability to attract men of above-average intelligence and intellect for senior management positions within the company. Even when such men are found, they are retained only with difficulty and tend to move on within a short time. There is usually a lack of research facilities and no opportunity for "team research" within the organization, both factors which encourage product innovation(5). Another characteristic of small firms also militates against product development, in that senior managers are often not brought in from outside for reasons just outlined, but are promoted up through the company. Often promotion is dependent both on the efficient execution of a particular line management function over a number of years and, more ominously, on an acceptable "conformity" of behaviour and acceptance of traditional organizational structures. As a result, new senior managers tend not to question or challenge the managerial system or company attitudes and this does nothing to encourage either organizational change or new product development. This promotional "conservatism" is particularly observable in tightly-controlled family businesses, in which the owners' paramount concern in bringing new members to the boardroom table is that their own position and attitudes are not challenged. The new manager, ideally, is required to be *plus royaliste que le roi*. Such motives clearly work against innovation, but can nevertheless be seen to exist today in many companies.

In the larger firm, the search and evaluation aspects of new product development are necessarily and easily separated. Search is a delegated responsibility for the R & D, sales and market research functions, while screening and feasibility studies remain in the final analysis with top management working groups called to review and evaluate present and future developments. In contrast, small company senior management needs to be closely involved not only in project evaluation but in new product search. This, in turn, requires that management needs to find a balance between specialist and generalist skills; specialist to meet the "search" responsibility, generalist for the "evaluation" requirement. Ideally, therefore, the top decision-making team should reflect a mix of managerial talents, both broadly and narrowly defined.

The second major internal factor in product innovation, and one that is critical for the small firm which has to innovate as best it can and without any formal research staff or departments fully devoted to the task, is the organizational structure of the firm, both formal and informal and its effectiveness as a vehicle for new product ideas and development. In contrast to large companies whose operational structures are formally planned and developed, the organization of the small firm is, in fact, often informal and custom-based. This does not mean, however, that the small company is necessarily more flexible and "open", for instance, in terms of ease of communication within the firm and inter-departmental staff liaison. Indeed, a company enjoying no formal managerial structure can, in spite of this, operate under a rigid and repressive hierarchical system established by custom over many years.

The small firm, by nature of its size, is a centralized productive unit in which power is concentrated at the top. This in itself can serve to repress innovation and diversification. Over-centralized management can lead to autocratic leadership dedicated to preserving an order and constancy in company affairs and organization. As already mentioned, internal promotion based on loyalty and behavioural criteria, rather than on creative merit, only serves to reinforce such a system should it exist.

Autocracy at the top often established itself by forming a rigid custom-based structure within the firm, significantly reducing the degree of open communications within the company. "Empire building" may, by inference, be encouraged, although such empires may not formally be defined. The process is essentially one of "divide internally and rule". Rigidity within the structure is promoted and, in consequence, its responsiveness to creativity and its ability to encourage new ideas becomes negligible.

Ease of communication within a firm is a critical factor in creating the right environment for product diversification and new product development. Communication, in fact, needs to be effective both vertically and horizontally within the organization for new ideas to be generated and developed. Vertical communication requires open discussion from top to bottom of the organization and must be the direct responsibility of top management. Horizontal communication is concerned with the relationship between departments and with the ease and frequency of "sideways discussion" *across* the organizational structure. Empire building, found in the small firm to an extent not generally acknowledged, clearly restricts the degree of communication, whether vertical or horizontal. Autocratic direction from the top restricts vertical discussion other than that between senior and middle management (which in any case tends to be one-way and "directive"); while the absence of organized or informal multi-departmental research groups within the firm contributes to the failure of horizontal communication.

Poor overall communications and a rigid organizational structure work against innovation in other ways. Managers throughout such a firm, seeking to protect their own position and to isolate their department from "outside interference", may refine and emasculate new product ideas coming from their own staff or from other departments, or simply reject them outright without any real consideration of their possible merits and potential. In seeking to achieve senior management status, managers of different departments within the firm attempt to diminish each other's initiative and originality. The individual manager, in other words, may see two threats to his own position : the first from subordinates within his own area of responsibility, the second from managers of other functions who are in a sense directly competitive with him. The former threat is a vertical one within the organization, the latter horizontal; both serve to restrict vertical and horizontal communications flows and reduce the effectiveness of the innovator at non-managerial levels within the company and, indeed, at middle and lower management levels themselves.

Having looked at the major obstacles to innovation within the firm, conditions conducive to new product development and product diversification are self-evident :

1) creative senior management, responsive and accessible to *all* employees throughout the company

2) recruitment of some senior and middle management from outside the company (to avoid "inbreeding" and the conservatism that goes with it)

3) open promotion based on operational performance and creative contribution; promotion in no circumstances to be based principally on years of service

4) open communications, both vertical and horizontal, at all levels within the company

5) incentive programmes linked to innovation and new product ideas

6) product line review groups (multi-departmental), comprising managerial and non-managerial staff at all levels, for periodic assessment and evaluation of market and company developments.

Managerial and structural constraints on product diversification are reinforced by "external" factors which restrict new product development. New ideas may be generated within the firm by feedback from the market place, regarding technological change and developments or new consumer requirements. In the larger organization, with its considerable number of technical contacts built up through R & D departments and market research units, and with its sizeable sales and engineering staff supplying continuous and widespread feedback from both customers and suppliers, the information flows necessary to generate such developments are readily available. In contrast, the small firm, with little or no research and development facility and with comparatively small sales and engineering

departments incapable of achieving the depth and breadth of contact
maintained by the larger company, cannot hope to receive the same
degree of feedback from the market. Consequently, information on new
developments is restricted essentially to that transmitted by distributors
and suppliers, and perhaps also by end-users of the company's products
communicating directly with the company. However, this is, in reality,
information reaching the firm at too late a stage for effective exploitation
through new products. The distributor or wholesaler is more likely to
feed back information on existing "new" products, rather than on
potential products still in the development stage. The same problem, of
course, faces the large organization (though not in fact to the same
degree : market feedback to large firms is highly organized and effective)
but the disadvantage here is offset to a large extent by the early knowledge of technological advances and the ability to use this knowledge to
fully exploit future product trends. These differing abilities to develop
and exploit external market changes reinforce the contention that, while
large organizations are able to *innovate* in technologically sophisticated
markets, the smaller firm can only *imitate*, a point developed in more
detail at a later stage.

   In contrast to internal constraints imposed on product development,
there is a limit as to how effectively the small firm can overcome external
factors which restrict the process. The problem is again one of limited
communications, this time due to market size and poor technological feedback. The latter can be remedied to some degree by liaison of small
firms with universities or other research centres, and the onus lies with
the company to cultivate such ties either directly or by taking advantage
of government-sponsored technological support for the smaller firm.
The needs of the smaller organization were recognized in the United
States in 1965, when the "State Technical Services Act" was passed to
assist small businesses in using technological information(6). In the
U.K., the availability of technical knowledge to the small firm has depended very greatly on the industrial liaison centres based on universities,
polytechnics and technical colleges and on the work of individual trade
associations. With regard to universities and other higher education
establishments, however, there is disappointingly little evidence to show

that creative innovation has been present to any marked degree when they are approached by small organizations seeking assistance with, for example, specific problems of product design(7). Universities are abreast of, and may, in fact, initiate, major technological research and development, but for the small firm the translation of these achievements into practical application in the new product field is usually notable only by its absence. It is the larger firm which again would appear to benefit most through liaison and joint research with the universities.

External constraints on innovation remain substantial, therefore, for the small organization. Their effects are minimized by :
1) frequent communications within the widest possible market and at all levels
2) active liaison with universities and other higher educational establishments, with industrial liaison centres and with relevant trade associations
3) inter-firm co-operation on technological changes and the development of new ideas; information-sharing schemes.

Diversification Alternatives : Analysis and Selection

Possible organizational and market constraints within which the small firm is obliged to operate have been examined, and it has been argued that communication and incentive are the two major factors influencing the flow of new product ideas. Given an open communications network, and the existence of appropriate conditions within the firm, this flow should prove satisfactory. The analysis now concerns itself with identifying the most attractive and realistic areas of innovative opportunity.

There are basically three major types of diversification for consideration(3) :
1) Horizontal diversification : covering the introduction of "new" products within the same general industry, based on an attempt to serve additional needs of existing consumers or to create entirely new markets by product diversification.
2) Vertical diversification : either moving backward in the production chain to produce components formerly purchased or, alternatively, moving down the line and taking up additional production, assembly or distribution functions.

3) Heterogeneous diversification : i.e.moving out of one's present industry altogether and developing new products unrelated to the previous line.

For the small firm, horizontal diversification is clearly the most attractive in terms of its demands on managerial, financial, productive and technological resources. Unless there is a high new technology element in the new product or products, it does not entail any radical change in the company's existing method of operation. In contrast, vertical diversification demands larger injections of development capital and requires that management and staff learn to develop and apply new technological skills. New plant and machinery, significantly different from existing facilities and equipment, may be necessary. Again, if vertical diversification moves down the line, there are major market development and distribution problems to be faced.

Heterogeneous diversification is, under normal circumstances, not for consideration by the small firm, in spite of Brion's claim that it can prove more attractive to the smaller organization than to the large firm. The financial burden of moving out of one industry and into another would often be crippling, made worse by the considerable expense of over-coming possible barriers to entry. Such diversification requires totally new managerial skills, a retrained labour force and new plant and productive facilities. It may be worthwhile only if the company, either by accident or design, has developed a new product, enjoying patent or similar protection, suitable for highly profitable exploitation in another industry, or alternatively if the company's existing industry is dying or in rapid decline and resources have to be reinvested in another unrelated and more buoyant field of operations.

HORIZONTAL DIVERSIFICATION

Having argued that horizontal diversification offers the best opport-unity for small firm new product development when assessed on a "least cost" basis (nearly always the critical factor for the smaller organization), how can such diversification be achieved? The first significant point is that horizontal development may be effected by either of two methods, i.e. by product or by market diversification. Product diversification is concerned with developing and broadening the range of products offered to actual and potential customers within the firm's traditional market, in the hope that these product additions or refinements will, in fact, increase sales revenue and profitability. Market development, on the other hand, requires new products to broaden the market base by attracting new customers from outside the company's traditional market. Of the two, product diversification requires little or no re-organization of existing sales and distribution systems. Market "broadening", in contrast, necessarily implies some reassessment of marketing supply channels.

Horizontal product diversification

This can be best achieved either through modification of existing products or through the development of products entirely new to the company range.

1) Product modification : modifications may be made first of all by alterations which do not change the overall nature and functions of the original products significantly enough for them to be classified as "new" products, but simply as "modified" versions of the original. The modifications are usually brought about either by changes in the "mix" of existing inputs (raw materials, etc.) and do not require the use of new materials, or through variations in the "quality", but not in the component parts, overall design or specifications, of existing products. The latter is, in fact, product diversification through quality changes, reflected in price variations rather than through changes in raw materials and component inputs. Change is again effectively only one of input "mix" variations, and hence, of quality; but this can be considered to broaden the range of products offered and is, in a sense, diversification. It also has the considerable attraction to the small firm of requiring no new material inputs (unlike product modification achieved through design or specification changes) and no new technology requirements at any level.

2) New product development : in contrast to "modified" products, "new" products are, by definition, significantly different, in some respects, from existing product lines, even though they may well serve the same functional purpose. They may take three forms : firstly, they may be functionally identical to existing products; secondly, functionally

similar; or thirdly, functionally "unique", i.e. unlike any other product past or present(9). Clearly, the functionally unique product calls for major financial and technological resource capabilities and their development is today, for the most part, the preserve either of large corporations or of smaller research establishments enjoying negligible financial constraints and with an extremely high level of technological expertise. By and large, the small firm's new product opportunities lie with the development and exploitation of functionally identical or function-ally similar products which can be achieved with more moderate inputs of managerial and technical skills. New products may originate from existing raw materials, from new material and technological inputs, or, more probably, from a mix of traditional and new inputs. A major internal source of possible new product development lies in the exploitation of by-products of existing production processes, particularly in the development of lower-cost functionally identical products.

An effective way in which the small firm can obtain a share of new markets, opened up by high-technology new products, is by imitation rather than by attempting to channel limited funds into often abortive technological research. Levitt(10) refers to this strategy as "innovative imitation", and argues :

"Imitation is not only more abundant than innovation but actually a much more prevalent road to business growth and profits (than innovation itself). If the smaller company imitates, waits for market development, then launches, it has floated a 'new' product at minimal risk."

The principal barrier to innovative imitation is clearly the possible existence of patents and copyrights taken out by the originating company. Even if they exist, however, it is often possible to circumvent such restrictions to market entry, by developing and improvising on the new product idea, rather than by attempting exact imitation of existing products or prototypes.

Finally, the small firm is again able to exploit high-technology product opportunities by taking up licensing or franchise agreements with larger organizations. The rising cost of research and development in recent years and the desire for the smaller firm to capture at least a share of the technologically more sophisticated markets has seen a marked rise in such arrangements. Whether in fact they are profitable to the small organization is dependent on the many cost/benefit aspects of the particular venture and on the prospects for substantial short- and long-term demand for the product or products in question. They are, however, a further option open to the organization whose size restricts its potential for developing and exploiting technical advances unaided.

Horizontal market diversification

Market diversification is concerned with broadening the sales base of a company, within the same general industry, by attracting new customers through product innovation. Inevitably, some new managerial and technical skills are required and sales and distribution organizations may have to be significantly adjusted to the nature and requirements of the new market segment. For the small firm, these technological and organizational changes cannot be too demanding, hence, new product search needs to be directed to those areas (a) where production and technical requirements can be easily accommodated within existing resources and capabilities, and (b) where the new distribution network necessary for market development is contained within acceptable limits. Markets can, in fact, be developed either by new-technology products sold through existing distribution channels, or equally by new products developed from existing technology but channelled through a modified distribution system.

Unlike product modification or new product development within a firm's existing market, diversification into similar yet distinct new market sectors, within the same general industrial field, depends to a great extent on the efficiency of market "feedback" from these potential trading sectors, concerning their present and future product requirements. Existing sales and distribution systems, the major source of market feedback in the small firm, tend, naturally, to change only if and when a new product or products are launched into new markets. Market development begins with the introduction of the products in question, where sales and distribution policies are concerned. New market information in the larger organization is the responsibility of market research, which can effectively close the feedback "loop" before a new product launch, thus reducing the risk factor to a considerable degree. In contrast, the small firm tends to have far more limited prior knowledge of new markets and market conditions. With no feedback from sales and with little or no market research capability, it must obtain information necessary for market evaluation before committing itself to new product development in unknown markets as best it can. Review of trade and technical publications, library-based research and informal market assessment by middle and senior managers are time-consuming and costly operations, and still fail to solve the major problem of word-of-mouth feedback through sales, distribution or organized market research sources, often the most reliable information relaying system with respect to present and future market trends and developments.

Various methods of horizontal diversification through both product and market development have been examined. Figure 1 summarizes the major policy options open to the small firm. These alternative strategies, together with their associated consequences in terms of their potential demand on new and existing company resources, need to be listed and screened in detail in order to assess their individual feasibility and attractiveness. The degree of financial, technical and managerial "flexibility" of the firm will determine which options can be considered realistic.

If company and market constraints are significantly low, then vertical diversification is, of course, a strategy option. As already mentioned, product development and manufacture in "new" areas of operation, even within the same industry, call for considerable capital expenditure which usually proves prohibitive for the smaller organization. However, should such diversification be feasible, an opportunity often lies in "backwards" expansion, as the firm is in a position to know what products and services are expected from its existing suppliers and may see a particularly good opportunity not as yet exploited by present raw materials producers and processors or components manufacturers. By moving backward in the production process, the company can hope to capitalize on any inefficiencies or inadequacies of existing suppliers. However, there are still major barriers to entry and only limited market opportunities. Backwards diversification on any scale requires the development of new markets,

FIGURE 1 : Horizontal diversification options

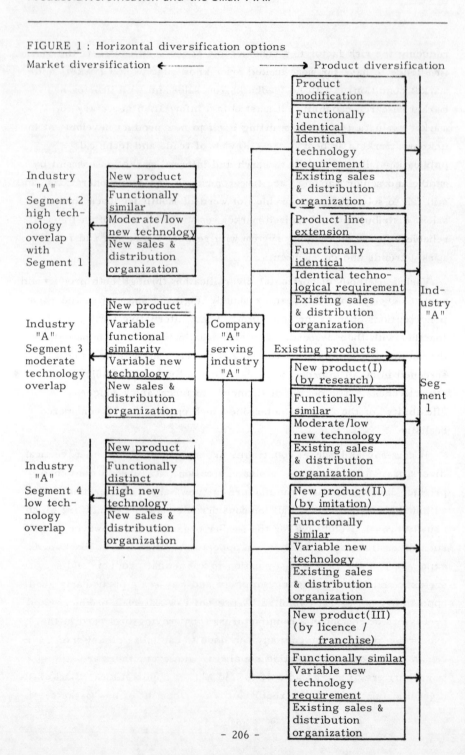

primarily among existing competitors; it is clearly in the interests of
these competitors to buy supplies only from "independent" sources.
(This problem need not apply to the large firm whose own raw material
or component requirements may be sufficiently large to justify plant
investment on the assumption that the operation will initially be based on
intra-group trading and sales. Market development can be achieved over
time to increase new plant utilization to an acceptable level and to widen
the market outside the group for the particular materials or components,
so that the new organization is not merely servicing group requirements
but taking an increasing share of overall market demand.) For the small
firm, vertical product diversification is always a high-risk decision, even
allowing for minimal managerial, technological and financial restrictions
on the company itself.

Summary

The interpretation of the process of product planning is markedly
different when viewed from the standpoint of the small firm, as opposed
to that of its larger counterpart. Lacking formal organization for product
and market research, effective new product development depends primarily on the ability of the small company to create an overall organizational
"climate" and structure, which itself acts as a catalyst for new ideas.
The level of communications which large organizations seek to achieve
within their R & D and market research divisions, in order to ensure the
flow of new product ideas, must be achieved on a company-wide basis
by the small firm. This, in turn, has to be reinforced by promotional
and financial incentives geared to reward creativity within the
organization, which leads to the adoption and implementation of new
ideas and ultimately to higher overall sales profitability.

Finally, the direction of diversification must depend to a great extent
on the various constraints affecting the firm. For the great majority of
smaller companies, heterogeneous and vertical diversification programmes
are, in normal circumstances, unrealistic. Horizontal diversification,
however conservative this may appear, is most appropriate to their
market situation and, when implemented on a continuing basis, offers
the best opportunity for such firms to adjust to changing market
conditions.

(1)   Stilson, P. & Arnoff, E.L., 'Product Search & Evaluation', Journal of Marketing, July 1957, pp. 33-39

(2)   Andrews, K.R., 'Product Diversification & the Public Interest', Harvard Business Review, July 1951, pp. 91-107

(3)   Brion, J.M., 'Corporate Marketing Planning', Wiley Marketing Series, New York, 1967, p. 88

(4)   Kline, C.H., 'The Strategy of Product Policy', Harvard Business Review, July-August 1955, pp. 91-100

(5)   Cooper, C.A., 'Small Companies can Pioneer New Products', Harvard Business Review, September-October 1966, pp. 162-179

(6)   Muse, W.V. & Kegerreis, R.J., 'Technological Innovation & Marketing Management : Implications for Corporate Policy', Journal of Marketing October 1969, pp. 3-9

(7)   Doutt, J.T., 'Product Innovation in Small Business', Business Topics, Univ. of Michigan, Summer 1960, pp. 58-62

(8)   Kast, F.E. & Rosenzweig, J., 'Diversification Planning : A Systematic Approach', Business Topics, Univ. of Michigan, Summer 1960, pp. 12 -22

(9)   Steele, R.J., 'Pricing & the Level of Newness', in Creative Pricing, Elizabeth Marting ed., 1968, p. 157

(10) Levitt, T., 'Innovative Imitation', Harvard Business Review, Sept.- October 1966, pp. 63-70

CHAPTER 6 : SUCCESSION AND DELEGATION

Introduction

In Chapter 5 it was suggested that strategies for survival and growth of the small business are invariably ad hoc and intuitive, if they exist at all. This theme continues to pervade the following three articles on delegation and succession : the authors warn that without effective delegation and planned succession the long-term survival of the small family firm is uncertain.

In the first article, Perrigo deals with both issues. Delegation is a necessary condition for management succession, in his view, for the sudden demise of a chief executive who has refused to delegate authority to his family or professional managers can result in a crisis of survival. But the archetypal entrepreneur tends to eschew delegation, preferring to safeguard his independence by retaining control. To him delegation implies loss of control and, to the extent that he is the embodiment of the firm, also loss of personal status. Perrigo reminds the reader that the clue to the understanding of the small business lies in an understanding of the entrepreneur.

The extent of delegation will also depend on the skills and abilities of the chief executive's subordinates. It follows that, since personal friends and family members may be appointed to executive positions in the small business, irrespective of their skills and abilities, when the time comes to delegate authority to these positions, there may be some reluctance to do so. But the willingness to delegate is still paramount, since training can rectify at least some of the deficiencies.

The confusion of personal and business objectives is frequently a source of succession problems. The owner-manager's desire for absolute control to the exclusion of even his close family tends to conflict with the needs of the business, particularly where these needs require the gradual transfer of power and ownership to younger family members or to professional managers.

The remaining two articles in this chapter address the dynamics and problems of management succession. The importance of choosing the right successor to the chief executive is reflected in the fact that a large number of business failures are the result of appointing the wrong person. McGivern illustrates the succession problem with two brief case studies and identifies three stages in the succession process, starting with the incumbent's willingness to make an appointment through to the actual appointment and its attendant problems. In McGivern's view, external advisers should consider five groups of variables in each situation, since the individual social characteristics of the small business will determine the outcome of succession in each case. These groups of variables include the firm's stage of development, its internal organisation and external environment, the owner-manager's motivation and not surprisingly, the extent of family participation in the business.

The final article deals in more detail with succession in the context of family businesses. Barnes and Hershon describe the contradictions and conflicts that characterise family business, which they claim are far more abundant than previously thought. Indeed, family control is extensive even in some very large firms. The conflicts arise because the interests of the family are not always in sympathy with the interests of employees, relatives, outsiders and the reality of the market-place. As the control of the business passes from the first to later generations of family owners, the outcome of these conflicts determine the success or failure of the firm. To ensure successful continuity in family management, Barnes and Hershon point to the need to develop dialogues between the interested factions so as to include all the relevant perspectives.

1. DELEGATION AND SUCCESSION IN THE SMALL FIRM

A.E.B.Perrigo

Personnel Management. Volume 7 Number 5. May 1975

Lack of defined objectives, ineffective delegation and lack of management skills are shortcomings common to many small firms. Indeed, in
surveys covering a wide range of such organisations, the Small Business
Centre at Aston University identified a number of such characteristics
which militate against the growth of the small firm. For example, the
chief executive (usually owner-manager) was often so preoccupied with
the day-to-day pressures and activities of the business that he devoted
little or no time or attention to the paramount tasks of the chief
executive. This meant that improving the efficiency of current operations
was overlooked and forward planning was neglected. Also, there tended
to be a lack of necessary skills and/or knowledge on the part of the
chief executive and his team to introduce and maintain effective, but
in general very simple, management controls and information services
which would aid sound decision-making.

The management training requirements to overcome these basic shortcomings differ considerably, quantitatively and qualitatively. In the case
of lack of defined objectives, they mainly involve recognition of where
the firm's potential lies, and the setting up of specific objectives for
the purpose of achieving that potential. This necessitates recognising
where one's personal requirements as owner are likely to clash with such
objectives and resolving situations of potential conflict. Where ineffective
delegation is concerned, the remedies will include change of management
style, of habits, and of relationships within the firm - as well as a
change of attitude. Where the problem is lack of necessary skills, the
training requirements are mainly limited to the acquisition of knowledge
of some relatively simple but appropriate management techniques.

It is therefore not surprising that delegation - or the lack of it - is
usually by far the most difficult for owner-managers of small firms to
rectify. Since our present brief is the problems of delegation and of
succession (which is the ultimate or supreme step in the delegation

process) we will briefly consider why this difficulty should arise and what the owner-manager can do to achieve effective delegation.

The owner-manager of the small firm will have his own personal objectives as owner. If the needs of the firm and his objectives conflict - and the owner-manager does not recognise this or is not prepared to subordinate his own personal objectives to the needs of the firm, or achieve his own desires by other means than through the firm - the firm will not achieve its actual potential. In such circumstances, the owner-manager can be an incubus to the development and improved performance of the firm. In many cases, the firm would probably be more successful as the subsidiary of some other private company where the owners would be prepared to help it achieve its potential or as the subsidiary of a public company with a capable board of directors and a remote and spread ownership.

Most of us will have come across the case of an owner-manager who has no desire for his firm to grow once it has reached the stage of providing him and his family with the material things they want from life. As long as the firm is meeting his needs he does not see why he should add to his responsibilities by developing the firm 'just to pay most of it over to the tax man'. To change such a person's attitude to growth one first has to facilitate change in his attitude regarding the firm and its employees. It needs to be pointed out to him that, whilst his own personal requirements are being fulfilled, it does not follow that those of his most valuable employees are. The more able and far-sighted of these - who are probably those who contribute most to the firm's performance - are likely sooner or later to recognise that their own ambitions will only be realised within the firm as it grows. In consequence, as they become aware of lost opportunities because of lack of exploitation of potential, they are likely to lose morale and leave. Such a possibility will probably not have occurred to the general manager.

Appointing a Successor

There are also many cases of the owner-manager who has had a very successful business life but who, in the interests of the firm, should relinquish his executive duties and appoint a successor as general manager. Too often in such circumstances, even where a series of suitable candidates have been found over a period of time for him to select from, he cannot make up his mind to offer anyone the appointment. Eventually, if the problem is discussed frankly and in depth with the owner-manager, he is likely to get clear in his mind the reason for his reactions, and to admit that, subconsciously, he had not wanted to make an appointment. It may be that he had not wanted to give up the personal satisfaction which he derived from being chief executive of the company or that he had a son - or, perhaps, nephew - as yet only in his teens whom the father wished to succeed him when he retired, and he was afraid that the appointment of an outsider as chief executive at this stage would block the young man's prospects of taking over executive control when the owner-manager retired.

Resolution of the problem is facilitated when the owner-manager is able clearly to recognise the difference between his own personal desires and the needs of the firm, and the conflict so generated. When this stage is reached, it is often possible to achieve an acceptable and satisfactory solution. For example, where it is the father's desire for his son to succeed him,it has often been solved by the recruitment of an experienced man of an age greater than was originally contemplated. In such circumstances, a definite date is planned for the assumption of executive control by the son. The advantage of this is that the outsider is fully aware of these proposals and signifies his willingness to play his part in the management training and development of the son.

Even when objectives and a course of action have been agreed and defined, success of the whole operation depends upon the ability and willingness of the owner to delegate responsibilities. This brings us back to our main topic of delegation, since lack of skill in this art can have an adverse effect upon the best-laid and best-intentioned of plans on the part of the owner-manager to ensure a smooth succession to executive responsibility - whether through promotion from within the firm or through bringing in an 'outsider'.

To the person who has spent his working life in the larger organisation it may appear strange that delegation often presents such a difficult problem to the chief executive, or owner-manager, of the smaller firm.

It has to be realised that, in many small firms, the chief executive runs the firm in a manner unchanged since the inception of the business. In fact, its early success might well have been due to his herculean contribution to the day-to-day activities of the company at that time, without which it might never have got off the ground. With the gradual growth of the firm, however, there inevitably comes a time when his pre-occupation with its day-to-day affairs is no longer appropriate, if he is to make his proper contribution to its prosperity. More of his time and energies are needed on forward planning, and on improving current performance.

Delegation of at least some of his daily tasks is therefore necessary, to permit him to devote more time to his paramount responsibility - that of ensuring the future prosperity of the firm. This inevitably necessitates organisational changes, with corresponding clearly-defined new areas of authority, responsibility and duties of some members of the workforce. The changes also need to be understood and observed throughout the firm.

These changes are much more difficult to implement in the small than in the large firm. It is not just a case of the owner-manager intellectually mastering the principles of delegation and organisation - which are so disarmingly simple - and how they should be applied within the firm. They also involve a change in habits, often long-standing and deep-rooted, of the owner-manager, and in the relationship between him and his employees, and between the employees themselves. Such changes may be resented and resisted by some employees - especially by those who, for the first time in their working life or since joining the firm, find themselves responsible to, and receiving instructions from, a fellow employee instead of the owner of the firm himself. The owner-manager also has to learn to adjust his style of management to meet new situational needs, and to develop the necessary flexibility in style to enable him to operate more effectively through direct subordinates.

It may be worthwhile reflecting here that, when a firm is young and very small, the owner-manager is usually highly dedicated to the job itself. In other words, he has a high task orientation but a low relation-ships orientation. He knows what he wants, how he wants things done, makes most or all of the decisions, and directly carries out or supervises most of the more responsible day-to-day operations himself. In consequence, he tends to gather round him employees who are content to be told what to do, rather than to share in decision-making.

He often achieves a level of success in these early stages which would not have been attained without his own direct day-to-day contribution, and it may well have been accomplished without sacrificing time or energies which ought to have been directed to the longer term needs of the business, and without creating significant resentment amongst his employees. Furthermore, at this scale of activities, with everyone in the firm directly answerable to him and with little or no specialist support, he generally does not need to develop much flexibility in his management style to meet the situational needs within the firm.

As the firm grows, however, with specialists joining the payroll, the owner-manager needs to develop and extend his management style to a more relationships-orientated style - i.e., because of the organisational and technological change in the subordinate situation - to enable him to delegate activities to the degree demanded by their increased scale. Unless he succeeds in this, he will be so stretched in contributing in the manner which has been his practice, that he will have less and less time available for his primary and longer term tasks as chief executive. When further growth of the firm becomes inhibited the owner-manager often succeeds in convincing himself that the static situation is the result of market forces.

Relief of the day-to-day pressures on the owner-manager of the small firm is not an easy task. He often needs on-the-job coaching in the practice of delegation, as well as advice and assistance regarding the implementation of those organisational measures necessary to make delegation effective and in the time-consuming training of subordinates in their new roles. The subordinates, as well as the owner-manager, have to understand the purpose of the new measures. This means that they should be made aware of the firm's objectives and potential, and once trained and suitably motivated, should be capable of assisting the owner-manager in the decision-making processes and the achievement of objectives.

Many an owner-manager who is aware of the benefits to be derived from effective delegation and would like to delegate more of his day-to-day activities, has confessed that he is afraid to do so because he considers that his subordinates would not do the jobs as well as he does them himself. Such owner-managers - who, like other normal people, often exhibit the weakness of having an inflated idea of how well they perform jobs, relative to other operatives - need to remember that the prime purpose of delegation is to free the owner-manager for more important activities : it is not for the purpose of trying to find someone who can do the delegated job better! In consequence, the owner-manager has to learn to be prepared to accept a level of performance which he does not necessarily think is as good as his own level. He should not confuse style with the substance of performance and he must avoid the temptation of competing with his subordinates.

In the first few weeks of such a programme, even with a sympathetic and experienced coach at his side, the owner-manager will probably find himself under greater pressure than before. Training one's subordinates and establishing new relationships takes a heavy toll on one's time, and breaking old habits and developing new ones is an exhausting process. In consequence, all but the most able of owner-managers need temporary personal assistance if they are to succeed. This can take the form of assistance from an on-the-job coach, who needs to be an experienced and sympathetic mentor. Such a person can be invaluable to the owner-manager by patiently and tactfully revealing to the latter when he returns to an old habit - e.g. giving instructions directly to someone on the shop floor instead of through the appropriate direct subordinate. Like all coaching, it is much more effective when the one being coached is shown the fault when it happens, rather than in retrospect.

Big Pay-Off from Delegation

The pay-off resulting from the achievement of effective delegation can be considerable. The owner-manager, often for the first time, has the opportunity of directing his attention in a relaxed manner to the longer-term aspects and prospects of the firm, and to means of improving the efficiency of the day-to-day operations. This helps him to plan ahead and thereby avoid the day-to-day crises of *ad hoc* management, with their expedient solutions and inevitable cost in emotional wear and tear throughout the firm. Instead of the day-to-day affairs controlling him, the owner-manager finds that it is possible for him to control most of them. This permits him to view the firm in proper perspective, and he is more likely to realise that the greatest assets which a firm can have are an effective chief executive with a team of able and willing subordinates to implement his plans - and that he cannot be effective without having or developing such a team. This should lead him to realise the importance of investment of time in the development of his subordinates as managers and supervisors and the considerable return provided from such an investment. If he starts thinking this way he will quickly see the vital importance of protecting and ensuring the continuity of the firm's management - and his own post in particular.

This leads him to making plans for his own succession. Where the owner-manager has achieved effective delegation, a continuous process of management development will have been occurring within the firm, and he is more likely to be able to select and groom a prospective successor from his team than otherwise would be possible. Where there has not been such delegation, the firm is not likely to be a breeding ground for a prospective successor and, at some time, an outsider will need to be brought in to assume the supreme position, and he will initially have the great disadvantage of having to operate without the support of such an experienced team as is developed through the process of effective delegation.

Therefore, we may with advantage conclude with the thought that, when an owner-manager initially embarks upon a programme of delegation to improve his own effectiveness within the firm, he may unwittingly be taking the first sound steps to cover his succession.

2. THE DYNAMICS OF MANAGEMENT SUCCESSION

Chris McGivern

Management Decision. Volume 16 Number 1. Spring 1978

The succession of the chief executive of any organisation is a critical event. In 1971 a study(1) revealed that in the U.K., management succession was almost equal to financial failure as the major cause of firms ceasing to exist as independent organisations. Dun and Bradstreet(2) calculated that in the U.S.A., 45% of all business failures are caused through the appointment of incompetent managers to chief executive positions.

A number of management thinkers have tackled the problem - yet the usual product of their labours has been a number of universal prescriptions which take little account of the complex reality of organisational life. These generalisations tend to be even less helpful in the context of the smaller, family owned firm, where the pressures are particularly intense and a choice of successors is almost non-existent.

This article, based on the author's research, describes a model for analysing succession situations. The model is intended for use by those involved in a company facing succession problems, either as members of firms or as external advisers. It attempts to show that a complex network of influences exists in any organisation at a time of chief executive succession. It argues that it is not possible to generalise about what firms should do, and suggests that it is ultimately a question of taking balanced decisions in the light of pressures from various sources. The main task should be that of ensuring that the future survival of the organisation is the main priority.

The research was carried out via a study of the available literature on the subject and intensive action research projects carried out in two fairly typical small firms. One was employing about 100 people, the other had around 90 employees. Brief details of the companies and their succession problems appear below (see Table 1). The model which was developed is discussed in the context of both the literature on succession and the two case histories.

TABLE 1 : Brief case histories of two firms with succession problems

Company A Barlows Ltd.	Company B Crawford Ltd.
Barlows is a small merchanting company employing about 100 people. Founded in the 1920s it had always been a family business. By 1958, when the founder died, his 4 sons were all working for the firm. The eldest son Bill then took over the firm, but found it a tough job. In 1964, after a move to a new, larger site, Bill resigned from his post as MD because he felt he did not possess the ability to continue. Meanwhile, a non-family member, John Brooks, had been promoted from salesman to sales director. The brothers decided that he & the youngest brother Ken should become joint managing directors. Ken would handle the storage & distribution functions, plus administration, while John would take on sales & marketing. As a result of this move, one of the brothers left the firm in disagreement with the others, taking his 25% shareholding with him. The two powerful, extrovert personalities of John & Ken had their ups & downs. A crisis was reached at one point when there was a major confrontation between the two. This was finally resolved with them moving into the same office and sitting behind a purpose built T-shaped desk. The partnership which then developed was effective. The brothers agreed that, for various reasons they would all like to retire at about the same time. John Brooks was to take on the day-to-day control while the other brothers would remain as non-executive directors. In 1970, at the age of 41, Brooks died & the plans were back in the melting pot. After a good deal of soul searching, the brothers decided to pursue their plans for	Crawfords began life in 1928 as a small scale, high quality furniture manufacturing business, based on the skills of its founder Andrew Crawford. The firm grew into shopfitting and during World War II it prospered through MOD contracts. Since 1945 the business grew slowly, moving in & out of various products until in the early 1970s it hit on a booming sector of the furniture market. In 1973 it employed about 90 people. Andrew's son, Paul was 36 when he took over the business in 1971 after his father suddenly decided to retire. Paul had had 18 years in the firm in a variety of positions, although it was not in his father's nature to delegate or share control. This was a business based entirely on the skill, knowledge & benevolent autocracy of Andrew Crawford. Paul had no experience of running the business therefore when he took over. Nor had there been a handover period. It was all done within a month. Andrew foresaw no problems. Business was booming & indeed for 3 years, as Paul put it himself, the firm virtually ran itself. There was time for sailing & golf & life was good. Paul's style was totally unlike his father's. Rather than issue detailed & specific instructions, he left people to sort things out for themselves. His one co-director, Bert Appleby (a craftsman friend & colleague of the founder) seemed to be able to keep things ticking over. By 1974 the storm clouds were gathering. There was a serious decline in business. The factory was running badly. Morale was low & things did not seem to get done as they should. Paul did not know what he could do. He called in

Company A

(cont...)

joint retirement, though they were
to delay it for a few more years.
Ken was to continue to be MD
until a time when he & his brothers
were convinced that the then middle
managers could prove their
capability to run the firm & to
provide a capable general manager.
They set 1976 as their deadline for
retirement & embarked on a
comprehensive programme of training for their middle managers. If
this failed, they were to sell the
business.
The programme was in many ways
a success. The middle managers
took on greater & wider responsibilities & after a year a general
manager-designate was appointed.
He was to be put in complete day-
to-day charge of the company
after 12 months.
Meanwhile the recession worsened
& the firm's profitability sagged.
The MD decided to remain & worked
in with the new GM. Two years
later (1977) he is still in post &
is talking of remaining two more
years - 'just to set the firm back
on its feet'.

Company B

(cont...)

various consultants who eventually
left without improving things much.
Bert was only concerned with the
technical excellence of the product.
Paul desperately tried to get
people more committed & involved
- but seemed to make no headway.
In mid-1975, a third of the workforce were made redundant & a
third more in 1976.

Succession is not a Simple Issue

Nobody has yet identified a set of variables which exist in all succession situations and whose effects are predictable. Most researchers have
concentrated mainly on the disruptive after-effects - and even then their
work has been primarily descriptive. The assumption seems to have been
that it is sufficient to provide generalised descriptions of succession
situations, coupled with generalised prescriptions for dealing with them.
So far there are few cases of contingency theory(3) applied to succession.
A contingency approach would suggest that as a means of designing a
strategy to cope with a particular succession problem it would be necessary first to identify the main variables affecting the situation and then

to work out how, individually and in combination, they influenced the
process of succession.

Any serious examination of succession in reality would suggest that
a contingency approach is necessary and that the universal generalisations
in much of the literature can serve only to provide a fairly superficial
understanding which cannot help much to resolve the problems in a
specific organisation.

The Succession Cycle

Before identifying the main variables which seem to be of particular
influence in succession situations, it is necessary first to look at the
stage that a particular succession has actually reached. This is important largely because it is usually possible to identify certain characteristic
problems occurring at various stages in the succession process.
Marrison(4) has suggested that there is in fact a *cycle* of stages through
which each succession passes. The cycle proposed roughly coincides
with the periods before, during and after the succession itself. (Marrison
argues that a firm is always at one of these stages, but it would seem to
be more realistic to include a fourth "dormant" stage, when succession is
not a live issue. Despite its crucial influence on the small firm, succession is a relatively infrequent occurence.)

The three stages when succession is a current issue can be seen as
follows :

Stage One - the chief executive (and probably others) will have recognised
the need to replace the chief executive at some time in the foreseeable
future.

At this stage there will probably be a debate about the future of the
business and whether it ought to continue or be sold. This is clearly
a time when feelings can run strong, particularly if people feel
threatened by the insecurity created.

Barlows, (see Table1) had almost passed through this stage. The fact
that they were prepared to sell the business if they failed to find a
convincing successor did create insecurity in the managers which affected
both their performance on the job and the way they behaved as contend-
ers for the job of general manager.

Stage Two - a decision has been taken to appoint someone at some time
(perhaps unspecified) in the future. This period gives rise to
problems such as :

- the selection of the successor
- his designation
- his training and development
- preparing the organisation(mainly other employees)
- the retirement process of the outgoing chief
  executive.

This represented the stage which the Barlow partners had reached in
their planning. Their novel way of announcing the decision to withdraw,
by giving the middle managers two years to prove themselves and to
show that one of them had leadership potential, represents an interesting
attempt to overcome many of the problems normally encountered at this
stage.

Stage Three - At the third stage, after the formal succession, a number
of new issues arise, for example :

- problems of taking control & introducing change
- developing an appropriate leadership style
- building effective relationships(& getting over
  unfavourable comparisons with previous chief
  executive)
- handling a continuing influence from the retired
  chief executive
- the development of the successor's technical
  management skill & knowledge.

Crawford Furniture manifested the main characteristic problems of stage
three. The successor had difficulty in assuming control at a time of
crisis. His leadership style did not seem to be effective. His relationships suffered because of unfavourable comparisons with his father.
Although his father did not have much influence even at the later stages
of the business crisis, Paul Crawford did suffer from a lack of management expertise. None of these problems had been anticipated in any way.

FIGURE 1 : A Model of Succession Issues & Problems & the Factors which Influence the Outcome of Decisions about Succession

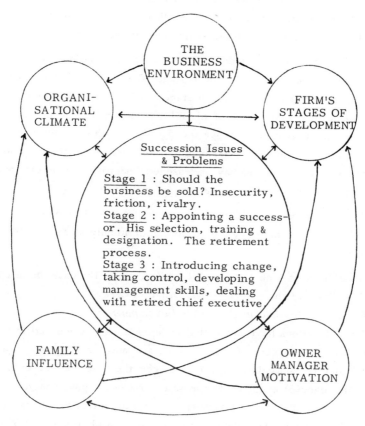

The Main Variables Influencing Succession Situations

There are five important groups of variables which will have some influence on most successions and must be built into any diagnostic model for the analysis of the problems involved. These are :

(1)   the stage reached in the firm's development

(2)   the motivation of the owner-manager

(3)   the extent of family domination

(4)   the organisational climate within the firm

(5)   the business environment

Any or all of these factors can have a major influence. They can have direct effects, and they can also, through various inter-relationships with other groups of variables, have different combined effects. The model (Figure 1) serves to illustrate some of these interactions.

At the centre of the model is the succession situation itself, which will have reached one of the three stages described. The problems manifested will depend firstly on the stage reached and secondly on the five influences identified. Each of the influences can have a direct effect on the way the succession is experienced. Most of the influences can also have effects on the other variables and as a consequence, their individual effects on the succession may be lessened, magnified or otherwise altered. (The arrows show the likely patterns of influence.)

There is no *one* way of using the model, it will all depend on the situation. It may help however to look individually at each of the influences.

Let us look at each in turn and relate them to the case histories outlined earlier and the evidence from other writers.

(1) *The Stage Reached in the Firm's Development*

Several writers have noted that organisations develop and in so doing pass through a number of stages which are more or less recognisable. One theory is particularly interesting from the point of view of the small firm. Kroeger(5) argues that the small firm develops through five stages, which he calls initiation, development, growth, maturity and decline. It should be possible, he believes, to place any small firm at one of these stages. The main implication for the student of succession however, is that, as Kroeger points out, each stage in this cycle creates a particular managerial role requirement on the chief executive. For each stage there is a parallel managerial role, thus :

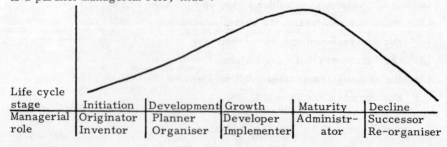

Life cycle stage	Initiation	Development	Growth	Maturity	Decline
Managerial role	Originator Inventor	Planner Organiser	Developer Implementer	Administr-ator	Successor Re-organiser

At the initiation stage, the "originator-inventor" creates an enterprise and the main problems relate to the exploitation of his ideas in a commercially viable way. The firm depends entirely on the founder. At the development stage, the chief executive must be able to cope with the problems of maintaining and developing the business. The top man must maintain the entrepreneurial flair and drive but must possess the quantitative and analytical skills needed to make the kind of decisions that will be required. At the third, or growth stage, the company will display a tendency towards a more stable organisation structure and will require managerial skills in co-ordinating activities while still growing. When the firm reaches maturity, the main role of the chief executive will be the effective maintenance of the *status quo*. Finally, the company will tend to decline, at which time it will fail altogether unless a "successor-organiser" is found. He will combine entrepreneurial talent as well as the financial and managerial skills of the "developer".

It would therefore seem reasonable to suggest that it is necessary to look at the successor in terms of whether he conforms to the role requirements of the chief executive at whatever developmental stage the firm has reached. In Crawford Furniture (Company B) the firm had, at the time of succession, reached the latter stages of the "mature" period. It was presumably for this reason that the founder decided to hand over to his son, believing that he would merely have to maintain the business as it was. In the then business climate (it was highly favourable) this must have seemed a reasonable decision. The question of the successor's competence as an able "administrator" seems not to have been questioned however.

There is evidence for Kroeger's theory in a study carried out by Boswell(6) who found that of the older firms he looked at, 53% were in a state of decline, and the majority of them, like Crawfords, were run by inheritor successors. (They, incidentally, accepted no responsibility for their firms' situations!)

(2) The Motivation of the Owner Manager

Levinson(7) sums up the psychological needs of the owner-manager by saying that his business is "essentially an extension of himself, a medium for his personal gratification and achievement above all". Other writers have identified owner-managers' powerful needs for independence as the main reason for the foundation of many businesses. Thus a good deal of evidence suggests that the owner-manager tends to use the business as a tool for satisfying his own personal needs and the firm exists more as an extension of his personality than an independent entity. A deliberate decision to withdraw may in the mind of the owner-manager be tantamount to a decision to deprive himself of his major source of personal satisfaction.

This problem became particularly evident in Barlows Ltd. when, having appointed a general manager, the previous managing director found a variety of reasons for deciding not to withdraw as he had previously agreed. This left the new general manager in the unfortunate position of being so in name only. How long he would remain in the previous chief executive's shadow thus became a serious problem, as did his own credibility in the eyes of the firm's employees.

Clearly, therefore, it is important to face up to the reality of the owner-manager's motivation and to work towards his acceptance of the fact that (a) the business must survive without him and (b) he must find other ways of satisfying his psychological needs. A personal counsellor may be an important part of this process.

(3) *Family Domination*

In the same way that the owner-manager may have personal reasons for not wishing to withdraw, or for not being concerned for the survival of his business without him, where other family members have a share-holding, their influence may be important. In one of the major works on succession, Christiansen(8) points out that when "....a family dominates a business, its members may have aspirations and demands at variance with the best interests of the enterprise". This is clearly of particular importance when the family demands that a successor be one of them, irrespective of competence. One need not labour the pitfalls of nepotism. If it is inevitable, the best that can be done is to plan thoroughly and carefully the training and development of the successor. It may also be necessary to ensure that he has access to sound professional advice.

This problem is particularly acute in some family businesses, where professional competence can be regarded as unnecessary. Despite the fact that several writers have suggested it, advocating a shift away from family domination towards a more professional approach seems to be a very faint hope however. What might be more realistic would be to change the attitudes of family shareholders towards professional competence and to do so over a fairly lengthy period before the succession takes place.

In the case of Crawford Ltd., this issue was probably not even considered. At Barlows, on the other hand, the family recognised, largely through experience, that their continued financial security and family management did not mix. It was primarily for this reason that they embarked on their programme of management development and devolution of management to non-family members.

(4) *The Organisational Climate* (9)

Defined crudely, the climate of an organisation is made up of individual members' perceptions of various of its characteristics. "The way things are in this firm" would be one way of describing it. The climate of an organisation can be a key to the understanding of its members' behaviour. In other words, people's perceptions of a firm's climate, (i.e. the way they see their working environment) will influence their behaviour.

The main problem with the whole concept of organisational climate how-ever is that there is no one set of common elements which applies universally. Different features of climate may be more or less important in different organisations. Significant features of organisational climates have included such things as : structural clarity, (i.e. the extent to which the organisation structure, roles and responsibilities are clear to members) the extent to which the organisation is perceived as achievement-orientated the nature of superior/subordinate colleague relationships, distribution of power and influence, reward and punishment systems and management and leadership style. These and other variables *may* be an important influence on employee behaviour, but in a succession situation in a small firm, the most important variable is often that of management style. Very often the chief executive totally dominates his firm and there is frequently nowhere in the organisation where his style is not all pervading.

In examining succession problems in the context of management style the key question relates always to the perceived appropriateness of the style to the situation. For example, the management style of small firms is often autocratic. This is usually seen as appropriate, particularly when the whole firm is based on the expertise of the founder. When a firm has grown larger however, the ability of one man to exercise full control becomes less. Consequently the autocratic style is less appropriate. The problem is often highlighted after a succession when, as with Crawfords, the founder cannot manage *effectively* (i.e. get the results he wants) as an autocrat. Yet employees frequently get so used to being managed in a particular way that they are unable to work effectively under any other regime. Further, it is often the implicit recruitment policy of small firms to hire people with a need to be dependent on others. As a consequence it can be well nigh impossible for a successor to achieve results using a different style of management to that of his predecessor. If, however, he does not possess the knowledge or expertise to do this and still tries to replicate the previous style he can still find it impossible to achieve the results he seeks - as was the case with Paul Crawford. It is therefore important, in the short term, to match the management style not only to the task, but also to the expectations and abilities of the employees. In the longer term it may be possible either to modify the company's recruitment policy, or the prevailing style - or both.

(5) *The Business Environment*

This factor can be defined as the extent to which the commercial prospects for the firm are either good, bad or indifferent. These prospects will be reflected internally in the company's accounts and particularly in its most recent profit and loss statement. They will also be seen in the order book, the willingness of the bank to lend money and the general economic environment.

In the context of the model described earlier, the business environment and the extent to which it is favourable at a particular time, will be a major determinant of the owner-manager's decision to withdraw, or to stay on in control. In both Barlows and Crawfords, the decision to withdraw was taken at a time when the business prospects were good. In Barlows particularly the decline in the favourableness of the business climate was a major reason for the previous managing director to remain in the company. A deteriorating situation therefore will usually tend to put plans for succession into suspension, or at least to slow them down. To some extent it was true that the downturn in the business climate was looked upon by Ken Barlow as an *excuse* for not retiring, a point that should be borne in mind in the current state of economic uncertainty.

A deteriorating business environment should also reinforce the need for developing the skills of a successor, as it will provide an early test of his abilities. It will also affect, for good or ill, both the organisational climate (especially in terms of morale and willingness to adapt to a new successor) and the firm's development. If the firm is at a critical stage of development, the business situation will be particularly influential because it will be that much more precariously situated.

Some Conclusions

The model described earlier is not of course a perfect representation of succession in the small firm. It identifies those factors which, both in the literature and in reality seem to be the main determinants of the outcomes of succession. It does so in a way which offers the possibility of understanding some of the dynamics involved, although these can only be truly understood within the context of an individual organisation.

Unfortunately, there is no *one way* the model can be used - would that there were! It is intended to be used as a guide to those involved in particular cases, either as members of the company, or as outside advisers. It could, for example be one way that an outgoing chief executive could get together with a counsellor from outside the firm to discuss the best way to plan for a succession. This is very much the kind of approach recommended by Perrigo(10), who is a strong advocate of external advisers. In such cases, a discussion of the model could well lead to a deeper understanding by the chief executive of the complex of problems with which he would have to deal. Similarly, members of a company, perhaps father and son or family directors, could use this approach as a means of making more carefully balanced decisions on succession problems.

It is also unfortunate that there will probably never be a totally satisfactory outcome to all parties involved. All this approach might do is to help them to arrive at a rather happier compromise than might otherwise be achieved.

(1) *Merrett-Cytiax Associates, The Dynamics of Small Firms, Committee of Inquiry on Small Firms, Research Report No. 12, HMSO, 1971*

(2) *Dun & Bradstreet, The Failure Record Through 1971, Business Economics Department, 1972*

(3) *For a fuller discussion of contingency theory, see Kast & Rosensweig, Organisation & Management – a Systems Approach, 2nd ed. McGraw-Hill, 1974*

(4) *Marrison, P., Chief Succession in the Small Business , unpublished MSc. dissertation, Univ. of Durham, 1975*

(5) *Kroeger, C.V., Managerial Development in the Small Firm , California Management Review Vol. XVII No. 1, 1974*

(6) *Boswell, J. The Rise & Decline of Small Firms, Allen & Unwin, 1972*

(7) *Levinson, H. Conflicts that Plague the Family Business , Harvard Business Review, March–April 1971*

(8) *Christiansen, C.R., Management Succession in Small & Growing Enterprises, Harvard Business Graduate School of Business Admin. 1953*

(9) *For one of the few thorough examinations of organisational climate see : Tagiuri, R., The Concept of Organisational Climate , in Organisational Climate : Explorations of a Concept, Boston, Harvard University, 1968*

(10) *Perrigo, A.E.B., Delegation & Succession in the Small Firm , Personnel Management, May 1975*

3. TRANSFERRING POWER IN THE FAMILY BUSINESS

Louis B.Barnes and Simon A.Hershon

One of the most agonizing experiences that any business faces is the moving from one generation of top management to the next. The problem is often most acute in family businesses, where the original entrepreneur hangs on as he watches others try to help manage or take over his business, while at the same time, his heirs feel overshadowed and frustrated. Paralleling the stages of family power are stages of company growth or of stagnation, and the smoothness with which one kind of transition is made often has a direct effect on the success of the other.

Sons or subordinates of first generation entrepreneurs tell of patient and impatient waiting in the wings for their time to take over the running of the company. When the time comes, it usually comes because the "old man" had died or is too ill to actively take part in management, even though still holding tightly to the reins of the family business. Often this means years of tension and conflict as older and younger generations pretend to coexist in top management.

As one second generation manager put it, speaking of these problems: "Fortunately, my father died one year after I joined the firm". Concerning another company, a prospective buyer said : "The old man is running the company downhill so fast that we'll pick it up for nothing before the kids can build it back up".

The transition problem affects both family and non-family members. Brokers and bankers, professional managers, employees, competitors; outside directors, wives, friends and potential stock investors all have more than passing interest as a company moves from one generation to the next. Some of these transitions seem orderly. Most, however, do not. Management becomes racked with strife and indecision. Sons, heirs, key employees, and directors resign in protest. Families are torn with conflict. The president-father is deposed. Buyers who want to merge with or acquire the business change their minds. And often the company dies or becomes stagnant.

Transferring Power in the Family Business

The frequency of such accounts and the pain reflected in describing the transfer of power from one generation to the next led us to begin a more formal research inquiry into what happens as a family business, or more accurately, a family *and* its business grow and develop over generations. Specifically, what happens in the family and company between those periods when one generation or another is clearly in control but both are "around"? In addition, how do some managements go through or hurdle the family transition without impeding company growth? And can or must family and company transitions be kept separate?

The research project on these questions began in June 1974 and is still continuing. It has included interviews with over 200 men and women and multiple interviews in over 35 companies, not all of which went beyond the first crucial transition test. This article contains some of the initial findings and conclusions.

Professional or Family Management ?

Some observers and commentators on family business believe that the sooner the family management is replaced by professional management in growing companies, the better. The problems just described can lead to disruption or destruction of either the family or the business, sometimes both, in the long run. Furthermore, the argument goes, an objective, professional management will focus on what is good for the business and its growth without getting lost in the emotions and confusions of family politics.

This rational argument for professional management in growing companies has many strong advocates. It has even been suggested that the family members should form a trust, taking all the relatives out of business operations, thus enabling them to act in concert as a family(1).

Like any argument for objectivity, the plea for professionalism has logic on its side. It makes good business sense, and in a way, good family sense as well. It guides a business away from mixing personal lives with business practices, and it helps to avoid the evils of nepotism and weak family successors who appear so often to cause transition crises.

Historically, the main problem with this rational argument is that most
companies lean more heavily on family and personal psychology than they
do on such business logic. The evidence is overwhelming. There are
more than one million businesses in the United States. Of these, about
980,000 are family dominated, including many of the largest. Yet most
of us have the opposite impression. We tend to believe that, after a
generation or so, family businesses fade into widely held public companies
managed by outside managers with professional backgrounds. The myth
comes partly from a landmark study of big business by Adolph Perle and
Gardner Means, who maintained that ownership of major U.S.companies
was becoming widely diffused and that operating control was passing into
the hands of professional managers who owned only a small fraction of
their corporation's stock. This widely publicized "fact" was further used
by John Kenneth Galbraith to build a concept which he called the
"technostructure" of industry, based in large part on the alleged separation of corporate ownership from management control(2).

There is evidence to the contrary, though. A study reported in
Fortune by Robert Sheehan examined the 500 largest corporations on this
question. Sheehan reported that family ownership and control in the
largest companies was still significant and that in about 150 companies
controlling ownership rested in the hands of an individual or of the
members of a single family. Significantly, these owners were not just
the remnants of the nineteenth century dynasties that once ruled American
business. Many of them were relatively fresh faces.(3)

The myth is even more severely challenged in a study of 450 large
companies done by Philip Burch and published in 1972. By his calculations, over 42% of the largest *publicly* held corporations are controlled
by one person or a family, and another 17% are placed in the "possible
family control" category. Then there is one other major category of
large "privately" owned companies - companies with fewer than 500 shareholders, which are not required to disclose their financial figures. Some
well-known corporate names are included in this category : Cargill,
Bechtel Corporation, Hearst Corporation, Hallmark Cards, and Hughes
Aircraft, among others. Burch notes that contrary to what one might
expect, the rather pervasive family control exercised is, for the most

part, very direct and enduring. It is exercised through significant stock ownership and outside representation on the board of directors, and also, in many cases, through a considerable amount of actual family management(4).

When one thinks more closely about families in big as well as small businesses, some well-known succession examples also come to mind, suggesting that family transition and corporate growth occur together even though there may be strain in the process. For example :

-- H.J.Heinz was founded by Henry J.Heinz to bottle and sell horse-radish, and today H.J.Heinz II, a grandson, heads the billion dollar concern.

-- Triangle Publications owns the *Morning Telegraph, TV Guide* and *Seventeen*. It was founded by Moses Annenberg. He was succeeded by his son, Walter, and a daughter, Enid, is now editor-in-chief of *Seventeen*.

-- The Bechtel Corporation was begun by Warren A.Bechtel, for building railroads. His son, Steve Sr., directed the firm into construction of pipelines and nuclear power plants. Today, Steve Jr. heads the $2 billion company, which is now further diversified.

-- Kaiser Industries, built by Henry J.Kaiser, includes Kaiser Steel, Kaiser Aluminium and Chemical, Kaiser Cement and Gypsum, Kaiser Broadcasting, Kaiser Engineering and Kaiser Resources. The present industrial giant is headed by Henry's son, Edgar, now over 65 years old. An obvious successor is Edgar Jr., president of Kaiser Resources Ltd.

Should a family business stay in the family? The question now seems almost academic. It is apparent that families *do* stay in their businesses, and the businesses stay in the family. Thus there is something more deeply rooted in transfers of power than impersonal business interests. The human tradition of passing on heritage, possessions, and name from one generation to the next leads both parents and children to seek continuity in the family business. In this light, the question whether a business should stay in the family seems less important, we suspect, than learning more about how these businesses and their family owners make the transition from one generation to the next.

Inside and Outside Perspectives

What are the implications when the transition from one generation to
the next includes both business and family change, and what are the
consequences also if business and family, though separate, remain tied
together in plans, arguments, and emotions? In considering these
questions, it might help to examine two perspectives in addition to age
difference. One is the family, the other is the business, point of view.
Both of these can be viewed from either the inside or the outside.

Exhibit I shows these four different vantage points from which to
observe family and business members. One viewpoint is that of the
"family managers" (inside the family and inside the business) as seen by
both old and young generations. When they forget or ignore the other
three perspectives, they can easily get boxed into their own concerns.
This kind of compulsion includes hanging onto power for the older
generation and getting hold of it for the younger. To both generations,
it implies the selection, inclusion, and perpetuation of family managers.

A second perspective comes from "the employees", again older and
younger, who work inside the business but who are outside the family.
Understandably, they face different pressures and concerns from those
of the family managers, even though many are treated as part of the
larger corporate family. The older employees want rewards for loyalty,
sharing of equity, and security, and they want to please the boss.
Younger employees generally want professionalism, opportunities for
growth, equity, and reasons for staying. Both age groups worry about
bridging the family transition.

A third perspective comes from "the relatives", those family members
who are not in the active management of the business. The older relatives
worry about income, family conflicts, dividend policies, and a place in
the business for their own children. The younger, often disillusioned
brothers and cousins feel varying degrees of pressure to join the business.
Both generations may be interested, interfering, involved, and sometimes
helpful, as we shall see later on.

Finally, the fourth perspective comes from "the outsiders". These
are persons who are competitors, R & D interests, creditors, customers,

EXHIBIT 1 : Pressures and interests in a family business

	Inside the family	Outside the family
Inside the business	**THE FAMILY MANAGERS** Hanging onto or getting hold of company control Selection of family members as managers Continuity of family investment and involvement Building a dynasty Rivalry	THE EMPLOYEES Rewards for loyalty Sharing of equity growth & successes Professionalism Bridging family transitions Stake in the company
Outside the business	THE RELATIVES Income & inheritance Family conflicts and alliances Degree of involvement in the business	THE OUTSIDERS Competition Market, product supply & technology influences Tax laws Regulatory agencies Trends in management practices

government regulators, vendors, consultants, and others who are connected to the business and its practices from the outside. They have various private interests in the company which range from constructive to destructive in intention and effect.

A curious irony is that the more "outside" the family the perspective is, as shown in *Exhibit 1*, the more legitimate it seems as a "real" management problem. Yet the concerns in the left column boxes are typically just as important as, and more time consuming than, the outside-the-family problems on the right. These inside-the-family problems tend to be ignored in management books, consultant's reports, and business school courses. Ignoring these realities can be disastrous for both the family and the company.

Our studies show that the transfer of power from first to second generation rarely takes place while the founder is alive and on the scene. What occurs instead during this time is a transition period of great difficulty for both older and younger generations. For the founder, giving up the company is like signing his own death warrant. For the son or successor, the strain may be comparable. As one of these said :

"I drew up the acquisition papers to buy my father out, because for a long time he has been saying he did not care about the business any more. However, when it was all taken care of, and we presented him with the papers, he started to renege. Everything was done the way he would like it. Yet he would not sign. He finally told me he did not think he could do it. He felt it awfully hard to actually lose the company. He said he felt he still had something to give."

And another commented :

"I can't change things as fast as I would like to. It is absolutely clear to me that things need to be changed. However, it is not easy. First of all there is the function of age and experience as well as being the boss's son. Every other officer in the company is in his fifties. What I am talking about now are deep sources of dissatisfaction. I would like more ownership. Now I have only 7%, my father has 80% and my family another 13%. In my position, I just cannot move the company fast enough. We argue a lot, but nothing seems to change. I have set a goal for myself. If I cannot run the company within two years, I am leaving. I'll do something else."

The Company Transition

While family managers feel the multiple strains as the generations over-lap during periods of transition, another related process is occurring as the company grows and develops. Various authors have tried to describe this process(5). But, where one describes a smooth procedural develop-ment, another sees a series of difficult crises. For some, it is the merging of functions with processes that count. Most writers do not tie business growth or decline to family transitions. However, the following points stand out for us in relation to company transitions :

(1)   Organizational growth tends to be nonlinear. Organizations grow
in discrete stages, with varying growth rates in each stage.

(2)   Periods of profound organizational development often occur *between*
periods of growth. These slower periods often are viewed with alarm,
but they force managers to examine what the company has grown toward
or into. These periods of development are the transition periods which
appear less dramatic (i.e., there is less growth) but may be most crucial
to a company's preparations for its own future(6). The apparent floun-
dering can provoke useful learning once management begins to adopt and
encourage new practices and procedures.

(3)   A typical management response to transitional strains is a total or
partial reorganization of the company. This sometimes helps shake up
old habits but rarely resolves a transition crisis. What is needed is time
for the social and political systems of the company to realign themselves
into new norms and relationships.

Exhibit II shows how a later growth stage differs from and builds on
the earlier ones. The first stage is characteristic of an entrepreneurial
company with direct management. The second is typified by a rapidly
growing product line and market situation with second-level management
set up in specialized functions. The third stage has divisional operations
with a diverse line of products and markets. Whereas the management
style of the first stage is highly personal and direct, the second tends
to become the more collaborative style of a boss and specialized peers.
The third stage typically involves a looser, impersonal, collective style,
with the chief executive managing generalists as well as functional
specialists. Under the patterns of the first stage, the core problem for
a small company is survival. The patterns of the roughly defined second
stage show a size and scope requiring such specialized functions as
finance, production, marketing, and engineering.

As the company's size continues to increase, it is likely to evolve
toward third-stage patterns of growth : at this point, different product
lines become separate companies or divisions, while, in multinational firms
the separation may also be on an area basis (e.g., Europe, North America,

EXHIBIT II : Characteristics of company growth

Organizational characteristic	Patterns of the first stage	Patterns of the second stage	Patterns of the third stage
Core problem	Survival	Management of growth	Managerial control and allocation of resources
Central function	Fusion of diverse talents & purposes into a unified company	Fission of general authority into specialized functions	Fusion of inde-pendent units into an inter-dependent union of companies
Control systems	Personal (inside) survival in marketplace (outside)	Cost centers & policy formulation (inside); growth poten-tial (outside)	Profit centers & abstract performance criteria (inside); capital expan-sion potential (outside)
Reward & motivation	Ownership, membership in the family	Salary, opportunities & problems of growth	Salary,perform-ance bonus, stock options, peer prestige
Management style	Individualistic; direct management	Integrating specialists; collaborative management	Integrating generalists; collective management
Organization :			
Structure	Informal	Functional specialists	Division organizations
CEO's primary task	Direct supervision of employees	Managing specialized managers	Managing generalist managers
Levels of management	Two	At least three	At least four

Latin America, Middle East, Far East) as well.

In between the box-like stages of growth shown in *Exhibit II* appear the transition phases which help to prepare an organization for its next stage. To cross the broken lines separating one growth stage from another in *Exhibit II* requires time, new inter-action patterns, and an awkward period of overlap. In effect, the broken vertical lines of *Exhibit II* represent widened time zones of varying and irregular width.

As we have seen, family transitions and company transitions can occur separately and at different times. However, we found that they usually occur together. As a company moves from the problem of survival to one of managing rapid growth, it must develop new control, motivation, and reward systems. It also requires a management style that can integrate specialists and their functions. This development cannot occur without a top management that wants to take the extra step beyond survival thinking. That is where an eager younger generation comes in. He, she, or they are more likely to want to go beyond traditional practices. This pent-up energy seemed to be a major factor in getting beyond company transitions in 27 out of 32 businesses we studied where the company had gone beyond the first growth stage.

Another kind of transition occurs between the second and third growth stages. Company and division units in stage three had general managers in both the head office and the decentralized units who had learned to work with both other general managers and functional specialists. This meant that they had to have or develop a sense of the complex inter-dependence that characterizes most major companies today.

These dual transitions seemed best catalyzed when the old management forces somehow helped to pave the way for the new. The following case is a good example :

When Max Krisch came to America in 1851, he brought an expertise in baking and an old family recipe for bread. Soon after settling, he established a small bakery. The business grew, and Max got help from his three sons as soon as they were old enough to operate the ovens after school and on weekends. When Martin, the oldest, graduated from college in 1890, he joined the business and soon started suggesting

changes which he was convinced were good for the company's growth.
His father refused, and the two men would often end up in disagreement.
Sometimes the arguments were long and bitter.

Eventually, Max's wife abandoned her role of neutrality and intervened
on Martin's behalf. She begged Max to give Martin a chance to implement
his ideas. Reluctantly, Max agreed and let Martin take the first step.

Martin's idea was to sell bread to milk peddlers who would offer it for
sale to their milk customers. It was a new concept at the time, and it
worked. The demand for Krisch's Bread increased sharply.

At this time, too, the second brother, Peter, was ready to join the
company. Martin realized that the company's production capability would
soon be unable to keep up with the increasing sales. He hoped that
Peter could take over, modernize, and expand production, but again Max
reacted strongly. He argued that the baking of Krisch's Bread could not
be done in volume without ruining the quality. Martin and Peter eventually promised their father that if the new methods harmed the bread's
quality they would discontinue them. Over time, Max again agreed to go
along with the change, and Peter worked closely with his father to
increase production while still maintaining quality. Again, too, the
mother was behind the scenes trying to keep peace in the family.

When the third brother, Kurt, joined the firm, Martin gave him the
responsibility for bookkeeping and financial affairs. Fortunately, Kurt
had a good head for figures and did the job well.

As Max became less active in the business, Martin was in charge, with
Peter heading production, while Kurt handled the financial end of the
business. The business flourished. Occasionally, the three sons felt
hampered by Max's continuing strong opinions on some aspects of the
business. At these times, the boys' mother would often referee the disagreements. Partly because she was a sensitive person and a good
listener, she was usually able to help the father and sons arrive at some
mutually satisfactory solution to their problems.

Our studies show that when the familial and organizational transitions
occurred together, as in the Krisch case, they typically took place in an
atmosphere of strain and uncertainty. Quite often, a mother was a

behind-the-scenes influence. More often, though, the transitions were not managed well either inside the family or inside the business. In the Krisch case, Martin guided the company into its second growth stage. But it was his mother's sensitive management of the family relationships that eased that process and eventually permitted the brothers to achieve an outstanding growth record for the firm. Although Max's time-tested ways and methods fell by the wayside as his sons took over, he became a useful adviser once both he and his sons accepted Martin as head of the business though not head of the family. The transfer of power inside the business took place when Max moved into a new working relationship with his sons and a new family relationship with his wife. With Martin managing the business transition and his mother helping to hold the family together, Krisch's Bakeries made both transitions.

The second transition period for Krisch Bakeries is also instructive. After an impressive growth record over a 30-year period, Martin Krisch and his brothers set the wheels in motion for the transition to the third generation. Martin's son, Max Krisch II, was the most obvious successor.

By 1925, the company had established an executive committee of both family and non-family managers who made decisions by consensus. The brothers believed that such an arrangement helped keep the family together and provided valuable inputs from non-family members on the executive committee.

In preparation for the transition, Martin, who was then 55, hired an outsider who suggested that a new role of coordinator be set up for the committee which he took on initially and then passed on to Max II, who had just been brought onto the committee as a member. Soon after, Martin was advised by the outsider that he should get off the committee and out of the company as much as possible.

Thus Martin began to spend more and more of his time away from the company in civic, volunteer, outside boards, and other business activities. At times, he was frustrated and unhappy over not being in the mainstream of the business, but he gained some satisfaction in watching Max II develop into a manager who set new wheels in motion for the company's expansion and diversification into new areas of business. New product lines were developed, the company was broken into divisions and a chain of other businesses was started. All seemed to be going well until the company was hit by an anti-trust suit which restricted and delayed some of its most ambitious plans.

Though the Krisch Bakeries' plans for wider ownership, diversification and expansion were stalled for a number of years, it seemed to again make the dual transition on both the family and the business levels.

The Single Transition

Even though most of the companies we studied changed top management and growth stages together, other companies showed one transitional change at a time. A stagnant company can get that way when the older generation gives way to the younger without any company transition. The Quinn Company was one of these.

In the Quinn family business harmony had been difficult to achieve. The founder, Josiah Quinn, established his industrial supply company in 1911. He began the business with a partner, and it grew steadily. As business improved, the partner took a less active role, and Quinn soon began to resent the partner's equal salary and taking of the profits.

When his wife suddenly died, Quinn impulsively sold the business to his partner and took his five children West. After several years there, he returned home and began a new business, remarried, and had two children by his second wife.

Eventually, Quinn's oldest children joined the firm. They worked well together, and the company prospered. When his second set of children also joined the company, however, jealousy and resentment increased. Conflict began to disrupt operations daily. The problems flowed over into family life, where his wife took the side of "her" children against "his". Finally, Quinn decided to set up a separate company for his wife's children. He founded it under another name, brought customers from the other company, and enjoyed helping it get started.

When World War II broke out, Quinn's most capable son in the first company was drafted. He was sent out West, married, and eventually set up his own company in San Francisco. This left the first company without a really capable successor, though the departed son's brothers and brothers-in-law worked to keep the company going. Again, dissension increased. While the company continued to operate after Quinn died, its performance levels never rose over the next 30 years.

The Quinn Company's transition from first to second generation was influenced by a major split within the family, by the loss of its key young successor, and the divisive role taken by Quinn's second wife. The family conflicts seemed to keep Quinn and his heirs from dealing with company transition problems, since all their energies were spent on inside -the-family problems. The result was a family transition without a simultaneous company transition. Such single transitions were even harder for those inside the family and the company than when the two transitions occurred together. Today the Quinn Company is heading painfully into another transition, its second generation having apparently suffered much, but having learned little from the first one. The older family managers find it hard to let go as the 66-year-old president steps aside uneasily, only to be replaced by a 68-year-old in-law whose sons wait impatiently and sometimes irresponsibly for their turn. Meanwhile, the company suffers.

Another type of single transition occurs when a company moves from one growth stage to the next within one management generation. Such growth occurs rarely, it seems, in the first generation, partly because entrepreneurs tend not to be reorganizers, and growth requires reorganization along with a shift in management styles. We found these company transitions without a family transition to occur more often during the second generation. Whereas first generation entrepreneurs had trouble shifting to high growth strategies and more collaborative styles; the sons were more flexible, possibly because the shift from a second to a third stage growth pattern involves letting go of less personal ties or possibly because they had more help in making the shift. Here is an example of such a transition :

When Wells Thomas died, his hardware supply business passed on to his two sons, Paul and Bing. Paul handled production, and Bing worked in sales. The two brothers built the family firm into a major hardware supply house. Paul became chief executive officer, and he and Bing eventually diversified the business into retail hardware stores, medium equipment companies, an electrical manufacturing company, and several unrelated businesses. Along the way, they brought in six third-generation members of their own and their sister's families. But these younger family members never quite made the grade. Paul, with Bing's approval, fired five of the six and handed the presidency of the corporation over to a man who had been president of one of the acquired companies.

His justification for discharging his sons, nephews, and sons-in-law was the good of the family business, and therefore in the long run the interests of all family members. Nevertheless, he had created a split in the family that never healed. Meanwhile, the new company president admitted that Paul had become like a father to him, and it was apparent that the father-son parallel was very strong for both of them. There was still one nephew in the company, and although he had an important position, it was clear that he had no inside track on succession plans.

Thomas Enterprises moved faster than most companies do in its growth cycle, possibly because Paul Thomas was willing to sacrifice family harmony for what seemed to be business efficiency. Ironically, though, the fired family members each went on to successful careers in outside jobs, most of them pleased in retrospect to get out from under Paul's reign. Whether any one of them could have taken over the sprawling company is hard to judge at this stage. What is clear is that Paul found another "son" who became heir apparent. In an artificial way, the "succession" transition actually came along only slightly behind the company transition.

The three patterns shown in the Krisch, Quinn and Thomas cases suggest some overall advantages of family and business transitions occurring at the same time. The Quinn and Thomas cases also show what happens when family managers, relatives, employees, and outsiders cannot form a power coalition to protect either the family or the business transition, whichever is jeopardized by family conflicts. In the Quinn case, the family managers withdrew in the face of destructive family pressures typified by Quinn's second wife. She not only divided the family but had a strong hand in dividing the company into two separate enterprises, each also competing with the other. In effect, the microcosm of family conflict became replicated in the macrocosm of the two companies. Without capable second generation managers, the original Quinn business never got beyond the first growth stage.

In the Thomas case, the opposite occurred. The relatives retreated "for the good of the family business" as Paul Thomas put it. They helped to destroy the family by abdicating in favor of the dominant older family managers, Paul and Bing Thomas. In the process, some competent family managers were lost. However, the point is not whether Paul and Bing were right or wrong, it is only that they made sure that they were never really tested or questioned by the intimidated relatives. Neither employees nor outsiders found a way to help either.

Under the distorted dominance of either family managers or relatives, not only crippled transitions but regression can set in. Consider one more case :

In the Brindle Company, a father had handed the business over to a son-in-law, did not like the results, and reclaimed the company, even though the son-in-law had done an impressive job of managing the company in terms of growth and expansion. Several years later, with the son-in-law out of the business, but still with a small ownership stake, Mr. Brindle sold the company at a fraction of the price that the same buyer had offered while the son-in-law was running the business. The business' growth had stalled and declined. The company had gone from second generation back to first generation, and the family was shattered to the extent that the two youngest grandchildren born to the son-in-law and his wife had never been permitted to meet their grand-parents.

Managing the Two Transitions

If, as in the Brindle case, a single dominant power force tends to cause lopsided transitions or regression, how can a constructive pattern be built for creating and managing both transitions? The answer seems to lie in a power balancing setup that prevents polarized conflict. Only in the Krisch case, of those described earlier, was this power balancing done effectively. Yet it also happened in at least some of the other companies we studied. It may help to look at some of the assumptions and mechanisms that were used to encourage and manage the two transitions.

The company will live, but I won't

The key assumption for growth was an almost explicit decision by senior managers that "the company will live, but I won't". This assumption, so often avoided by older family managers, is almost built into the forced retirement programs of established companies. But an entrepreneur or even his sons, as they get older, must somehow consciously face and make the decision that, even though they will die, the company will live. Often, that decision occurs not because they are pushed into it, or out of the company by the younger family managers, but because of the intervention of relatives, noncompeting employees, or trusted outsiders, who may find a way of helping to pull the old family manager into a new set of activities.

At some point, a critical network of family managers, employees, relatives, and outsiders must begin to focus upon the duality of both family and business transitions. Such talks should, in our opinion, begin at least 7 or 8 years before the president is supposed to retire. Even though the specific plans may change, the important assumptions behind those plans will not.

Mediation vs.confrontation

Time after time we saw cases in which an entrepreneur's wife played an important role in bridging the growing gap between father and sons, as happened in the Krisch case. It also happened that an entrepreneur's widow would step in as a peacemaker for the younger generation. But when it came to helping make both transitions occur, the wife was more important than the widow. As in the Krisch case, she would help or persuade her husband to look toward the (children's) future instead of his own past. In effect, she provided a relative's outside-the-business perspective. Such outside perspectives turned out to be crucial in transition management, because they helped to heal and avoid the wounds of family conflict.

Transferring Power in the Family Business

In some management circles over recent years, a cult of confrontation has been built. Confrontation is regarded as calling a spade a spade, not in anger, but as a way to move beyond conflict toward problem solving. The approach is reasonable and works in many business situations.

As we pointed out earlier, though, families and their businesses are not necessarily reasonable. The primary emotions tend to be close to the surface, so that conflicts erupt almost without reason. Attempts at confrontation by one party often fail, because they are seen as open or continuing attacks by the other.

When such nerve ends are raw, partly because of family jealousies and partly because of historical sensitivities, a third party or outside perspective can provide mediation and help to soften hardened positions. Relatives, outside directors, friends and key employees all take this role in family companies. But they do something else that is equally important. They can help to begin a practice of open dialogue that cuts not only across age levels, but across the different perspectives of family managers, relatives, employees and outsiders. The dialogues can aid in manpower planning and in managing the transitions. The question is how to develop such dialogues so as to include all the relevant perspectives.

Mechanisms for dialogue

None of the dialogue mechanisms we observed or heard of is a cure-all. But each brought different important combinations of people together. One company management had periodic family meetings for family managers and relatives. Another combined family managers and employees into project teams and task forces. Outside boards of directors executive committees, and non-family stock ownership (to be sold back to the company at the owner's death or departure) brought together family managers, employees, and outsider consultants on major policy problems in a number of companies. One family company had in-company management development programs, but invited outside participants and also gave periodic progress reports to the financial and civic community for comment and review. At one extreme, family managers and key employees did set up a series of confrontation sessions, but only after detailed planning. The ground rules were carefully worked out and over the years both family and company transitions made good progress. At the other extreme, companies would hold various lunches or social events where the open dialogue opportunities were limited but sometimes possible in an informal setting.

Future role building

Unwillingness to face the future stalls both family and business transitions, since in one sense the future can only mean death for an older family manager. But in a more limited sense it implies new but separate lives for the manager and his company. If some of the above assumptions and mechanisms begin to take hold, they will lead to the building of new roles. The older managers learn how to advise and teach rather than to control and dominate. The younger managers learn how to use their new power potential as bosses. Family managers take steps to learn new roles outside the business as directors, office holders and advisers. Employees learn new functional management skills as well as new general management skills. Relatives learn how to take third party roles to provide an outside perspective.

Beginning Near the End

We have been describing one of the most difficult and deep-rooted problems faced by human organizations. Family owned and managed concerns include some of the largest as well as most of the smallest companies in the United States and possibly the world. It seems point-less to talk about separating families from their businesses, at least in our society. Families are in business to stay.

However, as one management generation comes near its end, the life of the business is also jeopardized. Meanwhile, critics, scholars, and managers like to pretend that the "real" business problems lie outside of the family's involvement. This may be true in some cases, but it can also lead to and perpetuate four sets of tunnel vision. Family managers, relatives, employees, and outsiders adopt separate perspectives and separate paths.

Our studies, however, suggest that the healthiest transitions are those old-versus-young struggles in which both the family managers and the business change patterns. For this to happen, "the old man" must face the decision of helping the company live even though he must die. If he can do this, the management of transitions can begin. In effect, a successful family transition can mean a new beginning for the company.

Writers like to think that their work and words will have a lasting impact upon the reader. However, the history of the topic we are discussing provides little cause for such optimism. In fact, a truly lasting solution may come only from experience such as that described by an entrepreneur, who said :

"I left my own father's company and swore I'd never subject my own children to what I had to face. Now my son is getting good experience in another company in our industry before coming in to take over this one. Within five years of the day he walks in that door, I walk out. And everyone knows it - even me."

(1) *Harry Levinson, 'Conflicts that Plague the Family Business', HBR March-April 1971, p.90*

(2) *Adolph A.Berle & Gardner C.Means,'The Modern Corporation & Private Property' (New York:Harcourt,Brace & World,1968) and John Kenneth Galbraith,'The New Industrial State' (Boston:Houghton Mifflin, 1971)*

(3) *Robert Sheehan, 'Proprietors in the World of Big Business', Fortune, June 1967, p.178*

(4) *Philip H.Burch, Jr., 'The Managerial Revolution Reassessed' (Lexington, Mass. : D.C.Heath, 1972)*

(5) *George Strauss, 'Adolescence in Organization Growth : Problems, Pains, Possibilities', Organizational Dynamics, Spring 1974,p.3; Robert B.Buchele,'Business Policy in Growing Firms' (San Fran. Chandler Publ.Co.1965); Theodore Cohn & Roy A.Lindberg, Survival & Growth:Management Strategies for the Small Firm (New York:AMACOM, 1972); Lawrence L.Steinmetz,'Critical Stages of Small Business Growth', Business Horizons, Feb.1969,p.29; Bruce L.Scott, 'Stages of Corporate Development,Part 1', Harvard Bus. School Note 9-371-294, BP 798*

(6) *Larry E.Greiner, 'Evolution & Revolution as Organizations Grow', HBR July-August 1972, p.37*

PART IV

POLICY
PERSPECTIVES

CHAPTER 7 : PUBLIC POLICY

Introduction

The fourth and last part of this book provides a reprise of its main theme : a perspective view of the small business field. The first of its two chapters is concerned with a "policy perspective", and each of the three articles looks at policy from a different point of view.

The first article by Beesley and Wilson is an historical review of public policy towards small business in Britain since 1946, although it concentrates on the post-Bolton period. It outlines and comments upon the legislation and assistance given by official and semi-official organisations, and attempts to predict the likely future direction of public policy. One interesting observation is that, despite persistent denials that public policy towards small business seeks to discriminate positively in its favour, successive Governments have progressively evolved a de facto policy of direct preferential assistance to small business. This policy appears to stop short of the more overt attitude to small business prevailing in the United States, although the authors point out that further direct preferential treatment of small business, including the possibility of a representative body for small business, cannot be ruled out. Originally published in Italy in 1978, the article has been specially updated for this book.

The second article by Storey is devoted to regional policies and pursues a theme introduced by Beesley and Wilson, where the trend towards a more preferential small business policy on the part of central government is related to increasing official concern with the rising level of unemployment. The link between job creation and the encouragement of small business is given a regional dimension by Storey. He discusses the implications of encouraging small business growth as a method of dealing with unemployment and he suggests ways in which policies can be implemented if regions are to get their fair share of small business growth.

While Storey warns that without a small business dimension to regional policies, inequalities will persist, he provides several reasons why the regions of high unemployment in Britain suffer from a low birth rate of new ventures. In so doing, he exposes some of the limitations of public policy towards small business, particularly where local variations in the necessary conditions for the birth of new enterprise are unfavourably disposed to the emergence of entrepreneurs.

The last article in this chapter by Wilson and Gorb deals with one aspect of the interface between the large and small firm : the trading relationship between the small supplier and its large customer. It examines the characteristics which enhance and inhibit this relationship and points to the considerable influence held by large corporations over their small suppliers. The dependence of the latter on the large company has important implications for public and private sector policy to encourage the growth of small firms. For instance, buyer inertia tends to favour existing suppliers to the disadvantage of untried, new suppliers and the article points to the considerable benefits of orientating the procurement activities of large organisations in both the public and private sectors to the encouragement of small business.

1. GOVERNMENT AID TO SMALL FIRMS IN BRITAIN

M.E.Beesley and P.E.B.Wilson

Published with the permission of the Acton Society Trust

1. Introduction

The Government first recognised that small firms might face problems and have needs different from those of large firms in the 1960s. The appointment of the Bolton Committee in 1969 to investigate the problems of small firms and to make recommendations signalled the beginnings of an overt small business policy by Government. The publication of its report in November 1971 promoted an unprecedented interest in the small business sector, partly through its examination of hypotheses about the disadvantages widely thought to be suffered by small firms and partly through its recommendations for remedial action by Government(1). Most of the government measures covered by this article then began to emerge; and the genesis of public policy towards small business gained momentum.

The growth of concern about small business is shown by statements made by government spokesmen. Diagram 1 measures Parliamentary interest in terms of entries to Hansard from 1964 when small business first began to be debated seriously. It shows the beginnings of Parliamentary interest in the mid-1960s, the perceptible impact of the Bolton Report of 1971 and the subsequent rapid increase in the number of debates, questions and answers in Parliament, all reflecting a deepening interest in the contribution of small firms to economic growth and employment creation and a concern with the impact of government policies on the health of the sector.

Before the Bolton Report, assistance to small business was ad hoc, emerging as a by-product of policies towards industrial efficiency, training, technology, organisation or location. The prevailing philosophy at the time of the Bolton Report was one of bigness, exemplified by an industrial policy of rationalisation and reorganisation into larger units capable of exploiting supposed economies of scale. For instance, the Industrial Reorganisation Corporation (IRC), established in 1966, was charged with the reorganisation and development of firms in strategic

DIAGRAM 1 : INDEX OF PARLIAMENTARY INTEREST IN SMALL BUSINESS 1964-1980

Number of entries in Hansard, consisting of debates
and written and oral questions and answers

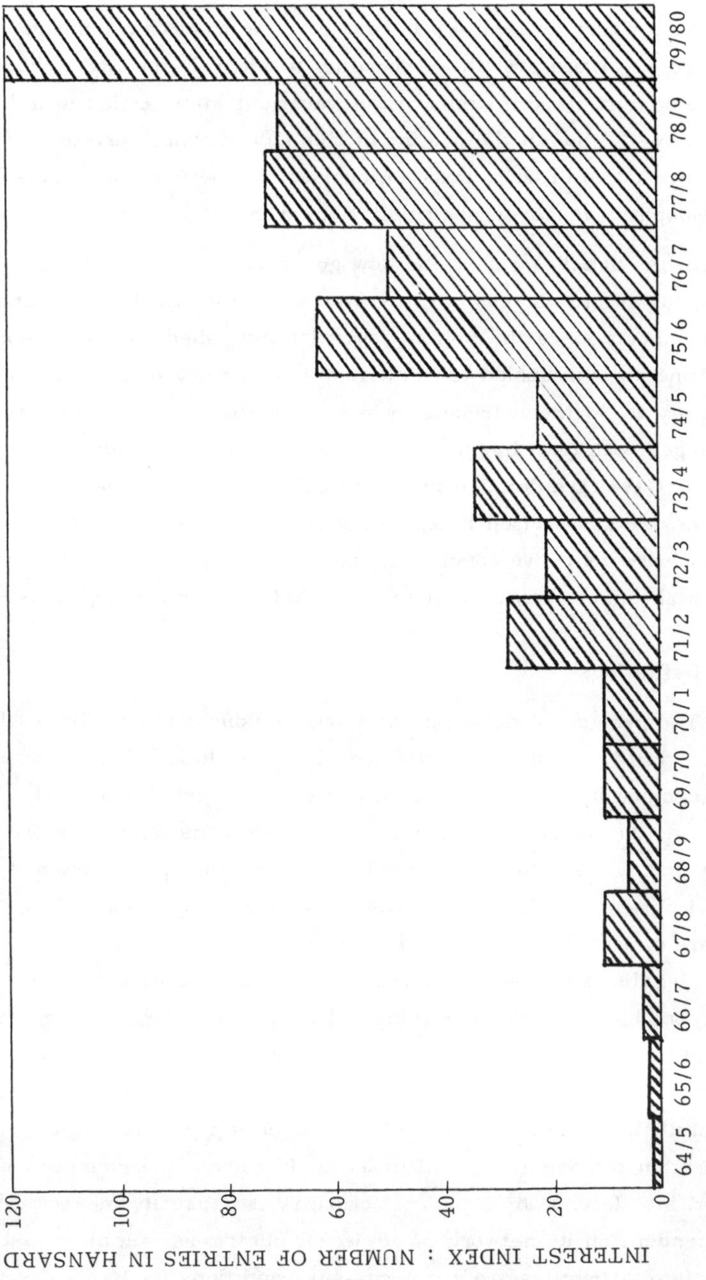

INTEREST INDEX : NUMBER OF ENTRIES IN HANSARD

PARLIAMENTARY SESSION

SOURCE : Hansard, Volumes 719-992

industries in order to ensure that Britain competed effectively in world markets where large size was considered a necessary minimum condition for survival and growth. According to Allen(2) the IRC embodied the development of more systematic government intervention in industrial activity; although the origins of this new approach are to be found in the promotion of large-scale enterprise, in them also lies the simultaneous development of government policy towards small business.

In the article we describe how government policy and assistance towards small business have evolved since the late 1940s; but particularly since the Bolton Committee published its findings in 1971. We confine our discussion to Britain, although much of the assistance applies equally to Northern Ireland, which, in addition, has its own agencies charged with local business development. The assistance measures until August 1981 are detailed in chronological order in Appendices A, B and C and are summarised in Appendix D. In the light of our findings, we draw some tentative conclusions about government policy and assistance to small business and point to some likely future developments.

2. Definitions

The problem of definition of a small business is usually resolved by referring to the Bolton Committee which concluded that a "small firm" is recognised by three broad qualitative characteristics(3). First, a small firm tends to have a relatively small share of its relevant market, implying that it has little or no power to affect either price, quantity or its environment. It is possible, however, for a small firm to have a large share of a small yet specialised market niche. Second, a small firm has no formalised management structure; rather the owner-manager is responsible for decision-making. The extent of formalisation will vary among firms, however, since as the firm grows, personal owner-management is replaced partially or wholly by professional management. Third, a small firm is independent of the control of a parent company, implying a certain freedom to make decisions. But even if management is free from interference by a parent company, it is usually inextricably dependent on its network of advisers, customers, suppliers and bankers. So these attributes are not necessary conditions for being deemed "small business", although most commentators assume they are.

In practice, only close observation will reveal whether the small business exhibits these characteristics. In fact, the behaviour and role of the owner-manager or entrepreneur are the key to a working definition. In most small firms, the behaviour of the owner-manager and the behaviour of the firm are synonomous. But in order to determine changes in the small firm population over time, numerical definitions are also necessary. These are given in Appendix G. Generally, small firms in manufacturing are defined as those with fewer than 200 employees and in other sectors, a variety of definitions applies.

3. Government Policy towards Small Business

In seeking to establish whether successive British governments have developed explicit policies towards small business and what the nature of these policies is, we look to three main indicators of public policy. These are :

    a) specific small business legislation;

    b) statements made by government spokesmen; and

    c) other general legislation and measures to assist small business.

Britain has no specific small business legislation, such as is to be found in the legislation of other countries, particularly that of the United States(4). For instance, the Small Business Act of 1953 which established the Small Business Administration was the culmination of a long history of legislation sympathetic to the independent business, starting with the Sherman Anti-trust Act of 1890(5).

Without the benefit of such obvious small business legislation, evidence must be sought elsewhere. The Bolton Committee, established by a Labour Government sympathetic to the needs of small business, is an appropriate starting point. When the Committee published its report of 1971, the Conservative Government welcomed its findings and recommendations and the Secretary of State for Trade and Industry at the time commented that he was well aware of the place of small firms in the economy and that he would ensure that "their interests be taken into account in the formulation of policies"(6). In June 1972, the Under-Secretary of State with responsibility for small firms(7), a new position recommended by the Bolton Committee, stated that he was "determined that small firms should be allowed to flourish and thrive in the freest possible environment, unhampered by unnecessary restrictions and unintentional discrimination"(8).

The Conservative Government acted on many of the Report's recommendations, although it was firmly against discriminatory policies in favour of small firms. It intended, rather, to remove past discrimination and to prevent discrimination being built into new policies, by considering measures necessary for the encouragement of individual enterprise and initiative(9).

These intentions were largely in sympathy with the Bolton Committee's conclusions that positive discrimination by Government in favour of the small business was unjustified and that the sector could perform its self-regenerative function unaided. It did find that Government had imposed a number of unintentional disabilities on the small business which amounted to discrimination(10). We discern a commitment to these sentiments by the Conservative Government, with policies oriented to two objectives : first, providing an environment in which the small firm could thrive, free from interference of any kind; and second, removing the discriminatory impact of existing legislation. Although evidence of the former is not presented here, and indeed would be hard to gather, there is evidence of the removal of discrimination and the exemption of small firms from certain statutory obligations which, it was alleged, bore more heavily on them than on larger firms. We point to this evidence in the following section.

The Labour Government of 1974 adopted the same objectives. The accent was to be on the avoidance and elimination of unintentional discrimination against small firms and the creation of a climate favourable to their growth, including protection from the alleged anti-competitive market practices of the giant companies(11). In June 1974 the Minister of State for the Department of Industry (DOI) pointed to the Labour Government's "unambiguous" commitment to an active small business sector, which was "important in regional terms as a seedbed of regional growth and a source of diversification and balance in the industrial structure".(12)

The Labour Government's attitude to small firms soon acquired a flavour of more direct support. The Secretary of State for Industry in 1975 signalled a "more vigorous" policy for small firms because of their local markets, their labour intensiveness and the close relationship between the owner-manager and the workforce. Indeed, he claimed to be "strongly sympathetic" to small firms and "strongly in favour" of their development(13).

This theme was further developed with the appointment in September 1977 of Lord Lever, a senior Minister in the Labour Government, and Robert Cryer, the Under-Secretary of State in the Department of Industry with responsibility for small firms, to make a special study of their problems and to recommend and initiate remedial action(14). Increased official concern for small business was clear and implied that existing policies were not adequate. As a result of Lord Lever's study, budgetary measures were announced in October 1977 and in April 1978 as "part of a developing policy in which Government was going to show a continuous responsiveness to the needs of small firms".(15)

In January 1977 the Government appointed the Wilson Committee to inquire into the role of the financial institutions and the provision of funds for industry and trade, and the Committee's study of the financing of small firms was published in March 1979(16). Some of the recommendations of the Committee were subsequently accepted, particularly those involving no apparent change in government policy. Of the recommendations which could be classified as discriminating in favour of small business, the proposals for Small Firm Investment Companies, an English Development Agency and a publicly underwritten loan guarantee scheme were the most extreme, signalling the Government's willingness to depart even further from its adherence to a non-discriminatory small business policy. In the event, the loan guarantee sheme and certain investment incentives were introduced, though in a more muted form than that proposed by the Committee; but no Agency has yet been sanctioned.

The Conservative Government of 1979 pursued the trend towards greater intervention in the affairs of small business started by the previous Labour Government, David Mitchell, Under-Secretary of State responsible for small firms, stated in July 1980 :

"There is a recognition on both sides of the House of the importance of small businesses as the seedcorn from which wealth creation and many jobs in the future will come. We have far too few such businesses. We need many more. The balance between the incentives to start a business, the hurdles which face those who start and the burdens they have to carry has been tipped so far that the logical person has not felt it worthwhile to start a business.

The Government are engaged in a threefold task. The first is to identify the burdens and to pull them down, to identify the hurdles and take them away, so that it is easier for people to start. Secondly, we have to increase incentives for them to do so. Thirdly, we have to look at the problems of financing those who have started, or are seeking to start, in terms of the money inside the business as well as incentive in terms of what one can take out in reward for success".(17)

We recognise in this statement the familiar references to the removal of discrimination. But for the first time a government spokesman also spoke of a need to encourage the birth of small firms (as opposed to their survival and growth) and to do so directly. Not only were incentives mentioned as an element of policy, but the allusion to the problems of financing new and small firms presaged further direct preferential assistance by Government. Although the Bolton Committee had expressed concern about the low birthrate of new firms, successive Governments had introduced few measures specifically oriented to new firms. Nevertheless there has been a consistent increase in the numbers of new businesses since 1974 and a clear upward trend in these numbers since the mid-1960s, illustrated in Diagram 2. Policy has changed simultaneously with this increase.

In spite of this revealed change of direction over the last few years, government spokesmen still do not espouse a policy of direct preferential assistance. For instance, in March 1981 the Under-Secretary of State for small firms reiterated the Government's policy of removing obstacles and burdens and changing the overall climate in which the small business operated(18). There was no allusion to direct preferential assistance.

DIAGRAM 2 : NEW FIRM FORMATION 1960-1979

New registrations of business names and companies

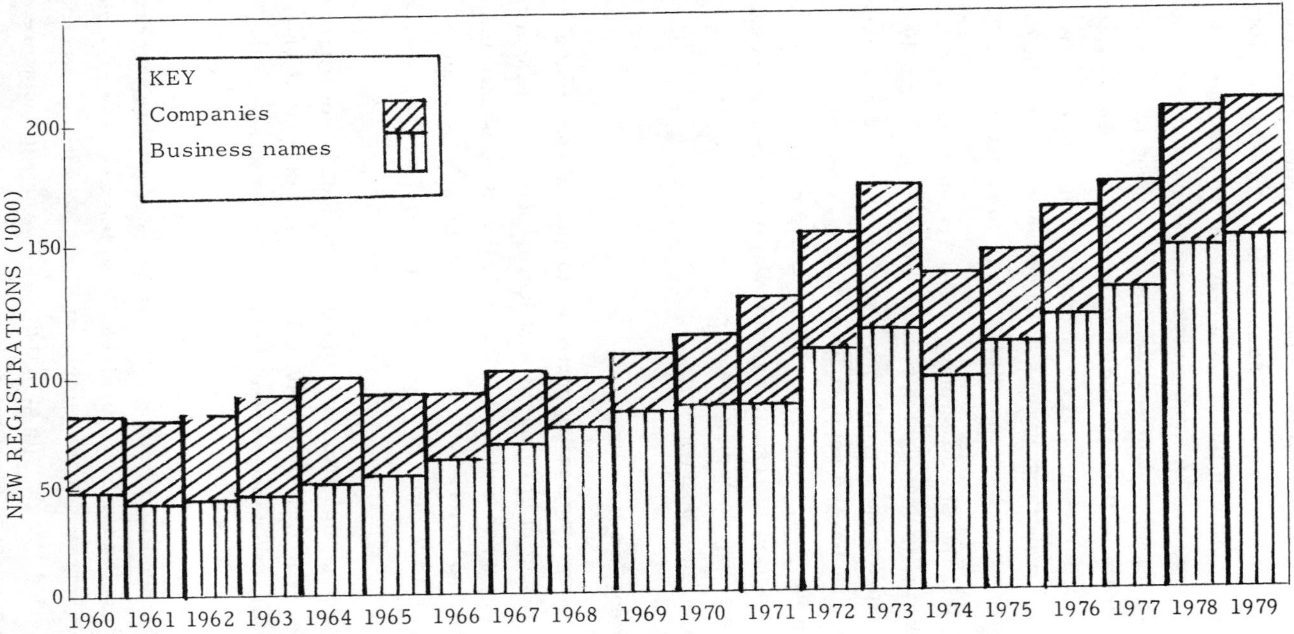
KEY
Companies
Business names
NEW REGISTRATIONS ('000)
200
150
100
50
0
1960 1961 1962 1963 1964 1965 1966 1967 1968 1969 1970 1971 1972 1973 1974 1975 1976 1977 1978 1979
YEAR

SOURCES : *Trade & Industry (now British Business) and Companies (Department of Trade)*

Yet the Business Opportunities Programme was launched by the Government in May 1981, following the measures introduced in the 1981 Finance Act, another example of direct encouragement of small business. The Programme's emphasis on raising national awareness of the opportunities and rewards of small business adds a new dimension to government policy : in order to stimulate the birth of more new ventures, the Government is pursuing an aggressive marketing campaign throughout the country. This Programme is described in more detail below, as are the other measures which constitute a de facto preferential policy.

In July 1981 the Chief Secretary to the Treasury outlined four elements of industrial policy, namely the reduction of inflation, "supply side" policies to improve market efficiency, privatisation and market-orientation of the public sector and support for industry in selected areas. It was intended to stimulate the economy by removing constraints to the efficient operation of market forces and by improving incentives to enterprise and rewards for effort, including the introduction of measures to stimulate the growth of small business(19).

4. Government Aid

In this section, we confine ourselves to general comments about the nature and extent of government assistance; individual measures are detailed in the appendices. With the exclusion of assistance that has either a marginal or no effective bearing on small firms at all, it is possible to identify three groups of measures and within these, a number of sub-groups.

These three groups also mark the three periods of government activity noted below. The first from 1946 to 1960 covers the period when there was no specific assistance to small business. The second period up to 1970 was characterised by government measures to remove discrimination. The third period covers the measures introduced since the publication of the Bolton Report, including most instances of positive discrimination. This period can be further sub-divided into two five year periods, and a perceptible increase in the number of direct measures is recorded in the latter period. Each type of activity, with varying incidence, has been continuous, once commenced.

Indirect Assistance

The first group consists of those measures that indirectly or inadvertently have a significant effect on small business, despite their intended
universal application. These are listed in Appendix A. They can be
further grouped into regional or locational assistance, such as the
Scottish and Welsh Development Agencies which have their own small
business units; assistance with production efficiency, training and
advice, such as the Industrial Training Boards; technological assistance
as with the National Research Development Corporation; and assistance
consistent with economic policy, as with industry aid under the Industry
Act of 1972. Until 1976 there was no marked trend in indirect assistance
although in the last five years there has been a perceptible increase over
the earlier period, which as we illustrate in the appendices has been
characteristic of all government assistance to small business.

Most indirect assistance falls into the regional assistance sub-group
and the bulk of this has been introduced since 1970. A substantial amount
of indirect assistance has been directed to small firms (Appendix A, A5)
and local authorities have also begun to orientate their employment
policies increasingly towards small business (Appendix A, A6) which
effectively gives small business policy a greater regional and local
dimension(20). Indeed pressures brought to bear by local government
organisations on central Government to devolve additional small business
powers down to the local level are increasing; many local authorities are
considering directly investing in small businesses through local enterprise
trusts set up for this purpose(21).

The introduction of training and advisory assistance, although directed at industry as a whole, can have a considerable impact on small
business. This has been recognised by successive Governments,
culminating in a more direct approach in recent years, which we discuss
below. The recognition that small firms are at a particular disadvantage
in the market for training and advice is based on the limitations of the
owner-manager with regard to personnel training expertise. Although
such expertise is available externally in appropriate amounts, for most
very small firms it would still be uneconomical to employ it. Despite the
availability of industrial training and advice from the public sector at

subsidised rates, small firms have not been successfully absorbed into training schemes.

The Removal of Discrimination

The second group has been imposed to remove discrimination against small firms, largely by exempting them from various statutory obligations. It is based on the proposition that management resources in the owner-managed small firm are lumpy : they consist essentially of one person. To add to them involves a disproportionately large increment, not easily achieved. The small firm, in this view, is placed at a considerable disadvantage relative to larger firms with respect to any given commitment requiring managerial attention. Large companies need only make relatively small adjustments in resources to deal with the duties and obligations imposed on industry and commerce by the Government.

Within this group are three distinct sub-groups. Regional exemptions cover industrial and commercial construction allowances to small firms; administrative exemptions such as disclosure exemptions under the Companies Act and the revision of statistical surveys of small firms; and exemption under economic and social policy, particularly the recognition that the smallest firms should not be subject to dismissal procedures under the Employment Act.

Direct Preferential Assistance

The third group of measures discriminates specifically or positively in favour of small business by providing resources and inducements. The majority of measures falls into this category, most being introduced after 1971 with a clear upward trend in the last five years. As Appendix C illustrates, direct assistance since the Conservative Government came to power in 1979 has accelerated further, despite the claim that such positive discrimination was never to be incorporated into government policy.

It is possible to distinguish three broad types of assistance within this group. The first type is designed to further the general aims of economic and social policy and consists of measures to promote exports, particularly among small first-time exporters, rural development, regional assistance and technological change. The second type is designed to favour small firms per se and consists of non-financial aid such as training and advisory services and the Small Firms Division of the Department of Industry, charged with overall responsibility for the sector. The third type consists of financial measures such as fiscal incentives to establish new ventures, increasing the rewards due to entrepreneurial activity, improving the supply of venture capital to new firms and providing a loan guarantee scheme for loans made by the private sector banks. We observe two main features relating to these financial measures. The first is the marked increase in direct financial measures relative to other direct measures over the last few years; and the second, the focus on new ventures relative to established small firms.

5. Summary and Comment : Future Developments in Public Policy

The large number of measures described in the appendices confirms that since 1946 there has been continuing government interest in small business. But until the 1960s assistance tended to be ad hoc, incidental and indirect. Thereafter, increasing official concern with small business was reflected in the introduction of direct preferential treatment - more than 75% of government measures are either direct or related to the removal of discrimination(22). Over two-thirds of all measures have been introduced since 1970 and over one-third since 1975.

The trend to greater direct assistance is likely to continue unabated. In the period 1946-70, 53% of all measures introduced were direct, while in the period 1971-1981 this proportion was 64%, rising to 72% in the five year period up to 1981. Successive Governments have implemented a de facto policy increasingly favourable to small business and the introduction of further measures that actively discriminate in its favour is possible. As an indication of future developments, the following policy-related issues and assistance are likely to concern small business in the medium-term. These fall into the categories:economic and social policy, regional assistance, government procurement, industrial deconcentration and legislative consolidation.

Economic and Social Policy

Based on the trends in small business policy observed above as well as on issues, currently neglected, which are beginning to attract attention, we can identify at least three areas of likely future activity. The first is further support for the introduction of advanced technology in small firms and the encouragement of advanced technology output by small firms, either through indirect assistance by the British Technology Group or through direct financial assistance and incentives. The new role for the National Enterprise Board as a catalyst in the promotion of advanced technology and small firms is likely to be further strengthened.

The second area is the promotion of co-operative enterprise through the Co-operative Development Agency and the Industrial Common Owner-ship Movement. Although the present Conservative Government is not disposed to encouraging co-operatives through preferential support, the opposition Labour Party and Labour-controlled local authorities have expressed their strong support for co-operatives. Similarly there is likely to be increased support for community business ventures.

The third area is the encouragement of minority-owned enterprise. While there is currently no specific assistance in this area, the attention of central and local government is increasingly being drawn to minority businesses(23). The rioting and general unrest experienced in 1981 have emphasized the special circumstances prevailing in areas occupied by minority groups, particularly those of West Indian origin. The deprivation and disadvantages allegedly suffered by small businesses owned by these minorities are likely to attract remedial assistance, principally from local authorities.

Regional Assistance

The further orientation of regional investment incentives and other assistance away from large to small firms is the likely consequence of the continued structural decline of some of Britain's older industries. Also the emphasis on the employment creation impact of small, rather than large, firms will tend to strengthen the flow of assistance to the former in the assisted areas and in nominated inner city areas(24). The intro-duction of Enterprise Zones in the 1980 Finance Act provides a further channel for more direct assistance. The Enterprise Zones are designed to attract industry into pockets of inner city need by offering a range of financial and other inducements, including greater flexibility in terms of planning regulations. Measures to assist specifically small firms could at a later stage be introduced alongside existing Enterprise Zone incentives.

As we have pointed out earlier, there has been an increasing flow of resources to small business at the local level through local authorities and intermediary agencies in which both central and local government are indirectly involved. The Association of Metropolitan Authorities for instance, has already called for greater powers at the local authority level to intervene directly in the establishment and growth of small firms. In London the founding of a Greater London Enterprise Board charged specifically with the development of new and small businesses, is evidence of the continuing trend to greater local intervention in the affairs of small business.

Government Procurement

Central and local government, the nationalised industries and quasi-government bodies provide a large untapped resource for exploitation by small firms in the form of procurement contracts. The Bolton Committee noted that certain government departments were unintentionally favouring large firms when placing procurement contracts(25), and recommended that purchasing policies be investigated by the Small Firms Division with a view to increasing the flow of products and services provided by small firms to the Government. A possible extension of a passive interest in the share of government contracts going to small firms is the system adopted in the United States whereby a minimum proportion of these contracts is guaranteed for small firms.

Policy has not proceeded this far. However, the present Government has stated that the flow of information to small firms about procurement contracts should be improved(26). To this end, the Small Firms Information Centres have produced a booklet on government procurement, while senior Ministers in all government departments have been questioned about their respective procurement activities(27).

Industrial Deconcentration

A further source of possible developments in policy is a coincidence of arguments in favour of small-scale organisation, growing in popular appeal, and the specific need of large firms to shed labour in response to economic recession, to make profit centres more responsive to the business and social environment and to accentuate entrepreneurial initiative. The activities of such nationalised industries as the British Steel Corporation in assisting small firms are only one step removed from hiving off certain production tasks into subcontract work, where executives and/or skilled workers might take severance or redundancy pay and start up a new enterprise supplying their former employers with the necessary administrative, managerial and other assistance provided by the parent company. Large private companies could, it is argued, be persuaded to act in a similar fashion where there were clear economic and social benefits, or where redundancies were inevitable at management and artisan levels. In these cases, tax incentives or holidays could be offered if benefits were clearly visible.

Consolidating Legislation & Small Business Representation

Although the introduction of a wide range of additional measures to assist small business cannot be discounted as part of the likely future direction of government policy, the current diversity and complexity of assistance described in this article are reaching a point where consolidating legislation for small firms is indicated. The plethora of assistance also raises the question of a national agency charged with representing small business at all levels of the public and private sectors(28). The Small Firms Division, based as it is in the Department of Industry, cannot easily perform this role. But no commitment by Government to a new institution has yet appeared.

(1) *Report of the Committee of Inquiry on Small Firms, Cmnd.4811 (HMSO 1971)*

(2) *G.C.Allen : The Structure of Industry in Britain, p.162 (Longman, 1970)*

(3) Op.cit. Chapter 1, pp.1-4

(4) For instance, see Stuart W.Bruchey(ed.):Small Business in American Life (Columbia U.P., 1980)

(5) Ibid. pp.21-23

(6) John Davies : Hansard, 3rd November 1971, Column 188, Vol.825

(7) See Appendix C, C15

(8) Anthony Grant : Hansard, 12th June 1972, Column 1061, Vol.838

(9) Trade & Industry, 13th July 1972, Volume 8, Number 2

(10) Op.cit. pp.87-91

(11) John Fraser, Minister of State for Prices & Consumer Protection, Trade & Industry, 28th October 1977, Volume 29, Number 4

(12) Eric Heffer : Trade & Industry, 27th June 1974, Volume 15, No.13

(13) Tony Benn : Trade & Industry, 28th February 1975, Vol.18, No.9

(14) Trade & Industry, 10th November 1978, Volume 33, Number 6

(15) Harold Lever : Trade & Industry, 21st April 1978, Vol.31, No.3

(16) The Financing of Small Firms. Interim report of the Committee to review the functioning of financial institutions. Cmnd.7503 (HMSO 1979)

(17) Hansard, 30th July 1980, Column 1553, Volume 989

(18) John McGregor : British Business (was Trade & Industry), 13th March 1981, Volume 4, Number 11

(19) Leon Brittan : British Business, 24th July 1981, Vol.5, No.13

(20) Greater detail is contained in : P.Wilson, Local authority assistance to small business (Conference paper, U.K.Small Business Management Teachers Association, Manchester September 1980)

(21) S.Windass(ed.) : Local Initiatives in Great Britain (Foundation for Alternatives, 1981)

(22) A notable feature of government assistance is the orientation to manufacturing. Only one third of assistance is oriented to non-manufacturing, reflecting the concern with the declining share of manufacturing in the economy.

(23) House of Commons, Home Affairs Committee. Racial Disadvantage : West Indians in Business in Britain (HMSO, 1980)

(24) D.J.Storey : Small firms & the regional problem, The Banker, Nov. 1980, Volume 130, Number 657

(25) *Op.cit. p.80. Public sector buying power amounted to £22,000 million in 1980 (The Times, 12th January 1981)*

(26) *Hansard, 27th March 1979, Column 128, Volume 965*

(27) *Hansard, 13th November 1979, Column 700, Volume 973*

(28) *G.Bannock : The Economics of Small Firms, p.123 (Basil Blackwell, 1981)*

APPENDIX A : INDIRECT ASSISTANCE

A1 National Research Development Corporation

The National Research Development Corporation (NRDC) was established under the Development of Inventions Act of 1948, in order to encourage
more effective exploitation of inventive ideas and through the licensing of
patents and know-how, to invest in the R & D activities of British industry.
The Secretary of State for Industry has general responsibility for the
NRDC, and he appoints the Chairman, Managing Director and twelve
board members.

Its function is to provide finance for industry specifically oriented to
the development and exploitation of inventions and technological innovation.
The NRDC assists many small firms established by inventors and innovators.
For instance, by 31st March 1977, some £7.8 million had been invested in
131 small and medium firms (defined as those with annual turnovers below
£5 million) representing respectively 38% of total financial assistance and
75% of all firms assisted. In addition, £1 million was provided to 19 small
and medium firms for licensing projects. Of the total number of small and
medium firms in the NRDC's portfolio, 45% received less than £20,000 each,
40% received between £20,000 and £100,000 each, and the remaining 15%
received over £100,000 each.

Financial support for innovation normally involves a joint venture with
the company, which retains the ownership of the invention and the
responsibility for its development and subsequent exploitation. The NRDC
may contribute a proportion of the development expenditure in exchange
for a levy on the sales of the resulting product or some alternative return
on its investment. Where a new company is established to develop and
exploit an invention or new technology, the NRDC may take an equity
stake as well as provide loans on a more conventional basis.

In September 1980 a new fund of £2 million was set up to increase
investment in small firms and new ventures through a range of financial
packages, while the NRDC and the National Enterprise Board (see below)
are now to merge into the British Technology Group with a more
aggressive approach to small innovative, high technology firms.

A2 British Productivity Council

The British Productivity Council (BPC) was established in 1952 as an independent body with government backing, to promote higher productivity in industry. At a national level this was through publications and films, and at a local level through 32 Local Productivity Associations, which organised courses and seminars on productivity. Direct government support was phased out in March 1973, although the DOI still sponsors the BPC. But many local associations have continued their work in industry through self-financing and voluntary work. Their activities are co-ordinated by the British Council of Productivity Associations.

A3 Industrial Training Boards

The Industrial Training Act of 1964 authorised the creation of 23 Industrial Training Boards (ITBs) under the Training Services Division (TSD) of the Manpower Services Commission (MSC), and the Employment & Training Act of 1973 extended their scope. Although industrial training is available irrespective of the size of the firm, certain schemes in industries with large numbers of small firms are designed to cope with their special training problems. Levies are imposed on firms for the services of the ITBs, but small firms were exempted from payment in certain circumstances by the Employment & Training Act of 1973 (Schedule 2, Part 1, para.10). The MSC pays the administration expenses of the ITBs and provides them with grants for training activities.

Examples of services to small firms are to be found in the Furniture and Timber ITB and Engineering ITB. The former provides training mainly in small manufacturing firms. Over two-thirds of the participants employ fewer than 100 persons, while over 40% employ fewer than 50 persons. The latter has group training schemes for small firms covering 750,000 employees. In 1965, 76 schemes were in operation covering 850 firms, while by 1972, 171 schemes were in operation covering 4,500 firms.

A4 Highlands and Islands Development Board

The Highlands and Islands Development (Scotland) Acts of 1965 and 1968 established the Highlands and Islands Development Board (HIDB) and gave it extensive powers to develop the economy of the Highlands and

Islands of Scotland. These powers extend to agriculture, fishing, industry, transport and tourism, and the HIDB provides finance, builds factories, establishes new ventures, and provides a wide range of advisory services. Although there is no limit to the size of firms eligible for assistance, the scale of economic activity in the region means that much work is done with small firms, including the craft industries and co-operatives.

The main forms of assistance are loans repayable over a five to ten year period, and grants which are only repayable in the event of failure. In 1977 the HIDB approved assistance of £8.8 million for 726 projects, which was supplemented by £12.5 million from private sources. Between 1965 and 1977, grant, loan and equity assistance of £40.1 million was approved for 4,608 projects, with private contributions of £55 million, creating or retaining an estimated 13,291 jobs.

Towards the end of 1980 the HIDB linked up with the Bank of Scotland and the Industrial & Commercial Finance Corporation (ICFC) to form Highland Venture Capital (HVC) using proven techniques from the U.S.A. to identify and assess individuals with new business ideas. HVC commissioned Venture Founders Corporation of Boston (U.S.A.) to seek out and evaluate entrepreneurs who could start their ventures in Scotland's Highlands. HVC were to provide individual injections of capital from £25,000 to £300,000.

A5 Industry Assistance

While selective financial assistance under Sections 7 and 8 of the Industry Act of 1972 is available regardless of the size of the firm, in 1979 small firms with fewer than 200 employees accounted for more than 50% of the offers of assistance under Section 7. State assistance for advanced technology projects was introduced in the 1965 Science and Technology Act.

Section 7 of the Industry Act is designed to provide financial support only in the assisted areas(1) for projects meeting criteria which include viability, employment creation and strengthening the regional economy. Between March 1974 and December 1978, 1923 small firms (with fewer than 200 employees) were provided with assistance creating 55,900 jobs at a cost of £8,753 per job, while 1,442 larger firms (more than 200 employees) were assisted, creating 154,500 jobs at a cost of £18,771 per job.

Section 8 assistance is available throughout Britain for projects concerned with, amongst others, launching new products, improvements in performance or an increase in scale of operation. Besides the financial support available from the Energy Conservation Scheme and the Micro-processor Application Scheme, since 1972 there have been 15 sectoral industry schemes covering a large number of small firms. The clothing industry is an example. Under the assistance package introduced in October 1975 (projects had to be completed by December 1978) rational-isation and restructuring were encouraged and £15 million was made available for grants of up to 25% of the cost of improvements. The minimum size for investment projects was £10,000. Financial assistance was also available for consultancy in firms employing up to 300 persons.

A6 Local Authority Assistance

The decentralisation of government assistance to the local authority level has its origins in the Bolton Report. Following the recommendations of the Report, the Government urged local authorities in 1972 to take into account the problems of small firms and to be fully aware of their role in the local and national community. Small firms are now eligible for local authority assistance under Section 137 of the Local Government Act of 1972, the Inner Urban Areas Act of 1978 (see below) and several other local Acts and ordinances. Many local authorities also employ Industrial Development Officers to encourage the retention and expansion of industrial activity in their respective boroughs, with the emphasis on the activities of small firms.

Small business benefits substantially from the Government's Urban Programme to assist inner city areas where "special social need exists". Assistance measures were proposed in the white paper entitled 'Policy for the Inner Cities'(2). The Inner Urban Areas Act of 1978 empowers local authorities, in partnership with the Department of the Environment, to make loans and grants for improvement schemes in areas designated "industrial improvement areas" where additional employment is created. In specified cases, grants can be made for rent payments and for building improvements up to 50% of the cost of the works, or an amount of £1,000 per additional job created, whichever is the lesser. Funds are also available for larger projects, many of which are designed to help small firms.

But local authorities have expanded their small business assistance policies in the past two years, moving beyond conventional industrial promotion to the active encouragement of new ventures and small firms through competitions, enterprise agencies and direct financial assistance. For example, in September 1979 Peterborough Development Corporation launched a microprocessor competition with prizes including free factory space, cash, marketing advice and access to venture capital from ICFC. In early 1980 Hull City Council opened an Innovation Centre to help entrepreneurs with new products or ideas. The long-term objective is to promote small new companies by nurturing them through their formation and early growth stages. The Centre provides workspace and services to the tenants, including business advice.

In June 1980 a group of representatives from central and local government was requested to review local authority assistance to small firms, particularly in view of the proliferation of local authority programmes, some of which were thought to be redistributing activity from one area to another and not adding to net economic activity. The Association of Metropolitan Authorities at the same time urged the Government to grant local authorities more power to help small firms through industrial mortgages, loans for capital expenditure, interest relief grants and grants for site preparation and other expenditure. The Association also suggested that local authorities be given powers to acquire equity holdings in small firms.

A7 Scottish Development Agency

The Scottish Development Agency (SDA) was established by the Scottish Development Agency Act of 1975 to further economic development, safeguard employment and promote industrial activities throughout Scotland. At the end of the 1980 financial year the Agency had investments totalling £160.4 million in industrial land, factories, equipment and loans to businesses.

A Small Business Division (SBD) within the SDA was established to replace the Small Industries Council for the Rural Areas of Scotland, although the SBD's services extend to urban areas as well, and to larger firms than those supported by the Council. At the end of March 1980, the SBD had 421 loans totalling £2.7 million outstanding to small firms. The services provided by the Small Industries Council are now provided by the SBD, and include advisory facilities, promotional events, export missions, technical and managerial assistance and a Small Firms Counselling Service based on the experience of retired executives (see C17 below). The SBD also has responsibility for the encouragement of crafts in Scotland, and the Crafts Consultative Committee, set up by the SDA, advises on relevant matters.

A8 Welsh Development Agency

The Welsh Development Agency (WDA) was established in 1976 to regenerate the Welsh economy. The Agency's Small Business Unit (SBU) was set up in April 1977 to take over the functions of COSIRA(3) in Wales, but its jurisdiction has been extended to small firms in urban areas. The SBU provides loans up to £50,000 and in 1979/80 had a net investment portfolio totalling £2.1 million in 120 small firms(4). Loans may be granted at subsidised rates to firms in rural areas creating new jobs. The Agency has adopted a positive role in nurturing new ventures and by 1980 had supported more than 50 start-up enterprises.

In 1979 the WDA set up experimental loan guarantee schemes with the National Westminster, Barclays and Lloyds Banks. The WDA undertakes a feasibility study of the business proposal requiring finance and, if acceptable in terms of the relevant criteria, agrees to guarantee the loan up to a total of £50,000. A small charge of 1% per annum is levied for the facility and loans are available for a period of 10 years.

The WDA has launched several new initiatives, including enterprise competitions to identify new products and ideas among Welsh universities and colleges and the construction of nursery units and advance factories for small firms, usually in association with local authorities.

A9 Development Board for Rural Wales

The Development Board for Rural Wales (DBRW) was established by the Development of Rural Wales Act of 1976 and came into operation in April 1977, to promote the economic and social welfare of mid-Wales. The Board assumed the role and responsibilities of the now defunct Mid Wales Development Corporation. Since February 1978 the Board has operated a special loan scheme for small businesses creating new jobs and employing not more than 20 skilled persons. Loans are limited to £30,000 and interest rates vary from $7\frac{1}{2}$% for five year loans, to $9\frac{1}{2}$% for loans over 15 years. Applicants are normally required to contribute at least 20% from their own sources. The Board approved 15 loan applications in 1977/78 at a total cost of £270,100. The DBRW builds factories with short-term leases for new enterprises and also assists local authorities with advance factory construction for small firms.

A10 National Enterprise Board

In recent years, the government-backed National Enterprise Board (NEB) has intervened more actively in the small business sector, mainly in the assisted areas. In September 1978, for instance, the NEB launched Newtown Securities in partnership with the Midland Bank to provide loans of between £5,000 and £25,000 to customers identified by the Bank. This scheme was closed shortly thereafter due to a lack of interest by small firms.

In March 1979, together with Collinson Grant Associates, a firm of management consultants, the NEB formed Sapling Enterprises to assist promising small firms in the north-west region. Launched as an experiment, Sapling Enterprises offered rapidly growing firms funding of at least £50,000 from the NEB, supported by advice and consultancy from Collinson Grant.

In August 1980 the NEB was given a new set of investment guidelines and a "catalytic investment role" in promoting specified industries in the assisted areas. Besides its involvement with advanced technology, the NEB launched Oakwood Loan Finance in April 1981, to provide loans of up to £50,000 to small firms. Oakwood's loans are for a period of 5 years at a commercial rate of interest with deferred repayments. Each loan is accompanied by a warrant giving Oakwood an option to subscribe for up to 20% of the equity of the borrowing company between the 5th and 7th years. The company can repurchase the warrant at any time. By September 1981, Oakwood had received applications from over 300 firms, of which 15 received loan assistance.

At the same time the NEB formed a subsidiary, Grosvenor Development Capital, to act as a holding company for its existing portfolio of small business investments. Grosvenor will manage and develop the portfolio of 10 small companies and invite institutional investors to participate in its growth. The NEB has also linked up with a Californian venture capital company to develop advanced technology firms in the assisted areas, based on "seedcorn" investment funds and an entrepreneurial management approach to foster new ventures. This new initiative, Anglo-American Venture Management, is to seek out high technology in the U.S.A. for transfer to Britain and to identify British entrepreneurs who would launch new ventures. The venture capital is to come from Anglo-American Venture Fund.

A11 European Investment Bank

The European Investment Bank (EIB) will lend up to 50% of the cost of fixed assets for projects undertaken by small and medium sized companies in manufacturing in development and special development areas. The projects must create additional jobs. Introduced in 1978, the scheme covers firms employing fewer than 500 employees and with fixed assets below £20 million. The maximum loan is £2.5 million and the minimum £15,000. The loans are made for up to 7 years at a 10% fixed interest rate in a mix of foreign currencies, usually dollars and deutschmarks. For a small premium, insurance cover against exchange risks is available.

The Government acts as an agent for the EIB and negotiates the loan facility annually. In 1978 the £20 million facility was fully taken up by 31 projects creating 8,800 jobs, and in 1979, 66 projects creating 9,500 jobs accounted for the £30 million facility. In 1980 another £20 million was made available.

The Government found that the response from the smallest firms was disappointing and in 1980 EIB loans were made available through ICFC at an interest rate of 13.5% to cover exchange risks. The upper limit is £50,000 and the lower limit £15,000, with a maximum limit of £5,000 per job created. Funding is available for 50% of the fixed capital costs of a project for a period of 8 years. A 2½ year moratorium on capital repayments is optional.

The European Coal & Steel Community (ECSC) has similar loan facilities, lending up to 50% of the fixed capital cost of a project which creates employment for ex-coal and steel workers. An interest rebate of between 0% and 3% is also available.

Appendix A - References

(1) *The assisted areas cover most of Scotland and Wales and the whole of Northern Ireland, and parts of England where unemployment and industrial decline are particularly severe. These areas are divided into special development areas and intermediate areas where financial and other forms of assistance are available to firms creating or saving jobs.*

(2) *Cmnd. 6845, HMSO 1977*

(3) *Council for Small Industries in Rural Areas (see C3 below)*

(4) *Defined as recipients of loans below £50,000*

APPENDIX B - THE REMOVAL OF DISCRIMINATION

B1   Industrial Development Certificates

Under the Town and Country Planning Act of 1962 and subsequent legislation, the Government has wide powers to correct the regional industrial imbalance through Industrial Development Certificates (IDCs) issued by the Department of Industry. New and extended factory space over specified limits requires an IDC stating that the proposed development is consistent with policy. As most small extensions below the limits set out in Table B1 are undertaken by small firms, they are effectively in many cases excluded from the provisions relating to IDCs.

TABLE B1 : IDC Limits and Revisions Since 1970

Date of Revision	Upper Limits per Project in :	
	Non-assisted Areas (sq.ft.)	Midlands, South-East (sq.ft.)
Up to 1970*	5,000	3,000
December 1970	10,000	5,000
May 1976	15,000	12,500
November 1978	60,000 (total per district)	60,000 (total per district)
August 1979	50,000	50,000

The Hunt Report on the Intermediate Areas in 1969 (Cmnd. 3998) recommended further relaxation of the limits.

There has been a progressive relaxation of the limits since 1976 to allow local authorities to promote small factory developments. For instance, in November 1978 the limits were raised to 60,000 square feet per local authority district. At present IDCs are only required in the non-assisted areas where one firm intends to occupy more than 50,000 square feet. In addition, IDCs will not be granted where a firm moves from an assisted area.

B2   Office Development Permits

Under the Control of Offices and Industrial Development Act of 1965, local authorities were unable to grant planning permission for office space above specified limits in the South-East, Eastern and Western Regions of Britain, without an Office Development Permit (ODP) issued by the Department of the Environment. The specified limits and revisions since 1970 are set out in Table B2. ODPs were finally abolished in July 1979.

TABLE B2 : ODP Limits & Revisions since 1970

Date of Revision	Upper Limits in :		
	Eastern, Western Regions (sq.ft.)	South East (sq.ft.)	London (sq.ft.)
Up to 1970	10,000	10,000	3,000
December 1970	no limit	10,000	10,000
June 1976	no limit	15,000	15,000
June 1977	no limit	30,000	30,000

B3   Companies Act Disclosure

Prior to the Companies Act of 1967, nearly all small private firms with fewer than 50 members were exempt from certain provisions, such as published accounts and the requirement to employ an independent and qualified auditor. Following the Jenkins Committee on Company Law[1] the Companies Act of 1967 abolished the exempt status, though continued to exempt unlimited companies from filing accounts and reports, provided they were not subsidiaries or holding companies of a limited company. The 1967 Act made further concessions to small limited companies which were amended by later legislation as detailed in Table B3.

The Government proposes to introduce new legislation to allow companies to purchase their own shares. The intention is to facilitate external equity participation in the small business by increasing the options open to private investors when disposing of the equity. It is also intended to reform the company accounting and disclosure provisions of the Companies Act by providing for three tiers of company. The smallest tier comprises proprietory companies with a turnover below £1.3 million, a balance sheet total below £650,000 and fewer than 50 employees. They will not be required to publish their accounts in any detail, nor will they be subject to rigorous auditing requirements. The proposed new forms of incorporation are designed to remove legislative constraints affecting the internal organisation of and the disclosure requirements for the small firm.

TABLE B3 : Disclosure Concessions to Small Firms

	Upper Disclosure Exemption Limits in respect of :				
Year	1.Turnover (£ t/over)	2.Exports (£ t/over)	3.Directors' Total Remunerat'n (£ total rem)	4.Average No.of Employees & Total Wages (employees)	5.Employees' Individual Earnings (£ earnings)
1967	50,000	50,000	7,500	100	10,000
1972	250,000	*	15,000	*	*
1980	1 million	*	40,000	*	20,000

* No change

B4   Employment Legislation

Section 27(1)(a) of the Industrial Relations Act of 1971, and paragraph 9(1)(a) of Schedule 1 to the Trade Union and Labour Relations Act of 1974, provided special treatment for small firms. A firm employing fewer than four persons was exempt from the unfair dismissal provisions of the Act where an employee had been continuously employed for thirteen weeks or more. The Employment Protection Act of 1975 (paragraph 14(1)(a) of part III of Schedule 16) repealed this provision

Rule 130 of the DOI's Code of Industrial Relations Practice relaxed the formal disciplinary and dismissal requirements for "very small establishments". In 1978 only 1/1000 small firms were likely to face a tribunal decision requiring compensation for an unfair dismissal; only 1/300 went to a tribunal hearing; and only 1/100 were faced with unfair dismissal applications.

The 1980 Employment Act changed this legislation. Section 2 exempts an employer of up to 20 employees from the provision requiring firms to enable recognised trade unions to hold secret ballots on the premises. Section 6 requires an industrial tribunal to take into account the size and administrative resources of the firm when deciding whether dismissals have been fair or unfair. Finally Section 8 exempts firms with up to 20 employees from the unfair dismissal provisions of the Act for persons employed for fewer than two years.

B5 Value Added Tax

Small firms with an annual turnover below a specified limit are exempt from VAT. Exempt firms can opt for VAT registration if they so wish, and firms may deregister where past or anticipated future turnover does not exceed a specified amount. The registration turnover limits and changes since 1972 are detailed in Table B5.

TABLE B5 : VAT Registration Limits since 1972

Finance Act	Registration Limit £ (annual turnover)
1972	5,000
1977	7,500
1978	10,000
1980	13,500
1981	15,000

The Commissioners of Customs and Excise have been simplifying VAT procedures, with small businesses in mind. The changes include modification of the rules for partial exemption in order to increase the number of traders eligible for full deduction of input tax; simplification of the VAT return form; removal of restrictions on the alignment of VAT accounting periods with traders' accounting years for firms with a turn-over of £50,000 or less; encouragement to small businesses to simplify their VAT accounting by using cash book records for input tax purposes and an increase in the limit for less detailed tax invoices from £10 to £25.

B6   Price Code

The Counter Inflation Act of 1973 relaxed reporting requirements and control levels under the Price Code for small firms. These requirements and the Price Commission have now been abolished. While larger firms had to report on a quarterly basis and notify the Price Commission of price changes in advance, small firms only had to keep appropriate records of price changes and produce them for inspection when required. These lesser obligations applied to Category III firms under the Price Code, but did not include very small firms with annual turnovers below £1 million in manufacturing industry, below £250,000 in distribution and services and below £100,000 in the professions. These firms were not wholly exempt from the Price Code's regulations, but were not obliged to keep records.

B7   Collection of Statistics

The Bolton Committee recommended changes in the collection of stat-istical and administrative data from small firms, to minimise the burden of form-filling. The Finance Act of 1973 exempted many very small firms from statistical inquiries and allowed the Business Statistics Office to utilise data collected by the Customs and Excise Department in the administration of VAT. This information related to the name of the company, its address, industrial classification, turnover and legal status. Forms and surveys were to be reviewed and all new surveys for more than ten respondents were to be vetted by the Survey Control Unit of the Central Statistical Office. Inessential or unjustified surveys were to be rejected, and greater use of sampling was introduced in the collection of statistics.

In July 1978 the Prime Minister launched an inquiry into the number of forms that industry and commerce were obliged to complete, and instructed government departments to review once again all administrative and statistical forms, to ensure that they were necessary, relevant and simple, and to assess whether small firms could be exempted entirely from their scope. At the time there were 241 statistical surveys each year and the Department of Employment's annual census, amounting to some $1\frac{1}{2}$ million forms sent to small businesses. The Department of Trade reviewed form filling at the end of 1979 and many forms were either simplified or scrapped altogether. The number of forms sent to small firms was reduced by 18% and another 22% were simplified; 15 surveys were discontinued and another 5 were to exclude small firms.

B8   Competition Policy

The Competition Act of 1980 gave new powers to the Director-General of Fair Trading to allow investigations of anti-competitive practices that made it difficult for firms - especially small firms - to compete effectively. Investigations under the Act may lead to references to the Monopolies and Mergers Commission. Small firms' practices are exempt from the terms of the Act, however, where small firms are defined as those with an annual turnover of less than £5 million. They cannot be found to be anti-competitive unless they have at least a 25% share of the relevant market or are part of a larger company.

Appendix B - References

(1)   *Cmnd. 1949, HMSO*

APPENDIX C - DIRECT PREFERENTIAL ASSISTANCE

I ECONOMIC & SOCIAL POLICY

C1 Small Exporter Policy

Introduced in the early 1960s by the Export Credit Guarantee Department, the Small Exporter Policy was designed for manufacturers with no export experience and for other exporters with an export turnover up to £100,000 per year. Premium charges were higher under this policy than under normal policies. In June 1971 the policy was discontinued as it had received very little support, there being only twenty policies current at the time.

C2 Low Cost Automation Centres

The Low Cost Automation Centres were set up in the early 1960s and were one of the first measures in the small business field. The eighteen centres run by the Ministry of Technology were designed to persuade small industry of the benefits of low cost automation, to provide information and advice on the subject and to provide training and consultancy at a small fee. Few small firms actually utilised the service and it was eventually phased out.

C3 Council for Small Industries in Rural Areas

The Council for Small Industries in Rural Areas (CoSIRA) was established under the Development Commission in 1968, taking over the functions of the former Rural Industries Bureau (founded in 1921), the Rural Industries Loan Fund (founded in 1940) and the County Organisers of the Rural Community Councils. Its purpose is to regenerate depopulating and disadvantaged rural areas in England(1), through financial, advisory, consultancy and training assistance offered from 32 county-based offices. Small manufacturing and service businesses are eligible for assistance provided that not more than twenty skilled workers are employed and the business is located in a rural area or country town up to a maximum of 10,000 inhabitants. Locational priorities are accorded firstly to "areas of pull" in the assisted areas, secondly to small firms in locally identified "pockets of need" and third, to small firms generally.

Small tourism enterprises are also eligible provided they are located in
the assisted areas. C oSIRA's services do not extend to agriculture or
the retail trade.

C oSIRA is funded by the Development Commission, a part of the
Department of the Environment. Loans are available for buildings,
equipment and working capital, but Co SIRA expects the major financial
contribution to come from the banks or other sources. Loans below £250
are not normally considered and there is an upper loan limit of £50,000.
The repayment period for building loans is twenty years and for equipment and working capital, five years. Interest charges are specified
by the Treasury but a concessionary rate is available at 3% below market
rates in certain areas of Britain. Borrowers are normally required to
provide security to cover loans for buildings, working capital and larger
plant and equipment. In 1979, aggregate loan financing amounted to
some £12 million to more than 12,100 firms, representing over 77,000
employees.

C oSIRA provides non-financial assistance too. Locally based Small
Industries Organisers provide information and general assistance with
business problems; a consultancy and advisory service offers management and technical skills; and training courses are arranged on a wide
variety of subjects for apprentices, journeymen and mastermen employed
in eligible small rural businesses. CoSIRA also builds a large number of
small factory units.

C4   Export Award

The British National Export Council introduced the Export Award(2)
for Smaller Manufacturers in 1969. It is now sponsored by the British
Overseas Trade Board and the Association of British Chambers of
Commerce, amongst others, and has the support of the Small Firms
Division of the DOI, the TUC (Trades Union Congress) and the CBI
(Confederation of British Industry), amongst others. The award is
made annually to five independent manufacturers or groups employing
not more than 200 people and not previously having won the award. The
value of exports must exceed specified amounts in succeeding years; for
instance, in the 1979/80 financial year exports had to exceed £50,000 in

the year to March 1979, and £100,000 in the year to March 1980.

C5   Crafts Advisory Committee

The Crafts Advisory Committee, established under the Department of Education and Science in 1971, is responsible for the promotion of the crafts and the provision of loans and grants to craftsmen. Some £400,000 is provided annually by the Government to the Committee which is distributed to craftsmen and crafts organisations in England and Wales. In Scotland, the Scottish Development Agency provides for the crafts.

There are five grant and loan schemes. Grants are made to craftsmen setting up workshops for the first time. Up to 50% of the cost of equipment is provided, and a maximum of £1,120 per year is available for working capital. Second, annual grants of £1,120 are awarded to established workshops to take on graduate students and other potential craftsmen. Third, grants between £100 and £1,000 are made for special projects and new activities. Fourth, annual bursaries of up to £2,800 are available to craftsmen who wish to take a sabbatical period to reassess their work or to take on a specific project. Eligibility is confined to craftsmen with at least eight years experience. Fifth, loans between £500 and £3,000 are available to established craftsmen. Although the interest rate on these loans is 10%, if repayment is made within a five year period, the interest paid is refunded to the borrower.

The Committee provides other supportive assistance in the form of exhibitions, publications, craft conservation and information on crafts courses, suppliers of materials and equipment, and the regional activities of various associations.

C6   Export Educational Visits

A scheme to help small firms familiarise themselves with a new market in Western Europe was established in August 1974. Trade associations, chambers of commerce and similar organisations capable of sponsoring group export educational visits are given a sum of £50 per participant. The scheme applies to small firms employing not more than 200 persons, and not already exporting to the country visited. Visits to trade fairs, workshop meetings and other similar events are covered, provided they extend over a period of at least three days. The sponsoring organisation is expected to undertake preliminary market investigation, establish local contacts, monitor follow-up action taken by the firms, and arrange a feedback meeting six months after the visit to assess the value of the exercise.

C7   Co-operatives and Common Ownerships

Most assistance to co-operative and common ownership enterprises is to very small ventures. The Industrial Common Ownership Act of 1976 empowered the Secretary of State to provide grants and loans up to a total of £250,000 over a period of five years, for the furtherance of common ownership aims. The loan fund is administered by Industrial Common Ownership Finance Limited. Small grant-assisted loans are made mainly to manufacturing co-operatives for five years. The rate of interest on the loans is specified by the Secretary of State and adequate security for repayment must be provided. The Industrial Common Ownership Movement (ICOM) provides advice and assistance to small common ownership enterprises and promotes the establishment of new common ownerships.

The Co-operative Development Agency (CDA) Act of 1978 enables grants of up to £1.5 million to be made to the CDA to promote the principles and practices of the co-operative movement. Aid is channelled indirectly to new and existing small co-operative enterprise, in the form of legal, financial and other advice. The CDA assists local agencies throughout the country by sponsoring feasibility studies into the establishment of local co-operatives, often with local authorities.

C8   Small Firms Employment Subsidy

The Small Firms Employment Subsidy was introduced by the Department of Employment in July 1977, applying initially to manufacturing firms with fewer than fifty employees in special development areas only. It was subsequently extended to firms with fewer than 200 employees in the assisted areas and inner city partnership areas. For each additional fulltime job created, a subsidy of £20 per week was provided for a period of six months. An allocation of £35 million was made to the scheme which lapsed on 31st March 1980. In the first year of the scheme, 2,228 firms received £2.6 million, creating 8,587 jobs; after two years 18,920 firms had received subsidies creating 50,500 jobs.

C9 Computer Aided Production Management

The Department of Industry introduced a scheme in September 1977 to finance consultants who would look at computer aids for the management of production in small manufacturing firms employing up to 500 persons. The Scheme, known as Computer Aided Production Management, lasted for three years.

C10 Market Entry Guarantee Scheme

The Market Entry Guarantee Scheme was launched by the British Overseas Trade Board in January 1978, specifically for small and medium manufacturing firms. In August 1981 the scheme was extended to non-manufacturing exporters. Launched initially for an experimental period of two years, but later extended, the scheme was designed to minimise the risk of small companies entering or operating in overseas markets, and some £2 million was provided for financial guarantees. The scheme contributes 50% of the eligible costs of a venture in return for a levy on sales in the overseas market. The maximum contribution of £150,000 to any one project spread over five years effectively limits assistance to small firms : in 1978 some 70% of the beneficiaries had annual turnovers below £2 million. The minimum contribution is £20,000.

Eligible costs are the overhead costs in the export market. The investment and subsequent recovery periods are set in relation to the levy, so that the scheme recovers its contributions with a return of 2.5% above the clearing banks' base rate. The levy payments stop when this return has been achieved, or if the sales do not materialise, the payments stop at the end of the agreed recovery period. For the potential loss to the scheme, the company pays an annual premium of 3% of the contributions received. By August 1981, 275 applications had been made under the scheme and 80 agreements concluded.

C11 Business Opportunities Programme

The Business Opportunities Programme was launched in May 1981 following the measures to assist small business in the Finance Act of that year. The Programme is aimed at established business persons and emergent entrepreneurs; its principal objectives are to publicise the assistance available to small firms from government sources and to change the attitudes of the general populace to self-employment and small business. In launching the Programme, Sir Geoffrey Howe, Chancellor of the Exchequer, explained that Britain's social ethos did not recognise the importance of entrepreneurship, risk-taking and business initiative. The Government intended to change this. The DOI would step up its monitoring of the small business sector, ministers would seek the opportunity to talk directly to small businessmen and conferences on the issues facing the small business sector would be held periodically. Receptions have already been held by the Prime Minister for entrepreneurs, successful small business owner-managers, inventors and innovators. In addition, a range of booklets publicising assistance to small firms is available from the Small Firms Information Centres, described below.

II NON-FINANCIAL DIRECT ASSISTANCE

C12 Industrial Liaison Service

Established in the early 1960s the Industrial Liaison Service assisted smaller manufacturers with fewer than 500 employees, through 75 industrial liaison centres based on technical colleges, polytechnics and universities. Industrial liaison officers were on the staff of these colleges and the Department of Trade and Industry paid two-thirds of their running costs. The officers assessed the type of advice needed and showed firms what help was available, as well as providing assistance themselves. With the introduction of the Small Firms Information Centres, the Government terminated financial support for the Industrial Liaison Service in July 1973. Some centres closed but many colleges retained their officers and continued to provide a similar service.

C13 Production Engineering Advisory Service

The Production Engineering Advisory Service was established in 1967 and run on behalf of the Department of Trade and Industry by the Production Engineering Research Association. Technical advice and training were provided free to small engineering firms by mobile units, and a consultant could be employed at subsidised rates. The service was terminated in March 1971.

C14 Consultancy Scheme

In June 1968 the Board of Trade launched a consultancy scheme for small firms employing between 25 and 500 persons. The Board offered 50% of the cost of employing consultants up to a maximum of £5,000. The scheme was transferred to the Department of Employment in 1969. Although the Bolton Committee concluded that its services were costly and should be discontinued, the scheme was used by 227 firms between 1968 and 1972 and was deemed to be successful. It was subsequently discontinued.

C15 Small Firms Division

As a result of the recommendations of the Bolton Committee, a Small Firms Division was established in the Department of Industry in 1971, to ensure that the interests of small firms were taken into account by government departments, and to be responsible for the development and policy aspects of small business. A junior minister, designated as Parliamentary Under-Secretary of State for Industry in charge of small firms(3), heads the Division and acts as a focal point for small firm issues.

C16 Small Firms Information Centres

As a result of the Bolton Committee's recommendations to set up advisory bureaux for small firms, eleven Small Firms Information Centres have been established since 1973 on a regional basis throughout Britain, under the aegis of the Small Firms Division. They were established to act as a signposting and local information network by making contact with local sources of advice and assistance and either advising small firms themselves, or directing them to available sources of assistance. Several publications on various aspects of starting up and running a small business are available at no charge from the Centres.

They were staffed by 60 civil servants and were operated at a cost of £1.8 million in the 1980/81 financial year. By April 1978 well over 326,500 enquiries had been received from small firms or from people wishing to start a business. Of these enquiries, 27.7% came from manufacturers, 47.1% from services and 25.2% from new enterprise. In 1981 the Centres were expected to provide free advice and assistance to some 100,000 enquirers.

C17 Small Firms Counselling Service

The Counselling Service was announced in April 1976 and a pilot service was introduced in the South-West Region in November. This proved to be successful and was extended to the rest of England and Wales. In Scotland counselling is provided by the Scottish Development Agency. The service uses retired, experienced businessmen to advise small firms on their problems and to guide them to further sources of assistance. There were 127 counsellors in March 1981. Although the first counselling session is free, subsequent sessions are charged at a rate of £15 per day up to a maximum of ten days per year. In the year to March 1981, 10,126 appointments were arranged (6,324 in 1979/80) from 50 area offices. The Counselling Service was expected to assist about 10,000 cases in 1981. An independent evaluation of the service commissioned by the Small Firms Division revealed that it was highly cost-effective, practical and valued by its users.

In November 1979 the Small Firms Counselling Service linked up with the Post Office superannuation fund to provide venture capital to small businesses. Initially limited to the Eastern Region as a pilot project, counsellors were to identify suitable investment opportunities, to undertake feasibility studies and where appropriate to recommend investments to the fund. It was intended to establish a nationwide facility for financial institutions to invest in small firms.

C18 Collaborative Arrangements

In April 1976 the Department of Industry introduced a scheme to provide financial aid for feasibility studies into collaborative arrangements for small firms. The scheme required that four or more firms or organisations (such as trade associations) should be willing to collaborate, and the Department paid 50% of the cost of each study up to a maximum of £5,000. By March 1978, of the £100,000 originally available, only £35,000 had been taken up, so the scheme was extended for a further period. It applied to independent firms in manufacturing employing not more than 200 persons; in retailing and services with annual turnover up to £100,000; in the wholesale trade with turnover not exceeding £400,000; in road transport up to five vehicles; and in catering.

By January 1978 four studies had been completed - a voluntary buying group for small retailers in drapery and the fashion trade; a centralised safety advice service; common services for small grocery outlets; and the provision of an integrated marketing organisation for small firms. The scheme was closed on 31st August 1980 after 25 studies had been supported at a cost of about £80,000.

C19 Management Education

Although the Bolton Report recommended that attention be given to management education for small business, little improvement in the facilities available materialised until the late 1970s. Educational institutions have since devoted increasing resources to small business management education and the Government has contributed to the formation of new firms through the New Enterprise Programmes (NEP) and Small Business Courses (SBC).

These courses and programmes are sponsored by the Training Services Division of the Manpower Services Commission. The NEP is a 16-week programme run at four business schools where potential entrepreneurs with firm ideas are taught essential business skills and are assisted with their individual projects up to, and in some cases, beyond, the launch of the new business. The SBC is a similar 12-week programme run at 25 other educational centres. Since inception in 1977, some 61 courses have been run producing 536 small firms with 2,857 employees. The courses have cost the Government £4,425 per head, amounting to some two and a quarter million pounds annually.

C20 Manufacturing Advisory Service

This service is designed to help small and medium manufacturing firms in the engineering industry employing from 100 to 1,000 persons. The Production Engineering Research Association (PERA) has operated the MAS on behalf of the Department of Industry since September 1977, with the object of increasing the efficiency of firms by adopting modern and proven technology and management practices. Retired engineering management executives visit interested firms with a PERA representative, and a suitable course of action is identified, after which consultancy is provided either by PERA or by other specialist organisations and consultants. Up to fifteen man-days of consultancy are provided at no charge, and a further fifteen days are available at half the normal cost.

C21 Small Factory Units

The provision of very small workspaces and small factory units has been encouraged by the Government through a number of indirect incentives and direct assistance. The English Industrial Estates Corporation (EIEC) has undertaken the construction and letting of small factory units on behalf of the Government, ranging from 500 square feet to 2,500 square feet. The EIEC has formed Beehive Workshops to build and manage these small unit developments. The regional development agencies have also provided small factory units as have many local authorities and new town corporations. Much of the funding for these construction programmes comes from a combination of private and public sources. The Midland and Barclays Banks, for instance, have contributed substantial funds to the building programme; by September 1981, some £30 million had been raised to fund small factory construction programmes. Between 1978 and 1980 the National Coal Board pension fund built 750 million square feet of nursery and small units at a cost of some £15 million.

The Department of Industry commissioned Coopers and Lybrand (Management Consultants) and Drivers Jonas (Estate Agents) to investigate the market for small industrial premises. Their report in 1980 found that a national shortage existed; much of the Government's commitment to providing small units is a result of these findings. The 1980 Finance Act, for example, enabled capital expenditure on the construction, improvement, alteration or extension of industrial buildings providing workspaces of 2,500 square feet or less to quality for a 100% initial allowance. This scheme is to operate for 3 years. The relaxation of planning controls over changes of use between light industry and warehousing has further increased the supply of small factory units.

III FINANCIAL DIRECT ASSISTANCE

C22 Capital Gains Tax

The Finance Act of 1965 introduced retirement relief for owners of small firms. A person over the age of sixty years is exempt from Capital Gains Tax (CGT) on gains up to a specified value, accruing on the disposal of a family trading company or of shares in a family company either by way of sale or gift. The respective limits and changes since 1965 are set out in Table C22.

TABLE C22 : Retirement Relief from CGT - Exemption Limits since 1965

Finance Act	Exemption Limit for each year over sixty (£)	Maximum Exemption Limit at age 65 (£)
1965	2,000	10,000
1974	4,000	20,000
1978	10,000	50,000

The Finance Act of 1978 contained two further provisions relating to small family firms. Capital gains arising on the gift of assets used in a business, or of shares in a family trading company, can be rolled over to the donee where the donor and donee are in agreement. Retirement relief will be given to the donor first. An appropriate proportion of gains qualify where assets are not used wholly for the purposes of the trade. Second, rollover relief from CGT for business assets disposed of and replaced by a person carrying on two or more trades, is granted as if the trades are a single trade. Similar relief is given to a shareholder of a family trading company who replaces an asset, if both the old and new assets are for the purposes of the company's trade.

C23 Corporation Tax

The 1972 Finance Act first proposed a small companies rate of Corporation Tax to fall on profits below a specified amount, with tapering relief between this and a higher specified amount. The Finance Act of 1974 introduced a small companies rate of 42%; the standard rate was 52% at the time. The Finance Act of 1980 reduced the small companies rate to 40% and the lower and upper limits on profits have been progressively amended in the Finance Acts since 1972. Details are supplied in Table C23.

Tapering relief on profits between the lower and upper limits is applied by reducing the standard rate according to the formula $(M-P) \times \frac{I}{P} \times$ a fraction specified by Parliament, where :

M = upper limit; P = amount of profits; I = amount of income.

The relevant fraction is given below.

TABLE C23 : Small Companies Corporation Tax - Upper & Lower Limits and Relevant Fraction, 1972-1981

Finance Act	Lower Limit (£)	Upper Limit (£)	Fraction
1972	15,000	25,000	none
1974	25,000	40,000	1/6
1976	30,000	50,000	3/20
1977	40,000	65,000	4/25
1978	50,000	85,000	1/7
1979	60,000	100,000	*
1980	70,000	130,000	*
1981	80,000	200,000	*

* No change

C24 Close Companies

The 1972 Finance Act revised the shortfall provisions for small firms. At the time of the Bolton Report, close companies (companies controlled by five or fewer persons or by their directors) were subject to shortfall provisions which made them liable to additional taxation on distributions that fall short of their "required standard", and this shortfall could be apportioned to the directors for surtax purposes. Special relief for small firms was available where trading income after Corporation Tax was less than £5,000,and tapering relief was available for trading income between £5,000 and £15,000. New apportionment rules were introduced in October 1977. The exemption limit for apportionment was raised to £25,000 net of Corporation Tax, and where the relevant income was between £25,000 and £75,000, it was abated by one-half of the difference between the income and the upper limit. In addition, for those close companies within these limits, the cost of acquiring a business counted as a requirement of the company's business for apportionment rules. The net effect of the new apportionment rules was that directors of close companies could leave more money in their businesses.

The 1980 Finance Act abolished all the above apportionment rules, the restrictions applying to interest paid to the directors of close companies, and the requirement that, to qualify for tax relief on money borrowed to invest in or lend on to a close company, the borrower had to work for the greater part of his time in the company. Now to qualify he must control more than 5% of the ordinary shares. The 1981 Finance Act extended this provision to partnerships and co-operatives.

C25 Rating Relief

In 1974 certain classes of mixed hereditaments (i.e. combined shop and residence) were allowed to benefit from domestic rate relief, where the domestic value of the property exceeded 50% of the total value. In April 1981, local authorities were required by the Government to assist small firms by allowing the payment of rates by instalment.

C26 Capital Transfer Tax

Capital Transfer Tax (CTT) was introduced by the 1975 Finance Act. Many of the subsequent amendments were designed to relieve the owners and shareholders of small businesses of the liability to pay CTT on the transfer of business assets or shares to their successors or members of their families. By so doing, the intention was to remove any severe disincentives that might exist to the reasonable accumulation of assets in small businesses. The position currently obtaining is as follows, with previous years' figures in brackets :

a) Exemption from liability to CTT was granted by the Finance Act of 1976 to transfers of value below £2,000 in any one year. (The 1975 Finance Act set the figure at £1,000)

b) The Finance Act of 1980 set the threshold for liability to CTT on lifetime transfers of value at £50,000. (The 1975 Finance Act introduced CTT for transfers over £15,000. This was revised in October 1977 to £25,000)

c) The 1975 Finance Act relieved certain lifetime transfers of capital from CTT. Transfers relating to sole ownership, partnership or controlling shareholdings in a company were granted relief at 50% (initially introduced at 30% in 1976 but revised in October 1977), and relief at 20% was given to minority shareholdings in unquoted companies.

d) The Finance Act of 1975 provided that payment of CTT can be deferred.

e) The Finance Act of 1978 exempted gifts of shares by an individual to an employee trust from CTT and qualified them for CGT rollover relief if the trust obtained the majority of the ordinary shares and voting control.

C27 National Health Service Dispensing

The Department of Health and Social Security introduced a new payment system for National Health Service dispensing in January 1978. Small pharmacies were to receive a higher rate of payment on prescriptions than their larger competitors.

C28 Income Tax

Successive Finance Acts have sought to promote small businesses through fiscal inducements to start ventures and incentives to invest in new and small firms. The 1978 Finance Act encouraged new entrepreneurs by offering carry back relief for initial trading losses of unincorporated businesses. A trading loss sustained in the first or subsequent three years can be set against taxable income of the previous three years, including earnings from employment. This applies to losses sustained in 1978/79 or later.

The venture capital scheme, introduced in the 1980 Finance Act, was designed to encourage private investment in small companies. Capital losses on shares in unquoted trading companies incurred after 5th April 1980 can be set off against income. Although this relief was to be available to individual investors only, the 1981 Act extended the provisions of the scheme to investments by companies. The 1980 Act also enabled the cost of raising business finance, certain pre-trading business expenses and redundancy payments to be allowable deductions to tax.

The Finance Act of 1981 introduced the business start-up scheme which allows an individual investor to obtain relief against taxable income on investments between £1,000 and £10,000 in any one year in a new independent business, or in one which has been in existence for fewer than 3 years. The investment has to be maintained for at least 5 years. This new incentive is available to investors who do not have a controlling interest in the business.

The 1981 Finance Act, in setting out to encourage redundant employees to start their own small firm, also increased the limit up to which redundancy payments are not liable to tax from £10,000 to £25,000.

Successive Governments have been concerned about the incidence of high marginal rates of taxation on the decision to invest in small firms. The present Government reduced the marginal rates of income tax from their levels under the previous Government on the basis that lower rates would encourage entrepreneurial enterprise and the growth of small firms. The recent changes in income tax rates are provided in Table C28.

TABLE C28 : Income Tax Rates 1978-1981

1978/1979 Taxable Income	Rate	1979/1980 Taxable Income	Rate	1980/1981 Taxable Income	Rate
£	%	£	%	£	%
0- 750	25	0- 750	25	0-11,250	30
751- 8,000	33	751-10,000	30	11,251-13,250	40
8,001- 9,000	40	10,001-12,000	40	13,251-16,750	45
9,001-10,000	45	12,001-15,000	45	16,751-22,250	50
10,001-11,000	50	15,001-20,000	50	22,251-27,750	55
11,001-12,500	55	20,001-25,000	55	27,751 & above	60
12,501-14,000	60	25,001 & above	60		
14,001-16,000	65				
16,001-18,500	70				
18,501-24,000	75				
24,001 & above	83				

C29 Loan Guarantee Scheme

The Finance Act of 1981 introduced a pilot loan guarantee scheme in co-operation with the clearing banks and ICFC. Several other banks have since joined the scheme, which is covered by funds provided under Section 8 of the Industry Act of 1972. The scheme was introduced to benefit firms with inadequate security and lack of a track record, which would normally prejudice their chances of obtaining bank finance. Under the rules of the scheme, the banks are responsible for evaluating loan requests and if acceptable, they are passed on to the Department of Industry for approval.

Loans up to £75,000 for 2 to 7 years qualify for a government guarantee of 80% of the loan. A premium of 3% is charged by the Government to ensure that the scheme is self-financing. There is a ceiling of £50 million on each year's lending. The scheme opened on 1st June 1981 and in the first 3 months, 540 guarantees were provided for loans totalling £18 million, of which £10.6 million was allocated to new ventures.

Appendix C - References

(1) *CoSIRA's activities in Wales and Scotland are part of the small business activities of the Welsh Development Agency and Scottish Development Agency respectively.*

(2) *The Award consists of a holiday for employees nominated by the winning companies, a trophy for the chief executive and a certificate for the company.*

(3) *The present imcumbent is John McGregor, M.P.*

APPENDIX D - SUMMARY : GOVERNMENT ASSISTANCE 1946-1981

A. INDIRECT ASSISTANCE

1946 - 1960

- A1 National Research Development Corporation (1948, manufacturing) (1)
- A2 British Productivity Council (1952, manufacturing)

1961 - 1970

- A3 Industrial Training Boards (1964)
- A4 Highlands and Islands Development Board (1965, retailing and services excluded)

1971 - 1981

- A5 Industry Assistance (1972, manufacturing)
- A6 Local Authority Assistance (1972, mainly manufacturing)
- A7 Scottish Development Agency (1975)
- A8 Welsh Development Agency (1976)
- A9 Development Board for Rural Wales (1976)
- A10 National Enterprise Board (1978, manufacturing)
- A11 European Investment Bank (1978, manufacturing)

B. THE REMOVAL OF DISCRIMINATION

1961 - 1970

- B1 Industrial Development Certificates (1962)
- B2 Office Development Permits (1965)
- B3 Companies Act Disclosure (1967)

1971 - 1981

- B4 Employment Legislation (1971)
- B5 Value Added Tax (1972)
- B6 Price Code (1973)
- B7 Collection of Statistics (1973)
- B8 Competition Policy (1980)

C. DIRECT PREFERENTIAL ASSISTANCE

I. Economic & Social Policy

1961 - 1970

    C1   Small Exporters Policy (1961, manufacturing)

    C2   Low Cost Automation Centres (1961, manufacturing)

    C3   Council for Small Industries in Rural Areas (1968, manufacturing, services and tourism)

    C4   Export Award (1969, manufacturing)

1971 - 1981

    C5   Crafts Advisory Committee (1971, manufacturing)

    C6   Export Educational Visits (1974)

    C7   Co-operatives & Common Ownerships (1976)

    C8   Small Firms Employment Subsidy (1977, manufacturing)

    C9   Computer Aided Production Management (1977, manufacturing)

    C10 Market Entry Guarantee Scheme (1978, manufacturing)

    C11 Business Opportunities Programme (1981)

II. Non-Financial Direct Assistance

1961 - 1970

    C12 Industrial Liaison Service (1961, manufacturing)

    C13 Production Engineering Advisory Service (1967, manufacturing)

    C14 Consultancy Scheme (1968, manufacturing)

1971 - 1981

    C15 Small Firms Division (1971)

    C16 Small Firms Information Centres (1973)

    C17 Small Firms Counselling Service (1976)

    C18 Collaborative Arrangements (1976)

    C19 Management Education (1976)

    C20 Manufacturing Advisory Service (1977, manufacturing)

    C21 Small Factory Units (1977)

III. Financial Direct Assistance

1961 - 1970

    C22 Capital Gains Tax (1965)

1971 - 1981

   C23 Corporation Tax (1972)

   C24 Close Companies (1972)

   C25 Rating Relief (1974, retailing and services)

   C26 Capital Transfer Tax (1975)

   C27 National Health Service Dispensing (1978, retailing)

   C28 Income Tax (1978)

   C29 Loan Guarantee Scheme (1981)

SUMMARY OF ASSISTANCE : Number of Measures per Period

1946 - 1960	:	2
1961 - 1965	:	8
1966 - 1970	:	5
1971 - 1975	:	15
1976 - 1981	:	18

Appendix D - References

(1)   *Year refers to year of inception; manufacturing refers to industry coverage; where no industry is mentioned, the assistance applies to all, or most, industries.*

APPENDIX E – SPECIFIC DEFINITIONS RELATING TO GOVERNMENT ASSISTANCE

Type of Assistance	Definition (upper limits)
1. Definitions relating to employment	
EIB loans	500 employees
Proprietory company (proposed)	50 employees
Employment Act exemptions	20 employees
CoSIRA aid	20 employees(skilled)
Export award	200 employees
Export visits	200 employees
Employment subsidy	200 employees
Computer Aided Production Management	500 employees
Industrial Liaison Service	500 employees
Consultancy Scheme	500 employees(min.25)
Collaborative Arrangements	200 employees (manufacturing)
Manufacturing Advisory Service	1000 employees(min.100)
2. Definitions relating to annual turnover	
Companies Act disclosure exemption	£1 million
Proprietory company (proposed)	£1.3 million
VAT registration	£15,000
Price Code exemptions	£1 million (manufacturing)
	£250,000 (distribution, services)
	£100,000 (professions)
Competition Act exemptions	£5 million
3. Miscellaneous definitions	
EIB loans	£20 million (fixed assets)
IDC exemption	50,000 square feet
ODP exemption	30,000 square feet
Proprietory company (proposed)	£650,000 (bal.sheet total)
Small Exporter Policy	£100,000 (export value)
Corporation Tax reduced rate	£80,000 (profits)

APPENDIX F - FINANCIAL LIMITS TO GOVERNMENT ASSISTANCE

Type of Assistance	Lower Limit	Upper Limit
Highland Venture Capital (HIDB)	£25,000	£300,000
Industry Aid	£10,000	–
WDA Small Business Unit Loans	–	£ 50,000
WDA loan guarantee scheme	–	£ 50,000
DBRW loans	–	£ 30,000
Newtown Securities (NEB)	£ 5,000	£ 25,000
Sapling Enterprises (NEB)	£50,000	–
Oakwood (NEB)	–	£ 50,000
EIB loans	£15,000	£2.5 million
CoSIRA loans	–	£ 50,000
Market Entry Guarantee Scheme	£20,000	£100,000
Loan Guarantee Scheme	–	£ 75,000

APPENDIX G - STATISTICAL DEFINITIONS OF SMALL BUSINESS

Industry	Definition (upper limits)(1)
Manufacturing	200 employees
Retailing	£185,000 p.a. turnover
Wholesale Trade	£730,000 p.a. turnover
Construction	25 employees
Mining and Quarrying	25 employees
Motor Trade	£365,000 p.a. turnover
Miscellaneous Services	£185,000 p.a. turnover
Road Transport	5 vehicles
Catering	All except multiples and brewery managed public houses.

Appendix G - References

(1)   *Limits have been revised upwards since the Bolton Commission
        originally published these definitions. Figures are at 1978 prices.
        (Interim Report of the Committee to Review the Functioning of
        Financial institutions op.cit. p.43)*

2. SMALL FIRMS AND THE REGIONAL PROBLEM

D.J.Storey

The Banker. Volume 130 Number 657. November 1980

For nearly half a century governments have tried to minimise the gap
between the rates of unemployment in the assisted areas and elsewhere
in Britain. During periods when the economy was buoyant, this gap has
been reduced, but it has never been eliminated. In the present
depressed state of the British economy, therefore, what hope is there
for the unemployed in assisted areas; in particular what contribution can
small and new manufacturing firms make to the creation of jobs in these
areas? Does the government's emphasis on small firms need a regional
dimension?

Policies designed to reduce rates of unemployment in Northern England
Scotland, Wales and Northern Ireland have been in operation for almost
half a century. The Special Areas Act of 1934, following a set of reports
describing vividly the fate of the unemployed, was the first in a series
of Acts which attempted to bring work to these areas. This, and the
legislation which was to follow, up to and including the current 1972
Industry Act, offered financial inducements to firms to expand by opening new plants in areas of high unemployment.

It was thought that the introduction of more modern industry would
diversify job opportunities for the workforce and inject a new dynamism
into declining areas. The assistance which firms currently receive in
regional development grants is directly linked to investment in buildings,
plant and machinery, on the assumption that investment creates jobs.
In 1978-79 £417 millions was paid in the form of RDGs under the 1972
Industry Act, and together with regional selective assistance payments
of £124.3 millions, constituted the vast majority of the government's
regional budget.

A third weapon in the government's armoury was the control of
industrial development certificates (IDCs). Firms in prosperous areas,
wishing to extend their existing premises more than marginally were
required to obtain a certificate. Pressure was then exerted upon the

firm to expand into an assisted area rather than on its existing site or elsewhere in the non-assisted areas, with refusal of an IDC as the ultimate threat. Recent changes, however, have raised the minimum requirement for a certificate to 50,000 square feet, substantially weakening this weapon.

Missed Targets

Estimates of the numbers of jobs created in assisted areas by these and other, now discontinued, policies have been the subject of some debate. Moore and Rhodes[1] estimated that regional policy created approximately 240,000 jobs in the assisted areas of Wales, Scotland, Northern Ireland and northern England between 1960-76. Ashcroft and Taylor[2] suggest the number is rather lower but it seems likely that at least 10,000 jobs were created per year. In the 1970s however, the sluggish performance of the British economy and the relatively lower incentives meant job creation in the regions was only about half that of the late 1960s and by the late 1970s the regional disparities in unemployment were as high as ever. Since 1976 the unemployment rate in the South East has, until very recently, fallen whereas it has risen virtually every year in Northern England and Scotland.

Clearly traditional regional policy, whilst there have been periods of success, has failed to achieve its objective. With the slow down in economic activity fewer companies are now moving to the assisted areas. Directing expanding companies towards the assisted areas now risks either choking off that expansion altogether, or inducing a compensating loss in the donor regions. The assumption that the South East and the Midlands will be unharmed by channelling expansion elsewhere is no longer realistic, if only because of the high levels of unemployment in the inner urban areas of London and the West Midlands.

Regional policy, as traditionally practised, has then to be reviewed, since it is less relevant to a stagnating than to a growing economy. In particular, the effectiveness of the financial incentives must be questioned. Table 1 shows that payments of regional development grants are geographically very unevenly spread. For example, the county of Cleveland, home of Britain's petrochemical and steel industries, is a

TABLE 1 : RDG Payments 1975/76 - 1977/78 and RDG Payments Per Capita

Region	RDG(£M)	RDG/HEAD(£)
Cleveland (a)(b)	269.50	471.15
North(Rest)	126.90	49.72
Yorks & Humberside	63.71	13.02
East Midlands	4.13	1.11
South West	17.17	4.05
West Midlands	0.76	0.15
North West	152.46	23.22
Wales	179.81	65.01
Scotland	311.65	59.86

SOURCE : *Regional Statistics. Population figures are the average for 1975 and 1976.*

(a)   Data for Cleveland were obtained from information on individual companies receiving assistance in excess of £25,000, published in *Trade & Industry*. In the 3 years Cleveland took 69.2% , 69.3% and 65.6% of the totals allocated in the North. These percentages were then applied to the total RDG paid to the North, published in *Regional Statistics*.

(b)   Cleveland population was estimated to be 571,600.

massive recipient of government aid, yet within that county is Hartlepool with currently a rate of unemployment in excess of 15%, and Cleveland itself has the third highest rate of unemployment of any English county.

In short, the link between government finance, investment and jobs has to be re-examined. Is traditional regional policy likely to lead to self-sustaining economic growth in regions such as Tyneside and West Central Scotland, even if the British economy were yet again to prosper? There are a number of reasons to believe that it would not.

The number of new manufacturing firms formed in an area has been shown to be directly related to the proportion of the working population employed locally in small manufacturing firms. Johnson and Cathcart(3) show the probability of an individual employed in a manufacturing firm having less than 10 employees starting in business, is fifteen times greater than an individual employed in a firm employing more than 500. Unfortunately the vast majority of new manufacturing jobs in assisted areas in the 1960s and early 1970s were created by giant enterprises establishing large plants. Regional policy was, therefore, ossifying the existing size structure of industry, with large firms in heavy industry being replaced by large firms in lighter industry. In so doing the policy may have depressed the rate of indigenous new firm foundation, a healthy rate of which is a necessary (but not sufficient) condition for self sustaining growth.

Regional policy has been directed towards encouraging the transfer of manufacturing units of a company to the assisted areas. Very rarely, however, was there a transfer of headquarters functions and, because of modern communications, the branch plant has rarely obtained much autonomy. Purchasing is often centralised and hence the impact upon local firms is minimal.

More seriously in the long run, externally-controlled branch plants may have drained the assisted areas of managerial talent. Take for example the case of an ambitious young local man entering a company at 18, as a trainee manager. By age 25 he will recognise that the only way to advance further within the company is to move to headquarters or at least to another plant elsewhere. The absence of a real opportunity to 'manage' at a branch plant, other than at the very top, means the area may lose its most ambitious and talented individuals. Bearing in mind that many new firm founders are educated and managerially trained, it means the area is also losing a potentially successful entrepreneur.

Boost from Small Firms?

Enterprises relocating into assisted areas often require large sites which are found on trading estates on the outskirts of major new towns and conurbations. The concentrations of unemployment, frequently, tend to be in central areas, and travel via public transport to outer areas is often difficult. Hence, newly located firms claim they are unable to acquire suitable labour as they are competing with other firms in the area. To overcome this problem female labour is often used, thus raising female activity rates but doing little to assist the unemployed males.

These issues raise doubts about whether, even if boom conditions were to recur in Britain, regional policy in its traditional form will ever generate self-sustaining growth in the assisted areas. Instead of trying to induce established firms to locate new branches in the assisted areas should we not look to the small indigenous business to create new jobs? Surely small businesses will spawn more new businesses? Surely small businesses will be created in inner areas where the unemployed live? Surely small businesses will keep individuals in the area rather than enticing them away to headquarters jobs in London, Brussels or New York? Before, however, becoming too excited about the possible contribution of small businesses to the regional problem we should examine the results of recent British studies on new and small firms.

A number of studies have recently appeared which have quantified and catalogued the contribution of small firms to employment change in recent years(4). in Britain the studies have concentrated exclusively upon manufacturing firms with the following broad trends being common (5) :

(a) In general the small manufacturing sector shows a net tendency to increase employment whilst larger firms, in aggregate, seem to be shedding labour. However, most firms which were small in the 1960s continued to be small ten years later, with the vast majority of the remainder going out of business. The growth in employment in the small firm sector was due to the outstanding performance of a relatively few firms. In the East Midlands, for instance 85% of the gross job gains by 1976, in single plant independent firms employing less than 25 people in 1966, were in 15% of firms. Indeed 38% of gross job gains were in 3.3% of firms. In Cleveland the average growth of firms employing less than 50 in 1965, was 17% by 1976, at a time when establishments employing more than 50 people declined, on average by 20%. It is instructive, however, to see in Table 2 the composition of this 17% growth. We find that, of the firms employing less than 10 people in 1965, 87% either stayed in this size category or went out of business by 1976. For those employing between 10 and 24 this proportion was 80.4% and for those employing between 25 and 49 the proportion was 67%. The concept of 'average' growth rate is, therefore, very misleading since the arithmetic mean is 'distorted' by the performance of the few.

TABLE 2 : Employment Change by Size in Cleveland's Manufacturing
Establishments 1965-76

Size in 1965	1976 size					
	Out of business	1-9	10-24	25-49	50+	Total
1-9	35	81	13	2	2	133
10-24	20	16	50	16	5	107
25-49	21	3	8	23	11	66

This table includes all establishments - not simply single-plant independent firms. If only small firms were included the employment
performance of the small firm sector would be correspondingly poorer.
SOURCE : *Cleveland Establishment Data Bank*

(b)   Most wholly new manufacturing firms do not create many jobs over
a decade. The average (and here use of the arithmetic mean is valid)
surviving firm after a decade employs around 16 people. The chances
of such a firm growing to more than 100 employees within a decade would
seem to be between a half and three quarters of 1%.

(c)   Rates of new firm formation have risen almost continuously according to most indices since the mid 1950s. Table 3 shows that business
names registered have risen in every five-year period since 1950, whilst
company incorporations have also risen in every period apart from 1966-
70. Fothergill and Gudgin show that for Leicestershire new manufacturing
firm formations were 50% higher in the 1968-75 period than for the 1947-56
period. It should also be stressed that the observations of the Bolton
Committee in 1971 on the decreasing importance of the small firms have
not continued in the 1970s. It is now recognised that the relative decline
of the small firm sector has certainly been arrested, and probably
reversed - although whether this is due to the 'good' performance of the
small firms sector, or the 'bad' performance of large firms is less clear.

(d)   There are however, considerable regional variations in the numbers
of small firms and in the proportion of the labour force employed in these
small firms. For instance, Cleveland has 4.4% and Tyne & Wear 7.1% of
its manufacturing labour force employed in units of 50 or less employees.
The average for the South East is 15.4%. The importance of this statistic

is that, as shown above, it directly determines the number of new firms formed in the locality.

TABLE 3 : New Firm Formations in England (annual average)

	Incorporated Companies	Business Names Registered
1950-1955	13,773	27,939
1956-1960	23,873	32,930
1961-1965	37,661	41,326
1966-1970	26,065	67,378
1971-1975	47,704	89,256
1976-1979	57,565	116,731

SOURCE : *Annual Report of Registrar of Companies, Department of Trade London, HMSO*

(e)   It has been shown that the successful new firm is more likely to be run by an educated and managerially trained founder(6).   The distribution of educated manpower and managerial talent is, however, uneven. The South East in 1971 had 10.4% of the population in the managerial and administrative class whilst the North had 7.7%.   The North in 1971, also had only 10.5% in the 25-29 age group qualified to degree or equivalent level, compared with 14.1% in the South East.

The above research results demonstrate that it would require a revolutionary transformation for new manufacturing firms in assisted areas to make a major impact, within ten years, upon total employment. In no assisted area for which data are available did wholly new firms contribute even one quarter of jobs created by openings in a decade and in no area of Britain did they create more than 15% of all new jobs per decade.   During the next few years jobs created by new and small firms in the regions will have to be offset against the reduction in movement into assisted areas as well as against the increase in job losses through contractions and plant closures.

Regional Dimension

Despite these reservations on timescale, a regionalised policy to assist small firms does recommend itself on three levels.   The first is that the

small firms sector is the only sector which, in manufacturing, is currently showing a net tendency to increase employment. Secondly, it offers,
as we have seen, the best opportunities for self sustaining growth.
Finally, and most importantly, it is all we have.

The impact of policies to assist small firms will, however, be slow. In
areas currently experiencing high rates of unemployment the major
influence on that rate over the next decade will be the performance of
the major employers in the locality. Specifically it will depend upon
metal manufacturing, ship-building and heavy engineering firms.
Wholly new manufacturing businesses, in aggregate terms, will be virtually irrelevant.

Policies adopted today are directed at a time horizon well in excess of
a decade. Nevertheless, the regions must obtain their share of new
businesses or risk lagging behind the prosperous areas for the foreseeable future.

Unfortunately, policies to assist small firms are not, at present,
regionally differentiated, with the possible exception of the initiatives on
premises taken recently by the English Industrial Estates Corporation.
Even the enterprise zone plans are not intended to be restricted solely
to the small firm. Until the incentives are greater in the assisted areas,
small firm policies risk being regionally divisive, in the crude sense that
the rate of responsiveness, or take-up, will be greater in the South than
in the North, i.e. in areas which require the employment least. A
regional dimension to small firm policy is essential.

Four issues appear to be of major concern to the small firm. The
first is the availability of premises, the second is access to finance, the
third is the level of rates and the fourth is access to information and
advice. In all four, central government could offer greater incentives
to small firms currently in assisted areas. Indeed a comprehensive
policy to assist these firms might include the following items :
(a) Rates levied by local authorities in assisted areas on business
premises could be reduced to the standard domestic rate for the area(7).
The local authorities could then be reimbursed for any loss of revenue
through the rate support grant formula. This would, of course, be an
expensive 'option' since nearly 60% of rate income for local authorities

comes from non-domestic properties.

(b)   Central government could issue interest free loans to local authorities in assisted areas for the construction of starter premises. Very often the local authority is in a better position to develop land than government agencies such as the English Industrial Estate Corporation whose sites may be in the outer rather than the inner areas.   In addition the importance of a lead being taken by local authorities is underlined by the major financial institutions, which may be prepared to invest in small premises in the prosperous South, but are unwilling to undertake such investments in the regions and in the inner areas.

(c)   Tax thresholds and payments could also be varied regionally. There would, in my view, be little value in regionally differentiating income tax, since it is unclear whether this affects rates of new firm formation, but a higher threshold level of VAT payments, or a lower rate of corporation tax could be valuable to a small manufacturing firm in an assisted area.   These should be accompanied by a simplification of the system, with the matter given wide publicity.

(d)   The Chancellor of the Exchequer is considering offering tax incentives to firms intending to hive off plants to act as independent concerns. The process, called either 'deglomerisation' or 'management buyouts', is apparently becoming substantially more important with ICFC alone expecting to set up 50 such enterprises this year, compared with five in 1977.   These tax incentives could be limited to plants currently in the assisted areas.

(e)   Government should limit its consideration of a loan guarantee scheme to small firms in assisted areas.   It is argued that the development of small firms is inhibited by a shortage of loan capital (rather than equity) and that such a scheme would overcome the absence of a track record of infant firms wishing to obtain capital.   The success of the scheme in other countries suggests it can be an effective way of inducing expansion although the lukewarm attitude of the clearing banks to bearing part of the risk has cast doubts upon its feasibility.

(f)   Most small firms serve a local market so their potential for expansion is, to a considerable extent, determined by the size and wealth of their locality. Again small firms in assisted areas are at a disadvantage compared with firms in more prosperous areas. To assist the small firm local authorities and other public organisations in assisted areas could be encouraged to review their purchasing arrangements to discriminate in favour of local small firms. Central government should then be prepared to reimburse these organisations for any financial penalty incurred.

(g) The above incentives are directed primarily towards encouraging the more rapid growth of existing small businesses. The critical consideration in assisted areas is to encourage individuals to start in business but currently this is not an area requiring intervention since the registrations and formations of new businesses are at an all-time peak, presumably because of the high rates of unemployment. There is also no evidence in the assisted areas of a shortage of agencies prepared to offer advice to the budding entrepreneur. Perhaps the problem may even be too many. An individual considering establishing a firm on Teeside, for example, could obtain advice/assistance on a variety of relevant topics from up to twenty five different agencies within a 40-mile radius.

Resources for the above programme could be obtained by raising taxes, to which the government is opposed, transferring from other forms of public expenditure or readjusting the existing regional policy budget. We have argued that most regional expenditure is incurred on capital projects and that attracting to the assisted areas branch plants may not, in the long term, generate self-sustaining employment growth. It might, therefore, be prudent to reduce these incentives and channel funds to assist the indigenous small and new firm. The system of regional grants should not be changed for firms currently located in the assisted area, and who were presumably attracted to that area by the availability of grants etc. The assisted areas cannot risk losing jobs associated with already established firms either investing elsewhere, or relocating because of changes in the regional grants structure.

Long-Term Expectations

Regional policy, despite its fifty-year life, has not substantially reduced the gap between the rates of unemployment in the prosperous

and in the less prosperous areas in Britain. A policy of attracting large
manufacturing branch plants to assisted areas is likely to be even less
effective in creating jobs than previously. Such areas will have to rely,
in the long run, increasingly upon small local firms to create employment.
The conditions for the growth of such firms are more favourable in the
prosperous areas of Britain, so it is necessary to have a regionally
differentiated small firms policy. Greater assistance has to be given to
small and new firms in the assisted areas than elsewhere. Even then the
contribution to total employment which small firms make in a decade is
not high. The rates of unemployment, in assisted areas, in the next
five to ten years depend not upon the enterprise and initiative of small
businessmen in those areas, valuable as it is, but upon the fortunes of
the metal manufacturing, heavy engineering and shipbuilding industries.
Beyond that time scale the small firms look a promising creator of
employment. The regions must ensure they obtain their share.

(1) B.Moore,J.Rhodes & P.Tyler, 'The Impact of Regional Policy in the
     1970s', C.E.S.Review No.1 pp.67-77

(2) B.Ashcroft & J.Taylor, 'The Movement of Manufacturing Industry &
     the Effect of Regional Policy', Oxford Economic Papers(1977)pp.84-
     101

(3) P.S.Johnson & D.G.Cathcart, 'The Founders of New Manufacturing
     Firms:A Note on the Size of their "Incubator" Plants', Journal of
     Industrial Economics, December, 1979, Vol.XXVIII No.2

(4) The most frequently quoted (or misquoted) is that by D.L.Birch,
     'The Job Generation Process', M.I.T. This study showed that 66%
     of net new jobs were created by firms employing less than 20 people.
     It is normally misquoted by failing to include the word 'net'.

(5) See S.Fothergill & G.Gudgin,'The Job Generation Process in Britain'
     Centre for Environmental Studies, Research Report No.32, D.J.
     Storey, 'Job Generation & Small Firms Policy in Britain', Centre for
     Environmental Studies, Policy Series No.11

(6) N.R.Smith, 'The Entrepreneur & His Firm', B.Nicholson & I.Brinkley
     'Entrepreneurship Characteristics & the Development of New

Manufacturing Enterprise', Regional Studies (forthcoming).

(7) *In 1979/80 the non-domestic rate exceeded the domestic rate by this figure having fallen from a peak of 40% in 1975/76.*

3. SMALL FIRMS AND THEIR LARGE CUSTOMERS

Peter Wilson and Peter Gorb

INTRODUCTION

The encouragement of small business now occupies a central position within the broad framework of public economic and social policy, while private sector activities to encourage new businesses and the growth of established small firms have also proliferated in recent years. It could be argued that this proliferation has tended to obscure rather than illuminate the importance of the interface between the small firm and its external environment. Certainly one important feature of this interface which has consistently been overlooked is the extent and nature of collaboration between buyers and sellers particularly where the large organisation is a buyer from the small one.

The interdependence of small and large firms has far-reaching social and economic consequences. Indeed, the impact of a change in the relationship between buyer and seller bears not only on the corporate existence of the small firm itself, but also on its employees, their families and ultimately on the local community. Furthermore the importance of local markets to small firms draws local government into the network of interdependent relationships, both as a source of influence and also as a major purchaser in its own right. And central government agencies can have the same influence on small firms in their local markets. The consequences of the actions of these large organisations in the market-place are likely to impinge heavily on the existence of the small firm, in some cases resulting in the formation of new firms and the successful growth and development of established firms, and in others, the death of the firm through bankruptcy or insolvency.

Previous discussion has dealt with some of the problems of state procurement and only superficially with the impact of the purchasing policies of large firms on their small suppliers(1). The overall finding is that both state and private sector purchasing inevitably discriminates against small business, although this view is based on circumstantial evidence. Attention has been devoted mainly to two aspects of this problem : large companies withholding payments to their small suppliers, and an equitable share of state procurement contracts for small business (2). But little attention has been devoted to the wider significance of this trading interface.

Here we review the trading relationship between large and small firms by presenting empirical evidence of some of the major issues at this interface by examining both the dependence of small firms on their markets and the commercial behaviour of large organisations in relation to their small suppliers. A consideration of this evidence has led us to the view that the dependence of small firms on large customers makes them particularly vulnerable to the strategic plans and business policies of these customers. In our conclusions we make some tentative suggestions about this vulnerability and point to its likely consequences. The evidence we describe below arises from a study undertaken in the London Borough of Camden between October 1979 and April 1980(3).

THE ANATOMY OF DEPENDENCE

Many of the small firms in the study were single-product firms (even in the case of some multi-product firms, their products tended to be sufficiently undifferentiated as to render them effectively single-product firms) but we propose to ignore the direct consequences of product dependence and to concentrate on trading dependence. A firm is said to be "dependent" in the market-place when it sells a substantial share of its total output to another firm, or to a very few firms, or into a local market; by "substantial" is meant that level of output which, if lost to the dependent firm because of the withdrawal of the buyer (or buyers) from an agreement to purchase, would force the seller either to cease production and leave the industry (permanently or temporarily) or to reorganise itself in such a way as to change fundamentally its character, for instance by changing its fixed cost structure, its products or its markets.

The study set out to examine the extent and nature of this dependence and where possible, to point to the likely consequences for the birth and growth of small firms and the implications for large public and private sector organisations. Dependence was examined mainly in terms of the number of customers per firm and their share of the firm's total output, and the importance to the small firm of local and regional markets vis-a-vis national and export markets. In addition, we tried to evaluate the firm's reliance on non-price competition in the market-place and the consequences and implications thereof and to assess the importance of different market-related problems to the small firm at the time of the interview.

1. Dependence on one or a few customers

The firms in the survey tended to be dependent on a very small number of customers; many were highly dependent on one or a few major customers who in some cases were large organisations either in the public or private sectors.

TABLE 1 : Number of Customers per Firm

No.of customers	% of Firms	Cum.%
1 - 10	19.2	19.2
11 - 50	18.3	37.5
51 - 100	12.5	50.0
101 - 200	11.5	61.5
over 200	38.5	100.0
Total	100.0	100.0

TABLE 2 : Share of Annual Turnover with Major Customers

% of Turnover	With Major Customer		With 5 Major Customers	
	% of Firms	Cum.%	% of Firms	Cum.%
100	7.0	7.0	16.8	16.8
75 - 99	9.0	16.0	10.9	27.7
50 - 74	6.0	22.0	17.8	45.5
25 - 49	13.0	35.0	7.9	53.4
10 - 24	11.0	46.0	3.0	56.4
1 - 9	54.0	100.0	43.6	100.0
Total	100.0	100.0	100.0	100.0

Tables 1 and 2 illustrate the extent of dependence in the market-place. Table 1 shows that nearly one fifth of the firms had fewer than ten customers each, while nearly two-fifths had fewer than fifty customers. On the other hand, as much as one half of the firms had over 100 customers each.

Table 2 is even more revealing. While most firms (54%) were dependent on their major customer for less than 10% of their turnover (which in terms of our earlier definition can be considered to be a measure of relative independence), a significant proportion was heavily dependent on the major customer. Some 7% of the firms had only one customer and nearly one quarter was dependent on their major customer for over 50% of total turnover. These proportions increased considerably when the share of turnover with the five major customers was used as a measure of dependence. The last column in Table 2 shows that one sixth of the firms was wholly dependent on their five major customers while nearly one half was dependent on their five major customers for more than 50% of total annual turnover.

Even within the sample of small firms, the degree of dependence was highly variable which seems to indicate that there are certain factors limiting dependence, characteristic of either the industry (or sector) or the firm, or both. Although these factors are still to be thoroughly investigated, at this stage our evidence leads us to conclude that the firm will tend to be more dependent on one or a few customers the young-er it is, and the smaller it is in terms of numbers employed. Having established this, we need to consider dependence in more depth.

External Determinants of Dependence

Besides the strength of competition and the structural state of health of the industry in which the small firm operates, historical ties between buyer and seller will also determine the extent of dependence. The cloth-ing industry, for instance, combines the traditional relationship between large and small manufacturer with the more recent one between the large retail or wholesale group and the small manufacturer. The close relation-ship between Marks & Spencer and its small suppliers is a notable example. In addition, because competition in the clothing industry is generally very strong and entry and exit are relatively costless, there is a greater tendency for small sub-contractors to submit themselves to the tutelage of larger companies where at least a small measure of protection is afforded against competition. In this case, the large partner has special responsibilities to the small partner and its workforce largely because of the vulnerability of the latter in the short-run to sudden changes in supply conditions.

Such changes are possible where the undiversified small firm has all or most of its customers in an industry which is structurally unstable. The "domino" effect of a substantial decline in performance of a few large firms in one industry can be devastating on the survival of their small suppliers. For instance, it has been argued that the employment impact of withdrawing state support from certain large British manufacturers (such as British Steel Corporation and British Leyland) would extend far beyond the large firms themselves to their small component suppliers. The combination of such large-scale failure of both small and large firms would then impact undesirably on the environment and the local community.

Although the small firm is allegedly highly flexible and adaptable to changes in economic conditions, the extent of dependence on its existing customers and its marketing innovativeness will ultimately determine its survival in the longer-run.

The mythical qualities of flexibility and adaptability which led earlier writers to believe in the self-regenerativeness of the small firm sector, must be challenged in the light of the extent of dependence recorded here. At least one implication is that buyers in large private and public sector organisations must seek to collaborate responsibly with their small suppliers if they are not to erode Britain's industrial seed-bed.

Internal Determinants of Dependence

Small firms limit their dependence in the market-place by their operational circumstances or by deliberate managerial volition. Operationally, small firms have relatively short planning horizons with little or very often no marketing strategy that allows them to mitigate the worst effects of dependence.

In some cases this is simply because of the strong production orientation of the market-place. But increasing the marketing effort requires a substantial commitment by the small business, either through the redeployment of existing resources or the employment of additional ones. It is a fundamental characteristic of resource allocation in the small firm that many of the incremental resources required in the process of growth are indivisible and at the margin they constitute an unwanted overhead. The owner-manager tends rather to redeploy internal resources (of perhaps lower quality) to meet any marketing need, until the small firm reaches the threshold where it can readily absorb the resources required to widen its markets. Thus the indivisibility of incremental marketing resources tends to strengthen the dependence of the small firm on its existing customers.

On the other hand, the owner-manager of the small business may pursue a deliberate policy of no-growth and therefore submit his firm to a high degree of dependence. It is very often the case that the owner-manager does not wish to expand the firm beyond his own locus of control either because he is unable to or unwilling to delegate responsibility to his employees or because he is content to accept the constraints on growth imposed by the nature of the market. In either case, he is likely to depend heavily on a few major customers or a local market.

Benefits and Costs of Dependence

The benefits and costs of the dependence of small suppliers on large customers vary according to the size and age of the firm. In general, while dependence may be necessary for new firms at the entry stage, it may or may not be detrimental to the longer-term growth and development of the firm. In determining the effects of dependence on individual small firms, it is important to bear in mind that the owner-manager may have limited skills in dealing with the uncontrollable element of his environment. Unlike the large firm, where the response of management is to extend the frontiers of control into the unknown, the small firm owner-manager generally lacks the specialist skills of, inter. alia, marketing, strategic planning and financial forecasting. Thus his external environment remains largely outside his control and he cannot easily predict it(4).

His likely response therefore is to collaborate with the large customer whom he knows and trusts.

Some of the benefits of collaboration are :

(a) it facilitates entry into the industry by guaranteeing a market for the products of the new firm and reducing the impact of competition. This in turn provides leverage for raising finance, securing premises and for meeting the other commitments at the entry stage. By reducing the costs of marketing, dependence also lowers the general overheads in the new firm thus reducing barriers to entry brought about by high unit costs and an absence of economies of scale;

(b) for established small firms, the higher the degree of dependence, the lower are marketing costs and hence general overheads. Furthermore the closer the collaboration, the more likely are there to be other externalities, such as advice on product development and technical assistance, to the extent that the boundaries of the small firm merge with those of the large firm creating, as far as the external environment is concerned, a unitary structure. Within this structure, the small firm may be nurtured to conform closely to the goals and objectives of the larger "foster parent". Collaborative agreements may cover the use of the larger firm's reputation in financial and other markets to provide leverage in procuring operating resources at favourable rates;

while some of the costs are :

(a) in a structurally declining market or one which is inherently unstable, the small supplier may find itself without an outlet for its goods or services with no prior warning if it depends on one or two customers. For instance, this is typical of parts of the clothing industry where small subcontractors can lose their market overnight;

(b) a high degree of dependence is not conducive to entrepreneurial behaviour and may even induce complacency in the small firm through a lack of incentive to sell in the open market. It is important here to distinguish between opportunism within the relationship with the large firm and entrepreneurial behaviour in relation to the outside world. At the interface the small firm owner-manager will often continue to act entrepreneurially in his selling and negotiating stance. But in a macro-economic sense he may become insufficiently responsive to change to ensure the long-term survival of his firm <u>outside</u> the relationship with his large customer;

(c) by imposing specific product and technical requirements on the small supplier, the large customer constrains the supplier in its approach to research and development and prevents it from fully assimilating the impact of trends in the market. If subsequently the small firm wishes to increase its independence in the market-place, it may face substantial barriers to growth when confronted with the realities of competition.

2. Dependence on Local & Regional Markets

We found that the firms were generally dependent on local and regional markets; they considered that the main locational advantage of the area was its proximity to the market-place. The very smallest firms (employing fewer than five persons) were relatively more dependent on proximate local markets than the larger firms in the sample, where the local market is defined as the area within a two mile radius of the firm. The regional market was defined for the purposes of the survey as the Greater London area, covering all 32 London Boroughs.

TABLE 3 : Location of Customers

Location	Major Market (% of Firms)	All Markets (% of Firms)*
Local area	21.2	48.1
Rest of Greater London	53.8	82.7
Rest of U.K.	22.1	56.7
Exports	2.9	26.9
Total	100.0	100.0

* Firms could be supplying more than one market location

Table 3 shows that about one fifth of the firms (21.2%) was dependent on the local area for its major market while nearly one half had penetrated the local market at least to some extent. Some 75% of all firms were dependent on the local and regional markets for their major customer and only a small number of firms (less than 20%)were not supplying the regional market at all. Very few firms were currently operating in export markets. These findings support the contention that small firms tend to depend on local and regional markets and many of the reasons for this dependence are to be found in the internal marketing weaknesses of the firm described earlier, as well as the constraints imposed external- ly to the firm by the market itself. As with the small firm's dependence on one or a few customers, its dependence on proximate markets is not necessarily a disadvantage. One major benefit is the local firm's independence of costly distribution channels which is likely to be reflect- ed in lower unit costs.

Besides the problems posed by this dependence for the survival and growth of the small firm, the most important implications of these findings concern public sector intervention to promote small business. Because of the dependence of small firms on local markets and their contribution to local employment, organisations with a local presence are likely to be more effective at intervention than national bodies. It was found, for instance, that the smaller the firm, the greater the proportion of local residents employed in the firm (rather than commuters from outlying suburbs).

It was also established that there were differences in dependence on local markets between very small or new firms and larger, more mature small firms. The smallest firms had somewhat stronger linkages with national and international markets. Similarly the youngest firms were more dependent on local and regional markets than the oldest firms which in turn had strong linkages outside the region.

One of the consequences of strong local dependence, particularly for the smallest firms, is that local events and changes in the intrastructure and other trading conditions (such as roads, bus routes, parking provision, industrial premises and rates) are likely to impact more heavily on small than on large firms. It is entirely logical, therefore, that changes in the physical nature of the local market-place have historically been one of the major causes of the decline of small firm activity in our inner city areas. It is sufficient that local authorities permit even a relative decline in local trading conditions for many small firms to move away. But for planners and policy makers, one implication is that local government, as well as large companies with a sense of social responsibility for the welfare of local communities, can more easily influence the growth of small firms through intervention in the local economy.

Indeed, local authorities and private companies are now devoting increasingly larger quantities of resources to the encouragement of small firms. Paradoxically, however, this intervention can be counter-productive since the needs of the local economy (intervention to promote the local market-place) and the long-run needs of the growth-orientated small firm (reduced dependence on local markets) are in conflict.

3. Non-price Competition

The firms did not in general compete in the market on price alone; they were more dependent on non-price competitive criteria such as quality, service and personal contacts. Because they operated in small but clearly defined market niches where direct competition with larger firms was avoided, they tended to increase their dependence on non-price competition. However, many of them saw this as giving them a competitive edge against larger suppliers to the same customers.

When asked how they competed in the market-place, less than 10% of the firms gave lower prices as the major reason for their competitiveness. Most claimed that the superior quality of their products or services (23.2%), or better service and delivery schedules (35.4%) were the major reasons their customers supported them. A number of additional reasons were given, including personal contact between the buyer and seller, reliability of the product or service and local monopoly of the product.

Although it is frequently stated that small firms are price takers(they operate in markets where their size prevents their exercising any perceptible market power) the findings support the opposite view, i.e. that price was relatively unimportant. Many of the markets were highly monopolistic with the result that there were no uniform market prices. Since many of the firms were service-based, the high degree of product differentiation militated against price taking. Ultimately, however, the dependence of the small firm on one or a few products selling to one or a few customers produced a strong sense of vulnerability to the vagaries of the market, whether the firm was a price taker or not. Part of this uncertainty was the impact on the market of the behaviour of buyers in large organisations, which we discuss in more detail below.

4. Marketing and Customer Problems

In order to ascertain the relative importance of the issues described above, the firms were asked about their major market- or customer-related problems. They were also asked to rank their major overall problems in order of importance.

The most significant findings were the large proportion of firms with no major market-related problem at all; the extent of bad debts and slow debtors as the most important problem; and the vulnerability of some firms to deteriorating demand. The absence of a market-related problem among so many firms was remarkable because of the depressed state of the economy at the time of the interviews. There are several possible explanations. Because many firms operated in niches in the market where the impact of a general economic decline was not directly perceptible, or where the lags of the business cycle acted to restrain the impact in the short-run, problems relating to cyclical decline were relatively unimportant. A number of firms mentioned that one marketing problem was that large customers withhold payments for unduly long periods. Several others specifically mentioned their dependence on a few large customers as a major marketing issue. But "no marketing problem" as an answer from nearly half the respondents suggests that small firms tend to find ways of dealing with and overcoming the problems of selling to the large customer which they have not made explicit in their responses.

THE LARGE CUSTOMER

In order to explore the interfirm relationship from the side of the large firm, interviews were undertaken with seven prominent large firms in the private sector and four public sector organisations located in and around the local market area of the small firms interviewed above. These organisations included hotel groups, national retailers, manufacturers, a construction company, the University of London, a hospital, the British Library and the Local Council. The organisations were chosen arbitrarily but were identified as likely to have a significant impact on their small suppliers through their buying policies and general business plans.

1. Purchasing Policies

The purchasing criteria were in most cases very comprehensive in theory, requiring the supplier to produce bank and trade references as evidence of an acceptable track record, evidence of the quality and reliability of the product or service and an adequate guarantee of the firm's ability to produce the goods or services in the required quantities according to agreed delivery schedules. Additionally in some cases the supplier had to submit his factory premises to scrutiny, particularly where very specific health standards were required. Once these criteria had been met, and prices had been agreed, the firm was generally placed on an approved list of suppliers or in an approved catalogue and this ensured future consideration as a preferred supplier to the organisation.

Were these criteria strictly adhered to, there is no doubt that many small firms would experience considerable difficulty in ever gaining recognition. As one chief buyer observed, however, "there are no hard and fast rules in the buying game" and much would depend on the individual buyer, the determination of the potential supplier and the embryonic relationship at a personal level between the two parties. Despite this assertion, the rigid application of these criteria could discriminate unfairly against small firms in a number of ways :

(a) For a new firm there are no trade references or a track record to gauge its credibility. Neither the quality and reliability of the product nor the ability of the firm to meet required quantities can be accurately evaluated;

(b) For established small firms, there remain the problems of meeting quantity criteria. If the proposed order requires a large incremental adjustment to the operating systems and resource consumption of the small firm, it may not seem evident to the buyer that the firm could meet the increased production throughput. It has already been noted that the allocation of resources in the small firm necessitates the redeployment of existing resources or the employment of additional lumpy ones, neither of which may be the most efficient solution in the short-term. Thus the small business will require a firm commitment from its large customer before the additional resources are employed, for should the buyer withdraw the order, the overheads imposed by the new resources may jeopardise the survival of the small firm;

(c)   Several of the large organisations did not have a policy of multiple sourcing. This would inadvertently tend to discriminate against new and existing firms because for large national contracts the required quantities and consistent throughput could not be met by firms with small production capacities. Buyers would, on the grounds of cost or inertia, be disinclined to turn to multiple sourcing when one large source was available.

2. Negotiating Costs

The extent of collaboration between small and large firms depends largely on the nature of the allocation process since resources are scarce in an absolute sense, and on the costs of buying from, selling to or advising the small firm which are relatively large because of the indivisibility of negotiating inputs. These disproportionately high costs impose constraints on the birth and growth of the small firm. There are several costs in the negotiating process :

(a)   There are substantial and largely fixed transactions costs which involve identifying, investigating, evaluating and either rejecting or accepting new small suppliers. Not only do several small suppliers have to be identified to meet a large purchasing requirement, but the acknowledged paucity of published and readily accessible data on small firms contributes to the high investigatory costs;

(b)   The administration costs of monitoring and maintaining contact with suppliers are larger the greater the number of small firms currently on the approved list;

(c)   The costs of the risk of small suppliers not being able to perform adequately tend to be larger the younger (and therefore the smaller) the firm. A very high proportion of new and young firms do not survive the first few years and the costs of lost or late supplies may be substantial. The recognition of supply contracts when existing suppliers fail is an additional cost to the large firm.

The importance of these negotiation costs will vary according to the role or price in any agreement between small supplier and large customer. Clearly it will be economical to procure from small suppliers where the benefits of local deliveries and short distribution channels outweigh the combined disadvantages of higher transactions costs and loss of economies of large-scale production. Moreover, as we have seen earlier, small firms tend not to compete on the basis of price alone, but rather qualitative factors are given more weight in the buying decision. Thus the advantages of rapid delivery, personal service, small but specialised production runs and local availability of supplies will tend to outweigh the costs of dealing with small firms. It is also arguable that the benefits of dependence on a secure market confer a long-term financial gain on the small supplier and this will be reflected in the short-run in a more competitive price. In this way the small firm is able to use its dependence on the large firm to its own advantage as a quid pro quo for more favourable negotiating terms.

3. Helping the Small Supplier

The policies and attitudes of the large companies towards their small suppliers varied from the supportive to the obstructive. It was the deliberate policy of two organisations not to take on suppliers who would need to devote their entire production to the large customer. One organisation would not purchase more than 60% of a supplier's output although in the light of the extent of dependence observed earlier, it is immaterial whether the proportion is 60% or 20%, since dependence on the large customer is assured in either case. Thus such procurement policies tend to discriminate against the small firm, albeit inadvertently. Nevertheless many established, dynamic firms owe their initial success to their complete dependence on one customer and the special advantages that accrue from this relationship.

The "cultural" differences between small and large firms help to explain some attitudinal and behavioural issues. To the small firm owner-manager

the large company milieu is often quite alien. The flexibility of short
lines of communication and an opportunistic negotiating stance on the
part of the small firm contrast sharply with the formal and lengthy
decision-making process of the large customer. The institutionalised
buyer may not easily coexist with the entrepreneurial seller in the market-
place.

A further inhibiting factor is the "inertia" found in large organisation
buying departments. Buyer inertia, a lack of interest in the products
or services of new suppliers, combined with a reactive buying stance, is
reflected in the tendency (usually reinforced by buying policy) of buyers
to opt for "value for money" as their primary buying criterion. Such
buying behaviour is inherently conservative and failure-averse, and not
conducive to the birth and growth of small firms, many of which are one-
product, one-market firms with little appreciation of the market and the
behaviour of buyers. Their products or services may still be at the
prototype stage requiring buyer feedback, or advice may be needed on
product presentation and pricing. In all these cases the buyer is the
critical link between the survival and growth of small firms and their
failure.

The survey of large organisations revealed that in some cases they
were prepared to extend direct financial assistance to their small suppliers.
For instance, one large firm was prepared to assist its small suppliers
with purchases of equipment and raw materials where its considerable
market power could effect reductions in price. But such a sympathetic
attitude was not usual. The reverse was more often true. Several
buyers admitted that their organisation were slow in paying their small
suppliers particularly where they were supplying a non-essential
commodity. The impact of slow debtors on the working capital needs of
the small firm can be highly detrimental, given their relatively greater
dependence on short-term capital.

A final point was that most large organisations saw little value in
having their small suppliers located in close proximity to them, usually
because their contracts were for national distribution but also because
there was no requirement for rapid delivery or for close contact between
buyer and seller. In the absence of any significant advantages of having

their suppliers on their door-step, inertia generally prevailed among the buyers, inhibiting closer collaboration with local small firms.

CONCLUSION

The traditional view of the small firm as an independent entity providing much of the flexibility and adaptability required in a modern industrial economy is open to question. There is evidence that many small firms are highly dependent on relatively few large customers, which reduces their flexibility and adaptability to change. Not only do many small firms depend on a few major customers for a large proportion of their turnover, but they also rely on collaboration with large firms for technical, marketing and financial assistance. We have recorded their dependence on one or a few products and have produced evidence of strong reliance on local and regional markets too. It should be added that dependence in the market-place is only one facet of overall environmental dependence in which the small firm finds itself. The commitments to financial institutions, advisers, suppliers, landlords and employees imply further states of dependence for the small firm, and help is certainly on offer in all these fields.

With British industry becoming increasingly concentrated, much of the market-place will continue to be dominated by larger and more powerful organisations. For instance, state procurement now amounts to some £22 billion a year. It is crucial therefore that large organisations recognise the impact of their purchasing policies and practices on the survival and growth of their small suppliers.

(1) *See for instance :*
     Report of the Committee of Inquiry on Small Firms (Cmnd. 4811, HMSO 1971);
     Voluntary Collaboration vs Disloyalty to Suppliers (D.H.Farmer & K.MacMillan (Journal of Purchasing & Materials Management. Winter 1976, Vol. 12 (4).)
     Large Customers and their Suppliers, K.J.Blois (European Journal of Marketing Vol. 11 (1) 1977)

Big Firms Get Together to Help Small Suppliers, P.Walker (Chief Executive, December 1978)

(2) *See for instance :*
'Ironing out the pay squeeze', The Guardian 14th Dec. 1979
'Larger slices for small mouths', The Guardian 28th Nov. 1980

(3) *Employment & Small Business in Camden : A Survey, P.Wilson, (London Business School 1980).*
The research was carried out in the London Borough of Camden, an inner city area of London stretching north-west from the centre. There were 104 firms in the study, most of which were independent and employing fewer than 50 employees. The average size of the firms in the sample in terms of numbers employed was 23. Average turnover in the 1978/79 financial year was £1.66 million and the average profit before tax was £81,000. Manufacturing industry accounted for 51.9% of the responses, distribution, catering and repair work accounted for 26% and the remaining firms were in various service industries.

(4) *The Management Development Needs of Small Business : Farmers & Hunters, P.Gorb (Management Education & Development, Dec. 1978)*

CHAPTER 8 : THE FUTURE OF SMALL BUSINESS

Introduction

The interweaving of technology and small business, particularly in the new fields of micro-electronics and bio-technology, are topical themes. The articles in this final chapter take a look at the future of small business in the context of technology. They are concerned with the ways in which technology will affect small business and its growth, and also the extent to which small business is likely to be in the vanguard of technological change.

The first article, by Gibbons and Watkins deals with innovation in the small firm. Written ten years ago, it was one of the first comments on small business as an appropriate place in which to encourage the rate of technological change. The authors note the tendency towards the concentration of small innovative spin-off firms in the now famous Silicon Valley and Route 128 outside Boston, although a greater degree of geographical dispersion exists among such firms in Britain. One possible reason for this difference is that in the United States the pre-vailing environment is more supportive of technological spin-off, and the authors point to the necessary elements of this environment. But they warn that other more subtle factors are involved in Britain. Although finance does not appear to be one such factor, the earlier article by Stevens on venture capital financing is complementary to this article.

The second article by Rothwell was written more recently and deals with the same subject. It questions some of the assumptions which had gathered force during the 1970s (and are still with us) about the size and nature of the contribution of small and medium sized firms to tech-nological innovation. Historical surveys of inventions and innovations show that small firms have accounted for a disproportionately large share thereof, although since the 1930s the rise of the very large corporation with its extensive R & D facilities has eclipsed the earlier primacy of small firms in promoting technological innovation. This does not deny their importance, however, and there is some concern that government policy in Britain does not sufficiently recognise this.

The concluding article in this book is The Coming Entrepreneurial Revolution by Macrae. Published at the end of 1975, it remains the classic piece of futurology in the field, anticipating much of the current policy debate on the future of small businesses. Deliberately provocative and controversial, it interweaves the themes of entrepreneurship, technology and social and economic change. In proposing that the era of the large corporation may now be passing into history, to be replaced by entrepreneurial individuals and other small-scale activities, it provides a most appropriate tailpiece to this book.

1. INNOVATION AND THE SMALL FIRM

M.Gibbons and D.S.Watkins

R & D Management. Volume 1 Number 1. October 1970

Transfer Mechanisms

The question of the *mechanism* by which ideas get from a predominantly research environment to a commercial one is an important one. It is being increasingly observed that such ideas diffuse primarily by the movement of people from one environment to another. For example, in a recent study of technological innovation by Langrish, Gibbons, Evans & Jevons (1971) (see Table 1) it was found that of 158 important technical ideas contributing to the innovations which won Queen's Awards for technological innovation during the years 1966 and 1967, 102 originated outside the firm. Of these, approximately 20 were brought into the firm as a result of a new person joining it. Similarly, Burns (1969), summing up the results of a conference on technological innovation, pointed out that the most important single achievement of the meeting had been the establishment of the fact that "the mechanism of technological transfer is one of agents not agencies : of the movement of people among establishments rather than of routing information through communication systems".

Crucial to the process of translating a novel technical idea into a commercial proposition is the entrepreneur. With the rise of the modern large corporation, it has often been assumed that the entrepreneur is of less importance than he was in the earlier part of the century. However, there is a growing body of evidence tending to support the contrary view, that such men are just as vital to the innovation process as they ever were.

For the purposes of the present paper it is useful to distinguish two types of entrepreneur by the environment in which they choose to work. The first type, frequently called a product champion, performs the entrepreneurial function within the existing framework of an organization, although he often works through informal rather than formal channels.

TABLE 1 : Method of transfer of 102 important technical ideas (a)

Transfer via person joining the firm	$20\frac{1}{2}$(b)
Common knowledge via industrial experience	15
Common knowledge via education	9
Commercial agreement(including takeover & sale of knowhow)	$10\frac{1}{2}$
Literature (technical, scientific and patent)	$9\frac{1}{2}$
Personal contact in U.K.	$8\frac{1}{2}$
Collaboration with supplier	7
Collaboration with customer	5
Visit overseas	$6\frac{1}{2}$
Passed on by government organization	6
Conference in U.K.	$2\frac{1}{2}$
Consultancy	2
	102

(a) *Taken from Langrish, Gibbons, Evans & Jevons*

(b) *The half integers arise because, in some cases, the method of transfer involved more than a single route.*

The second type - the technical entrepreneur - is an entrepreneur in the full sense since he leaves his company or research establishment and sets up his own business. The organization resulting from the latter process is often referred to as a spin-off company; it is with certain aspects of such firms that the remainder of this paper is concerned. It is worthwhile to note at the outset that spin-off is a characteristic of both the British and American industrial environments; it is often wrongly assumed that spin-off is a uniquely American phenomenon that somehow reflects a greater propensity for investment in advanced technology.

The Importance of Small Firms in an Industrial Economy

A question often asked of small companies, be they spin-off or not, is, how can they possibly compete with the resources of capital and manpower available to the giants? One answer, quite simply, is that a large, well-established corporation is often committed to a product or range of products which is well-defined technologically and finds itself constrained (by factors such as the need to maintain a good dividend to its shareholders) to change technologies only slowly. In many cases, the entire management structure is oriented towards coping with the day-to-day difficulties of a given technology and could not easily throw the weight of its expertise behind one which was strikingly different. In this sense, size may be a handicap rather than an advantage and the small company scores because of its faster reaction time. There is, too, the sort of product that is either too complex (or too simple) technically or aimed at too limited a market to be commercially attractive to the large firm. But, because it is of little interest to the giant, this may not mean that it is universally unattractive as a commercial proposition. Many small firms make very respectable profits for a time by supplying just these kinds of products, many of them technologically highly sophisticated, to what seems from the standpoint of large firms a some-what restricted market.

Technologically advanced spin-off firms tend to be formed when a scientist (or a group containing scientists) leaves a university or the laboratories of another firm, sensing a market opportunity which can be satisfied by his technological expertise and often armed with ideas that had previously been developed in the original organization. The point is, that unless these ideas are taken out of their existing environment (whether it be university laboratory or established firm) and placed in another environment more conducive to commercial exploitation, they are likely to be strangled by the structures and procedures of the original organization. In this way a small spin-off firm can provide an environ-ment for translating a novel technological idea into a commercial proposi-tion. On the other hand, when large-scale production facilities are required, many small firms sell out or are taken over by some larger organization which is well situated to supply the capital and management expertise in the quantities required. There is some evidence for a trend of this type among spin-off firms, particularly from America. The end result is that via the medium of the small company a new technology is now available in the economy which might not otherwise have been allowed to develop.

The Existence of Small Spin-Off Firms

That technologically oriented spin-off firms exist is now a matter of record. The growth of a scientific complex around Boston, Massachusetts

Route 128 has been thoroughly investigated by Roberts & Wainer (1968), among others. Similar complexes exist around other major industrial and educational centres in the country such as Palo Alto, California and Dallas, Texas and, according to some, the west coast complex surpasses in vitality the now famous firms on Route 128.

Contrary to popular belief, spin-off, of the Route 128 and Palo Alto varieties, does occur in Britain though it does not yet exhibit the degree of geographical concentration prevalent in America. In the United Kingdom, the Home Counties and southern Scotland seem to provide attractive sites for the technical entrepreneur; there is also evidence of some activity in the Oxford and Cambridge areas.

According to Mahar *et al* (1965), the conditions required to sustain a scientific complex like Route 128 include one or more of three major elements :

1. Science-based industry composed of :
   a) industrial research and development laboratories ;
   b) technically oriented manufacturing plants, that is, plant employing a high proportion of scientists and engineers, producing products embodying advanced and rapidly changing technology; &
   c) supporting suppliers and services
2. One or more major universities offering advanced studies in science, engineering and mathematics.
3. Government research facilities.

The Route 128 complex is the best known example of a full 'three-element complex-industry, university and government'. Palo Alto, on the other hand, is a two-element complex built around strong universities and science-based industries.

These major elements are present to some extent in the London and Edinburgh areas and may go part way to explaining why these two centres appear to be more active in producing spin-off companies in Britain. However, the fact that the same type of facilities are available, perhaps to an even greater extent, in Manchester and Birmingham where there seems to be virtually no university spin-off firms, suggests that other, more subtle, factors must be involved.

Some Comparisons Between the U.K. and the U.S.A.

Although the researches of Roberts & Wainer (1968) into the spin-off firms that originated from M.I.T.'s Lincoln and Instrumentation Laboratories are by far the most exhaustive treatment of the spin-off phenomenon, there is now available some work on the factors affecting commercial exploitation of research ideas from the Imperial College of Science and Technology with which some instructive comparisons can be made (Launder & Webster, 1969). In the Imperial College (I.C.) study, a survey was made of six departments - mining, mechanical, engineering, electrical engineering, chemistry, physics and botany. This survey determined, among other things, the incidence of commercially exploitable ideas at I.C., the type of idea involved (i.e. instrument, service, etc.), success with previous attempts at commercial exploitation, method of exploiting ideas, difficulties encountered and relations with industry. A similar study has been carried out by Peters and Roberts (1969) into the numbers of unutilized ideas in the Lincoln and Instrumentation Laboratories at M.I.T., the reasons why scientists there did not go into business for themselves, action taken on possible ideas, and factors impeding their successful development to the commercial stage. A summary of the comparisons made by the authors is listed in Tables 2 and 3.

TABLE 2 : The existence & utilization of ideas whose scope is outside the university

University	Sample	Claim to have ideas		Attempted to do something	
	No.	No.	%	No.	%
M.I.T.Lincoln(a)	161	72	44.7	25	35
M.I.T.Instrumentation(a)	138	75	54.4	24	32
Imperial College(b)	63	37	58.7	26	41.4

(a) *Peters & Roberts (1969), Table 1*
(b) *Modified from Launder & Webster (1969), Table 1, Appendix 1*

As may be seen from Table 2, roughly the same percentage of scientists in M.I.T. and I.C. had ideas which they felt were commercially exploitable. Of considerable interest is the fact that a somewhat higher percentage of British scientists actually attempted to do something about exploiting their ideas. In Table 3, we have tried to reduce the data in Peters & Roberts (1969), Table 4 and Launder & Webster (1969), Appendix 1, Table 2, to some common form. By and large this was successful, though as can be seen from Table 3 there were some categories with which comparisons could not be made.

TABLE 3 : Factors impeding attempts to proceed from initial ideas to the commercial stage (frequency and percentage)

	U.S.				U.K.	
	Lincoln Laboratory		Instrumentation Laboratory		Imperial College	
	No.	%	No.	%	No.	%
1. Lack of initiative by university personnel; Insufficient financial incentive.	15	22	15	21.7	27	21.3
2. Uncertainty of demand (fear that proposition may not be viable)	6	8.8	11	15.9	13	10.5
3. Insufficient official encouragement to develop ideas to commercial level	7	10.3	5	7.2	13	10.5
4. University restriction (including those imposed by teaching duties)	4	5.9	-	-	9	7.1
5. Lack of time & facilities to develop new ideas	28	41.2	22	31.9	10	7.9
6. Lack of adequate finance for development	4	5.9	9	13.0	42	33.0
7. Other	4	5.9	7	10.1	13	10.5
TOTAL	68	100.0	69	99.8*	127	100.8*

* *Error due to rounding*

One or two other interesting points emerge from this analysis. The largest factor impeding the successful development of commercially exploitable ideas in the U.S.A. was found to be a lack of the time and facilities to develop the ideas further, while in the U.K. the largest single factor was lack of adequate finance.

The American result is probably not unreasonable when one considers that the Lincoln and Instrumentation Laboratories, although administered by M.I.T. are heavily engaged in government contract work, thus implying that the scientists working there have less time to devote to their personal interests than they would have in a more traditional university laboratory. It also appears (though not from the tables presented here) that lack of management or business expertise is a greater factor impeding spin-off in the U.K. than the U.S.A.

An important distinction between the U.S.A. and the U.K. may be found in the degree to which people with ideas talk these over with suitably qualified people. Peters & Roberts (1969) have shown that scientists in the Lincoln and Instrumentation Laboratories tend to discuss the feasibility of their ideas : 32% of the replies to questions about specific action taken with ideas cited discussion with other qualified people (the largest single factor). By contrast, Launder & Webster(1969) found that : "One striking feature which emerged from the survey was that very few staff had attempted to enlist the help of Government research establishments or industrial research associations for development work. Some staff were unaware that research associations would undertake such work....It appears to the authors that collaboration between a university and such establishments would be an ideal way to undertake technically-advanced development work of an invention".

The fact that British scientists perceive a lack of adequate financial resources as one of the main impediments to developing their ideas into commercially viable products or services probably reflects their lack of awareness about how to obtain finance as much as an absolute short-age of money itself. A preliminary survey carried out by the authors would seem to indicate that the sources of finance, for the commercial exploitation of ideas embodying advanced technology, are both varied and relatively plentiful. If anything, there may be a shortage of people coming forward with suitable, commercially oriented ideas.

At the same time, it would be wrong to conclude that venture capital is as freely available to the would-be technical entrepreneur in the U.K. as it is in the U.S.A. One reason for this seems to be that it is relatively much easier for individuals to accumulate capital from income under the American taxation system. In addition, there are often tax advantages in investing this acquired wealth in small, rather than larger, companies. Nevertheless, high risk finance is available both from certain merchant banks and from companies such as Technical Development Capital Ltd. and Fulcra Finance which have specialised in investment opportunities involving inventive and technical entrepreneurs.

It is perhaps worth saying, however, that the belief in venture capital investments in high technology as a new and easy way of making money has been challenged recently by Welles (1970) and Rotch (1968). Rotch concluded that even the performance record of American Research & Development Corporation, which he described as "the most pre-eminent venture capital company of modern times", is far short of miraculous. A.R.D.'s return on capital invested was calculated as no more than 14% over the first 20 years of its existence. During a similar period, the average return on the securities comprising the Dow-Jones Index was only 2-3% lower at approximately 11.5%. If A.R.D.'s single most success-ful investment (that in Digital Equipment Corporation) is discounted, the return would be a mere 8%. When the extreme riskiness of investing in high technology penetrates the American money market there may well be less enthusiasm than at present to gamble away excess dollars.

Although in the U.K. a more cautious attitude towards financing high technology is adopted, there is still money available. If this is so, why does there appear to be relatively fewer Route 128 type companies in this country? It must be admitted that there is not nearly enough known about the problems of spin-off which have been encountered by small firms.

The authors are at present engaged in developing a programme of research into the problems associated with the birth, growth and diversification patterns of these companies. In addition, information is being gathered on the family and educational backgrounds of technical entrepreneurs who manage these firms as well as the attitudes of the various venture capital organizations towards high technology invest-ments so that international comparisons may be attempted.

If technological innovation is indeed dependent on the technical entrepreneurs, then policies should be developed to create an environment which fosters their activities. Far from being outmoded, the small firm and the individual technical entrepreneur are central to the innovation process and it would be unfortunate if preoccupation with size and economies of scale were to lead government to propose industrial policies which neglected this major area of potential for economic growth.

Burns, T. (1969), 'Models, images & myths', Factors in the Transfer of Technology, (ed. by W.H. Gruber & D.G. Marquis), M.I.T. Press, Cambridge, Mass. p. 12

Launder, B.E. & Webster, G.A. (1969) 'University Research & the Considerations Affecting its Commercial Exploitation', published by Technical Development Capital Ltd., January

Mahar, J.F. & Coddington, D.C. (1965), 'The scientific complex - proceed with caution', Harvard Business Review, Jan-Feb., pp. 140-155

Peters, D.H. & Roberts, E.B. (1969), 'Unutilised ideas in university laboratories', Academy of Management Journal, Vol. 12, No. 2, June, pp. 179-191

Roberts, E.B. & Wainer, H.A. (1968), 'New enterprises on Route 128', Science Journal, December

Rotch, W. (1968), 'The patterns of success in venture capital financing' Financial Analysts Journal, Sept.-Oct., pp. 1-7

Welles, C. (1970), 'Venture capital, the biggest mousetrap of the 1970s' The Institutional Investor, January

2. SMALL AND MEDIUM SIZED MANUFACTURING FIRMS AND TECHNOLOGICAL INNOVATION

Roy Rothwell

Management Decision. Volume 16 Number 6. 1978

INTRODUCTION

Governments in Western Europe are showing an increasing interest in the welfare of small and medium sized manufacturing firms (SMEs) and in the generation of new technology-based small firms. There are a number of reasons for this, two of the most important being :

(a) widespread belief in the potential of new technology-based small firms for producing radical new technologies that will open up new investment opportunities vital for future growth and employment

(b) increasing competition from developing countries, particularly in traditional industry sectors, the future competitiveness of which lies in producing more sophisticated and innovative products.

Thus, interest in SMEs is focused largely around their propensity for, and their ability to produce successfully, technological innovations. This article briefly presents empirical data which show the relative contribution SMEs have made to technological innovation during the post Second World War years(1).

THE ROLE OF SMEs IN INNOVATION

A great deal has been written concerning the innovativeness of SMEs in comparison with that of large companies. It has on the one hand been argued that large size and monopoly power are prerequisites for economic progress *via* technical change, while on the other hand it has been argued that small firms are more efficient at performing innovative activities and are, in fact, the major source of innovations. In this section the relative contributions of SMEs to both invention and innovation are discussed.

(i) Firm Size and R & D Expenditure

Innovations are generally the result of R & D endeavour, and it might be interesting here to discuss briefly the relationship between firm size and R & D expenditure. According to a recent literature survey, empirical evidence indicates that for those firms which undertake R & D, innovational efforts tend to increase more than proportionally with firm size up to some point that varies with industry sector. Beyond some magnitude, size does not appear especially conducive to either innovational effort or output(2). It is important to note, however, that most SMEs do not engage in formal R & D (probably less than 5% of firms employing under 200 perform R & D) while most large firms do so. The following figures provide some indication of the *concentration* of R & D expenditures in large companies :

> In 1970, firms employing more than 5,000 accounted for 89% of all industrial R & D expenditure in the U.S., 75% in West Germany and 60% in France.
>
> In 1961, firms in Britain with more than 10,000 employees accounted for nearly 60% of industrial R & D.

Taking *company-financed* R & D only (as opposed to *total* R & D performed which might include Government funded work), differences in R & D expenditure by size of firm become less marked (this, of course, relates to firms which *do* perform R & D). There are also large differences between industry sectors and in some sectors there is an inverse correlation between *research-intensity* - rather than absolute R & D expenditure - and firm size(3).

(ii)   Firm Size and Invention

Evidence concerning the relative contributions of firms of different sizes to *inventive* output is limited. Table 1 lists the results of several studies on the frequency of major inventions by small firms or independent inventors : it suggests that small firms and independent inventors have played a disproportionately large part in producing major 20th century inventions(4).

Re-analysis of the Jewkes, Sawers and Stillerman data showed, however, that while universities, independent inventors and small firms made the major contribution to the more radical type of 20th century invention before 1930, since 1930 corporate R & D has played the dominant role(5).

TABLE I : Research on the frequency of major inventions by small firms or independent inventors

Author	Type of inventions	%age of inventions by small firms or independent inventors
Jewkes, Sawers, Stillerman (1958)	61 important inventions & innovations of the 20th century	(more than) 50
Hamberg (1963)	major inventions in the decade 1946-55	(more than) 67
Peck (1962)	149 inventions in aluminium welding, fabricating techniques & aluminium finishing	86
Hamberg (1963)	7 major innovations in the American steel industry	100
Enos (1962)	7 major inventions in the refining & cracking of petroleum	100

SOURCE : *Prakke, F., The Management of the R & D Interface, Doctoral Thesis, Massachusetts Institute of Technology, 1974*

It is also worth noting that at least half the inventions in the sample produced by small firms and independent inventors subsequently owed their successful commercial exploitation to the development work and innovative efforts of large firms.

Data from the U.S. show that smaller firms produce a much higher - although declining - number of patents per dollar of R & D expenditure than large firms (Table II), which has been claimed as evidence of superior productivity of smaller firm R & D. However, one leading expert in the U.S. provides evidence that, contrary to general belief, large U.S. firms have a *lower propensity* to patent than small firms(6). In his view small firms cannot afford *not* to patent, and cannot afford to wait, so that patent statistics tend to exaggerate the contribution of small firms to inventive output. (Merely counting patents does not, anyway, give any indication of their relative importance.)

TABLE II : Estimated innovation rate in major innovations per R & D
Dollar

	Firm size (total number of employees)		
Time interval	1-1,000	1,000-10,000	10,000+
1953-59	100.0	29.5	3.9
1960-66	64.4	14.4	2.3
1967-73	35.1	9.0	2.0
1953-73 total	57.3	15.0	2.4

Numbers are relative to the innovation rate for companies of 1 to 1,000
employees in the 1953-59 period; this rate is assigned the value 100.

SOURCE : *Government Policies & Factors Influencing the Innovative
Capability of SMEs, paper prepared by the OECD, Secre-
tariat & Staffgroup Strategic Surveys TNO, OECD, May '78.*

(iii) Firm Size and Innovation

Probably the most detailed data relating to firm size and innovation
derive from the Bolton Committee of Inquiry on Small Firms in the U.K.
(7). The results of this study are shown in Table III.

TABLE III : Number & percentage share of innovations by size of firm
in United Kingdom

Years	Small firms (1-199)		Medium firms (200-999)		Large firms (1000+)		All firms	
	Number	%total	Number	%total	Number	%total	Number	%total
1945-53	17	9	25	12	160	79	202	100
1954-61	38	10	43	11	313	80	394	100
1962-70	54	11	53	10	399	79	506	100
Total 1945-70	109	10	121	11	872	79	1102	100

The study reached the following conclusions :

(a) Small firms contributed about 10% of all industrial innovations made
in the U.K. between 1945 and 1970. (This is greater than small firms'

share of R & D expenditure – about 5% or less.) In 1958 (the median year), small firms accounted for 25% of employment and 21% of net output (including construction and utilities).

(b) The share of small firms in innovation has been more or less constant, while their share of employment and output has been falling, e.g. in 1963 they accounted for only 22% of employment and 19% of output.

(c) Very large firms (employment over 10,000) accounted for 54% of all innovations. Large firms (employment over 1,000) accounted for 20% of all innovations.

TABLE IV : Share of small firms in innovations and net output of industries surveyed in U.K.

1958 SIC MLH Number	1958 SIC title of industry	%share of innovations by small firms 1945-1970	No.of innovations by small firms 1945 1970	No.of innovations by all firms 1945-1970	%share of net output by small firms 1963	Value of net output by all firms 1963 (£m)
471-3	timber & furniture	39	7	18	49	220
351	scientific instruments	28	23	84	23	154
431-3,450	leather & footwear	26	5	19	32	157
335	textile machinery	23	15	65	21	65
481-3	paper & board	20	6	30	15	317
339	general machinery	17	18	108	14	409
332	machine tools	11	4	38	18	100
411-15 417,419 492	textiles, carpets	10	6	63	18	670
364	electronics	8	13	160	8	320
211-29	food	8	3	38	16	814
381	vehicles, tractors	4	3	64	5	733
276	synthetic resins,plastic	4	2	52	12	77
370	shipbuilding	2	1	59	10	215
271(1)	dyes	0	0	22	7	35
272(1)	pharmaceuticals	0	0	44	12	124
463	glass	0	0	13	14	96
464	cement	0	0	18	0*	41
383	aircraft	0	0	52	2	185
321	aluminium	0	0	16	10*	100*
311-13	iron & steel	0	0	68	9	630
101	coal	0	0	23	0	655
601	gas	0	0	15	0	216
500,336	construction,earthmvg. equip.&contractors'plt.	12	4	33	53	1931

* estimated   SOURCE : (7)

The share of small firms in innovation varied a great deal from industry sector to industry sector (Table IV). Generally speaking, in the capital intensive industries, both product and process innovations were produced mainly by large firms. (The major exceptions were aerospace, shipbuilding and pharmaceuticals where, although capital intensity is low, the development costs for most new products are very high.) Small firms made their major contribution in machinery and instruments where both capital intensity and development costs are low, and where entry costs for new firms are also low.

A second study, this time of 380 important (importance was determined by an expert panel who chose the innovations out of an original total of 1,310) innovations produced in five countries, which were introduced onto the market between 1953 and 1973 looked, among other things, at the relative contributions made by firms of different sizes to the total number of innovations(8). The results of this study are presented in Table V.

TABLE V : Share of 352 major innovations by firm size in five countries

Country	Small firms(a) No.of innovations (Ns)	Ratio Ns : Nl	Medium firms(b) No.of innovations (Nm)	Ratio Nm : Nl	Large firms(c) No.of innovations (Nl)	Ratio Nl : (Ns+Nm)	Total No.of innovations
U.S.	90(35%)	0.70	37(15%)	0.29	129(50%)	1.02	248
U.K.	8(23%)	0.35	3(3%)	0.13	23(67%)	2.09	34
W.Germany	5(26%)	0.42	2(10%)	0.17	12(64%)	1.71	19
Japan	1(4%)	0.05	4(16%)	0.20	20(80%)	4.00	25
France	5(31%)	0.71	4(26%)	0.57	7(43%)	0.78	16
TOTAL	109(31%)	0.57	50(14%)	0.26	192(54%)	1.20	352

(a) *Sales less than $5 million*
(b) *Sales $5 million to $50 million*
(c) *Sales greater than $50 million*
SOURCE : (8)

Table V shows that :
(a) Averaged over all countries, small firms contributed about one-third of all innovations (31%) the majority share being taken by large

firms (54%).

(b) Medium sized firms played only a minor role, except in France, where they contributed 26% of innovations.

(c) Small firms' contribution was highest in the U.S. (35%) and France (31%), followed by West Germany (26%) and the U.K. (23%).

(d) Small (and medium) firms in Japan played a very minor role as producers of major innovations.

The study also looked at the comparison of firm size with the "radicalness" of the innovation. The results of this comparison showed that :

(a) In the United States small firms produced a reasonably even distribution of "radical breakthrough", "major technological shift" and "improvement" type innovations (27%, 30% and 37% respectively of all small firm innovations). A similar pattern was found for large firms.

(b) The output of small firms in the U.K. was entirely composed of radical breakthrough type innovations. The emphasis in large firms was also on this type of innovation (56% of all large firm innovations in the U.K.).

(c) In West Germany, Japan and France the emphasis for firms of all sizes, was on the less radical types of innovations.

Finally as regards firm size and radicality of innovation, a recent study of 50 or so post-war innovations in the European textile machinery industry has shown that the size of firms successfully producing technically radical innovations was about three times that of firms producing non-radical incremental innovations (750 employees - radical innovators; 220 employees - incremental innovators) (9). This pattern was a consequence of the ability of the larger firms to mount a formal R & D effort and to employ graduate level technical specialists. In the smaller firms technical developments were undertaken mainly by non-graduate technicians and draughtsmen working in a less formal design and development department.

SMEs AND RADICAL NEW TECHNOLOGY

Having considered the role of SMEs as producers of innovations, it is relevant to discuss the role they have played, and might play in the future, in advancing whole new radical technologies. (This does not refer to the production of a specific radical innovation, but rather to advance on a broad technological and economic front once a basic innovation such as electric power, polymerisation or the semi-conductor has been made.)

The question is, is such an advance best served by a few very big firms which possess large R & D, production and marketing resources, or by many small firms or by some combination of both? Perhaps the leading example of the successful advancement of such a technology is the case of semi-conductors in the U.S., and an analysis of this might go some way towards providing an answer to the above question.

According to one recent commentator :

".... on Route 128 and in Silicon Valley Technology Oriented Companies (TOCs) were created which consisted of a large number of entrepreneurial firms. These firms had strong relations with universities and government laboratories in the region. Many of them were started as spin-offs from government laboratories. These institutions also provided a continuous flow of highly specialised engineers. Moreover, communication between firms was guaranteed by that peculiarly American habit of job-hopping. Fortune (27 February 1975) at one time estimated the job turnover in Silicon Valley at 15% to 20% per annum. Risk capital was amply and expertly provided by local venture capitalists, many of whom were graduates of the small firm experience. Apart from the highly visible effects such as industrial parks and stock market values, these firms had a profound effect on the structure of the American electronics industry......none of the leading vacuum tube manufacturers in the U.S. survived to similarly lead in the production of semi-conductors. In Japan, however, the established firms were able to make the switch to semi-conductors without interference from small firms. In Europe the traditional firms were also able to maintain their position.

It seems that two explanations are possible. They both throw a different light on the role of small firms as sources of technological change. The first explanation is that the success of the TOCs reflects a particularly American phenomenon. It is based on a culture that puts a low value on company loyalty and a high one on individual entrepreneurial activity. Innovation activity in large firms would be discouraged because

of the threat technological change might present to individual job
security. If this analysis is correct it would be unwise to expect much
from recent European efforts to create TOCs......It would then be
wiser for Europe and Japan to concentrate their efforts on improving
the performance of established firms.

The second explanation of the difference in the development of the
U.S. and non-U.S. semi-conductor industry lies in the fact that the
U.S. firms were at all times in the forefront of technological development
in this area and that their European and Japanese counterparts can be
said to have had the less risk entailing task of following the leader.

A strategy of being second-to-market involves less uncertainty than
being at the forefront. The question can be posed whether large firms
in Europe and Japan would have been equally successful if U.S. industry,
characterised by the large role of small firms, had not paved the way.
There is a proposition in general systems theory which says that only
complexity can destroy complexity.

Translated to our area this could mean that in an area of rapid
technological change, of which the outstanding environmental property
is complexity, the most successful organisational response will also be
characterised by complexity. Such organisational complexity seems to
be better provided by a system of many small firms than by a few large
ones. The conclusion would be that Europe and Japan will not be able
to compete successfully with the U.S. in advanced technology by
concentrating technological development in their established firms.
These firms may be quite advanced scientifically through close co-operation with European university laboratories. They may be quite successful commercially through use of a second-to-market strategy....but if
the above explanation of the small firm phenomenon is correct they will
go on being dependent on technical know-how developed in a system
which tends to assign a specific place to small firms as creators of new
technology." (10)

In the light of the above, it might be possible to speculate on the
impact of the most recent radical advance in semi-conductor technology
- the microprocessor - on the competitiveness of small firms *vis-a-vis*
large firms. It seems reasonable to postulate that in the U.S. small

entrepreneurial firms will play a leading role in developing new "smart" products and process utilising microprocessors, while in Europe and Japan they will be produced, at a later date, by established large firms.

DISCUSSION

This paper has addressed itself to the question "What role do small firms play in producing technological innovation?" The answer to this question seems to be that SMEs play a significant part as generators of technological innovations and radical new technology. Having said this it is necessary to add the following qualifications to the answer :

(a) While SMEs appear to make a major contribution in such areas as scientific instruments and some branches of engineering (i.e. where capital costs are relatively small), in those areas where the capital cost of innovation is high, e.g. chemicals, pharmaceuticals, SMEs' contribution to innovation is small.

(b) In areas where economies of scale play a major role, e.g. automobile industry, SMEs' contribution to innovation is likely to be an *indirect* one *via* component (rather than complete system) innovations. In such areas innovation does, anyway, tend to be "production process" rather than "new product" orientated.

Finally, as regards to the role new technology-based small firms play in innovation and the economy, there is some evidence to suggest that they play a major (though declining) role in the U.S., but only a minor role in the U.K. and West Germany. This should be an area for some concern on the part of U.K. Government policy makers(11).

(1) *Rothwell,R. & Zegueld,W., Small & Medium Sized Manufacturing Firms:Their Role & Problems in Innovation in Government Policy in Europe, USA, Canada, Japan & Israel, Report to Six Countries, Programme on Innovation, June 1978*

(2) *Kamien,M.I. & Schwartz,N.L., Market Structure & Innovation:A Survey , Journal of Economic Literature,Vol.13,No.1,March 1975*

(3)   *Freeman,C., The Economics of Industrial Innovation, Penguin Modern Economic Texts, 1974*

(4)   *Prakke,F., The Management of the R & D Interface, PhD Thesis, Massachusetts Institute of Technology, 1974*

(5)   *Freeman,C., Science & Economy at the National Level , Problems of Science Policy, OECD, 1967*

(6)   *Schmookler,J., Invention & Economic Growth, Harvard University Press, 1966*

(7)   *Freeman,C., The Role of Small Firms in Innovation in the U.K. since 1945, Report to the Bolton Committee of Inquiry on Small Firms, Research Report No. 6, HMSO, 1971*

(8)   *National Science Foundation, Indicators of International Trends in Technological Innovation, NSF-C889, Washington, April 1976*

(9)   *Rothwell, R., Innovation in Textile Machinery : Some Significant Factors in Success & Failure, SPRU Occasional Paper Series, No. 2 June 1976*

(10) *Zegveld,W., Government Policies & Factors Influencing the Innovative Capability of Small & Medium Enterprises , Paper prepared for the Committee for Scientific & Technological Policy, OECD, 1978*

(11) *Little,A.D.,Ltd., New Technology-Based Firms in the U.K. and the Federal Republic of Germany, Wilton House Publications Ltd., 1977*

3. THE COMING ENTREPRENEURIAL REVOLUTION : A SURVEY

Norman Macrae

The Economist. 25th December 1976

TEN GREEN BOTTLES

This survey will set forth for discussion ten propositions :

(1) The world is probably drawing to the end of the era of big business corporations. These institutions were virtually created during 1875-1910. During 1975-2010 they may virtually disappear in their present form, and the interesting question is what will replace them.

(2) The main lesson from 1955-75 is that they will not be replaced by state capitalism, because state production of almost any service or good does not work in countries with access to a bewildering range of new technology. Many services now provided by governments will need to be "recompetitioned" and reprivatised. Unfortunately, unlike the retreat or reform of big business corporations, this will probably happen only slowly.

(3) The main reason why bureaucratic production can no longer work is that the decision-taker in any efficient productive system must now restlessly ask : "What is the best quickly-changing and labour-saving technology that I should use to accomplish this task?" In a state monopoly decision-blocking power quickly falls into the hands of people who can explain most suavely that anybody who keeps asking those questions is being a bad colleague by constantly rocking the boat. In some big business corporations, with layer of management sitting upon layer, decision-blocking power has fallen into the hands of similar middle bureaucracies. These will go bust.

(4) During the Henry Ford manufacturing age about 40 of the world's 159 countries had grown rich because they were temporarily able to increase productivity efficiently by organisational action from the top : i.e. executives sat at some level in the offices of hierarchically-run corporations and arranged how those below them on the assembly lines could most productively work with their hands. This method of growing

rich has now run into two rather fundamental difficulties : a "people problem" because educated workers in rich countries do not like to be organised from the top; and an "enterprise problem" because, now that much of manufacturing and most of simple white collar tasks can be gradually automated so that more workers can become brainworkers, it will be nonsense to sit in hierarchical offices trying to arrange what the workers in the offices below do with their imaginations.

(5) In three successive waves of efforts to solve their "people problem" (or "alienation problem"), rich northern countries have (a) imported more amenable workers from the poorer south, (b) sent multinational factories down to the poorer south, (c) tried to persuade native workers to love factories more through worker participation. None of these three systems is conceivably going to work.

(6) Incentives to make workers happier will have to become much more individual, and be geared to allowing each human to choose his lifestyle - because choosing one's lifestyle is what freedom in future must mainly mean. So tomorrow's job applicant will sit at a computer console and answer questions. Do you want a major personal say in choosing your own working hours? My own answer : "usually, yes". But in emergencies do you mind sudden periods of frantic working for a day-and-night on end? My answer : "no, actually I rather enjoy that". Do you mind..... But we will pick up this parlour game again later. The point is the obvious one that the atmosphere which each individual severally enjoys at work is an important part of that individual's happiness, and there is bound to be worker alienation until each individual can shop around to seek something like the atmosphere he wants.

The marrying of job specifications to the individually-varied and constantly-changing patterns of lifestyles demanded - with the lower wages going to those who say they choose the less productive or more popular lifestyles - cannot efficiently be attempted by a hierarchical corporation, but will be a matter for constant experiment. This means that the tabulation and widening (through asking new questions etc.) of both "personnel choices" and "lifestyle choices" will be among the many big-growth small-scale-entrepreneur industries, on subcontracting to which larger firms will increasingly rely. A big productive and libertarian advantage of this individualisation of contracts is that it will surreptitiously but dramatically erode the power of the trade unions. That is one reason why businesses, once they realise what can happen, will probably introduce it rather fast.

(7) When people can chat to a friendly computer about the workstyles they would like, it will probably be found that there is a surplus of would-be, part-time, part-risk entrepreneurs. This will be exactly what is needed in order to take advantage of tomorrow's technology.

Even in manufacturing, a main feature of a computer-controlled system will be that it can be told, unlike a batch of mere human beings, to make some experimental changes in the 404th item coming along the assembly line. Successful companies will be those which see that the best experiments for this "custom-built production at mass production prices" are not likely to be found by a committee. They will instead be found by (e.g.) renting out time on the assembly lines to people with entrepreneurial ideas. In white-collar work the need for entrepreneurship is already more obvious and urgent, and is being even more obviously mishandled. In most big offices, most white-collar departments are not even approximately of the right size and shape. All businesses should already be experimenting every day to find which is the best for them of several thousand possible approach roads towards the paperless office.

(8) At a time when the appearance of so many alternative new technologies should make an increase in entrepreneurship so desirable and such potential fun - while threatening to make into absolute hell the life of any managing director who thinks he has to decide through a committee(which includes the trade unions) on one particular way of doing things - rich countries will be silly if they restrict entrepreneurship to the few brave fanatics who can take imprudent risks with their families' whole manner of life. Dynamic corporations of the future should simultaneously be trying several alternative ways of doing things in competition within themselves, and have on their payrolls a lot of individuals and group co-operatives of workers who are part-entrepreneurial sub-contractors and part-salaried staff but wholly neither. This is what will be meant by this survey's argument that successful big corporations should devolve into becoming "confederations of entrepreneurs".

(9) It is gradually becoming clear that ownership of the means of production is no longer a source of economic or political power, and may indeed now be a source of economic and political powerlessness. It is easy for an organisation to take action against sub-contractors by cutting off contracts; it is no longer easy to pass down orders to direct employees. Where it has hitherto been fashionable for a company to boast how many workers it employs, it will be fashionable henceforth to boast how much work it has contracted out to others all round the world. The next generation of whizz kids will be those who make big business grow efficiently-smaller during a boom, with large profits to shareholders from their sales of bits of the businesses.

(10) This is not to deny that some activities should pass under the management of bigger organisations, even while others become more entrepreneurial. During the eventide of the big business corporations, the most successful companies have been those restless enough to be unsure what their management styles should be. Successful big American corporations today will often centralise their policy-making, and get a significant initial gain in effectiveness; but then, as time passes, will find that this does not work because the central planners do not know what is really going on out in the field. So these corporations will then decentralise, and get a significant initial gain in effectiveness, but will then find that all their divisions are going in different directions. So they will then recentralise, and get a significant gain in effectiveness, but after a time...... This constant reorganisation is in fact very sensible, and is a main reason why I judge that big American corporations are still often the most efficient day-to-day business operators (though not investors) in the world. European and Japanese companies do not keep their executives on their toes by reorganising nearly as frequently.

Still, the present American corporation management system - of chop a little and change a lot - is a device for dealing with the problems set by bureaucracy, not for replacing it by entrepreneurship. For the near future my guess is that many of the things that have traditionally been left to small organisations - like professional services, hairdressing(which needs to become more automated), computerised tax-dodging advice, golf club management etc. - will be made more efficient and profitable if they are periodically taken under some larger organisations' control and run by some more disciplined process; but that many of the things that have traditionally been run by some disciplined process (manufacturing, office management of big corporations, government services) will need periodically to be made much more entrepreneurial in very odd ways.

Nobody in his senses will agree with all the guesses at trends that I scatter broadside through the next few pages. But it will be disappointing if there is not a germ of an idea in some of them. Let us begin with the alienated workers.

THREE LIGHTS FAILED

Middle class critics tend to assume that the great worries about factory jobs are boredom and monotony. But sometimes the restfulness of this monotony is rather welcome. A bigger worry lies in the ordinary man's resentment when he's "got a foreman riding his back". This resentment increases with income, education, but most especially with increases in the school-leaving age.

Since 1946 liberals have successively hoped that the shopfloor labour problems of the rich north of the world could be mitigated by importing workers from the poor south, or sending multinationals to the poor south, or waving the flag of worker democracy. It has now become clear that none of these three is going to work.

Why immigration won't work

First generation immigrants from Jamaica or Turkey are the most daring of their village, a marvellous entrepreneurial type. When they arrive in factories in Birmingham and Eindhoven, they are told that they must integrate into the customs of those with whom they are menially set to work, which means "become bloody-minded please".

The indignities piled upon them, as exacerbated by such absurdities as Britain's class consciousness and leasehold and rent control (i.e. urban decay) systems, are borne meekly by the immigrants, but not by their sons. Since immigrants enter in waves and when of child-bearing age, these sons arrive at awkward teenagehood in a generation bulge. They go mugging and call it revenge for 400 years of slavery, while bashing some old lady in Brixton whose sense of historical guilt is understandably small.

It is then discovered in Britain, as it has been in New York, that welfare states are divisive in pluralist societies, even though they can be unifying in the Swedish sort of homogeneous society (where unification is anyway not much needed). Barriers are then put up against immigration, and there is much more widespread illegal entry than anybody dares to admit. A large disenfranchised illegal immigrant subproletariat is today encamped in both north Europe and north America. They are not loved.

In Britain the anti-immigrant populist backlash is now of the nastiest nazi-type and Labour politicians who lose thereby and Tory politicians who reap therefrom will both edge to it like von Papens. In north-west continental Europe and north America there will also be no new attempts to integrate settler-immigrants as manual workers, but there will be increased hirings of deliberately short-term migrant workers. Britons are likely to be one of the main groups of these poorish, unintegrated, short-term migrant workers on the European continent, so they will be unwise to allow their own prejudices against immigrants to become loud.

Nor will multinationals

The second remedy for the alienation of ordinary workers in rich northern countries was supposed to be to export manufacturing industries to the poor south. This will proceed, although in an erratic way. The most successfully-exported industries will be for disguised re-import, like the American consumer electronics industry. This departed entirely to Asia in the 1960s, but is now coming back to America for automated and computer-controlled production, because the American trade union restrictions which would have prevented this have disappeared while the domestic American industry did not exist. It would be wise to treat large parts of British manufacturing industry (including all of subsidised motor car manufacturing) in this way.

It will now generally be most un-economic to build a factory to make widgets in areas which "have a long tradition of making widgets already". Manufacturing plants are worst built as cathedrals in already-built-up areas with large site-clearing costs, log-jammed access roads, trade union traditions, self-important town councils and local aesthetes who safeguard every Victorian relic - i.e. they are least efficiently built in existing industrial towns. They are most frequently built as one storey buildings stretching across many green fields.

The green fields in poor countries may by the late 1980s attract more of them because of a change in the age structure of poor countries, which may indeed be the single most important - but most disregarded - statistic for this next decade. in most of the poor two thirds of the world a majority of the population today is below the age of 21, which helps explain these countries' low incomes per head, since children largely produce nothing and teenagers largely produce riots. The age bulge will naturally pass on ten years over the next decade and by 1986 these countries will have lots of underemployed cohabiting couples in their 20s. Much will depend on whether during their underemployed 20s they become urban guerrillas or parents or (as experience with other mass-unemployed 20-year-olds suggests) more obsequious workers. I think that in some poor countries there will be a move in this latter direction, so some factories are likely to emigrate towards them, although their governments are unlikely to be obsequious at all.

It will, however, be surprising if these factories are established by another southward safari by multinational corporations. There will be a search for local entrepreneurs and profit-sharing arrangements. Compared with the moneymaking method of hiring out the knowhow, through some licensing agreement, the establishment of a multinational subsidiary in the 1960s was supposed to have the great advantage of maintaining the use of the process for the dear old firm. But multinational corporations failed to notice that, just as their emigrant boom took off, material ownership was becoming no longer a source of economic or political power, and was probably indeed becoming a source of loss of both.

An American multinational corporation has now become a device for taking up an artifically weak bargaining posture versus left-wing Marxists and right-wing nationalists among local politicians; and versus local competitors, whose normal practices (tax dodging in Latin European countries, giving bribes and arranging occasional coups d'état in poor countries) have to some extent to be copied for survival by the multi-nationals, who are then accused of flinging bribery about and toppling princes.

For a brief period they will now become even more unpopular in poor countries by not flinging bribery about, and by keeping so far out of politics in all countries that they will be criticised as insufficiently-concerned corporate citizens. The age of multinationals is coming to an end, which is one of the subsidiary reasons why the age of most really massive business corporations is likely to be ending too. The age of entrepreneurial sub-contractors and licensees will succeed it.

Nor workers' participation

The third remedy for worker alienation was supposed to be worker participation or "producer democracy" in the rich countries themselves. Enthusiasts say that workers must be allowed to vote for the committee that should run their workshop, just when the un-productivity of the public sector everywhere (see final article in this survey) has shown that voting for a committee to run anything is the most inefficient possible way to run a whelkstall.

Producer democracy would put more power into the hands of the trade unions, at a time when people all over the world are telling public opinion polls that they want the unions to have less power. It would bring a new and absurd, therefore fortunately soon over-throwable, combination of bosses and unions against consumers. As the average worker in many western countries stays in a job for only three or four years, his vote will most logically be against saving corporate money through such things as properly funded pension schemes, and in favour of spending it on himself. This swing against corporate saving and investment is proposed just when saving for investment is vital for growth.

The craze for worker participation may temporarily impede the economies of West Germany and Sweden - possibly to the competitive advantage of Britain if the coming Bullock proposals are fortunately lost within bumbledom - but it will not last. The apostles of worker partici-pation say that the arguments for it are the same as those for universal suffrage in the nineteenth century. Exactly. The arguments for it belong entirely to this land of look-behind. Voter control of anything in the twentieth century, like monarchy in the nineteenth century, is where the world is coming from, not where it is going to.

The place where the world is going to is called consumers' freedom.

COMPUTE YOUR LIFESTYLE

At present the market system of free misinformation (including mendacious advertisements) allows every worker's wife in Britain a marvellous choice of quite effective soapsuds at the supermarket, while the government-dominated system of bureaucratic registration of unfilled vacancies allows very few workers any intelligent choice of lifestyles at his job.

Within the God-given range of the human spirit, Robertson may just want £50 a week with the smallest possible attendance at work at times chosen by him, Mrs Buggins may want to gossip on the production line, Miss Jones to work under a father figure, Browne to be a lazily productive genius, and Braun a frenetically ambitious one, Smith to work without a foreman riding his back and Smythe without a shop steward bullying him to join in some protection racket. But none of them, when applying for a job, is enabled actually to say this.

On the other side of the hiring line the employer knows in which job slot he would like an entrepreneur, in which he needs a frenetic Braun and in which a dilettante Browne would be more restful, in which morale might be improved by an amiable gossip or a divine Miss Jones, and in which he just needs an obedient toad. But the tyrannies of conventional politeness and bureaucratic job classification prevent him from saying any such things. So he usually advertises for somebody with experience, thus probably getting an inadequate who has been shifted from one relieved ex-employer to another, and he thereby keeps unemployment among school-leavers unnecessarily high. In Britain the present system of not employing people as individuals is most especially harming those imprisoned in both dangerously over-extended schooling and premature retirement. It is now also harming women - among whom the equal pay law, though only patchily applied, has promptly caused a problem of female unemployment to appear for almost the first time in British history.

The road ahead must be through data banks. By the end of the century the job applicant should sit answering questions from a computer console. "Is flexitime important to you, and do you want some individual say in choosing your own working hours, immediate companions, targets for work?" My personal answer : "Usually, yes". "But, in emergencies, do you mind sudden periods of frantic working for a day-and-night on end?" No, actually I rather enjoy that. "Do you object to calling your superiors Sir or Herr Doktor?" If they pay me more, I'll call them Your Excellencies if they wish. "If this firm follows the economy in securing $4\frac{1}{2}\%$ real annual growth so that it is possible to double everybody's real income every 15 years, do you want your next doubling in twice your present accumulation of material goods or six months extra holiday a year?" My answer : "I'd like to decide as this advance progresses, so don't tie me into any generalised trade union wages and hours agreement please".

Then the computer would print out the information that I was a willing-ly obsequious, greedy and indecisive anarchist with erratic but output-oriented views. If there was a glut on the market of obsequious etc. anarchists, then I would be offered a less profitable contract than the scarcer supply of ruder but more regimentable women or men. But wise employers would then adapt their work schedules so as to be able to employ more of us obsequious output-oriented bargains, and we ourselves would be slightly toning down our demands for anarchy by them.

The marrying of job specifications to the individually-varied and constantly-changing patterns of lifestyles demanded will be a very major industry in the future. Although the central data banks may have to be produced initially by a government department, but preferably then performance-contracted-out as most government departments' jobs should be (see last article in this survey), the use of the data banks and the tabulation and widening (through asking new questions etc.) of both personnel choices and lifestyle choices will be an industry for a lot of small, competitive concerns.

Other developments will be increasing the worker's potential for freedom in space and time. First, many white-collar workers will grad-ually become telecommuters. Once systems for modern tele-communications are in place, the cost of using them should not vary greatly with distance. It will eventually be sensible for many white-collar workers to live in Tahiti if they want to, and telecommute daily to their offices in New York. This will bring a huge liberation in lifestyle choices, and also make voting for politicians or works committees a much less important ingredient of freedom than politicians and members of works committees pretend it is now. People will move to areas with the domestic lifestyles (and local governments) they like, and telecommute to offices with the workstyles they want. Sensible people will want different lifestyles and sometimes different workstyles at different periods of their lives.

Even at an early stage of this widening of horizons for white-collar workers, employers will have to start offering much more freedom of lifestyles for blue-collar workers as well. There will have to be a movement away from paying people for mere attendance at the workplace and towards paying people for modules of work done. Each business will eventually define and quantify the nature of the output it is aiming at from each service (a salutary exercise in itself, because in many non-assembly-line jobs nobody has ever measured, or even defined, the output the worker or group is supposed to be aiming at). Two purposes of measuring modules will be (a) to allow individuals within the corporation to become more entrepreneurial and (b) to allow those who seek communal group enjoyment (rather than individual achievement) in their work to form their own small friendly co-operatives to work at the pace they want.

There will be lots of other purposes, but concentrate first on entrepreneurship.

COLOUR ME ENTREPRENEURIAL

In the period of exciting experimental opportunities and probing ahead, rich countries should no longer rely on entrepreneurship only by people lucky enough to be able or willing to gamble on their families' security. Also entrepreneurship should not be the province only of those who have the organisational patience and ability to set up from scratch every bit of the infrastructure that a new business needs. The aim should be to give ordinary people more scope for becoming tycoons than they have had since the industrial revolution was young.

The mechanism should be for the management in each progressive firm to define the modules of work that it wants to be done, and then invite "bids" from parts of the staff who think they could achieve the module more efficiently and happily than under the existing corporate bureau- cracy. Sometimes the bids will be made individually, sometimes by groups of friends within the company.

In "far-out" ventures the bidder will say how much of the corporation's existing services (production, marketing etc.) he would wish to use; and how rights of decision eventually to sell off the venture, if success- ful, to an outsider should be shared. Some of these "far-out" bids would be from employees willing to take a risk with their own security - in effect, working for bare maintenance if the project failed, or even involving a loan which would have to be paid back to the firm over the years. In "closer-in" ventures, more of the bids would be from group co-operatives or executives who were willing to take the job over only while being paid something like their present salaries or wages, although with smaller profit participation.

Practical examples? A pioneer in rearranging work modules, although not in making them entrepreneurial, was Mr Robert Ford at the American Telephone and Telegraph Company. In the Harvard Business Review, January-February 1973, he described how in Indiana :

"33 employees, most of them at the lowest clerical wage level, compiled all the telephone directories for the state. The processing from clerk to clerk was laid out in 21 steps, many of which were merely for verification. The steps included manuscript reception, transcript verification, key punch, key punch verification, ad copy reception, ad copy verification, and so on - a production line as real as any in Detroit."

The system was also breaking down, like any in Detroit. In its last year, 28 new hirings were required to keep the clerical force at the 33- employee level. Whenever an employee left AT & T because of job dissatisfaction, bang went large training costs and in came new entrants' mistakes (which proliferated under the production line or nobody-is- responsible system, and in telephone books are horrid).

The Coming Entrepreneurial Revolution

The reform initiated at AT & T was to allow certain employees to "own" their own telephone books and be responsible for them, or in large city telephone directories to "own" particular letters of the alphabet. Labour turnover fell, errors were reduced because individuals knew they were responsible, and when the system spread to the yellow pages directory at New Orleans the employees by last-minute efforts allowed the sale of advertisements to continue for three extra weeks, bringing more than $100,000 in extra revenue. In Mr.Ford's article, it is argued merely that "an employee who takes the entire responsibility for preparing a whole telephone directory.....ought to be paid more, although a new clerical rating must be established". It could be a smallish step in practice (though a big step in motivation) from this to the system recommended in this survey, in which it is envisaged that an entrepreneurial contract for the compilation of the directory (or of a letter in the city directory) should be vested over the period of a performance contract in the individual or small group responsible for that letter - although probably, in this case, under one of the less ambitious "closer-in" contracts.

Manufacturers ?

The module in the production of telephone directories was fairly obvious, but in fields where it is less obvious the advantages should be bigger. It may be worth picking a manufacturing example from Mr. Ford's article in Harvard Business Review, rather than cite cases from other companies which could require different jargon to explain the same trends. In a manufacturing process at AT & T, a junior woman employee discovered a new and profitable system of quality control for dry-reed switches, at a time when :

"two men, a die maker and a machine operator, had the complete responsibility for producing each day more than 100,000 of these tiny parts, which are not unlike two paper matches, but much smaller. How can one make a life out of this? Well, they did. The six stamping machines and expensive photometric test equipment were "theirs". A fork-lift truck had been dedicated to them.....Compared with workers at a plant organised along traditional lines, with batches of reeds moving from shop to shop, these three employees were producing at a fourfold rate. In the future, when now undreamed-of computer capacities have been reached, management must improve its techniques of feeding performance directly to the employee responsible. And preferably it should be done *before* the boss knows about it."

When a computer can feed performance results of new methods directly to employees, after their experimentation, and before the boss sees them, the scope for searching and bidding for entrepreneurial performance contracts will be hugely enlarged.

Two other trends from the computer revolution should expand the surge to entrepreneurial performance contracts even more quickly. Oddly they are the two that are often mistakenly supposed to be likely to do the opposite - namely, the effects of computers on the economies of scale for (a) assembly-line production and (b) large-scale distribution.

Entrepreneurial assembly lines

The really big change that is coming through computer-controlled production - to quote Dr Ruth Davis, the czarina of computing at America's National Bureau of Standards - lies in :

"the slogan I have used, which is 'customised production at mass production prices'. This simply means that if we use a computer-controlled production line for discrete processes in manufacturing we can, at mass production prices, have the diversification of products that we have only to date been able to have through very expensive custom work."

This is because a computer-controlled system can easily be told, unlike a batch of mere human beings, to make some changes in the 404th item coming down the assembly line. More important, it can also be told, without expensive retraining, to make changes in various experimental batches coming down it.

One of two things should then happen. Either big companies will rent out some time on their assembly lines (as they ought to rent out time on their underused computers already) to people with entrepreneurial ideas about how to modify certain batches of their products in ways that might sell more profitably. Or, and I guess this will happen earlier, they will allow various of their own staff to push through such exper- imental ideas on a basis that is part-company-financed, but with the staff member most sensibly putting in his own extra work as a part- entrepreneur.

Experimental products in future will not only be easier to manufacture, but also to launch. New sorts of two-way telecommunication should become common in rich countries' households by the late 1990s.

One way in which to launch a new or modified product - whether a new model of a manufacture or an ingenious idea for a new sort of package holiday - will be to advertise it on television, with substantial discounts for orders placed immediately. Customers will then respond electronically from their homes, stepping up to their consoles to push the right buttons to make their commitment, automatically depleting their bank accounts in the process, with generous and sometimes equity-linked discounts for those who make instant payment for deferred delivery, because they will help to finance the venture.

The initial order for the product will then be assessable soon after its design has been proposed. Once a product is on the launching pad, the computers will be able to work out the costs and potential profits of proceeding from pad to launch, with profit-to-risk ratios dramatically reduced. The economic incentive will then be to launch more entrepren- eurial ventures.

At the beginning of the Henry Ford revolution, the Ford Motor Company was founded in mid-June, 1903, with a cash capital equal to today's price of a suburban house and with only 125 employees; it sold its first cars to customers that October, and made a profit from then on. Professor Kenneth Galbraith - whose best-seller in the 1950s talked of an inevitable trend towards "public squalor amid private affluence", just as public sectors everywhere began to pinch the lion's share of all new resources - assumed in his best-seller of the 1960s that that sort of opportunity will never recur, just as it is about to become the most significant business feature of the new age. Profit-to-risk ratios for new products will soon be lower than in 1903. Then the new small man's entrepreneurial revolution should begin.

What is the module of output that a business should set for its typing pool? Almost any guess here will be too conservative. Let competition decide. Most big businesses would already be wise to set several separate teams or co-operatives of typists-plus-people-in-the-computer-room to compete with each other to find what is the best way of reaching the re-organisation that is coming in today's paperwork, or rather in tomorrow's advance towards the paperless office.

Probably, most big businesses and all big government offices could already economically cut by two thirds their staff engaged in writing letters, through such systems as that tentatively in operation in some innovative firms like Unilever, as described in *The Economist* on July 3rd:

"typists are connected to a computer via individual keyboards, each with a video screen on which mistakes can be easily rectified (rework normally takes about 40% of a typist's time). Standard letters, held in the computer's memory, need only the name and address to be attached. The typist handles no paper or carbons, printing (and filing) being done by the computer."

And all this shortly before voice-activated typewriters come into effect. The right sort of reorganisation here is much more likely to be found by competition than by committee. There is going to be a mass production revolution in all clerkly operations, bigger than the mass production revolution in manufacturing at the beginning of the assembly-line-age. Presumably, this will make it sensible for some corporations to contract their clerkly operations out to other businesses, sometimes small ones, employing various piecework-earning telecommuting housewives in their own homes.

What would be the worst stance for a company to adopt, on the eve of this computer revolution which will eat up the clerks? It would be a stance of delaying reform, while trade unionism spreads among white collar workers so that they all be frozen with restrictive practices in their present jobs.

A senior colleague, who read the first draft of these articles on an airline flight, issued the challenge : "I bet that today an airline ticket clerk uses less imagination than she did before she had all that computerised machinery. How would you make her work more entrepreneurial, or hope to set confederations of entrepreneurs competing with mighty airlines that need to use jumbo jets? And how do you propose that small entrepreneurs can come into our own industry of newspapers?"

All right. On an intelligent critic's own chosen ground, with a warning that all my answers will be too conservative, here goes.

Although she won't admit it, that airline ticket clerk has a nicer and more productive job than in pre-computer days when she was the equivalent of a railway booking clerk. But, of course, she is not yet used productively or entrepreneurially enough.

The desire of most passengers is to get to their destination at some particular time, but with attachment to that time varying considerably according to ticket price. The marginal cost of putting an extra passenger on a half-empty flight going to that destination at a slightly different time is often nearly nil. Under a sensible system, her job with that computer should be to bargain so that she maximises for her airline the profits gained from going for all marginal revenue that is in excess of marginal cost.

It is a tragedy that cartels like IATA have pitched air travel on to the course pioneered by railways (which have all gone bust) instead of on to the course pioneered by minicab and lorry firms (whose most efficient practitioners will survive). The IATA cartel's controls forbid airlines to compete on price, so they compete instead on technology, with the result that, instead of utilising cheap secondhand aircraft, we all have to cross the Atlantic in enormously expensive high-technology aircraft which consequently fly half-empty. The cartel's prices are kept up to cover these costs, so in boom years there is created many an Air Ruritania, which then loses as much money per passenger as does Pan American during the subsequent recession, but Air Ruritania is then subsidised as Ruritania's favourite lame duck. We then fly round the world in highly technological lame ducks. So long as the IATA cartel subsists, every high technology private airline will unfortunately if gradually go as bust as every railway has done.

The cartel in airlines has been organised mainly by lavish taxpayer-milking governments, so it has been protective of high technology; and jobs have been shed even as airlines have multiplied. My guess is that even in the airways confederations of entrepreneurs will nevertheless break through, probably with lower technology, in the same way as mini-cab and coach operators will ensure that the high-speed train sends British Rail still further into deficit. What differences with newspapers?

End of editors

The cartel in newspapers is run mainly by trade unions which oppose high technology; and thereby temporarily keep in employment many more journalists and printing workers than any newspaper really requires. My guess is that confederations of entrepreneurs will nevertheless break through, using even more labour-saving technology than would have been used if the workers' cartel had not existed.

By the end of the century most of the news comment that a customer buys in written form, as distinct from on video-tape, may come to him individually, probably by facsimile printout from the back of his television set. The packages that readers order will then not be those put together by the editor of The Times or the Daily Mail. They will be packages put together according to each reader's individual wishes. Mr Jones will order, by pressing a button after seeing on a screen what is on offer, one of several competitive summaries of the news, plus comment advertised that day by tomorrow's Bernard Levin or Scotty Reston, everything written that day about the prospects for So Blessed in the 2.30 at Ascot, book reviews by particular known names, any pin-up pictures of nude redheads in leather boots (or whatever is Mr Jones's special hang-up). The paper that comes out of the back of Mr Jones's television set will be the Monday Mr Jones, not the Daily Express. Advertisements will be attached to the particular articles or items ordered, and probably a computer will have worked out from Mr Jones's stated preferences what extra advertisements to send particularly to him. Mr Jones will have to pay considerably more if he wants to get his articles advertisement-free.

It is just possible that the signed articles ordered will belong to the writers themselves, whose agents will buy time on the advertising screen

and buy access to the delivery system. But most journalists would find
this tiresome. Nearly all of us are able to write what we do write because
of the access we get to news sources and men of ideas through the
publishing houses or newspapers for which we work. But obviously a
system of this sort will make newspapermen much more like part-entre-
preneurs, with rewards varying according to orders for their own
individual work. When publishing houses have rising new stars, they will
send some of their writings down the delivery system to Mr Jones for
free, in the hope of securing repeat orders. I could tell you which
articles in this week's issue of *The Economist* I would send to some of
you free, as bait, and might like to bet entrepreneurially on the choice
(rather than be part of a committee that decides what to send out). Each
house or newspaper will be a different mix of salaried staff, nursery and
confederation of entrepreneurs.

These spotty examples - on airlines and presses - have been chosen
because a critic cited them. In other industries it is rather easier to see
how "confederations of entrepreneurs" could be created. That statement
is contentious. It will be argued that other enterprises - say, those
making motor cars - cannot move in the same directions as newspapers,
because a car is arguably less of an individualistic product than a newspaper article is. So the critics say that cars will continue to be mass-
produced by workers on assembly lines, and that those who put up the
money for these expensive assembly lines will want through some committee
called a board to continue to appoint the people who decree how these
assembly lines be used (although, in fact, of course, none of us small
shareholders in ICI can remember who the managing director is).

End of ownership?

The critics misunderstand what is happening. In these 1970s, it is
gradually becoming clear that ownership of the means of production is
no longer a source of economic or political power, and may indeed be a
source of economic and political powerlessness.

At one stage people would have supposed that newspaper owners
would be the last tycoons to become mere managers of confederations of
entrepreneurs, because the bait which attracted tycoons into the loss-

making but fun business of newspaper ownership was to gain influence upon the world. Since ownership now means disrespect instead of power, the reverse is now true. In every country the tide of opinion is now running most strongly against whatever interests happen to be charitable enough to bear the losses that provide public opinion with its newspapers. Countries where the newspapers are subsidised by big business (like Italy) are turning most virulently anti-big-business; countries where the newspapers are owned by idosyncratic press lords (Springer, Hearst, Beaverbrook) turn most sharply against these idiosyncracies; countries where the newspapers are owned by the government of the day are the countries most likely to suffer coups d'état; any country where control of the press is usurped too much by trade unions or advertisers will turn most sharply against trade unions and advertisements.

In the same way, in industry generally, ownership or direct employment increasingly means loss of control. It is easy for an organisation to take action against sub-contractors by cutting off contracts. It is no longer easy to keep control over direct employees. So there will be a switch towards sub-contracting.

Still, there will have to continue to be a certain number of direct employees. What contracts to offer them?

UP, THE DISORGANISATION

The great but temporary discovery in the old Henry Ford age was that productivity could be efficiently increased by organisational action from the top ("engineer faster production lines"). This is a main reason why such jobs are now becoming increasingly unpopular in rich countries, where most workers do not want to be organised from on top. Most people who have reached the average young American's or young north-west European's standards of education and living very reasonably want to do more of their own thing instead.

So in the bossed-about industries there have in the past 15 years been some expensive withdrawal symptoms : absenteeism of up to 20% in some American and European manufacturing plants on Fridays and Mondays, high labour turnover, little attention to the job, in north-west

Europe sometimes only immigrants will work the night-shift, some
deliberate waste, disruption of work routines and wildcat strikes. There
has also been an increase at plant level in pilferage and violence against
property and persons, which reversed itself a bit during the recent
world recession, but not by much.

These troubles at plant level have been greater than most businessmen admit, but are less deep-seated than most professional liberals and
amateur experts on alienation proclaim. In America, say researchers
from Harvard, pilferage and violence are "not reported in the local newspapers and there is little or no appreciation of it in corporate headquarters. Local management keeps quiet because violence is felt to
reflect unfavourably both on its effectiveness and on its plant as a place
of work". In Britain corporate headquarters know more of what is
happening under their noses, but pilferage and violence are sometimes
regarded as some trade unionists' perks, so "don't talk about them, or
there may be a strike".

These are both evidence of breakdown. But such blue-collar blues
are to a large extent yesterday's problems for rich countries, not tomorrow's. Remember that in 1900 about 45% of America's workforce was
in the two large employments of agriculture and domestic service, but
that proportion is down below 5% now; today only about 23% of America's
workforce is in manufacturing and it may go below 5% during the lifetime
of most people alive today. The present British government's "new
industrial strategy" of putting more emphasis on jobs in manufacturing
industry is like a strategy for teaching us all to become hansom cab
drivers in 1910. In America I have some sympathy with the attack by
Professor Jack Douglas on liberal journalists who have been too scared
about some possible crisis of shopfloor alienation :

"The alienation of industrial workers cannot possibly produce such a
crisis because industrial workers are rapidly disappearing as the automation of industry accelerates. Industrial workers now constitute only
about 25% of all workers and their number is shrinking fast. Instead of
getting more alienated from their jobs, most of them are acting through
the AFL-CIO to try to keep their jobs exactly as they are, through legal
constraints on foreign investment, imports, technological change and so

on. They seem downright nostalgic about industrial jobs, and certainly
shrink from exchanging them for the creative complexities and excitement
of post-industrial society. In the 1960s these liberal social analysts
became progressively alienated from the non-alienated industrial workers.
In fact, they started attacking the 'hard hats' as reactionaries who
wanted to use force to maintain the status quo."

But one trouble is that alienation is moving farther up snob hill.

The besetting sin of most liberal social analysts is that of assuming
that God made all men in our own interesting image. It is quite possible
that in this survey I have overestimated the supply of people who want
to be entrepreneurial. Anyway, it is going to be just as important to
think up contracts that will bring happiness and productivity at work to
those who seek communal group enjoyment, to the work-obsessed, to the
imaginatively lazy, to nature's craftsmen and artists and nannies, to
those who want father figures, to those who find status and seniority
and even self-importance important, to many other groups of people who
will be identified during tomorrow's mass psycho-analysis by computer.
Since a computer is skilled at finding what is the best next question to
ask (and the nicest next thing to say) on the basis of input to date, it
should do such psychological testing rather well. One group of software
specialists already tries to arrange that the computer's sign-off statement after psycho-analysing a boss (who will usually like wit but cling
to self-importance) is : "Well, I have rarely enjoyed one of these con-
versations so much. I take it that you must be a computer, too?"

In the rush back towards individualism, which individualists may push
too hard as the entrepreneurial revolution starts rolling, those who
devise successful group friendship co-operatives will do a lot of social
good, and perhaps will deserve some subsidies or tax advantages because
on ordinary human trends they are otherwise unlikely to be the most
highly paid. This is not to say that their task will be hard, because it
should be largely a matter of arranging modules, and leaving workstyle
choices to those who want this lifestyle. Semi-autonomous teams of
perhaps six to seventeen people, who choose to work together as friends,
should be told by market forces what module of output will be paid for
at what pay rate per unit of output, and then should increasingly be

allowed to produce it in their own way.

I think that the imaginatively lazy and the work-obsessed will fall fairly easily towards earning their longer holidays and moonlighting opportunities once the new entrepreneurial revolution has eroded the power of trade unions. But harrowing social problems may be set for the aggressively upward mobile, at least for those who are not of an entrepreneurial type.

One of the forms of satisfaction of the upward mobile has hitherto been to boss people about, perhaps as a foreman, within the hierarchical pattern of the modern business corporation. This is a form of satisfaction which foremen will have to learn to do without in future, because ordinary workers will not agree to be bossed. Or, rather, those who want to run their workplaces like neo-nazis will have to pay much higher wages than their competitors.

Any company which allows its eagerly upward mobile workers to feel disgruntled will be wasting one of the rarest of human assets. There should therefore be a deliberate policy for re-gruntling them. This will include some whose upward mobile instincts so far have not been towards making money within the company, but towards acquiring power in opposition to it, such as many shop stewards. The more idealistic of these may make good entrepreneurs or organisers of co-operatives, but the more militant and the most conservative may prove too corrupt.

Nannies and artists

Strangely, much less good entrepreneurs may be made by some who have become more senior executives in hierarchical corporations, just when hierarchical corporations in their present form may be due to fade away.

The last years of the corporation age have not been years of rat race, but more of embarrassed avoidance of unpleasant decisions. Many of the worst inefficiencies and also personal strains in American and European business spring from unwillingness to offend a nice guy's amour propre. The Japanese, who in their personal tradition usually put more store on amour propre than westeners, have adopted a business system which gets around this difficulty rather better. The Japanese executive rests his status and pride in life on his age and length of service with the firm; he is Mr Nakamura, a graduate entry into the firm of the class of 1957; he regards it as peripheral that his present office is as sales director in charge of marketing circular widgets in south-east Asia, or in charge of internal distribution systems; the result is that if south-east Asia does not want circular widgets he is happy to recommend that this activity be reduced, and if internal distribution systems suddenly become more difficult for him to handle (perhaps because he does not really understand the new computerisation of them, or perhaps just because he is better at administering smoothly functioning departments than areas with sudden difficulties) then he is very happy to pass the hot potato to somebody else. But the American or European vice-president in charge of marketing circular widgets or of distribution systems feels his whole pride wrapped up in his office; he will often resist to the death any proposal to reduce his department's services even when nobody wants them.

It will often not be possible to make these vice-presidents into entrepreneurs, because (like civil servants in departments of industry) their inclination might be to suggest schemes for entrepreneurially cosseting the production of better but still unsaleable circular widgets. But they might sometimes operate as "nannies to the artists" - as organisers of another type of wasted non-entrepreneurial executive.

The "artists" are those with special knacks, or talents for bright ideas, whose maverick abilities are today not well used within the rigid bureaucracies of giant corporations, but who might not themselves be very good entrepreneurs either. It might often be best to set up subsidiary companies which use these people's talents as the small new companies' principal capital.

This is especially true for corporations which are entering new fields. In computers, there is a sort of artistry in the man who has really grasped how best to use them. In laboratories there is an artistry in those rare research scientists who can think the new technologies through into products that will actually serve a purpose. Designers in industries where fashion is rapidly changing could often best be hived into subsidiary companies. In salesmanship, there are people with rare sales ideas, but who are not naturally extrovert enough to make good salesmen themselves; often they should be set up in subsidiary companies to serve the whole group, and should also sell their services outside, with the right mix of doers around them. Unless ideas men also have all the qualities you want in an organiser or entrepreneur - and generally brilliant ideas men won't (sometimes because of inability to suffer fools gladly) - they might best be nurtured by a small supporting staff of a salesman of their talents plus a nanny. The nanny could often be the former vice-president in charge of circular widgets.

Containing craftsmen

While maverick ideas men should often be hived off into separate small companies, craftsmen should not. Craftsmen - whether working by brain or hand - are those who positively want a father-figure or father-organisation. It is possible that longer-term contracts help to breed these useful people; the tradition in Japan of lifetime employment with particular firms may have helped to make the breed more normal there. In America and Europe companies should probably aim to give long-term contracts to people of this group, both because it will make them happier and also make them more useful. It is often already more desirable and important that the office chauffeur should sign a contract (because one wants him to be an input-oriented but reasoning being), rather than that the finance director should do so (because one wants him to be an entrepreneurial type). Because finance directors draw up the terms for contracts, they are often slow to see this.

The various sorts of contracts suggested in these last three sections would cause big business corporations to move towards becoming confederations of smaller ones. The next section discusses a more fundamental reason why this would be wise.

BIG WON'T WORK

Some modern and much-criticised sociobiologists believe that man is an animal who has a genetic urge to hunt in packs, but also to make those packs less than 100 strong. Fifty thousand years of human history suggest they are right, as is witnessed by the idealisms which have been constantly mobilised to try to counter this urge. Most state or established religions (Confucianism, Islam, church-led Christianity) have been attempts to make men feel they want to belong to packs larger than 100, for the greater good of either society or the ruling classes : so have most fanatical political movements (nationalism, communism etc.) and attempts at demanding hero worship (men on white horses, Maos).

Big business corporations now face the difficulty that they are too large to inspire people to hunt together as a pack, so, behind many of their facades, the employees from just below the managing director to those around the shop steward are forming separate packs to hunt each other. It has also become clear that in the west there is no possibility of persuading people to enjoy working in overlarge packs by beating the drums of idealistic industrial religions, either of socialism or free enterprise. You do not set even Welsh miners to singing Japanese-style company hymns in love of the National Coal Board by saying it belongs to them.

The top 40 or so executives in a really big corporation do hunt together as a pack for the good of the dear old firm, even when stock options etc. do not tie their personal fortunes to its prosperity. The reason is that 40 or so (with good management, more) probably is a natural size of pack to make co-operative work into fun, even cooperation with unsympathetic people. Thus, as a parochial example of this parochialism, in each of my 1400 weeks at *The Economist* since 1949, the editorial staff, usually about 40 prima donnas strong, of very different political views, ranging during those years from intermittent Marxists through subsequent ministers in both Labour and Conservative governments rightwards to usually three or four Friedmanites at any one time and even me, have hunted with genuinely united desire to set the best possible 50-60 editorial pages (with remarkably little disagreement about what are the best possible articles) on to the presses each Thursday night.

Usually, the top two score or so executives in each of the world's large business corporations have the same sort of fun motivation for what they are doing, and often the same cohesion on behalf of the dear old firm. However, there is for them an awkwardness of objective. The healthy driving force behind most efficient great international companies is competition (or, better, rivalry) against certain other great international companies in wanting to grow faster. But then, awkwardly, when they do grow, there is often a decline in their efficiency.

In Britain there is now fairly clear evidence that the larger the workplace in any particular business, the worse and more frequent the industrial disputes, or the higher the absenteeism, including obviously bogus sickness. This shows itself in "idealistic" social services as well as in unidealistic British Leyland. In British hospitals, those with under 100 beds have shown between a half and two-thirds the sickness rates among nurses as those with more than 100 beds. Moreover there are signs that this deterioration in industrial efficiency continues right up the line.

It is just worth noting governments' reaction to this, while promising thereafter not to mention things so irrelevant as governments' policies towards industry again. The one successful sort of government intervention in industry since the war has been trustbusting by mistake. The foundations for Japanese and German miracles were laid by the victorious allies' "punitive" action in splitting the old zaibatsus into more and originally smaller groups; they thought they were limiting German industrial power for the future, but were instead increasing it, when they broke up I.G.Farben into three smaller and therefore more efficient firms. The right aim for an Industrial Reorganisation Corporation in Britain would be, as Management Today's Bob Heller once suggested, to trisect ICI.

Instead Britain's IRC and National Enterprise Board have nonsensically done the opposite. The IRC in the 1960s looked out on most British industries, typically tenanted by two sinking hulks and a smaller firm that was less inefficient. It then said to the dynamo behind the latter that a merger would make him the biggest force in the industry. If he was a nice man like Lord Stokes of Leyland or the former managers of Geo Kent, he agreed to have the hulks tied round his neck, and unsurprisingly sank.

Over most of the world, however, big businesses have grown bigger and therefore often worse through the normal processes of growth or takeovers, instead of through government force-feeding. Their usual explanation of why bigger means badder is to blame the middle management.

The aim of the middle bureaucracy in big business is to rise to the top bureaucracy, greatly heartened by the recent swing back to gerontocracy as exemplified earlier in the 1970s when a man of 63 finally made it to the presidency of General Motors. But a large middle bureaucracy in a company cannot succeed either as an imitator or as an operator under most present business systems.

When a big organisation, whether government department or business corporation, says it believes in "planning", this now usually means that a changing mix of top people take haphazard decisions on the nominal or even actual basis of advice submitted by their internal bureaucracies – who, however, now devise that advice principally so as to fit the known prejudices of their changing mix of top people, and who today use computers mainly to disguise the fact that this is what they are doing.

Any journalist nowadays has to be bewildered by the way in which official bodies and so-called learned institutions draw up computer models of, say "energy economics in the 1980s". Those models could not conceivably reflect the range of problems and answers in the way a free market will anyway do even if they had several billion factors, and usually they have something like 43. More worryingly, the corporate planning departments of supposedly profitmaking companies nowadays draw up similar models, which the corporate planners must know to be nonsense.

Alternatively, a large middle management may be used not to justify the initiatives that fit in with the prejudices of those who fix their salaries, but to block any initiatives at all.

The result is an increasing lag between the conception and completion of any investment project – which is absurd because one of the few things that "computerised planning" really should be able to do is very sharply to cut the time between the design of a new product and its delivery from the production lines. The lag is now shorter in Japan than in America or Europe. One reason is that in the west we have so many votes about everything, which lead quickly to disagreements about words. In Japan and the east they have agonising discussions about everything, in which nobody wants too sharply to disagree with anybody else, and this leads to slow but definite consensus about action. Surprisingly, the latter is now proving a quicker road to action than is voting.

In many large American and European companies, the mechanism for taking entrepreneurial initiatives has become stifled either by hierarchical orders from on top or by over-participation through committees and memo-writing. If trade unions' representatives are soon to join in every entre-preneurial decision, this stifling by over-participation will become a garrotting.

What makes for big?

Many big businessmen today agree that smaller organisations can inspire more dynamic motivation, but say that "increasing returns" from size are a function of (a) modern management, (b) modern manufacturing and (c) the "inevitable trend towards making more industries into the equivalent of public utilities". There are three different concepts here, and each is slightly muddle-headed.

I agree that central managements should periodically pull smaller entrepreneurs' diverse experiments together, impose terms for the successful experiments, and later decentralise again. Successful big new businesses in the past two decades have often been those that imposed central management systems in industries formerly diverse (e.g. retailing, hotels). Successful big new businesses in the next two decades will often be those that impose central management systems on industries at present diverse (e.g. sports clubs, and the very computerisable professional bodies called law firms, accountants, and health maintenance organisations or doctors). But the industries that have hitherto been centralised will be equally wise to decentralise into many new entrepreneurial experiments for a while, unless technology pulls the other way.

In manufacturing, technology will not pull the other way. It will favour experimental entrepreneurship. On an earlier page I said computer-controlled factories will provide opportunities for "customised production at mass production prices"; and the same should be true of what will grandiloquently be called "industrial robots", but are much better called general-purpose jigs. Present manufacturing plants contain a lot of machine tools, which are special-purpose jigs that temporarily have to be constructed in many shapes and sizes, mainly because a human being cannot hold work against a cutter with the required accuracy and strength. When there is a general-purpose jig that can be programmed to keep repositioning work against a cutter, with the same nous as a human would show if he were quickly-reacting and strong and accurate enough, then many present machine tools will be unnecessary. Once this general purpose jig (probably called an industrial robot) is mass-manufacturable, it should allow manufacturing industry to have a very small number of types of machine tools flexibly deployable in small factories, instead of a very large number of types of machines used in ones or twos in large factories. Factories should then become cheaper to establish and more switchable. If a strike at Longbridge is creating a shortage of certain parts, then re-programme some industrial robots in Angola to blackleg it for the next few weeks, by following the software instruction in databank entry XYZ/1234. If you have an entrepreneurial idea for a new manufactured product, then programme and produce it as software instruction ABC/5678 so that some firms with general-purpose jigs and spare capacity can take it on.

Some futurologists, while agreeing that in some manufacturing processes "more technological may mean smaller", argue that a new family of "increasing returns" (and therefore large) industries will nevertheless grow because of a "trend to public utilities". The increase in gross world product during the past two centuries has depended on a growth of (a) technological knowledge, based especially on erratic spurts in (b) new forms of transport and in (c) control over energy. In the next few decades there is likely to be an acceleration in all three - a knowledge revolution (based on data processing), a new transport revolution (based on telecommunications), a new energy revolution (based initially

on the surplus of fossil fuels into which the present committee system
of decision-taking is now moving us by assuming the opposite, but then
on solar-geothermal-fusion etc.). These three will share one overwhelming economic characteristic. That characteristic is high initial investment
of a public utility type, then very low marginal cost (including virtually
nil resource-use-cost) as the solar or whatever energy and the data
banks and the telecommunication systems are used.

There will then presumably be a spurt of other "increasing returns"
and "low marginal cost" industries, allied to these revolutions. Industrial
structures by the late 1990s may tend towards two main types, with
many existing but bankruptable big corporations straddling uncomfort-
ably in between : (a) a steadily-decreasing number of steadily-huger but
low-employment and automated "public-utility-type" plants in steel, some
basic chemicals, some basic engineering components, plus the infrastructure for the data banks, telecommunications systems, solar energy
etc. (all of these will have the constant economic problem that they will
be able to produce at lowest cost only when they are pumping out their
products in such glut that low market prices may make their whole
operation seem a loss-making one); and (b) a rapidly-increasing number
of steadily-smaller new entrepreneurial businesses that will be best-fitted
to experiment in using the exciting new low-marginal-cost products(above
all computerised and telecommunicated knowledge) in the most imaginative
way.

Switching contracts

Many people will say that the giant public-utility types of plant should
be government-owned and government-operated. This will be a mistake,
but not a tragic mistake. At present, almost all public utilities are less
efficient than they easily could be. The second worst system - next
worse only to government or local government operation - is local monopoly
private operation, especially with a government regulatory agency,
which soon becomes a client-oriented bureaucracy, operating price
controls and yet trying to protect jobs. The failure of this method is
important, because it is really the model of both so-called nationalised
industries in Britain and so-called private utilities like electricity in

America. The growth of a lot of new increasing-returns industries in the next three decades might provide the temptation for this bad system to spread. But the cure is obvious.

Instead of price controls designed to allow utilities a, say, 10% return on assets, sensible regulatory agencies should merely keep measuring the real value of a utility's capital assets. Then any organisation which convinces some regulatory body (preferably the electorate) that it could provide a better service at lower cost, while leasing those assets and paying the original owner a rent of 10% or whatever per annum, should be allowed to take the job over. It is possible to switch operators of public utilities, as witness when commercial television franchises were switched in Britain.

Performance contracts using the leasing system will probably become common for totally new sorts of privatisation of present public services : e.g., perhaps in urban transit with a contract promising the commuter that some transport mode will take him from city centre to some named suburb in under 30 minutes at any time of the day, provided the contractor can keep traffic moving by charging private cars for each use of city roads. Eventually, most spending decisions in what is now the local government sector should be taken in this way. Competitive bodies will stand at elections and persuade the electorate to grant them performance contracts of these kinds, and promise that they will levy lower payments of rates or property taxes if performance is not provided. I would already prefer to elect a business to run nine-tenths of the work done by my local council, rather than have to choose whichever party (Tory or Labour) puts on the tribal performance that temporarily annoys me least.

But this brings the argument into the field of government - where the biggest, most delayed but perhaps most essential part of the entre-preneurial revolution should break through.

THE WASTE LAND

An opening proposition of this survey was that public monopoly production of almost any service or goods is proving ludicrously inefficient in most rich countries during this age of advancing alternative technologies and is especially harmful for the poorest people in them. As current politics assume the opposite, this is socially awkward but entrepreneurially interesting.

One section will now be devoted to justifying this argument; one to suggesting what should be done; and one to saying why it won't be done quickly, but will eventually come.

In Britain we now pick the competitive providers of about half of our services (e.g.supermarkets, systems for getting clothes washed) by spending money, which means by a system of "plutocratic choice"; and we pick the providers of the other and often more essential half of our services (e.g. systems for prevention of crime, environmental protection education) by the democratic process of voting. It is now clear that in a technological age most systems commanded by plutocratic choice become steadily better-provided for the working class; and that most systems provided by state monopoly production become steadily worse-provided for the working class. The rich lose least from nationalised services, but today gain least from mass plutocratic ones.

This is because nationalisation or bureaucratisation slows the advance of competitive technology, while private enterprise's competitive technology in a mass production age strains hardest to move downmarket to where the main body of customers is. Consider, for example, the wash as a private industry, and crime prevention as a public monopoly one.

The toil and time taken to wash clothes have probably been cut by three quarters for the British working class woman in the past three decades, with an onrush of laundrettes, washing machines and "biological" detergents (entrepreneurially pushed by mendacious advertising and dreadful television jingles, which are jingled because working women like them). For the richer woman, servants have disappeared, so she's been hit.

In crime prevention, productivity per rich country's policeman has declined by perhaps around 75% in the last 30 years; it has been typical for crime rates to more-than-treble while police establishments have risen by over one third. Prisons across the developed world have gone further, and achieved the almost-unbelievable result of actually negative gross production; most penitentiaries now create more recidivists than they cure criminals. In most rich countries' courts of justice the processes of law have become steadily less expeditious - "to try a case now takes nine or ten times as long as when I started", said a recently retired New York judge - while also becoming more frequently fooled. Court procedures are adapted to an adversary game for upper-middle-class lawyers, not to the questions "did he do it?" and "how do we best stop this being done again?"

The rapidly declining productivity of public services like crime prevention and town hall bureaucracy has hit hardest at the poorest, because it is in poor areas (first in America, but now followed by Britain) that the danger of being mugged or raped has risen many times over during these past 30 years, it is in inner city schools that the sickening apprehension has mounted that one's son may be made delinquent or one's daughter made a slut, it is among the poorest that protection of environment has broken down.

In some rich countries such as Britain the proportion of gnp taken by public expenditure has gone fantastically over 50%, even while ever-more-expensive public squalor has mounted and ever-cheaper private affluence grown. The political process for ameliorating this has collapsed. Progressive governments (e.g.Mr Heath's) look out on public squalor amid private affluence, and want to curb the squalor. They therefore move net labour resources out of the private sector where marginal productivity is reasonably high and rising, into the public sector where it is now often negative. Conservative governments (e.g.Mr Callaghan's) then look at the mess which high public expenditure has caused. They therefore cut public expenditure, while trying to maintain public sector employment; and thereby make even bigger the backlog of urgent public needs which the long record of low productivity in the public sector has built up. So long as present low productivity persists in uncompetitive public services, there will be no way of preventing many of the most essential services in rich nations from growing steadily worse.

Recompetitioning

The cure to mass unproductivity in the public sector must be whole-sale recompetitioning. The need is to measure and state the output of every unit and eventually every employee in the public sector, and then always provide some mechanism whereby any outside private bodies or alternative public departments may submit competitive bids that they could on a performance contract produce more at lower cost. It is some-times said that this sort of competition would most obviously infringe human rights in the basic four public services - which are crime preven-tion, military defence or offence, succour of the underprivileged and public administration. So consider them first, thus agreeing to bat precisely on what the Establishment regards as the wickets on which "even you won't suggest that competition and output-measurement would work".

Crime : A prison in Britain is a place that spends around £4,000 a year per inmate, and has an unbelievably high recidivist rate but never measures it. If it was measured and published, then judges would steer prisoners away from the institutions with the lowest rehabilitation records, and those prisons would close down. If £4,000 a year per inmate was offered to any approved private or alternative public institution or indeed private person who looked after prisoners while achieving a lower recidivist rate than the worst existing public prisons, then of course recidivism and thus crime would be reduced. There are a lot of private people in rural areas who could take in some constantly re-convicted old lag on postdated payment of £4,000 for every year in which he didn't commit a crime again. Again, in notorious muggers' streets in New York and Brixton, it should be worth offering several thousand dollars a year to any performance contractor for each one per cent by which street crime fell, with no payment if it continued to rise. The rich in their offices and New York apartment blocks have private guards with now quickly-improving technology and efficiency (electronic surveillance, tactful reshaping of means of ingress and egress). Why should not the poor in particular streets be able to vote for similar competitive organisation of security if residents want it?

Defence : An index of unproductivity among rich countries' military is that the United States spent today's equivalent of $\$\frac{1}{2}$ trillion losing a war to slightly ridiculous North Vietnam. If the output being achieved in Indochina had at any time been analysed (movement towards total defeat, spread of drug culture and internal revolt in the United States, betrayal of millions of people eventually even to the barbarities of the Khmer Rouge), it would have been rather easy to suggest better ways of spending $\$\frac{1}{2}$ trillion - such as, at unimaginable crudest, giving $70,000 to each North Vietnamese household and asking them politely to become capitalists please. Vietnam was an instance where two sets of public authorities - the military and the related policy-creating establishment - were making such a mess that it became too embarrassing, became too insulting, for anybody else to apply common sense. This happens nowadays in many of the very widest fields of public affairs (crime prevention, welfare policy, overstaffing of public administration); and is increasingly also the story of really large catastrophes in big business corporations (Rolls-Royce, Slater Walker, the present failure of the major oil companies to follow a competitive buying policy to break Opec).

Welfare services : Across the industrial world, welfare states are now too often crippling their clients instead of rebuilding their self-reliance. In social security the main emphasis in a free society should be on a negative income tax. But any personal social services should be competitive, with the client using some voucher system to choose who seems the most sympathetic adviser on her or his rights - although with withdrawal of the facility of cashing vouchers from any consultant who aids a client to try to cheat the state. At present the handling of personal social problems is often a lottery, with a client liable to draw from the local authority anybody from Mr Bumble to Ms Trendy, both largely unchecked, and with nobody disciplined when there is a nonsense committed because at no stage in most bureaucracies is anybody's career affected by making appalling mistakes.

Administration and utilities : In town halls and central government offices across the rich world, almost every service would be provided more efficiently and humanely if subjected to competition. In public utilities the competition should come through the sorts of performance contract discussed in the previous section.

The Coming Entrepreneurial Revolution

The barrier

Reprivatisation will come in local government first, but it will not come quickly even there. There is an understandable bureaucratic barrier in the way. Public servants have chosen their jobs on the assumption that theirs are the safest forms of career. But recompetitioning can work only if public servants are subjected to sudden unemployment much more cruel than need hit most other people.

When consumers turn their favour from one soapsud to another, the conversion is usually gradual enough to allow a civilised pace of redundancies. But competition in public servics must mean that one performance contractor will often have to yield overnight to a totally different contractor with a totally different system and staff.

Until the 1920s, when governments spent only around 10% of gnp, American cities, in particular, were ruled by boss politicians' machines which are today regarded as having been incredibly corrupt, but were then regarded as natural - and which could anyway be, and were, voted out with all their cronies. Today most of the top politicians in rich countries (though not in poor ones) are honest and rather liberal, especially in most American politics. But voters do not greatly affect their own lives by playing the adversary party game of voting for one mayor or another.

The spending of the two fifths or one half of gnps handled by governments is really arranged by a huge, permanent and increasingly trade-unionised block of government employees. This system has insensibly become so corrupt that the public service itself honestly does not believe that it is anything but public-spirited, either as regards its loading of its own pensions or as regards its productivity. Often "establishments" in bureaucracies and other public service jobs have been set according to some empire-builders' convenience combined with trade union rules, and not according to marginal productivity which is not measured at all.

A key paradox is that the switch from market-oriented to bureaucrat-dictated spending is usually philosophically supported by the political party that draws its votes from the oppressed proletariat, but is a switch that gets its own support mainly, as Professor Irving Kristol has pointed out, from the fastest growing segment of the new middle class. Today "this new class consists of scientists, lawyers, city planners, social workers, educators, criminologists, sociologists, public health doctors, etc. - a substantial number of whom find their careers in the expanding public sector rather than the private. The public sector, indeed, is where they prefer to be. They are, as one says, idealistic - i.e., far less interested in individual financial rewards than in the corporate power of their class".

Three things will happen slowly to alter this. First, mass working class movements in rich countries will turn right-wing-populist rather than socialist. Indeed, this is happening already.

Secondly, however, big business corporations will not become more beloved, because they are equally annoying bureaucracies.

Thirdly, reprivatisation will spread through bureaucracy only after the entrepreneurial revolution in the rest of industry begins to break through. In the profit-seeking sectors, individual businesses can start experimenting with the new entrepreneurial revolution now. Those that do not may regret the delay.

INDEX